Public Poetics

TransCanada Series

The study of Canadian literature can no longer take place in isolation from larger external forces. Pressures of multiculturalism put emphasis upon discourses of citizenship and security, while market-driven factors increasingly shape the publication, dissemination, and reception of Canadian writing. The persistent questioning of the Humanities has invited a rethinking of the disciplinary and curricular structures within which the literature is taught, while the development of area and diaspora studies has raised important questions about the tradition. The goal of the TransCanada series is to publish forward-thinking critical interventions that investigate these paradigm shifts in interdisciplinary ways.

Series editor:
Smaro Kamboureli, Avie Bennett Chair in Canadian Literature, Department of English, University of Toronto

For more information, please contact:

Smaro Kamboureli
Professor, Avie Bennett Chair in Canadian Literature
Department of English
University of Toronto
170 St. George Street
Toronto, ON M5R 2M8
Canada
Phone: 416-978-0156
Email: smaro.kamboureli@utoronto.ca

Lisa Quinn
Acquisitions Editor
Wilfrid Laurier University Press
75 University Avenue West
Waterloo, ON N2L 3C5
Canada
Phone: 519-884-0710 ext. 2843
Fax: 519-725-1399
Email: quinn@press.wlu.ca

PUBLIC POETICS

Critical Issues in Canadian Poetry and Poetics

Bart Vautour, Erin Wunker, Travis V. Mason,
and Christl Verduyn, Editors

WILFRID LAURIER
UNIVERSITY PRESS

This book has been published with the help of a grant from the Canadian Federation for the Humanities and Social Sciences, through the Awards to Scholarly Publications Program, using funds provided by the Social Sciences and Humanities Research Council of Canada. Wilfrid Laurier University Press acknowledges the financial support of the Government of Canada through the Canada Book Fund for our publishing activities. This work was supported by the Research Support Fund.

Library and Archives Canada Cataloguing in Publication

Public poetics : critical issues in Canadian poetry and poetics / Bart Vautour, Erin Wunker, Travis V. Mason, and Christl Verduyn, editors.

(TransCanada series)
Based on a conference held at Mount Allison University from September 20–23, 2012.
Includes bibliographical references and index.
Issued in print and electronic formats.
ISBN 978-1-77112-047-0 (paperback).—ISBN 978-1-77112-049-4 (epub).—
ISBN 978-1-77112-048-7 (pdf)

1. Canadian poetry (English)—21st century—History and criticism—Congresses. 2. Poetry—Social aspects—Canada—Congresses. 3. Poetics—Congresses. I. Verduyn, Christl, [date], editor II. Wunker, Erin, 1979–, editor III. Mason, Travis V., 1977–, editor IV. Vautour, Bart, [date], editor V. Series: TransCanada series

PS8155.1.P82 2015   C811'.609   C2015-902714-4
                                            C2015-902715-2

Cover design by Martyn Schmoll. Front-cover image by derek beaulieu. Text design by Daiva Villa, Chris Rowat Design.

"The House Which Is Not Extension but *Dispositio* Itself" is from *Insecession* by Erín Moure, published in one volume with the Moure translation of *Secession* by Chus Pato (BookThug, 2014) and is reprinted by permission of the author and BookThug. "Routine" is from *All the Daylight Hours: Poems* by Amanda Jernigan (Cormorant Books, 2013) and is reprinted by permission of the author and Cormorant Books. "September Still" is from *Old Hat* by Rob Winger (Nightwood Editions, 2014) and is reprinted by permission of the author and Nightwood Editions.

© 2015 Wilfrid Laurier University Press
Waterloo, Ontario, Canada
www.wlupress.wlu.ca

Every reasonable effort has been made to acquire permission for copyright material used in this text, and to acknowledge all such indebtedness accurately. Any errors and omissions called to the publisher's attention will be corrected in future printings.

No part of this publication may be reproduced, stored in a retrieval system, or transmitted, in any form or by any means, without the prior written consent of the publisher or a licence from the Canadian Copyright Licensing Agency (Access Copyright). For an Access Copyright licence, visit http://www.accesscopyright.ca or call toll free to 1-800-893-5777.

Contents

Acknowledgements ix

Introduction: Public Poetics 1
Erin Wunker and Travis V. Mason

SECTION I [THE CONTEMPORARY FIELD] 25

1 **Public Poet, Private Life: 20 Riffs on the Dream of a Communal Self**
Sina Queyras 27

2 **The Threat of Black Art, or, On Being Unofficially Banned in Canada**
El Jones 43

3 **The Counter/Public in Pain: The Making and Unmaking of Poetry in Canada**
Tanis MacDonald 51

4 **Writing the Body Politic: Feminist Poetics in the Twenty-First Century**
Heather Milne 65

5 **Rewriting and Postmodern Poetics in Canada: Neo-Haikus, Neo-Sonnets, Neo-Lullabies, Manifestos**
John Stout 87

Poetry I 107

The Sturdiness
by Sina Queyras   109

The Sexual Politics of Bluestockings
by Tanis MacDonald   111

Routine
by Amanda Jernigan   112

Volume
by Shannon Maguire   114

September Still
by Rob Winger   116

The inevitability of gravity on glass
by Vanessa Lent   117

Section II [The Embedded Field]   119

6 **The Ingeminate Eye: Peter Sanger's Public Poetics**
Amanda Jernigan   121

7 **Reading for a Civic Public Poetic: Toronto in Raymond Souster's "Ten Elephants on Yonge Street" and Dennis Lee's *Civil Elegies***
Will Smith   139

8 **To the Bone: The Instrumental Activism of Dionne Brand's *Ossuaries***
Geordie Miller   159

9 **Rearticulate, Renovate, *Rebuild*: Sachiko Murakami's Architectural Poetics of Community**
Emily Ballantyne   177

10 **"We jimmied the radio": Gillian Jerome, Brad Cran, and the Lyric in Public**
Kevin McNeilly   199

Poetry II   217

Hungry
by Kevin McNeilly   219

Potter's Hearing Is Not Khadr's Ruling
by Kathy Mac   220

The House Which Is Not Extension but *Dispositio* Itself
(from *Insecession*, an echolation of *Secession*, by Chus Pato)
by Erín Moure   223

The Avian Flu
by Brad Cran   225

Section III [Expanding the Field]   229

11   Formal Protest: Reconsidering the Poetics of Canadian Pamphleteering
Andrea Hasenbank   231

12   Radio Poetics: Publishing and Poetry on CBC's *Anthology*
Katherine McLeod   253

13   The Public Reading: Call for a New Paradigm
Erín Moure and Karis Shearer   271

14   We Are the Amp: A Poetics of the Human Microphone
Michael Nardone   289

15   Canadian Public Poetics: Negotiating Belonging in a Globalizing World
Diana Brydon   313

Nota bene; or, notes toward a poetics of work…
Bart Vautour and Christl Verduyn   333

Contributors   341
Index   347

Acknowledgements

Like many essay collections, this one started with a gathering of people in one place. The Public Poetics conference took place in Sackville, New Brunswick, in September 2012. Unlike many conferences, but characteristic of so much that takes place in Sackville, the conference was a real community effort that was made possible by people working in the university, by the people who make arts and culture such an animated part of life in Sackville, and by independent artists who gave of their time and talents.

We'd like to thank Paul Henderson, whose design savvy was visible on our programs, posters, and what are likely still the most beautiful conference bags around. We've since spotted Paul's collaborative work with derek beaulieu's visual poetry being carried across Canada and internationally. Thanks goes to Kaeli Cook, whose hand-painted birch tree pottery mugs, which were made in her Sackville studio, accompanied attendees to their homes across Canada and abroad. Without the support of the Vogue Theatre and the Owens Art Gallery the poetic performances would not have been accessible to so many conference goers and community members alike, nor would they have happened in proximity to such beautiful Atlantic Canadian art. Thanks, too, to the many friends who helped out. Especial gratitude to El Jones, Ardath Whynacht, Tanya Davis, and Chris Luedecke, who provided inspired performances at the Vogue Theatre before an audience of engaged listeners.

Neither the conference nor this collection would have been possible without institutional support. In particular, we'd like to acknowledge the support received from the Social Sciences and Humanities Research Council's Connection Program. We would also like to thank Rob Summerby-Murray, former Dean of the Faculty of Arts and Social Science at Dalhousie

University, for his support. At Mount Allison University, we would like to thank the Centre for Canadian Studies, the English Department, and Barkley Flemming (former VP Research and Academic) for their support of the initial Public Poetics conference. We would also like to thank Brittany Jones and Elaine Simpson for all their expert help, which kept the sailing smooth and on course.

derek beaulieu, the reigning poet laureate of Calgary, has given us his support and work from the very beginning. From his attendance and participation as a keynote speaker at the conference, to his generosity as an artist willing to share his work, derek embodies for us one crucial iteration of public poetics in action. It is his poem "Prose of the TransCanada" that graces the cover of this collection, and it is beautiful, blue, and modified because derek opened his work up to collaboration with designers and continually said yes when we asked "is it okay?" Thank you, derek.

We would like to thank Smaro Kamboureli for including *Public Poetics* in the TransCanada Series. Lisa Quinn at WLU Press has shown constant support and encouragement for this project. Thank you to the anonymous reviewers whose attentions, questions, and suggestions have made this a stronger collection. Rob Kohlmeier, also at WLU Press, has given us his keen attention towards the end of the publication process. Finally, and emphatically, we'd like to thank our contributors for being part of the conversation that enables poetics to happen. You were the first publics for these ideas. Thank you.

Introduction | **Public Poetics**

By Erin Wunker and Travis V. Mason

> "*Poetry makes nothing happen.*"
> —W.H. Auden

1. Situating "Public" "Poetics"

While Auden's line in his poem memorializing W.B. Yeats is familiar to the brink of being clichéd, it *still* matters. As a poetic statement that often circulates outside the context of Auden's poem and larger poetic project, it is too often used to fortify a notion that poetry circulates outside the economics of the everyday. This dislocation of poetry from both poetics and public praxis may shortchange the statement Auden makes, however. Here is what Auden writes:

> Mad Ireland hurt you into poetry.
> Now Ireland has her madness and her weather still,
> For poetry makes nothing happen: it survives
> In the valley of its making where executives
> Would never want to tamper, flows on south
> From ranches of isolation and the busy griefs,
> Raw towns that we believe and die in; it survives,
> A way of happening, a mouth.[1]

Poetry, for Auden, is an actant, an agent that hurts, that makes, that survives not outside the public but in a different place of its own making. That different place, we argue, needs to be inflected by both poetry and an attentive, critical (re)turn to poetics. We want to suggest that an expansive public poetics is "a way of happening" that makes the impossible—that nothing outside our knowing—happen. *Public Poetics: Critical Issues in Canadian Poetry and Poetics* emerges from a fundamental belief that public poetics is indeed "a way of happening, a mouth." Poetry makes its own mouth and, through that self-made megaphone, articulates alternative "publics." Public poetics bespeaks a kind of possibility and praxis that, as the essays in this collection variously suggest, has crucial insights to convey about the state of being, speaking, making, and cohabitating in this place called Canada. Poetry makes publics; poetics makes speaking and thinking critically about those publics possible.

And what do we, the editors of this collection, mean by the phrase "public poetics?"

In part, we take our cue from Michael Warner's postulations in his 2002 book *Publics and Counterpublics*, wherein he brings public and poetry into juxtaposition. We begin with Warner for two reasons. First, not unlike Auden's statement, Warner's concept of publics and counterpublics circulates outside and beyond the context of his book. While acknowledging Warner's text and context, we see possiblity in resituating his notion of publics within English Canada as a means of thinking through what we're calling public poetics. Second, Warner's statement that publics "do not exist apart from the discourses that address them" underscores a pernicious set of issues in Canadian history and culture that suggest that publics only exist as such when they are hailed by dominant discourses. This is a country with an ongoing history of racism, colonialism, and regional and linguistic tensions. Not all communities are hailed by discourses in easily recognizable ways; not all communities are recognized as publics. In short, Warner's postulation requires us to look at the moments cited in this collection as examples of public poetics, not as a complete representation of instances of public poetics in this country now called Canada. Indeed, the papers in this collection actively respond to some of the country's geopolitical and socio-historical idiosyncrasies.

A consideration of publics and poetics requires us to be attentive to the moments as well as the modes of their production. "Both the public sphere and the lyric mode," Warner writes, "found their ascendancy with print; both show signs of stress under the dominance of massified electronic media."[2] In other words, for Warner the privacy of the lyric and the ostensible openness of the public sphere are in a moment of flux; the digital turn has shifted the conditions under which both operate and under which they are experienced. Further, these two modes differ significantly when it comes to the relation between, for lack of a better pairing, speakers and listeners. Warner argues, on the one hand, that "publics do not exist apart from the discourse that addresses them";[3] that a "public is a relation among strangers";[4] and that a "public is the social space created by the reflexive circulation of its discourse."[5] He suggests that poetry, or the lyric mode, on the other hand, "appears to take no cognizance of its addressee whatsoever."[6] He might be correct about this anxiety of audience to the extent that poetry often seeks to communicate less than public speech does—if, that is, Warner is only thinking about siloed understandings of the function of forms such as the lyric. He suggests that "lyric speech has no time"[7] and that the readers or hearers of poetry themselves are unlikely to be the intended object/subject of the poems. While we are compelled by Warner's concept of publics and their counterpublics, we find ourselves wondering if he doesn't give the public power of both poetry and poetics short shrift. We are more inclined to align our understandings of the public power and possibility for poetry and poetics with arguments made by Charles Altieri. Altieri posits that contra traditional understandings, the lyric has very particular possibilities for conveying public affect. "If texts are to be significant they have to affect how we think about the world," he writes. Further, he suggests that "we cannot oversimplify the specific ways lyric texts engage the world if we treat them as means of sustaining knowledge claims."[8] Like the contributors to this collection, we posit that lyric speech has the potential not only to cite specific temporal and geographic events, but also to activate the urgency with which those events are uttered. That is to say that poetry does have an audience, even if Warner mobilizes a figure such as Northrop Frye to suggest there is no word for that confluence.[9] Moreover, the way an audience responds to and circulates ideas about poetry constitutes a poetics—a living, breathing, and dynamic mode of public engagement. We are interested in thinking through questions immediate to the discourse of poetry and poetics in Canada, particularly discourses that occur outside of well-worn formats. That is to say, we want to have the discussion of poetry's potential in public. In the initial conceptual stages of this project our guiding questions were these: How does poetry inhabit other forms and media to gesture towards conversations relevant to political, cultural, and historical moments? How do commentators in public and academic fields construct space for poetry? In both the conference we held at Mount Allison University in September 2012 and the contributions to this collection of essays and poems, these questions have been variously (directly and indirectly) addressed, reframed, and extended.

"Public poetics," for our purposes, comprises more than the circulation of poetry in public; it also includes those attempts to deliver poetry to a public and to generate discussion about poets and the work of poetry (particularly in relation to pressing social, environmental, and political concerns) as well as those moments in which poetic representational economies make changes in order to proffer alternative ways of knowing. In Canada, we argue, public poetics have been subtly positioned at the margins of cultural discourse about our society while at the same time profoundly, even necessarily, involved in the project of both forming and critiquing cultural nationalism. Further, the shape and degree of that involvement changes at moments of historical rupture as well as with technological shifts. Some events, such as the 2012 *Printemps d'érable* student demonstrations in Quebec and the Idle No More movement, which manifested themselves across Canada a few short months after the conference are sites from which future and ongoing critiques need to emerge. For example, while no single book can be held accountable for addressing all issues, it is significant that the editors received no submissions on events-based instances of public poetics and social justice beyond the ones published here. The contributors to this collection enter the conversation at different cultural moments, yet almost every contributor (much like Warner) pays attention to dichotomous framing of publics and counterpublics.

In his own moment of composition, Warner admits that the "extent [to which] the changing technology will be assimilable to the temporal framework of public discourse [remains unclear]";[10] Web 2.0 had not yet gained currency when Warner published his work, so the proliferation of comment threads on news sites, of blogs (and blog comments), and of digital archiving of print materials doesn't figure in his expression of publics and counterpublics. Which is to say, we envision this collection adding to the conversation about frameworks of public discourse by addressing, among other underrepresented critical considerations, that specific gap, albeit in the context of Canadian poetics.

2. Situating "Public Poetics" "At the Mermaid Inn"

What follows in this introduction is not a complete history of public poetics in Canada. There are other paths we could have followed; we have chosen this assemblage as a means to address a shift in poetic publics that has taken place in print-based spaces. Had we followed another path, such as public poetics that hinge around events, we might have begun with conferences such as Writing Thru Race (1994) or Women and Words (1983).[11] We might have also have traced instances of poetic activism such as Dorothy Livesay's work in the 1930s or Stephen Collis's more recent work with the

Occupy movement, the Enpipe Line poetry project, or Idle No More. These are crucial moments in Canadian cultural production that demand more sustained critical attention. This, then, is only a beginning.

To begin addressing critical issues in public poetics in Canada, we would like to think through, for a moment, the original "At the Mermaid Inn." When we sought a print-based point of origin, this column emerged as a logical place to begin (because of its proximity to Confederation) as well as an anachronistic one (because of its reliance on outmoded media). The serialized column that ran weekly on Saturdays in Toronto's *Globe* from February 1892 to July 1893 was given—we must admit—an odd title for a column on Canadian cultural production. Yet like Auden's elegy for Yeats, when read both for its poetics and for its nation-based concerns, the column has some important things to tell us about Canadian apprehensions surrounding the production of publics as well as poetics. First, the column has transnational reach. The name is certainly meant to hail the Mermaid Tavern in London's Cheapside, where the Friday Street Club, founded by Sir Walter Raleigh and whose illustrious membership included Ben Jonson, John Donne, and likely William Shakespeare, met to discuss literature and the arts.[12] Indeed, in his inaugural piece for the 1976 revival of the column, Hugh MacLennan refers to these literary spectres when citing Keats's poem "Lines on the Mermaid Tavern" as a source of inspiration for the Canadian columnists. MacLennan writes: "Happy men they seem to have been, they of the old Mermaid column, at least to the extent that they did not have to worry about politics. And they swallowed whole Keats' legend about the Mermaid Tavern: *Souls of poets dead and gone. / What Elysium have ye known, / Happy field or mossy cavern / Choicer than the Mermaid Tavern?*"[13] The desire to align the column with the fabled Mermaid Tavern betrays the paradoxical concerns of the column's original authors, who were preoccupied with what we now call the Confederation project. "At the Mermaid Inn" acknowledged the looming phantasm of England's literary heritage while insinuating that the newly minted Canadian state finally had something to offer its readers, both at home and abroad.

While "At the Mermaid Inn" is regularly flagged as a crucial "milestone in the development of Canadian literature and criticism"[14] during an "age of crisis,"[15] it is interesting to note that it has rarely been the focus of sustained critical discussion. A part of this dearth of critical attention can be attributed to the column's *raison d'être*.[16] Barrie Davies, who edited the collected columns for publication in 1979, describes "At the Mermaid Inn" as a project that "rivets our attention to peculiarly Canadian complexities."[17] Notably, we learn in a letter written by Archibald Lampman that this endeavour was not started as a conduit for cultural nationalism but as a gesture of generosity.

Duncan Campbell Scott and Lampman conceived of the weekly column as a way for their co-writer William Wilfred Campbell to earn regular payment.[18] While both Scott and Lampman were gainfully employed as civil servants, Campbell was sporadically earning money, and never enough at that. In an announcement dated 5 February 1892, *The Globe* ran the following announcement:

> THE GLOBE will in to-morrow's issue begin a new feature which is altogether unique in Canadian journalism and has been seldom attempted anywhere. It is the establishment of a literary column or department to consist of contributions from three of the brightest lights of Canadian literature, vis., Messrs. W.W. Campbell, A. Lampman, and Duncan Campbell Scott. These gentlemen need no introduction to readers of THE GLOBE, which has on several occasions had the pleasure of printing and commending their different productions in prose and poetry. They have made names for themselves as representative Canadian writers, and the public will doubtless be pleased to be brought into contact with them oftener than has hitherto been possible. The department will be known by the title "At the Mermaid Inn," a name chosen by the authors themselves. It will be started to-morrow, and will form a permanent feature of THE SATURDAY GLOBE.

In this introductory announcement, the *Globe* editors introduce the column as a "department," an institutional structure built to bring the private lives of poets into public contact with their readership. Further, "At the Mermaid Inn" is framed as a unique experiment. This "altogether unique feature" is, we argue, significant precisely because it is a conscious attempt to bring poetics into public discourse around nation and culture *and* because it was born out of a private act of generosity. Interestingly, the column promptly ended when Campbell was hired for a well-paying government job just over a year after it first appeared.[19] As Laura Boone observes, it is also possible that "At the Mermaid Inn" was already dead in the water, and again, Campbell is to blame. His final contribution appears to have been "a rash one" in which he imitated Lampman's poetry, thereby possibly insulting him and leading to the end of the column.[20]

What then to make of this cornerstone of Canadian literary culture, especially one that occupies so public a space? Considering the column critically more than a century after it was written, it is difficult to imagine how the writers conceived of their public readership. Perhaps precisely because it emerged, at least in part, as a scheme to hoist Campbell out of poverty, the column lacks cohesion, focus, and sometimes coherence. The topics of discussion range from the need for Canadian literary magazines to flora and fauna, from household pets to fireplaces. As Davies notes, there's a disparity in the number of submissions as well. Lampman and Scott wrote for it far more regularly than did Campbell, whose dire straits were, as we note, at least in part the inspiration for the column. Indeed, Campbell is described by one of his co-columnists as erratic and unlikable. Shortly after the column began, Lampman wrote a letter to E.W. Thomson in which he painted a rather unfavourable portrait of Campbell:

> One of my nextdoor neighbours is the poet William Wilfred Campbell. He is an odd fish. His first impression is unsatisfactory, and does not inspire confidence, but I find myself gaining in respect for him as I get to know him better. His mind is erratic and slovenly, but there is some good stuff in it, which comes out now and then in an accidental and unexpected kind of way. Campbell is deplorably poor...Partly in order to help his pockets a little, Mr. Scott and I decided to see if we could get the Toronto *Globe* to give us space for a couple of paragraphs and short articles weekly at whatever pay we could get from them; they agreed to that; and Campbell, Scott and I have been carrying on the thing several weeks now.[21]

The double gesture of reaching out towards a public while simultaneously pulling together to help a friend can be read as a paradox of a public and private poetics: private actions can have public impact.

Born of private generosity or not, we're taking "At the Mermaid Inn" as a foundational moment of public poetics in the intellectual history of Canadian cultural production. First, *The Globe*, in which the column appeared, was one of the most widely read newspapers of the day, with readership in Canada and abroad; it was read by both cultural intellectuals (later called the *literati* in F.R. Scott's irreverent "The Canadian Authors Meet") and by the general public. In short, the medium for the column was inherently public. Second, the content of the column itself betrayed a public kind of poetics. In the preface to Volume 1 of *An English Canadian Poetics*, Robert Hogg explains essays such as the ones found in "At the Mermaid Inn" as poetic essays. He suggests they are "an attempt by the poets, for the most part, to address the writing process itself; but they also discuss, either directly or indirectly, a number of other concerns intimately associated with the arts, culture and politics of their time."[22] What we see in the jumbled collection of entries that make up "At the Mermaid Inn" are observational or meditative pieces that focus on "goings on about town," the likes of which were common in the "society and culture" sections of earlier publications like *Atlantic Monthly* (1825) and were serialized in later magazines such as *The New Yorker* (1925) and *The Paris Review* (1953). These cultural observations can be read as self-conscious attempts to *make* a literary readership in Canada. Further, in the submissions by Lampman and Campbell, we see overt evidence of a genuine public praxis.

Archibald Lampman—the only author mentioned by name in MacLennan's contribution to the revivified column—leads the trio in entries penned; he wrote eighty-seven columns.[23] Credited with what D.M.R. Bentley calls "the most famous Eureka moment in Canadian literature,"[24] Lampman realized, upon reading Charles G.D. Roberts's *Orion and Other Poems*, that poetry of the highest calibre "could be done by a Canadian."[25] Indeed, as is documented well and often, Lampman's correspondence with Roberts almost certainly led to the surge in literary cultural production in the Confederation period.[26] Yet Lampman's writing for "At the Mermaid Inn" seems to flounder in its purpose. Certainly he calls time and again for a "really good literary magazine, including a department of criticism conducted in a spirit of serious appreciation and uncompromising candor."[27] However, the literary magazine, although an "act of patriotic duty," is always set up in opposition to the literary and cultural production of the United States.

Given Lampman's reluctant comments about his colleague's abilities, in addition to his own multiple missteps in the short-lived column, it is perhaps unexpected that Campbell's writing appears most attuned to what we're calling public poetics. Campbell, who once had to write an apology to *Globe* readers after offending their religious sensibilities, returns time and again to the function of literature—and crucially for our purposes, the *discussion* of literature—in forging not only culture but also community. Campbell regularly focuses his writing on the need for public poetics. Importantly, he writes time and again of the need not just for a textual public space, but also for a physical public space in which to enact a public poetics. He notes that "we hear a great deal said about the (so-called) influence of our universities, of which we have many, in the different provinces," but he wonders "what these colleges are doing on behalf of the national life? To be direct *what are they doing for the national literature?*"[28] For Campbell, the burden of responsibility was not on the poets to create an international and cosmopolitan literature, but on the public to create a critically engaged national space into which poetics could be delivered. "No class of literary workers in the world today need so much encouragement as do the Canadians," he reminds *Globe* readers.[29] The first few essays issued from the new literary department cover book reviews by Lampman and meditations on

Canadian weather and the Canadian psyche (*pace*, Atwood). Perhaps the most rhetorically interesting essay comes from Campbell himself. It is a short piece that diagnoses the increasing economic divide among Canadians in an era of emergent capitalist ideology: "The concentration of wealth into the control of a few, and the gradually growing poverty of the working classes, is becoming more apparent every day," writes Campbell. "Here in Canada [class culture] is dying out as a result of the absorption of capital." Campbell goes on to align the rise in capitalist culture with the denigration of the majority of the public. He caustically calls for an infusion of humanities into what he sees as a rising conservatism rife with hypocrisy. "Religionists may cry out about the hopelessness of mere humanity as a religion," observes Campbell, "but it would be better did they put a little more hope into the anguish of this world by putting more of the humanities into their religion."[30] Campbell's invective against the then-emergent national cultural climate enacts a public praxis that we are calling public poetics. A private voice speaks in a public space in the hopes of creating the conditions for critically engaged public discourse.

3. The Contemporary Field

What *has* happened in the decades between the two Mermaid Inn columns? And after? And why is the first one, which lasted a little over a year, so much more discussed, admired, and canonical than the later one, which ran for thirteen years? In short, other than historical context, how are the two columns different, and how can we account for those differences? What might these differences tell us about issues in the contemporary field of poetry and poetics in Canada?

In Canada, the most palpable changes to state-sanctioned federal support for and facilitation of cultural production occurred in the wake of the *Massey–Levesque Report,* released in 1951, which ushered in an era of cultural nationalism, taken up in the literary world by established and emerging publishers. The report shifted where and how conversations about poetry and poetics in Canada took place, but it did not create a totalizing discourse. Notwithstanding the tendency of literary historians to focus narrowly on poetic discourses taking place in little magazines like the *McGill Fortnightly Review* and the CCF-affiliated *Canadian Forum* before the report's publication as though they were the sole sites of critical discussion, there is a long history of public poetic discourse in Canada that is now beginning to receive more sustained critical attention. Journals such as *Masses* and *New Frontier* deliberately elided critical discussions of poetry and poetics with political and social commentary. Candida Rifkind characterizes *Masses* as a "counterpublic sphere,"[31] while Colin Hill observes that publications such as *Masses* and *New Frontier* addressed the need for socially engaged discourses around poetry and poetics that attended to the lived experiences of the working publics.[32] Without rehearsing the effects of the *Massey–Levesque Report* on cultural production in detail, we want to draw attention here to the ways in which public discourses about poetics in Canada have both public and counterpublic histories. Further, we want to suggest that attentiveness to the public shifts with the changing landscape of publication venues.[33]

An example of these shifting attentions can be seen in the decade following the *Massey–Levesque Report*, which saw some attention-grabbing developments on the West Coast. For example, George Woodcock introduced the journal *Canadian Literature* in 1959, writing in the inaugural editorial that the new magazine was "the arriving guest, anxious to exert whatever attractions it may possess on its potential host—the particular *public* to which it has chosen to appeal."[34] Two years later, Daphne Marlatt, Fred Wah, George Bowering, Frank Davey, Lionel Kearns, and Jamie Reid utilized mimeograph technology (and "free" paper from UBC's English Department) to produce and distribute the little magazine *TISH*, which ran until 1969. Both these examples were situated at UBC, and they offer but two examples of the "particular public" to which each effort appealed. As Michael Warner says: "University presses and journals are mulish compromises, half professional and half public. Their products are widely available to any stranger who can buy or borrow copies, and in that sense they address publics. But they also take care to maintain a close fit between their circulatory ambit and the private realm of the professions."[35] What differs from Warner's distinction in the examples of *Canadian Literature* and *TISH* is that while the former survives, housed as it is within UBC, it is not a university press. While *TISH* made important interventions in Canadian discourses on poetry and poetics, it may not necessarily have done more than *Canadian Literature*. Done differently, yes. Done more? Questions of impact on and interactions with publics are more complicated than a simple "yes-or-no" response can ever offer, and certainly more complex than an inside/outside approach to universities and publics in Canada.

If we jump ahead again to the 1976 reiteration of "The Mermaid Inn," we find an exemplary, if brief, exchange between the poets John Glassco and Milton Acorn. It's exemplary for the way Acorn responds to Glassco's conservative take on poetry as primarily a written form. On 12 September 1977, Glassco takes on a site of public poetics directly, questioning the value of poetry readings (recitations, he calls them) when assessing a poet's work.

He writes that "for better or worse, we are still in a typographic era, and our final judgments should be literate instead of audio-visual, and arrived at privately rather than *en masse*."[36] Glassco's *Selected Poems* won the Governor General's Literary Award in 1971, in the Poetry *or* Drama category, so perhaps the conjunction implied for him an essential distinction between the two forms of writing rather than an essential similarity, that is, performance. Anne Compton maintains that poetry actually inhabits publics insofar as it inheres as performance, and that performance in turn inheres in a public. "Performance is public," she writes. "The audience is entitled to ask questions."[37] Acorn would likely agree. In his column from 17 December 1977, he argues that "poetry is encountered both in voice and print. It should be written for both."[38] And of course changing print technology contributes to public poetics in different ways. Would Acorn's response have carried more weight had it been published fewer than three months after Glassco's column, as social media would encourage today? Or would a more immediate response have been less substantial, less thoughtful? And what do non-professional writers contribute to current versions of public poetics that might have been missing from the two formalized, time- and paper-bound Mermaid Inn columns?

Just as Northrop Frye extolled the role of the narrative in poetic conversations for fear of lyric becoming "too entangled with the printed page" in an era of increased radio presence,[39] in *Public Poetics* we want to foreground the cross-platform, outward-looking, transnational aspects of Canadian poetry and poetics. Much of the published, scholarly work on poetics in Canada relies heavily on contributions from poets themselves, as in Hogg's *An English Canadian Poetics*, Vol. 1, *The Confederation Poets* (an anthology of public writing preceded by a critical introduction). Where this is *not* the case, collections have tended to filter a discussion of poetics through one of many possible theoretical lenses or formal approaches, as in Butling and Rudy's *Writing in Our Time: Canada's Radical Poetries in English (1957–2003)* and Eichhorn and Milne's *Prismatic Publics: Innovative Women's Poetry and Poetics* (both of which compile interviews with poets alongside critical biographies and short, contextualizing introductions from the editors). Of particular import to this current collection, however, is the fact that a great many contemporary conversations about poetics in Canada emanate from the Internet, and specifically from *Lemon Hound*, the blog (and as of 2012 full website) started and maintained by Sina Queyras. Thus we contextualize the contemporary and future-looking portion of this collection within and against *Lemon Hound*'s strategies and influence.

4. Lemon Hound, More Bite Than Bark; or, Mind the Comments Section!

Fast-forward to the contemporary moment. Move through the Canadian sojourn to New York and the collective negotiations of cultural anti-modernism of the *Song Fishermen's Song Sheets*.[40] Move past the McGill group, student-poets who "became their own historians,"[41] salute the countercultural vitality of *Masses* and *New Frontier*, move past the aesthetic and ideological arguments held publicly in the pages of *Preview* and *First Statement*. Acknowledge the work of E.J. Pratt and the Crawleys in editing *Canadian Poetry* and *Contemporary Verse*. Give a nod to 1951 and the *Massey–Levesque Report* with its claims that there is no definitive Canadian literature but there will be, gosh darn it! Note that post–*Report*, the question of whether Canadian literature exists seems to shift dramatically. Move on. 1957: A.J.M Smith's anthology *The Book of Canadian Poetry*, first published in 1943, is revised and republished; 1958: R.E. Rashley claims that the Confederation poets are the first poets in Canada;[42] 1961: the advent of *TISH*, an anagram for *SHIT*, a literary journal that asks its readers to respond to its poetry newsletters—"*TISH* wants to know how you're REACTING to it. Surely you do something when you read *TISH*. Then TELL us about it. Or SEND it to us."[43] And, comparable perhaps to letters to the editor in newspapers, readers comply. They send comments, and criticisms, and sometimes they talk about poetry.

Now, move all the way to Sunday, 9 May 2004, and onto the Internet, where the following appears:

> Now she is blogging. Now she is sitting on the black couch listening to the sirens wail and the rain fall. Now she is thinking of oysters. Now she is wondering why this is worth sharing. Now she is thinking how to decipher what is worth reading? Who is to say? Sifters. She thinks we have become a nation of sifters. We dial up and sift through the wreckage. And what is the use of adding one more paragraph to the motherload? She supposes that soon she will find out.[44]

This is the first post made by poet Sina Queyras on her blog *Lemon Hound*. It is now an indispensible website for public debates about politics and poetics—debates that often spill out to other social media—yet Queyras is ambivalent about starting (and continuing) the blog, albeit her move into this most public of spaces is not unprecedented. Queyras works across genres as well as borders and regularly does work that brings poetics into the public space. She edited *Open Field: 30 Contemporary Canadian Poets*, a rare instance in this long contemporary moment when a small American press asked to publish a Canadian-centric text, and one with important transnational reach. She co-curated the feminist *belladonna* reading series in New York and has fostered cross-border discussions about Canadian writing through her position as resident blogger for the Poetry Foundation in the United States. Queyras's *Unleashed*—a selected collection of her blog posts—can be read as a whole to consider the shifting nature of cultural production in a hyperlinked world. Importantly for our purposes, she maintains a resolutely Canadian perspective while also speaking from a resolutely gendered position. There are other important sites of digital discourse in the Canadian context—rob maclennan's long-running blog, the Canadian content on *Jacket 2*, and the Buffalo Electronic Poetry Centre—but Queyras's writing is an intervention that calls attention to the asymmetrical power relations in poetic production and subsequent critical interventions.

As a medium, the blog functions as what Desiree Lewis describes as a space that "opens up limitless opportunities for communication, writing and thought, and in the way that it galvanizes the proliferation of text freed from the mastery of authors... It makes all information the ownership of everyone."[45] Or, if it doesn't always offer ownership to everyone, it certainly offers anyone with access to the Internet the opportunity to join the conversation. Indeed, although blogs may not necessarily have been what Derrida had in mind when he was thinking about the theory and function of an archive (although he does give a nod to his little Macintosh computer), the fact that blogs are often designed to archive themselves could be read as a nifty enactment of both the "commandment and commencement" of the archive: the archive "coordinates two principles in one: the principle according to nature or history, *there* where things *commence*... but also the principle according to law, *there* where men and gods command, *there* where authority and social orders are exercised."[46] In a similar vein, the creators of the Independent Media Center (or Indymedia) note that the open publishing forum offered by Indymedia news websites—and also by blogs—creates what we've been calling publics in several ways: it opens up the media-making process to multiple progressive voices; it flattens the hierarchy that exists whenever news is presented as the "active" product separate from the "passive" audience; and it claims not to represent "the monolithic truth but an assembly of many people's views."[47] Which is to say: like it or not, poetics are public, and the public is commenting.

We've chosen to move from "At the Mermaid Inn" to Queyras's *Lemon Hound* because it marks another (re)turn to public poetics. Queyras's site is a space of just such an assembly Indymedia describes. In a 2010 post addressing changes to her site (which included, among other things, a regular roster of emergent writers as guest posters, a series of interactive Canadian poetry reviews, and an ongoing series of "how to read a poem" guest posts), Queyras acknowledges the shifting ground public poetics inhabit. "Here's to more changes in the new year," she writes,

> here and elsewhere. Print is dead they keep saying. Sure, fine. So [go] reinvent it. Here's to being open to reinvention. Here's to the will to bend to and be bent by the future. Here's to finding ways to make books relevant. Here's to the peak of Internet consumption, may it integrate into our lives well. Here's to the peak of the eBook, may we find balance in the ways we read. Here's to print. Here's to online magazines. Here's to social networks fraught and otherwise. Interesting times. Thanks for making this site part of them.[48]

Here's to collections of publics gathering to think, talk, and perform poetic events as well. One aim of this collection is, in other words, to trace a historicity of public poetics in Canada while marking out its current manifestations. We would like to suggest that, following Warner, "publics act historically according to the temporality of their circulation,"[49] but we are less sure about Warner's subsequent dismissal of poetry because it "has no time."[50] We argue that a historical trajectory of public poetics in Canada can be traced. We start here with the first iteration of "At the Mermaid Inn" and move through the changing mediascape of the twentieth century, to the current era of Internet blogging and digitized archives. Contributors to this collection reposition discourses about poetics in Canada so that they inhabit traditional literary-critical spaces as well as non-traditional and technological critical spaces. For example, in his contribution Michael Nardone considers the ways in which the collective voices of protesters act as both a human microphone and a radical revision of publics *and* poetics. In this collection, poetics and politics meet in three overlapping sites: the contemporary field[51] (represented by the survey papers in Section I); the embedded field (represented by the "poet as makers of publics" papers in Section II); and the adjacent field (represented by the papers in Section III, which recognize the work of poetics outside of dominant encounters with "traditional" poetry).

The opening section of this volume comprises contributions that consider the shifting landscape of Canadian poetry and poetics in our contemporary moment. The authors of these contributions cast their nets widely. Sina Queyras situates the poet at the interstices of gender, genre, and nation. What happens when the poet is gendered woman? What happens when public discourses around poetry and poetics get mapped onto the gendered body? What is the role—and responsibility—of the critic? For Queyras, these questions must be addressed dynamically with an eye to both the past and the future. Her concerns hinge on a kind of crisis-ordinary moment in contemporary Canadian poetics that echoes an ongoing national wobble around the relations between cultural production, criticism, and the nation. El Jones takes up the poet's public persona to consider the ways in which poetics are mapped onto a racial identity. Working with rhetorical strategies borrowed from slam poetry, Jones demonstrates the ongoing and systematic racism in Canada generally and in poetry communities more specifically. Tanis MacDonald surveys the contemporary field by framing the poetic public and counterpublic as bodies in pain, while Heather Milne addresses the shifting landscape of feminist poetic discourses in the Canadian context. The final contributor to this first section, John Stout, returns to earlier discourses of Canadian postmodernisms and documents their revision by way of neo-genres.

Section II in this collection, "The Embedded Field," is composed of contributions that consider the ways in which individual poets are makers of publics. In contrast to Lampman's comparative criticism, several of the essays in this volume focus on national and regional frameworks within which individual poets enact a public. The section opens with Amanda Jernigan's careful consideration of Peter Sanger's work. Her analysis grapples with his private life and public poetic output. Sanger's negotiation of gaps between private and public, poet and critic, reader and writer, functions for Jernigan as a strategy for challenging readers' expectations—for clarity, for authority, and for a sense of how the poet positions himself vis-à-vis history and tradition. Although Sanger is not an obvious or immediate choice for a public poet, Jernigan suggests that the intimacies forged between poet and reader extend outwards to create instances of public intimacies. Will Smith inverts the focus on the private life of the poet in his contribution, which considers the public civic poetics of Raymond Souster and Dennis Lee. For Smith, Souster and Lee enacted situated civic poetics in urban Toronto, where each poet functioned as either official or *de facto* poet laureate; this serves as a model for thinking about poetic–public engagements municipally, regionally, and nationally. Geordie Miller's contribution focuses on another former poet laureate of Toronto, Dionne Brand. However, rather than considering her civic poetics, Miller discusses her *Ossuaries* as instrumental instances of public activism. This communal involvement animates Smith's and Miller's readings. The poets they discuss have all been Poet Laureates of Canada's largest city (although in an unofficial capacity, in Souster's case), and the public aspect of this role shapes how Smith and Miller frame their discussion of the poets' work. Smith locates public poetics locally, arguing that the Toronto evoked by Souster and Lee serves as a model for thinking about poetic–public engagements municipally, regionally, and nationally. For Miller, Brand's long poem *Ossuaries* extends civic-mindedness outwards to consider social and ecological justice in the light of neoliberal policies and global capitalism. Each of these discussions would likely have found space in the early "Mermaid Inn" column, likely in the writing of Campbell. In a related discussion of public activism, Emily Ballantyne addresses Sachiko Murakami's *Rebuild* as a poetic practice refusing neoliberalism and gentrification in Vancouver. Ballantyne concerns herself, too, with Vancouver's particular influence on a poet whose work inhabits both a conventional bookishness and a digital realm open to multiple authorship. Ballantyne articulates an important relation between Sachiko Murakami's collection *Rebuild*, which confronts the shifting architecture of Vancouver housing, and her online project *Rebuild*, which aligns poetic efforts to inhabit the city's idiosyncratic "Vancouver specials" with the Internet's capacity for enabling revision—that is, Murakami's Web-based project invites from the public "renovations" of poems attuned to Vancouver's suburban architecture. Kevin McNeilly closes this section with a reading of the ways in which Vancouver-based poets and activists Gillian Jerome and Brad Cran move the poetics of the lyric into public praxis. He posits them, in their collaborative work and in their individual poetry, in dialogue with a lyric tradition. However, the lyric in Jerome's and Cran's poetry foregrounds its public audience, both aurally and politically, and does so with awareness of how living in Vancouver—the site of Canada's wealthiest *and* poorest postal codes—informs a particularly fraught poetic–public dynamic.

The contributors to Section III of this collection, "Expanding the Field," look beyond the traditional structures of poetry and nation. Each pushes at the borders of these signifiers and asks the reader to reconsider how we understand the terms. Andrea Hasenbank's examination of 1930s pamphleteering makes an argument for the political pamphlet itself as a site for witnessing material and radical poetics—poetics as a purposeful and public shift in language economies outside of hegemonic discourse. Katherine McLeod's contribution extends the borders of how we often consider poetics by looking at CBC's long-running poetry-based broadcast *Anthology*. For McLeod, the radio broadcast enacts a new field of public poetics that extends far beyond the page, yet functions in a related way by forming intimacies with a broad audience. McLeod's essay "listen[s] to the audio archive of CBC radio's literary program 'Anthology,'"[52] a critical project apposite to Frye's observation that "in an age when new contacts between a poet and his public are opening up through radio, the narrative, a form peculiarly adapted for public reading, may play an important role in reawakening a public respect for and response to poetry,"[53] even if MacLeod's focus is less on the narrative that radio might enact than on what she calls "radio poetics." Erín Moure and Karis Shearer's "Call for a New Paradigm" of poetry readings enacts a similar poetics of listening, one that confronts not just the poetry reading as an event worthy of critical engagement but the role of public funds in shaping models for readings and, concomitantly, critical responses to them. Moure and Shearer consider the function of the audience/poet, but from a decidedly different angle, reading the event of the poetic reading through the Canada Council's guidelines to suggest that the reading itself is an artistic happening that fundamentally forms and informs publics and public poetics. Michael Nardone continues on the thread of audience creation of poetic praxis as he thinks through the function of the human microphone in cross-border moments of activism. Finally, Diana Brydon's contribution picks up echoes of the opening section and extends them beyond well-worn critical narratives of nation. Surveying the ways in which some Canadian poets engage in planetary issues, she posits that contemporary Canadian public poetics reach out towards an imbricated engagement with the global. She considers the reach of Canadian poetry and poetics beyond the national and transnational. For Brydon, the most pressing issues to consider are those that situate Canadian cultural production in conversation with global conditions. All of the chapters in this collection situate themselves among political discourses by way of the public poetics we identify as having occurred and as still occurring within nation-making and nation-questioning frameworks. There are, however, large gaps in this collection. The lack of First Nations perspectives and the dearth of discourse about poetic publics in Quebec are but two absences that tell us much about the ongoing need for discourse and discussion across publics.

This collection is, as we have noted, the collective product of a particular time and place. The essays here were each presented first to a group of scholars, creative practitioners, and members of the public in Sackville, New Brunswick. But there weren't only "traditional" scholarly presentations at the Public Poetics conference. Several of our keynote speakers were poets who presented readings of their work. derek beaulieu and Erín Moure performed a collaborative reading of each other's recent publications. beaulieu read in Galician from Moure's *Unmemntioable*, and Moure read aphorisms and exhorations from beaulieu's *How to Write*. The final evening of the conference was held in the Owens Art Gallery; beaulieu's "Prose of the Trans-Canada"—which graces the cover of *Public Poetics*—was hung on the walls alongside Evan Rensch's "Enterprise." The monochromatic visual poetry by beaulieu was a strangely complementary companion to Rensch's series of black-and-white portraits of ironworkers at the Fawcett-Enterprise Foundry in Sackville: a typographic homage and critique of urban modernity standing shoulder to shoulder with local workers. Against this backdrop, the conference organizers facilitated an open reading. Participants—be they poets, members of the public, or academics—could read two poems. More than two dozen people performed. In one case, a presenter was reciting a Bruce Springsteen song and forgot a line; without missing a beat, a member of the audience provided it. We wanted to represent a version of that collaborative crosstalk in this collection. We have attempted to do this by including two clusters of poetry submitted by conference participants and, in the case of Brad Cran, a poet whose work with Gillian Jerome is explored in this collection as an example of public lyricism. The poems create interstices in the collection. They neither bridge the sections nor stand wholly apart from them. They speak alongside one another, and sometimes they provide the missing lines.

5. Towards Poetic Publics

We began this introductory essay on familiar—if often misread—ground. Citing Auden's claim that "poetry makes nothing happen," we argued that in fact this is a generative claim that opens out to the possibilities and potentials of poetic discourse and poetic language. While we acknowledge the partiality of this collection, we offer it as a gesture towards the possibility of poetry inviting engagement with publics. We offer it as evidence that participants in poetic publics remain attuned to the critical importance of thinking through history, media, and the politics of place. We will close the preface by offering an example of what we mean: On the second evening of the conference in Sackville, New Brunswick, that inspired this collection, participants gathered with members of the public in the old Vogue Theatre on Bridge Street. Nearly 250 audience members watched as spoken word poets El Jones, Tanya Davis, and Ardath Whynacht performed. Among other things, Jones addressed the pernicious racism in contemporary Canada, Davis queried the ongoing heteronormativity, and Whynacht addressed Canada's shift towards an American-style prison-industrial complex. Three of the four editors of this collection stood at the back of the theatre, watching, while the fourth sat at the front with the poets, rather nervously introducing each in turn. "No one is leaving," one of us at the back whispered. And indeed, no one was leaving. Instead, here in this small Maritime community, publics and counterpublics were watching lyric events. Together. As Jones, Davis, and Whynacht finished their portions of the show, we again experienced some trepidation. How would the audience react to the next performer, Old Man Luedecke, whom we'd invited thinking about his affiliation with folk poetics? Moreover, how would his fellow performers react to this radically different poetic? Here is what we saw: a theatre full of people leaning forward in their seats. Three performers who, having finished their own presentations, sat in the front row clapping, cheering, and shouting encouragements to their co-performer. If poetry makes nothing happen, then that nothing must be that which—until it enters poetic language—is inarticulable. What we saw that night, standing in the back of a full theatre in a small town in the Maritimes, a few kilometres from places that inspired Campbell's coterie, were public poetics in action.

Notes

1 W.H. Auden, "In Memory of W.B. Yeats (1939)," in *The Norton Anthology of Poetry*, 5th ed., ed. Margaret Ferguson, Mary Jo Salter, and John Stalworthy (New York: W.W. Norton, 2004), 1472.
2 Warner, *Publics and Counterpublics*, 82.
3 Warner, *Publics and Counterpublics*, 72.
4 Warner, *Publics and Counterpublics*, 74.
5 Warner, *Publics and Counterpublics*, 90.
6 Warner, *Publics and Counterpublics*, 79.
7 Warner, *Publics and Counterpublics*, 81.
8 Altieri, "Reading for Affect in the Lyric," 40.
9 Warner references Frye, who suggests that the lyric exists outside time. This is a contentious statement—and, we think, a problematic one—insofar as it divests the lyric of its political and situational efficacy. That said, Warner references Frye in the same section in which he is outlining the shifts and pressures on the lyric and the public sphere. So while Warner references Frye to underscore the changing conditions for both the lyric and the public sphere, we want to retain the reference for its problematic depoliticization of lyric poetry.
10 Warner, *Publics and Counterpublics*, 98.
11 These two conferences were significant interventions in public and poetic discourses of the day. Writing Thru Race, organized by Roy Miki, was predicated on reserving a safe space for discussion for writers of colour only. The restrictions on conference attendance and participation generated a great deal of controversy; ultimately, though, it was a landmark event that drew attention to the ongoing racial inequity in Canadian literary culture and in Canada more generally. Similarly, Women and Words, organized by FILL IN, brought together women writers from French and English Canada, as well as some women from Indigenous and diasporic communities. As with Writing Thru Race, attendance and participation at Women and Words was restricted. These conferences and the controversy and historical and cultural legacies they generated underscore the ways in which not all publics are equal.

12　Halliday, *A Shakespeare Companion*, 164.
13　MacLennan, "They May Think." MacLennan is referring to Keats's "Lines on the Mermaid Tavern."
14　Boone, *William Wilfred Campbell*, 161.
15　Davies, *At the Mermaid Inn*, xi.
16　Although, as Bart Vautour and Christl Verduyn go on to suggest in the conclusion to this collection, the climate of Canadian review culture continues to be fraught at best. For thorough statistics on the gender inequities of Canadian reviews culture, see the work of Canadian Women in the Literary Arts (www.cwila.com). For a survey of the cultural climate of review vis-à-vis the ever-evolving project of cultural nationalism, see Laura Moss, "Measuring Canadian Support on the 'Literary Assembly Line'" (http://cwila.com/wordpress/measuring-canadian-support-on-the-literary-assembly-line).
17　Davies, *At the Mermaid Inn*, vii.
18　Each contributor was paid a salary of three dollars per week. Boone, *William Wilfred Campbell*, ix.
19　Davies, *At the Mermaid Inn*, viii.
20　Boone, *William Wilfred Campbell*, 161.
21　Archibald Lampman, Letter to E.W. Thomson.
22　Hogg, ed., *An English Canadian Poetics*, 12.
23　Davies, *At the Mermaid Inn*, vii.
24　Bentley, Introduction," 37.
25　Lampman, *Essays and Reviews*, 94.
26　In one instance of correspondence, the two discuss the desire to "get together literary and independent Young Canada, and to spread...[the] doctrine...with untiring hands" (*Essays and Reviews* 29). In "Two Canadian Poets," Lampman outlines the poetic project of the day: "In the climate of the country, we have the pitiless severity of the climate of Sweden with the sunshine and sky of the north of Italy...A Canadian race...might, combining the energy, the seriousness, the perseverance of the Scandanavians with something of the gayety, the elasticity, the quickness of spirit of the south. If these qualities could be united in literature, the result would indeed be something novel and wonderful" (*Essays and Reviews*, 93).
27　Davies, ed., *At the Mermaid Inn*, 38.
28　Davies, ed., *At the Mermaid Inn*, 32–33, emphasis added. Notably, a CBC broadcast produced by Phyllis Webb, Earle Birney echoes Campbell's sentiment that universities are *the* public spheres in which to enact public poetics and public intellectualism. He observes that "the North American campus is the only place where established writers themselves can be found in a state of accessibility to student-writers...In Canada, where else but around the universities? All older Canadian writers aren't professors, but the handy ones are" (53).
29　Davies, ed., *At the Mermaid Inn*, ix.

30 Davies, ed., *At the Mermaid Inn*, x.
31 Rifkind, *Comrades and Critics*, 57.
32 Hill, *Modern Realism*, 159.
33 For more thorough considerations of these changing landscapes, see Smaro Kamboureli and Kit Dobson, *Producing Canadian Literature* (Waterloo: Wilfrid Laurier University Press, 2013).
34 Woodcock, *Canadian Literature*, 3.
35 Warner, *Publics and Counterpublics*, 148.
36 Glassco, "The Poet as Performer."
37 Compton, *Meetings with Maritime Poets*, 14.
38 Acorn, "Try Writing a Growl."
39 Frye, *The Bush Garden*, 156.
40 See Mount, *When Canadian Literature Moved to New York*, and Vautour, "Modernism, Antimodernism, and the Song Fishermen."
41 Queyras, *Unleashed*.
42 Rashley, *Poetry in Canada*, ix.
43 Qtd. in Butling and Rudy, *Writing in Our Time*, 54.
44 Queyras, *Unleashed*, 13.
45 Lewis, "African Gender Research and Postcoloniality," n.pag.
46 Derrida, *Archive Fever*, 1.
47 Breitbart and Nogueira, "An Independent Media Center," 19.
48 Queyras, *Unleashed*, 57.
49 Queyras, *Unleashed*, 96.
50 Queyras, *Unleashed*, 81.
51 In the Bordieuian sense. Barbara Godard suggests that in the Canadian context a survey of the literary field requires moving across interconnected nodes of cultural production. See Barbara Godard, "Notes from the Cultural Field," *Canadian Literature at the Crossroads of Language and Culture* (Edmonton: NeWest Press, 2008), 235–72.
52 See, in this volume, McLeod, "Radio Poetics," 253.
53 McLeod, "Radio Poetics."

Bibliography

Acorn, Milton. "Try Writing a Growl. It's Not Nearly as Effective as the Real Thing." The Mermaid Inn, *Globe and Mail*, 17 December 1977, editorial page.

Altieri, Charles. "Reading for Affect in the Lyric." In *Poetry and Pedagogy: The Challenge of the Contemporary*, edited by Joan Retallack and Juliana Spahr. New York: Palgrave, 2006.

Auden, W.H. "In Memory of W.B. Yeats." In *The Norton Anthology of Poetry*, 5th ed., edited by Margaret Ferguson, Mary Jo Salter, and John Stalworthy. New York: W.W. Norton, 2004. 1472.

Bentley, D.M.R. "Introduction." In *An English Canadian Poetics:* Vol. 1: *The Confederation Poets*, edited by Robert Hogg. 37–74. Vancouver: Talonbooks, 2009.

Boone, Laurel. *William Wilfred Campbell: Selected Poetry and Essays.* Waterloo: Wilfrid Laurier University Press, 1987.

Breitbart, J., and A. Nogueira. "An Independent Media Center of One's Own: A Feminist Alternative to Corporate Media." In *The Fire This Time: Young Activists and the New Feminism*, edited by Vivien Labaton and Dawn Lundy Martin, 19–41. New York: Anchor Books, 2004.

Butling, Pauline, and Susan Rudy. *Writing in Our Time: Canada's Radical Poetries in English (1957–2003).* Waterloo: Wilfrid Laurier University Press, 2005.

Compton, Anne. *Meetings with Maritime Poets.* Markham: Fitzhenry & Whiteside, 2006.

Davies, Barrie, ed. *At the Mermaid Inn: Wilfrid Campbell, Archibald Lampman, Duncan Campbell Scott in* The Globe *1892–93.* Toronto: University of Toronto Press, 1979.

Derrida, Jacques. *Archive Fever: A Freudian Impression.* Chicago: University of Chicago Press, 1998.

Frye, Northrop. *Anatomy of Criticism: Four Essays.* Princeton: Princeton University Press, 1990.

———. *The Bush Garden: Essays on the Canadian Imagination.* Toronto: Anansi, 1995.

Geddes, Gary. *Out of the Ordinary: Politics, Poetry & Narrative*, Mackie Lecture and Reading Series No. 6. Vernon: Kalamalka Press—Kalamalka Institute for Working Writers, 2009.

Glassco, John. "The Poet as Performer Debases his Art. You Hear Him, Not His Poetry." The Mermaid Inn, *Globe and Mail,* November 12, 1977, editorial page.

Godard, Barbara. "Notes from the Cultural Field," *Canadian Literature at the Crossroads of Language and Culture.* Ed. Smaro Kamboureli. Edmonton: NeWest Press, 2008. 235–72.

Halliday, F.E. *A Shakespeare Companion 1564–1964.* Baltimore: Penguin, 1964.

Hill, Colin. *Modern Realism in English-Canadian Fiction.* Toronto: University of Toronto Press, 2012.

Hogg, Robert, ed. *An English Canadian Poetics,* vol. 1, *The Confederation Poets.* Vancouver: Talonbooks, 2009.

Kamboureli, Smaro, and Kit Dobson. *Producing Canadian Literature.* Waterloo: Wilfrid Laurier University Press, 2013.

Lampman, Archibald. *The Essays and Reviews of Archibald Lampman,* edited by D.M.R. Bentley. Ottawa: Canadian Poetry Press, 1996.

———. Letter to E.W. Thomson, 16 February 1892. Parliamentary Archives Collection #29940, Ottawa, Ontario.

Lewis, Desiree. «African Gender Research and Postcoloniality: Legacies and Challenges,» In *African Gender Scholarship: Concepts, Methodologies, and Paradigms*. Council for the Development of Social Science Research in Africa, Gender Series, Vol. 1 (November 2004). http://codesria.org/IMG/pdf/LEWIS.pdf.

MacLennan, Hugh. "They May Think the Same Thoughts as Shakespeare at the CBC. But Only the Lesser Ones." The Mermaid Inn, *Globe and Mail*, 25 September 1976, editorial page.

Mount, Nick. *When Canadian Literature Moved to New York*. Toronto: University of Toronto Press, 2005.

"New Look, Links with Past for Saturday Globe Editions." *Globe and Mail*, 25 September 1976, front page.

Queyras, Sina. *Unleashed*. Department of Critical Thought no. 2. Toronto: BookThug, 2009.

Rashley, R.E. *Poetry in Canada: The First Three Steps*. Toronto: Ryerson Press, 1979.

Rifkind, Candida. *Comrades and Critics: Women, Literature, and the Left in 1930s Canada*. Toronto: University of Toronto Press, 2009.

Vautour, Bart. "Modernism, Antimodernism, and the Song Fishermen." *Canadian Poetry: Studies, Documents, Reviews* 70 (Spring–Summer 2012): 15–44.

Warner, Michael. *Publics and Counterpublics*. Brooklyn: Zone Books, 2002.

Woodcock, George. Editorial. *Canadian Literature* 1 (1959): 3.

Section I
[The Contemporary Field]

I

Public Poet, Private Life: 20 Riffs on the Dream of a Communal Self

Sina Queyras

1.
In the summer of 2012, on the heels of the launch of Canadian Women In Literary Arts (CWILA), and at the height of a public quarrel between Jan Zwicky and Michael Lista over reviewing, I wrote a blog post titled "On Misdirected Energy" in which I suggested that, rather than argue about negative or positive reviewing, critics should show a basic level of respect for *any* book and author under review, a basic level of understanding, a fact that is much more relevant than whether or not the critic is or is not a fan.[1] Further, I mourned the sidetracking of such an important event—the launch of CWILA—with an old, divisive, and inaccurate depiction of good criticism as necessarily skeptical and negative, making bad criticism, by default, "positive" and therefore "uncritical." Shortly after this exchange, a Canadian poet of some significance emailed me to thank me. She would comment herself, she said, but she has an extreme fear of public speaking. She went on to recount several horrifying experiences that occurred when she attempted to take up some public space. She concluded that she was glad there are people like me. Several other female poets emailed me to express similar sentiments with similar stories—again, concluding that they were glad there are people like me.

A month later, I participated in a virtual round-table discussion on the *Best American Poetry*[2] blog with American poets Juliana Spahr, Vanessa Place, Danielle Pafunda, Shana Compton, Elisa Gabbert, and Sandra Simmonds on the topic of women and criticism. An American poet published a link to our conversation on Facebook with the initial comment, "Read this." A few minutes later she added, "I have a lot to say too if I could bring myself to speak publicly"; then a few minutes later she noted, "I confess I was invited to participate but I thought, 'All white women of a certain background... I don't want to be just another same voice...'"[3]

Yet another poet of some significance emailed to say "Right on," she totally supported me, but she herself felt more inclined to respond indirectly, in a way that suited her aesthetically and gave her pleasure.

As the Zwicky–Lista controversy mushroomed in the *National Post* and on social media, another woman who had initially been excited to see Zwicky speak out emailed me in frustration to say, "I get it. I understand why so many women remain silent."

An ironic outcome, given that the advice Zwicky offered women also suggested that they "remain silent," rather than be negative, and that this "silencing" was the effect Lista's public rage had on so many.

Still, one might ask, why so much resistance to taking up public space? Isn't that part of the poet's job description? Speaking out? And who is this "other" braver sort of person some women seem to see me as?

Some weeks later the novelist Sheila Heti offered slant support for my position in an online interview, echoing my own uneasiness about the assumptions the discussion had unearthed about women writers' sense of victimization when facing our predominantly male critical establishment. Women need to "evolve in public," Heti said. "It's like a romantic relationship. You don't make yourself perfect and then enter in it. You fuck up in it, and you get better at being [in] it by fucking up in it."[4]

2.
I don't remember "not" being a feminist, nor do I recall a time when I didn't feel a little uncomfortable addressing sexism. I do recall the first flicker of desire to speak out about something that really didn't feel safe to do. This desire came at the moment I discovered poetry was a live art and something that could be written by women too.

Here is what happened: I came across a magazine called *Poetry Canada Review* in our high school library. The magazine ran in Canada from 1979 to 1994 and for a long time was a central source of discourse, though at the time I had never heard of it. Nor had I *heard* of contemporary poetry. If I recall correctly, the issue that I saw facing up at me had Margaret Atwood on the cover. Or at least her name on the cover—she and the *Four Horsemen*. It's a tricky issue to locate, and the magazine folded almost two decades ago.

I might just as well have been encountering pornography in our high school library. Certainly, it was a kind of provocation. Looking at the magazine seemed scandalous, as if the act of reading poetry, even thinking about poetry, could not be a public one.

And that a woman was on the cover—that was even more scandalous to me. So I wrote a paper on the poetry of Margaret Atwood for my tenth-grade English class. She was the first poet I read as a poet, period, and certainly the first writer who reflected, even remotely, aspects of my contemporary life and thinking. It took me weeks to write that essay, and unlike most of the things I had to do in high school, I was completely engaged by it. Yet, the morning I was to present it to class I stood in the hall with a hand on the doorknob and froze. I stood while the teacher took roll call, and I stood when he began to talk, and then called the first person up to do her presentation, and then the second person, and then I wrenched my hand from the knob and ran. I needed to be sick.

I don't recall handing in that paper.

3.
For the record, speaking in public still makes me sick.[5]

4.
Thinking about the Lista–Zwicky affair, and the ongoing silence of women in public poetic discourses, particularly in Canada, I asked the oracle that is Facebook what constitutes taking a risk for Canadian poets. Toronto poet Paul Vermeersch responded quickly: "writing a poem."

Really? Is it really a risk for a white, male poet of a certain background to write a poem? To take up public space in poetry? To offer his opinion of anything, in public? Really? If poetry in general is made of *risk*, show me the risk. Show me.

5.
In Montreal in 1948, painter Paul-Émile Borduas lost his job for writing his *Refus global* manifesto. Many consider this manifesto to be one of the

early catalysts for the Quiet Revolution in Quebec. Four hundred copies appeared on 9 August 1948. Borduas was dismissed from *l'École du meuble* on 2 September 1948.

6.
As I am writing this essay in the summer of 2012, three members of the Russian feminist punk rock collective Pussy Riot are on trial in Russia. The women are paraded in front of a judge, photographed, chastised, displayed in a glass box. All around the world these images appear, the women are discussed. For what? For speaking/singing out and interrupting the most sacred of ancient rituals: the passing of male power. All the oaths we put faith in.

7.
I took an oath to place once. This was around the same time I made a vow to writing. I decided that writing and Canada's west coast were limits for me, what I was not willing to give up. I would do whatever I had to do, despite constant pressures of gentrification and development, to stay and to protect and be part of the landscape and the people that I love; to resist overdevelopment of the land, air, ocean, cities, people. And I would do this by writing about it. Drawing a line so that I know who I am and what my territory is.

I had a line for difficult poetry too. I thought it was self-indulgent. Like the most bourgeois art forms with clever little explanation tags, difficult poetry was not for the people. I remember reeling after my first encounter with Jeff Wall's conceptual photography at the Vancouver Art Gallery. Equally confusing were early encounters with work by poets I am lucky enough to consider colleagues today. Take Erín Moure for example. Why, when I finally heard her read, did her ramblings between poems make more sense than the poems themselves? Or Fred Wah; why did I need to know his social circle in order to understand his poems?

And then one day I saw through the surface of the poem I was writing and into the poem I wanted to be writing and realized that I was completely wrong. Poetry is about more than content, even radical or socially active content. Poetry has to be radically conceived of "in form," radically in conversation with other poetry, it has to have context. It has to be deeply rooted in the history of people and place, yes, but also deeply rooted in poetry.

To try to understand where my roots begin, or end, I would have to risk cutting myself away, damaging important systems. I had to risk my comfort to see my own poetry.

To hear my own voice. I had to reach. I had to fail.

Shortly thereafter I kicked my soggy self out of paradise.

8.
In August of 2012 I emailed Stephen Collis at Simon Fraser University to ask about the relationship of poetry to the Occupy movement as the anniversary of the massive Occupy Wall Street that took place in 2011 fizzled and sparked in various cities around the world. I know poets who are involved in various Occupy and student movements, I know that there was some brutal behaviour in Montreal, and I watched as tensions rose, but had anyone in Canada been arrested, or suffered consequences from speaking in public or for actually reading or writing a poem in relation to this moment? Or the Enpipe Line protests?

No, Collis said, no one had been arrested for poetry.[6] No one had lost his or her job. No one had been chastised, though Christine Leclerc had staged a performance in the offices of a corporation, and been removed, but there had been no arrest, and the late Robin Skelton had placed a curse on Brian Mulroney, but this, Collis reminds us, was more part of his work as a witch than a poet.[7] In an interview on TV a few days later, Collis said that while there was no discernable or immediate outcome of the Occupy movement, the effects of the movement would linger. Great movements don't necessarily achieve their goals overnight. Information seeps in whether we want it to or not. Change is incremental. It moves in fits and starts. To riff on what Kalle Lasn, provocateur and founder of *Adbusters* expressed: the fire is lit, it will spread.

9.
I like Michael Warner's thinking: "A public is a relation among strangers."[8] If that is the case, how much contemporary poetry is actually being written for "a public"?

Warner cites Northrop Frye: "There is no word for the audience of the lyric."[9] Lyric speech, Warner goes on to say, has no time: "we read the scene of speech as identical with the moment of reading."

Public speech, on the other hand, makes us conscious of "the temporality of its own circulation,"[10] so public speech not only has a consciousness of time but of space and, one might assume, of audience.

10.
I have described my poetics as a poetics of collision[11] and as lyric conceptualism.[12] There's something combative about both of these statements, and not only outwardly.

Opposing forces are at play in my work—and in my thinking; both about my work and others.' Dialogic, some have called it: call and response, statement and reflection, repetition and variation, affirm and squirm. I would argue that both statements about my poetics reflect a centrifugal position—a term Lynn Keller makes use of in her look at pedagogy in the classroom.[13] The essential component here being a deep interiority looking outward.

Perspective isn't everything. Recently I've started writing backwards. Every morning I open my desktop, open my document, scroll back to the beginning, and start again.

I find this a bit disconcerting.

But maybe it shouldn't surprise me since I know I try to think backwards. To entertain dissent. To embrace doubt. To keep ideas airborne, aloft, as long as possible. Lucy Brock Broido describes wanting her poem to be a palpable coffin:[14] I want the exact opposite. I don't want my poem so refined that it has become polish. I want it barely containable. Active.

I have both a longing for and horror of the domestic and domesticated.

Horror especially at domestication that keeps the work, or the thinking, shut inside. Yet I understand and want to show that I understand that we all still crave the crib.

11.
In an issue of *Art Forum* the artist Ai Weiwei points out the democratizing aspect of Twitter. "We are all here together," he says. "You can be in the worst place in the world, and still be in this social space. Warhol could not have predicted this." On the other hand, he points out, it's almost inhuman "because being human should confine us to being 'in one place at one time.'"[15]

William Gibson has said, "Facebook is the mall, Twitter is the street..."[16]

Critic Dwight Garner has written about how together Facebook and Twitter are deadening our critical capacities.[17] I don't agree with all that he had to say...wait, what was I saying?

I don't agree with all that he had to say but...what was I talking about?

Yes, we should wonder about the impact of social networks, and indeed all technologies, on our thinking, but easy statements such as "the great literary correspondence is no more because people aren't writing letters by hand and mailing them..." are overblown, just as declarations of the death of the novel, poetry, the book, the audience, and so on.

In April I tweeted "Lyric is over," and in August I tweeted, "the secret goal of Twitter is to destroy poetry."

If Twitter kills poetry, at least we will all mourn together.

12.
In my experience critical and conceptual writing are the architecture that helps to get poets outside of themselves and that gives us frames to make public work.

13.
In 2004, I started a blog, an act that has, to my great surprise and probably against all odds, made me a public poet.

The decision to blog was one of the easiest and most difficult decisions of my life. Easy in terms of the technology available: I went to Blogger, chose a name, signed up, chose a theme, drafted a post, all in less time than it took to finish my cup of coffee. All I had to do was hit "publish." Which I did: no editors. No editorial apparatus. No assessment—at least not till much later when comments started trickling in.

A few days later I did it again, and then, overcome with that horror—of taking up public space, or speaking out—I left it idle for nearly a year.

The form of the blog was almost *too* liberating. Too exhilarating. I could do whatever I wanted. Say whatever I wanted. Particularly, at that point, because no one was listening. No one was reading. And there is great freedom in obscurity.

As I wrote in the introduction to *Unleashed*, a selection of posts from that blog edited by Kate Eichhorn and published by BookThug in 2009, there is nothing difficult about the fundamentals of blogging itself. Nor is there anything inherently difficult about taking up public space.

Except that it is terrifying.

14.
Maria Vladimirovna Alyokhina.
Yekaterina Stanislavovna Samutsevich.
Nadezhda Andreyevna Tolokonnikova.

During their trial, these three members of Pussy Riot were held in a glass cage, which it turns out is common for defendants in Russian courtrooms. They seemed very girlish in their dress and with their giggling, appearing to reflect, in turn, nerves and disbelief. They were arrested and ultimately charged for hooliganism, which I am told also has a long history in Russia, a catchall charge used from the time of the Czars for political control.

Angela Davis points out that during radical political protests men are sent to jail but women have their children taken away from them.[18] Québécoise artist Marcelle Ferron, a signatory of *Refus global*, had her children taken away from her for signing Borduas's manifesto, for effectively calling out politicians and engaging in art of "spontaneity and resplendent anarchy."[19] Since August 14, 2012, Alyokhina's and Tolokonnikova's children have been in the custody of their lawyers for fear of being taken by the state.

15.
Back in the early 90s I was deep in retreat, pushing myself into a series of prose poems that would ultimately become my master's thesis. Money was tight. I had to go back and forth to Vancouver where I worked with street kids—a job I had been doing for several years, along with other jobs like bartending, waitressing, house building, and gardening. My writing life wasn't coming together in my estimation and I decided to do a master's degree, hoping for some new contacts, some new skills, a sense of new possibilities.

I had been suffering from panic attacks. The quiet life that I had craved and crafted for myself was, despite how much I claimed to love it, becoming a straitjacket. It wasn't the right time for isolation or retreat.

I wasn't developing as a writer. I couldn't read my work in public without great, debilitating amounts of stress that often made me feel I could not have a life as a poet or writer. Furthermore, having glimpsed the writing that I wanted to do, I had absolutely no idea how to get myself there.

Though, to be fair to that early self, I did begin to find a voice that I didn't hate, and published a few poems from that work in *The Malahat Review* before leaving for Montreal.

My anxiety was so extreme I tried to get off the plane as flight attendants were closing the doors. I feared that what I wanted was impossible. That I was a bad writer. That I lacked the intelligence to narrate my own thinking, my own life. That the price of this path would be too steep. That I would lose control of myself. That I would not be able to come back home once I left.

I entered grad school hoping to be changed to the core.

But, like most people, I didn't want this change to happen in an inconvenient way. I wanted to offer up select parts to be changed, the parts I was frustrated with, the parts I could spare. I wanted to partition off other parts to keep untouched.

My experience of post-referendum Montreal of the mid-90s—empty stores on Parc Avenue, a sense of economic scarcity and defeat everywhere in terms of materiality—was hostile and agitating rather than inspiring. The poetry world I encountered there and then was even more depressing.

My master's thesis was my first exploration of the long prose poem, and like most creative writing master's theses of the day, it was based on my life and reading at the time. At my defence, one examiner found my "lack of formal attentiveness" offensive, but not as deeply offensive as the "content itself." The way my work represented the lives of girls and women was not accurate, he told me. He had girls and women in his life and their lives were represented nowhere in my poems.[20] He suggested that my thesis exhibited "Mastery of nothing."

Unfortunately the master's degree didn't help with my fear of speaking, or reading, in public. Not in the short run in any case. Even though that critic of my thesis retracted his objections a few weeks later saying that, in retrospect, I had done what I set out to do and he accepted my thesis as is, without revision (largely because he didn't believe it redeemable, I think).

Despite the fact of having support from the other reader of my thesis, a man who prefaced his comments with an early, hostile review of Walt Whitman, and the support of my adviser who had read and described the poems as moving, effective, and so on, the barrage of hate that visited me that afternoon lingered for years and realized my worst fears: if I make myself vulnerable in my work, if I give my work to the public, I will be attacked. My inability to defend myself effectively, to understand that publicness is a kind of veil, didn't help.

There are those who say that such moments are good for weeding out the weak. And for a while it seemed that was the case; that I *was* weak and would be weeded out, or weed myself out. I have been weeded out many times in my life.

16.
"I am afraid of being changed," my students often explain when they resist new or unfamiliar work. Once an idea "is inside" there is no "getting it out," a poet, and author of three books of poetry, confessed recently. She wasn't about to read conceptual writing because she was afraid of the influence, that she couldn't undo it.

There is some truth in that.

17.
Douglas Coupland writes: "A good teacher teaches you what to love, a bad teacher teaches you what to hate."[21]

18.
In 2003 I finally changed the poetry channel. I did so at a retreat in Vermont. It came after a particularly gruelling year teaching where I thought I would never have my own thoughts again, let alone write. For one month I had nothing but my own time. I wrote every morning, and then spent the afternoon reading—Gertrude Stein, Virginia Woolf, Lisa Robertson, Erín Moure, Anne Carson—and the evening, from dinner on, in conversation with thirty other artists and writers, looking at their art, listening to them read.

In my little studio, on my laptop, I wrote fluidly the entire time I sat. It was the most instinctive and unsettling experience I had ever known. I was writing very close to my thinking. Closer than I had ever allowed. Fast and loose, not worrying, as I did with my thesis, about what I was revealing about myself and not letting myself be vulnerable in the same way. Letting instinct, not reason, guide me, but in a very mindful or intentional way. I was allowing my experience, my "story," and the stories of the lives of those I knew and loved, those stories and emotions that inspired me to write, to transform, and mingle with other stories, and other writing. I was working with great purpose and direction, even though I was allowing my thinking to take leaps, to have gaps. My work has always had these leaps, but where I had previously seen myself as being limited by them, not quite achieving the conventional structures, now I allowed myself to consider that these leaps might be good.

I wasn't sure who was speaking anymore. I was no longer I and yet it was more I than ever. The text was no longer bogged down by my old expectations of what a text or a poem should or should not be, or any of the reading I had done.

Just because you love sonnets, it doesn't necessarily mean you should be writing them. You can love Oulipo, it doesn't mean you should be writing like that. You can love Emily Dickinson, or Fredrick Seidel, or Erín Moure—it doesn't mean you need to write like them.

Loving all kinds of poetry doesn't mean you can write all kinds of poetry.

But it might expand your view of things because you write your own poetry in relationship to other poetry, it makes your poetry more your own.

When I read what I had written that summer in Vermont—which eventually became the collection of poetry, *Lemon Hound*, published in 2006, and *Autobiography of Childhood*, the novel I published in 2011—out loud in readings in New York, I felt utterly transported to a new space. This space was entirely of my own creation—clearly built in relation to what I had been reading and thinking—and yet my own, very solid, inhabitable space. As if the poems billowed out around me, expanding me, but also protecting me. The poems were of me, but also, palpably, outside of me. I felt, perhaps for the first time, that I was expressing myself the way that I think, the way that I process my experience of living.

It was terrifying and deeply pleasing.

The line I had drawn earlier, I realized, was a line within me. A line I carried. I honoured and I pushed further when I needed to grow.

19.
When people—okay, mostly when women—tell me they don't blog, don't comment, or otherwise take up public space, the primary reasons they give are variations on the theme of "being changed." How can we know how sharing our thoughts on a regular basis will change us?

And it's true. To blog is to change mediums. It's to change the act, the space, and pace of writing and publication as much as it is speaking out.

Every time we change the way we compose we are changing our relationship to our work. But I would argue that even when we change locations, or projects, never mind mediums, we are also rewiring our brain. It is partly technology, yes; at the time of my initial blog post in 2005 I was still adjusting to the fact of having Wi-Fi access on my laptop, never mind composing "in public."

There was a time when I refused to compose poems on my little Mac Plus. I could transcribe, I could write "essays," but not compose poems. And I swore I would never do revisions of essays, or of poems, on a computer because it was too easy: revision amounted to cutting and pasting, not rethinking or "re-envisioning," which I take to mean starting over on a clean page. I remember all the anxiety about the space of writing. Trying to control what came in, what I saw, what was potentially influencing me.

I saw a vintage ad the other day calling for people to turn off the television and read a book, which reminded me of a quaint time when one could say, I don't want a television in my house, and take the television out of the house.

There is no longer anywhere away from screens. As Marshall McLuhan predicted, instead of television most of us are glued to our screens, we carry them with us, and we can do everything from listen to the radio, pay bills, shop for shoes, book travel, talk to our friends, visit libraries, watch movies, and television, buy, sell, publish our work, and—sometimes—write our poems.

Now the space of composition has shifted to even more micro and mobile composition modes such as Twitter. Here the form is the sentence, the constraint, 140 characters or less. There are many excellent conceptual projects under way—Nick Montfort's palindromes, Literary figure accounts such as Emily Dickinson, Sylvia Plath, Proust, and poets retweeting whole novels (@VanessaPlace tweeting *Gone With the Wind*). There are also people beginning to post original poetry on Twitter (see Martha Jane Canary @CanaryCalamity, Liz Bachinsky @ebachinsky and Matthew Tierney@ hayflick). There are poets who do amazing mash-ups (Kim Kierkegardashian @kimkiergardashian) or astute social commentary (Teju Cole @tejucole).

My latest poems—the poem offered in this collection, for example—are being composed on Twitter. Now I have a word processing "app" on my iPhone and I write while I walk, which is often the only time I have. I save them to a cloud as I cross the street, taking a photograph of my feet on the curb. Was the Twitter composition a leak or a leap? Is this a pubic or private mode of composition? Discuss.

I should add that I no longer compose on my blog—Lemon Hound has served me well, but is no longer mine. Well, the old blogger version is, but it's past tense. The new version, launched while the Public Poetics conference was happening in Sackville, NB, is as a literary journal with reviews, correspondents, and space for curators to work and gather archival materials related to visual art, poetry, and poetics, and will be written and maintained by many. I is finally, truly, a communal I. I is we.

Further, my partner, Danielle Bobker, gave this paper shape when I flagged at the conference deadline. We are rarely the single I. We are two I's joined by the arms, if you can imagine the small I with its dot as an arm and hand reaching out. IiiI = W as in We.

20.
As Kenny Goldsmith points out in *Uncreative Writing*, both Yoko Ono & Sol Lewitt suggest that "art should exist only in the mind."[22] To the extent that art helps shape our thinking, how we interact with the world. We ingest art. We are our thinking. Our thinking is art. Lucy Lippard wrote about this in *Art Forum:* how her practice of social activism is closely aligned with her art practice.[23] The poet Mary Burger is becoming a landscape designer. Many poets have similar folds between practices. For others—Jean Valentine, Kazim Ali—there is a mingling of prayer or meditation in their poetic practice. The performance artist Vito Acconci moved toward architecture because, he says, "something that starts private ends in private."[24] If one wants a poetry that is "public" one needs to begin in "public."

We are what we do. Or, as Diana Brydon notes in her contribution to this collection, we are *where* we think.

"If u don't share u don't exist," Calgary poet derek beaulieu says. To the extent that the Internet can be said to be public, we are writing ourselves in this virtual space.

Not that to be interior is necessarily silent, but to not take part in the public world of poetry is, in effect, remaining silent. The poem is a bowl of silence composed in public.

If you never risk speaking in public, to a public, then you may feel safe in your practice, but you may also feel alone and anonymous and mute. You might also not have a critical voice. It's like not voting. And if you don't vote you're a hypocrite to complain about the outcome. If you don't like the paucity of women taking up critical public space and you yourself take no risk to speak out, you are part of the problem.

Notes

1. Queyras, "On Misdirected Energy."
2. *Best American Poetry,* "Women Who Write Poetry and Criticism."
3. For the record, this is a poet whom I have offered space on Lemon Hound to publish her critical opinions repeatedly, and a poet who Tweets really smart, essential opinions on many feminist concerns, repeatedly, if on a protected (read, non-public) account.
4. *CWILA*, "Interview with Sheila Heti."
5. I have always been terrified of public speaking, yet one of my first jobs was as a reporter. I had my first byline on my sixteenth birthday, but for a year before that my writing appeared almost daily in the paper. So already I had a willingness to speak out.
6. Collis had legal actions brought against him, with his writing cited as "evidence," in the fall of 2014.
7. Stephen Collis, email to author.
8. Warner, "Publics and Counterpublics," 417.
9. Warner, "Publics and Counterpublics," 81.
10. Warner, "Publics and Counterpublics."
11. Thompson, "Talking *Expressway* at Truck," 26 February 2009.
12. Queyras, "Lyric Conceptualism."
13. Keller, "FFFFFalling with Poetry."
14. Brock Broido, "Myself a Kangaroo."
15. Ai Weiwei, "Editorial."
16. Gallagher, "William Gibson."
17. Garner, "A Critic's Case."
18. Davis, *Women, Race, and Class.*

19 CBC Digital Archives. "Le Refus global."
20 Sina Queyras, *Someone From The Hollow*, M.A. thesis, Concordia University, 1995.
21 Coupland, "Some Practical Writing Advice."
22 Goldsmith, *Uncreative Writing*, 18.
23 Lippard, "Lucy Lippard."
24 Acconci, "Designer of the Year."

Bibliography

Acconci, Vito. "Designer of the Year." *Whitewall Magazine*. Accessed 18 June 2013 at http://whitewallmag.com/all/design/vito-acconci-design-miami-designer-of-the-year.

Ai Weiwei. "Editorial." *Art Forum*, September 2012, npag.

Best American Poetry. "Women Who Write Poetry and Criticism." Accessed 18 June 2013 at http://blog.bestamericanpoetry.com/the_best_american_poetry/2012/08/women-who-write-poetry-criticism-roundtable.html.

Brock Broido, Lucie. "Myself a Kangaroo among the Beauties." In *American Woman Poets in the Twenty-First Century: When Lyric Meets Language*, ed. Claudine Rankin and Juliana Spahr. Middletown: Wesleyan University Press, 2002.

CBC Digital Archives. "Le Refus global." Accessed June 18, 2013 at http://www.cbc.ca/archives/categories/arts-entertainment/visual-arts/le-refus-global-revolution-in-the-arts/automatists-suffer-backlash.html.

Collis, Stephen. Email to author, 28 August 2012.

Coupland, Douglas. "Some Practical Writing Advice from Douglas Coupland." *LitReactor*. Accessed 18 June 2013 at http://litreactor.com/columns/some-practical-writing-advice-from-douglas-coupland.

CWILA. "An Interview with Sheila Heti." Accessed 18 June 2013 at http://cwila.com/wordpress/an-interview-with-sheila-heti.

Davis, Angela. *Women, Race, and Class*. New York: Vintage, 1983.

Gallagher, Aileen. "William Gibson on Why He Loves Twitter." *Vulture*. Accessed 18 June 2013 at http://www.vulture.com/2010/09/vulture_transcript_william_gib.html.

Garner, Dwight. "A Critic's Case for Critics Who Are Actually Critical." *NYTimes.com*. Accessed 18 June 2013 at http://www.nytimes.com/2012/08/19/magazine/a-critic-makes-the-case-for-critics.html?pagewanted=all.

Goldsmith, Kenneth. *Uncreative Writing: Managing Language in the Digital Age*. Chicago: University of Chicago Press, 2011.

Keller, Lynn. "FFFFFalling with Poetry: The Centrifugal Classroom." In *Poetry and Pedagogy: The Challenge of the Contemporary*, ed. Joan Retallack and Juliana Spahr. London: Palgrave Macmillan, 2006.

Lippard, Lucy. "Lucy Lippard As Told to Lauren O'Neill-Butler." *Art Forum*. Accessed 18 June 2013 at http://artforum.com/words/id=46694.
Queyras, Sina. *Autobiography of Childhood*. Toronto: Coach House, 2012.
———. *Lemon Hound*. Toronto: Coach House, 2005.
———. "Lyric Conceptualism, A Manifesto In Progress." *Harriet a poetry blog*. Accessed 18 June 2013 at http://www.poetryfoundation.org/harriet/2012/04/lyric-conceptualism-a-manifesto-in-progress.
———. "On Misdirected Energy." *Lemon Hound*. Accessed 18 June 2013 at http://lemonhound.blogspot.ca/2012/07/on-misdirected-energy.html.
———. *Someone From The Hollow*, M.A. thesis, Concordia University, 1995.
———. *Unleashed*. Ed. Kate Eichhorn. Toronto: Book Thug, 2009.
Thompson, Jane. "Talking *Expressway* at Truck." *FFW Weekly*. Accessed 9 September 2014 at http://www.ffwdweekly.com/article/life-style/books/talking-expressway-at-truck-3367.
Warner, Michael. "Publics and Counterpublics." *Public Culture* 14, no. 1 (2002): 49–90.

2

The Threat of Black Art, or, On Being Unofficially Banned in Canada

El Jones

Chris Rock has a joke about how in every town there's the White mall and the Black mall. In the slam community in Canada there is the White scene and the Black scene. In bigger cities this can happen in *quietly* racist ways: there's the team everyone knows, a.k.a. the White team, and then there is the other team, a.k.a. the Black team. The Black team is always considered to be the other team even if it came first and even if it is more successful. In cities that supposedly have one scene, the Black scene may be unofficial, like the way Black people in Halifax nod our heads at each other in acknowledgement and solidarity, but everyone knows what it is.

In Halifax, where I live, the Black scene means never being covered by the weekly alternative news and entertainment periodical, *The Coast*. It means having won two national championships and being paid less than the Canada Council minimum to speak and perform at government events while a White man with no credentials gets paid half a million dollars to perform consultations with the same agencies that praise the brilliance of your work but would never think of paying you fairly for it. It means having to measure your work by those national championships, because Black-based art forms are not respected on their own terms. It is sending the first all-Black team to Nationals and winning. It means having your labour undervalued because Black people are never considered to be artists, just entertainers. It is the assumption that Black people create naturally, from instinct, so therefore you are not compensated like White artists. It is the expectation that you will perform for free because your work is labelled political. It is only being asked to perform in February. It means hosting the national slam and having the Black artists from the rest of Canada discover that Black people cannot get cabs in downtown Halifax. It means every Black artist being late to the slam on a rainy night because of this. It means sharing that experience in poems performed at the next year's slam. It is Lawrence Hill coming to speak about the *Book of Negroes* at Dalhousie University and having the seats in the room all filled with White people while Black people are standing at the back or left outside. It is nobody questioning this hierarchized use of space or rearranging this audience structure. It is nobody insisting the event stop until we do.

It is White audiences being centralized even for a Black author and Blackness being pushed to the margins.

It is also providing a political, spiritual, and emotional touchstone for Black poets in the rest of Canada through the presence of Africville. It means carrying that legacy in your poetry. It means living and working and speaking within and from and to a Black community who see the work of Black artists in a continuum with daily life, with preaching in church, with educating, with honouring, and learning about history culture and so there is no real place where Black life ends and Black art begins. The Black scene means community centres and political rallies and African Canadian Studies classes and Black Youth Fellowship and performing your poem about Malcolm X at the Black Cultural Centre for one of his pallbearers and it only kind of means the stage where you host your series. It means that the public I speak about when I consider the theme of "Public Poetics" is not the same as the public you envision, not only because the faces in my imagination are not the same colour, but also because being a Black spoken word artist in Nova Scotia means that there has never been a time that poetry and performance have not been bound up with whatever we mean by the public, by the people, the ancestors, the collective. It means that I have never considered not having poems that junior high school students can relate to and that the craft it takes to accomplish this is never acknowledged.

It means performing in church even if you are not Baptist. It means having your poem take twice as long when you do because listening in the Black community is an active and shared experience. It means being integrated into the verbal life of the community so that performance flows from and with and into daily experience, so that to even write out this contribution and try to define something that is so naturally understood as part of lived life is to assign Eurocentric categories and labels to an artistic experience that by its very nature is holistic. It is being the only city in Canada that competes in the National slam that does not hold a monthly slam series because it is more important to provide a venue and voice for marginalized people to speak. It is recognizing that the value of this speech cannot be rated by audiences, validated by competing, or measured by a score. It is calling your series SPEAK! in recognition of silencing. It is to live on the margins of a Canadian slam scene dominated by teams from Ontario and for that scene to be happy to exclude you.

Being a Black slam artist in Canada means the belief that everything that happens at the National slam in the States is better. It is participating in an organization that directs all its policies towards copying that slam. It is these policies working to devalue and silence the styles that grow out of cultural and regional and social difference. It is fighting against policies aimed at depoliticizing slam and making it less Black. It is believing that a poetry founded out of the legacy of Africville is profoundly Canadian. It is the representatives from the slam cities agreeing at Nationals that the winners of the slam will be booked by all the participating cities that perform, and then never being booked when you win, except by the other Black scenes. It means the shared experience of sitting in the hotel with your team before the competition editing poems so they are not too Black to perform in front of a majority White audience. It means knowing all the other Black teams and artists are doing the same thing. It means sharing those same poems unedited, or the poems you could not do, with those other Black artists after the competition. It is never being asked how you write a poem, but always how you memorize all that. It is people asking if you freestyle your poems. It means knowing what the coded language of White artists means when they talk about how they prefer to do work that is more artistic rather than political. It means having your work characterized as ranting, as angry, as militant, no matter the form or content of that work. It means having the wide range of Black experiences written about by Black artists reduced to being "just poems about race" as if every poem from a Black perspective is the same. It means originating and innovating an art form that works its hardest when in the hands of the White majority to study, copy, and then erase you.

To be a Black artist in White spaces is to win a National Championship in your home city in front of a Black audience with Black-centred poetry and have the White poets openly say you only won because you are Black. It is for the names of this championship team to mysteriously be left off the website documenting the history of the slam. It is to be a founding team at the first national festival and to have no representatives on the board. It is to be pushed out and told that you jumped. It is to be expected to believe that these repeated slights are accidental. It is to be part of an organizational structure that operates with no understanding of history, or in whose footsteps you walk because they have the privilege of believing that history is irrelevant. It is constructing histories of slam that ignore Black artists. It is a similar festival being moved to the same dates that "When Brothers Speak" has inhabited for a decade and to have the White poets claim ignorance of this event. It is for White artists to be able to be ignorant of a Black-centred event that draws audiences of thousands. It is to have them see no reason to change it when they are informed. It is for no one to see a problem with the absence of these Black poets as a result. It is for a Black team to win that year anyway. It is to realize that you are not supposed to say the words "White people" in poems about racism. It is White poets performing poems about social justice and injustice without saying the words White people. It is to never have serious discussions about institutionalized racism in spoken word. It is the preference for art that offers cultural flavour without the threat of Black politics. It is being asked if you sing. It is to create a Black-centred poetry space and to have it appropriated anyway. It is for Black people to stop coming but White audiences to continue to believe they are participating in a Black space. It is White people always believing they are entitled to speak. It is the recognition that performing poems about racism itself becomes a commodity in a racist society, and having that consumption take the place of actual conversation about race. It is to be viewed as interchangeable with other Black artists and to know that you can be replaced by another Black artist and to have it make no difference no matter what the actual difference in quality or content of your work is. It is to always be forced into competition with other Black artists as a result. It is to be recused from every Black poetry series application to the Canada Council when you serve on the jury because you are cited in each one. It is to not be cited in any of the White ones. It is for no White jury members to be recused from White artists' applications. It is to be present as a token who is not even allowed to advocate for tokenism. It is to still have publication as the measure of worth in an oral and performance art form. It is having "The Beats" identified as the originators of the genre. It is being left out of what studies there are of slam poetry and spoken word or treated as marginal. It is being marginalized because you participate in an art form that is coded as Black at the same time as the art form is being whitewashed because you participate in an art form that is coded as Black. It is to have the term "spoken word" as though it were not poetry.

To be a Black female slam poet is to join all the other Black women who have left slam. It is nobody noticing these disappearances. It is being erased and forgotten the second you leave. It is nobody asking why women, particularly Black women, disappear. It is the sexual exploitation of women by male artists being sanctioned and the women who leave the scene. It is receiving death threats. When you refuse to perform in the same room as a White male artist who poses a racist and violent threat it is being told in reply that another woman performed at a slam that her rapist attended, as though that is the way things ought to be. To be Black and a woman and a slam poet is to be literally forced to compete against racialized representations of womanhood. It is to be judged by audiences who hold White ideals of femininity and to be scored in relation to one's ability or inability to conform to these ideals. It is to encounter, and find reinforced, the stereotype of the strong Black woman and to have your own performances be rewarded for playing into this myth. It is to not be allowed any other range of expression or mode of being. It is to perform art while not being permitted to perform your own humanity. It is to perform poems about your feelings in a society that does not allow Black women to express feelings and that does not recognize the full and human range of feeling when it applies to Black women. It is to be judged as angry whether or not you are actually angry and whether or not you are always angry and no matter how and why that anger is justified because to White audiences the very act of your speaking is confrontational and threatening. It is being expected to be freely available at all times to justify and explain your poetry. It is the expectation that White people somehow have the right to engage you in these discussions. It is the belief that if you refuse to respond, or if you respond, with anything except complete and total patience, that you are angry. It is being scared to demand what you are due for fear of being labelled an angry bitch. It is being constantly told by male artists that Black female anger is a destructive rather than a creative force. It is being told by male artists that it would be better if you wrote some love poems or something funny to vary your set minutes after you receive a standing ovation from Black women who are grateful to have their own anger recognized and given voice. It is knowing as those women know that Black women sharing in anger about racism together is an act of healing. It is having Audre Lorde speak to you in the same way. It is young Black women approaching you after the show and hugging you silently. It is giving voice to their experiences, because these experiences are yours.

It is going to dinner with a colleague, also a woman of colour, who shares with you later that people asked her if she wasn't scared to meet and talk with you. It is feeling dehumanized by this image of yourself. It is being introduced by the uncle of one of the students you taught at the community barbeque to a friend with the words "she is all about helping the people" and feeling that what you do and sacrifice in order to do must be worth it. It is being aware of the difference between that version of you and the one held by the White people around you. It is to perform poems about police brutality at the community justice forum and to have the White male police lodge a complaint against you on the grounds that you are threatening when they carry weapons and possess the power of the state. It is never being invited back to community justice events as a result. It is winning the National Slam four months after you began performing and feeling happy and proud and sending the video to the White male professor who used to mentor and encourage you when you wrote page poetry in your undergrad and to have him write back that he thinks your poetry would be more effective if you didn't rant at the audience. It is noting that he assumes that your audience is White people. It is realizing that what to you was the most profound act of unsilencing in your life when you began writing poems about your experiences as a Black woman was to others a disappointment and a sign that you became like every other Black person with a chip on their shoulder. It is recognizing, not for the first or last time, that to speak about racism and to work against it means losing at various points parts of important things in life: friendships, jobs, money, and health. It is coming to term with those losses through poetry. It is to reassure yourself when these things happen that when you perform in front of a Black crowd it will be different.

It is performing for hundreds of Black women at "When Sisters Speak" and having a White male poet message you six months later and tell you that your performance and the applause you received were "disgusting" because you spoke about the silencing of racism and violence against Black women. It is him telling you what racism really is and how his oppression as a White man is more important. It is him writing a poem where he threatens to slice you up if you continue to speak. It is recognizing the racism and sexism in his message. It is responding angrily. It is having people tell you that because you responded with anger you are equally or more at fault. It is to be told that you deserve it because you perform poems that make White people uncomfortable. It is the conversation becoming about a White man's feelings and not violence against Black women. It is the organization refusing to do anything to address racism and telling you instead that you should just slam it out at Nationals. It is the belief that dialogue about racism can productively take place through the scoring of poems. It is the solution being that you perform the same poems about racism that you were told made you deserve death threats in the same place as that poet and being expected to listen to him threaten to slice you up at the same time. It is boycotting that Nationals. It is being joined by only one comrade and having all conversation or evidence of protest erased from any public space controlled by the festival. It is White poets performing poems at that Nationals about social justice but recognizing no solidarity with Black women. It is recognizing that it is Black art and Black artists and Black resistance that is constituted as a threat. It is not being invited to perform anywhere in Canada for the next two years. It is being silently removed from the board of *Spocan*. It is the atmosphere of denial surrounding this freezing out. It is the irony of being unofficially banned for performing poems about the silencing of racism against Black women and being silenced as a result. It is the complicity of poets across Canada with this silencing through passivity. It is disappearing like the Black women who left slam before you.

3

The Counter/Public in Pain: The Making and Unmaking of Poetry in Canada

Tanis MacDonald

> *The conception that artifacts create people is right. The conception that creative power originates in the artifact is wrong.*
> —Elaine Scarry, *The Body in Pain*

> *A kind of rough strength and a personal tang—the body odour of indignation—give a validity and virtue even to crude rhymes and popular doggerel.*
> F.R. Scott and A.J.M. Smith, "Introduction," *The Blasted Pine*

The terms of making poetry are the terms of making publics; this dual making is, in turn, inseparable from the role that power plays in the creation of a poetic public and of a public poetics. The creation of a poem as a cultural artifact—even one that recalls a time of extreme pain in Elaine Scarry's scenario, or carries forward "the body odour of indignation" in F.R. Scott and A.J.M. Smith's example—remains the concern for all three critics. Scarry's assertion that "artifacts create people" is very close to the idea that artifacts can create a public, but she is adamant that power remains with people even as those people are "made" by the poems. Scott and Smith's tongue-in-cheek contention that "rough strength and personal tang" attach to poems and can be the "making" of a (perhaps unearned) public approbation is aligned with this statement's context as part of an introduction to a collection of "disrespectful verse," but it is not so far from the usual acerbic tenor of Scott and Smith's poetic criticism. As examples of how a public poetics may be conceived as powerful or attention-grabbing, these statements note that pain can inspire an address of such a public through poetics.

In the realm of painful situations, there is nothing quite like stacking the deck against oneself with a title whose broad terms suggest the impossibility of a complete answer even as that same title is underscored by its urgent subject matter. The task of reading Canadian poetics as a public that converses, debates, and defines the terms of its own communal parameters and, simultaneously, perversely, and productively, as a counterpublic that works against itself to challenge and delimit definitions of "Canadian" and "poetry" engages an enormous topic: one that has been debated, in various forms, at least since the conversations about poetics in a "new country" between W.W. Campbell, Archibald Lampman, and Duncan Campbell Scott in their column "At the Mermaid Inn." The enormity and the scope of the subject, buttressed by the canonical positioning of sometimes creaky historical texts like "At the Mermaid Inn," are as likely to infuriate readers as they are to establish a readable and satisfying literary history, and some of these infuriating constructions have their uses as catalysts for thinking about the changing paradigm of Canadian poetry in the contemporary moment. For we could rethink our literary history in terms of literary movements other than the lyric mode, or different literary publics than the white middle class filtered through middle-of-the-road modernism as it was moulded by the *Massey Report* and its subsequent recommendations for Canadian culture in the years following the Second World War. The curiousness of Canadian modernism as a largely (though not exclusively) post-1945 phenomenon, exactly when Europe began its exploration of postmodernism, has been a thorn in the side of Canadian literature instructors for years. I will not list every possible turn of alternative trails, but the last decade has offered many examples of reading the publics of Canadian literature differently, including Di Brandt and Barbara Godard's essay collection *Wider Boundaries of Daring: The Modernist Impulse in Canadian Women's Poetry* (2009); Gregory Betts's *Avant-Garde Canadian Literature: The Early Manifestations* (2013); and George Elliott Clarke's *Odysseys Home: Mapping African-Canadian Literature* (2002). There is no shortage of alternative ways to read Canadian literary history and so reconfigure, or reframe, the concept of the public in Canadian literature.

But Canadian poetics is a special case of a public that repeatedly enacts its own paradoxical construction and undoing. The idea of a simultaneously existing public and counterpublic conjures an image of a knot that is perpetually tied and untied by an unseen hand. The knot is offered for examination, swiftly undone by the invisible hand, and just as swiftly knotted again. The rhetorical strategies for approaching the knot—and its alternating corollary, the loosened string—are important, for it seems as though those of us who participate in Canadian poetries (by reading, writing, discussing, and/or teaching) have to trick ourselves into this conversation every eight to ten years. Favourite recurring topics include the values or the costs of divisions in poetic practice, the definition and redefinitions of poetic terms and schools, the *bête noire* of regionalism, a prickly sense of ownership of concepts and methods, and a stout cliquishness especially when we have been a part of the establishment or the solidification of such territories. In the face of habits and propensities from which I cannot, in all good conscience, absent myself, what follows is in no way an answer or even good procedural advice but one reading of the dynamics of public and counterpublic as they shuttle back and forth in Canadian poetries and poetics, read through gestures of making and unmaking.

Some of these gestures originate from my own position as a poet–critic, and my rhetorical strategy requires my acknowledgement of self-reflexivity. In fact, I have tricked myself into approaching the subject with a methodological carrot-on-a-stick, proposing not only to analyze the contemporary moment but also to approach it mimetically, in Theodor Adorno's sense of mimesis: to assimilate myself, as speaker, into the text of the contemporary moment through "the infectious gestures of direct contact suppressed by civilization, for instance, touch, soothing...coaxing."[1] When this essay was a conference presentation for the Public Poetics conference in Sackville, New Brunswick, one of the "gestures of direct contact" was embedded in my presentation: the fact that I stood before people and spoke. The "touch" in this context was my voice itself, and my (reasonably) vulnerable physical person standing before an audience of practising poets and critics with a question-and-answer period bearing down on me. So the transfer of this paper to a written version changes the register of my argument a bit, but even so, the idea of "soothing" with this paper is especially ironic when I have proposed analytic tools that are bristling with blades with which I could cut my own argument to ribbons as much as cut a swath through the proposed material. However, the title and the terms of this contribution remain unchanged precisely because my aim is to examine the role of pain in shaping a discursive corpus of and about Canadian poetry, with a special interest in gestures of making and unmaking. The critic's pain (as criticism and as text) is written into this paper, as is an old—but excellent—question from Scott and Smith, the evil angels of Canadian poetic criticism, who ask in their introduction to *The Blasted Pine*, "Is it too sanguine to hope that...in the future the stubborn, subversive, intelligent reaction to the standardized life will continue to find a voice—at least from our poets and artists? Will anyone listen?"[2] I am reasonably sure that I live a standardized life according to Scott and Smith's standards for a university professor, but I live a very non-standardized life according to their standards for a woman, so I appreciate their question with the standard amount of Morton's iodized free-pouring sodium chloride, taken as necessary.

My research into the feminist politics of the elegy brings a certain rhetorical force to bear upon a historical continuum that positions the articulation of poetics as inevitably about pain and pain's pressures in the form of "ugly feelings," as Sianne Ngai calls them, and such a rhetorical position has, in turn, much to say about that shifting set of parameters we call Canadian poetry in the contemporary moment.[3] There were waves of painful news for Canadian readers and writers in the spring and summer in 2012, with seemingly endless aggressive challenges (political, professional, rhetorical, personal) to my dual practice from government, law, electoral practice, cultures of violence, and reports of desperately waning student, professorial, and literary mental health. The inequities facing women writers and women reviewers came to a head to in public debate—a sometimes toxic, sometimes invigorating series of exchanges that led to the establishment of the Canadian Women in the Literary Arts (CWILA)—even as the cruel misogynies of the Republican Party in the United States flooded our news media. Physical assaults on women in southwestern Ontario were rampant, and the revelations of depression and suicide in the lives of writers David Foster Wallace and Shulamith Firestone seemed like real-life manifestations of Joyce Carol Oates's traumatizing delineation of madness and responsibility in academia in her novel *Mudwoman*. The summer of 2012 was a season in which the forces of pain were acutely attenuated to inspire refusal or engagement from Canadian poets, and many struggled with bewildering combinations of both feelings, often with a dose of rage included. The autumn of 2013 saw an online debate about gender and reviewing in Canadian poetry that left many people stunned not only by the overt practice of privilege asserted by some critics, but also by the violent language that accompanies that privilege. With these forces in mind, I would like to foreground the idea that one of Adorno's "infectious gestures of direct contact" that has the currency of necessity is this discussion as it is situated as part of an ongoing conversation: a way to bring myself—and readers—to ground where a considerate consciousness may dwell, and in which thinking about publics as they act for (and act against) poetry in

Canada may proceed with a curiosity that will foster more talk rather than less. These four sets of gestures of making and unmaking by four very different thinkers (Elaine Scarry, Sianne Ngai, Michael Warner, and Marjorie Perloff) will serve as ways to approach some long-standing puzzles and truisms about writing and teaching poetry in Canada and about the role of pain as a force in the shaping of Canadian poetry communities.

Predicating Criticism: Elaine Scarry and the Visibility of Pain
The Body in Pain, Scarry's seminal 1985 study of pain's relationship to the structures of belief, is subtitled "The Making and Unmaking of the World," and Scarry justifies her use of these terms by explaining that just as the "story of *physical* pain" is "a story of the expansive nature of human *sentience*," so too does the story of "*expressing* physical pain eventually open into the wider frame of *invention*."[4] To follow Scarry down this affective rabbit hole we must be willing to consider the ways that painful experiences unmake the world for an individual—that is, the ways in which pain causes the individual to doubt the composition and reliable nature of reality. Scarry notes that the "verbal and material artifacts" of such suffering reconstitute or "make" the world. Most pertinently, Scarry examines "the way other persons become visible to us, or cease to be visible to us...the way we make ourselves...available to one another through verbal and material artifacts, [and] the way the derealization of artifacts may assist in taking away another person's visibility."[5] It is in that "derealization of artifacts" that Scarry's theory of affect bumps up against how Canadian poetry can be "unmade" in a very public manner.

On reading Louis Dudek and Michael Gnarowski's 1967 anthology *The Making of Modern Poetry in Canada*, a reader could be forgiven for concluding that gestures dedicated to "unmaking" have been the very constitution of Canadian poetry. In categorizing the gestures of unmaking in Dudek and Gnarowski's collection alone, I include fighting, backbiting, jealousy, cliquishness, class snobbery, gender cruelty, homophobia, sniping, carping, and a general willingness to call one's poetic colleagues "half-baked, hyper-sensitive, poorly adjusted and frequently neurotic individual[s]"[6] or possessed of "a facetiousness that springs out of an excessive self-consciousness."[7] One of my favourite dual-function gestures in *The Making of Modern Poetry in Canada* is the inclusion of A.J.M. Smith's "A Rejected Preface," a document that purportedly did not get a chance to "make" Canadian poetry because it was "rejected" from its intended position as the preface to the 1936 anthology *New Provinces*, when E.J. Pratt supposedly "objected to its contents."[8] The "rejected preface" was published instead in 1965 in *Canadian Literature* after Smith spoke about it to Michael Gnarowski, who also championed it for inclusion in *The Making of Modern Poetry in Canada*. Much in this story leans on a kind of manufactured happenstance, earmarked as it is by the kind of bubbling resentment that is passed from master to student—a legacy of revenge eaten cold that has kept literary history on the boil for centuries in most Western nations—and the kind of story that elicits from inheriting generations of poets' and scholars' responses ranging from laughter to high dudgeon. However, as a training tool for scholars in Canadian literature, this tale is offered as a 1936 unmaking or "rejection" that found purchase and justification in a later era, and its 1967 making or "inclusion" is offered in the anthology as an example of Smith's prescience about the direction Canadian poetry took in the decades between. With this in mind, we can see how "making" can be defined by its "unmaking," or by its elisions, rejections, and belated corrections, be they richly deserved, grudgingly granted, or audaciously executed.

When Scarry wrote *The Body in Pain* in 1985, her focus could not be upon thinking about "visibility" and "invisibility" as social media have defined and redefined these terms. But in her discussion of the "structure of belief and its modulation into material making," Scarry makes the very provocative statement that "the consent to have a body is the consent to be perceived and the consent to be perceived is the consent to be described."[9] Insofar as she is discussing the predicate as a tool of self-description, it may be more accurate and timely to refine these terms and say that the consent granted by self-description is the consent to be perceived, and furthermore, to be historicized. *The Making of Modern Poetry in Canada* (both the text and the process) has historically honoured declarative self-descriptions as the bricks and mortar of canon building. Scarry's work with the structure of belief outlines not only the way literature makes culture by offering descriptions of bodies in motion, in life, in death, in pain, but also the way that literature structures cultural belief in the value of such bodies and their accompanying poetic production. But as soon as we accept this as true, we must also consider how culture unmakes or even distorts bodies through a structure of belief: structures that can be as basic as the refusal to self-describe or resistance to declaring an allegiance to a school, group, or poetic practice. How much of making exists in the investment in and occupation of a space that is finite (geographically and institutionally, for example), so that the effort of definition becomes a gesture of making that actually unmakes that which is not perceived to be present? Or is the space of making now infinite by definition, as cyberdistribution, e-books, digital access, social media, and other useful technologies often promise? Even if space has become infinite, can we say the same of our attention?

A strategy that involves casting aspersions as a means of declarative self-definition (what I will call "predicating criticism," based on the examples from John Sutherland—to whom *The Making of Modern Poetry* is dedicated—and A.J.M. Smith) is not exclusive to Canadian literature, but we would do well to examine how we perform these gestures and others like them on social media, whatever the future of social media may hold in form, tone, or shifting context. In the opening decades of the twenty-first century, these gestures can range from the issues we choose to address and how we address them, to who we "friend" on Facebook or count as a Twitter "follower," to the declarations made in the status updates we choose to "like," to who we deem worthy to take up in debate and who we dismiss as uninformed, or as incidental to the conversation, to the repetitiveness evident in our ceaseless self-promotion and the degree to which we perceive the ubiquitous "friend" or "follower" as an audience member or as a posthuman soapbox on which we will stand rather than as a reader, a colleague, or a sounding board.

Desultory Pain: Sianne Ngai's Non-Cathartic Emotions as Aesthetic Ma(r)kers

Aesthetic judgements based on clashing feelings, in particular, mirror the disputes between subjects or groups that underlie them: a state of social conflict that not all aesthetic categories make equally transparent.
Sianne Ngai, "Our Aesthetic Categories"

The Body in Pain underscores the creation of artifacts that "make and unmake" a world view on parallel beliefs in a structure of language and Wittgenstein's paradox of the vitality but inexpressibility of pain. If the "world" that is made by such contradictory forces is what we know as Canadian poetry (poems as artifacts and the discourse surrounding publication, canonicity, and history), then the role of pain—and its attendant "ugly feelings," in Ngai's sense of chronic non-cathartic feelings like envy and irritation—makes a large contribution to destabilizing, enlivening, and ironically preserving the framework of Canadian poetry.

In trying to identify "ugly feelings" of contemporary Canadian poetry, again and again I came up against a familiar feeling: an often unfocused, unmethodical, and disconnected feeling that can result from the externally imposed (and sometimes inwardly aligned) demand to define Canadian poetry, to justify one's existence within Canadian poetry, to devise a survey course on Canadian poetry, or to align oneself with a particular school of Canadian poetry. This "desultory pain" makes and unmakes Canadian poetry because it seems to accompany predicating criticism as both a catalyst and a shadow. It is close to but not equivalent to Ngai's term "stuplimity," which she defines doubly as a "strange amalgamation of shock and boredom"[10] and as "the mixture of shock and exhaustion produced and sustained by" texts that have the power to "aesthetically overpower" the reader.[11] Like stuplimity, desultory pain is caught between two uncomfortable affects, but the desultory pain of Canadian poetry is caught between urgency and overwhelm: the canon-building need to situate a text as impressively intellectual or aesthetically awe-inspiring, while at the same time feeling overwhelmed by the breadth and variety of Canadian poetic production, and made insensible to subtleties that are the very wealth of the tradition.

But, while Ngai notes that the "obstructed agency" of true stuplimity makes it one of the "weaker and nastier" of the non-cathartic emotions,[12] there is room in the public of Canadian poetics to consider a possibility that is more expansive: that desultory pain has a subversive agency as a counter-refusal, a responsible fogginess that does not flaunt its impotence as Ngai's non-cathartic emotions do, but rather makes its presence felt through its refusal to adhere to a single system or timeline in Canadian poetry. If, as Ngai notes, "dysphoric affects often seem to be the psychic fuel"[13] that runs an ideology, then desultory pain drifts, like fog, through Canadian poetry, unfocused in aspect but with the strength of ubiquity. Desultory pain is, then, absolutely germane to Ngai's identification of "the question of relevance" as "a very old predicament [that] haunts the discipline of literary and cultural criticism,"[14] haunting the structures of national literatures and their accompanying poetics in particular.

It is a psychological and poetic commonplace to think of pain as a process in art, a process that clarifies even as it devastates, like Gerard Manley Hopkins's "Heraclitean fire" that burns away dross to reveal the essential. But desultory pain appears to be just the opposite of such clarifying pain; desultory pain is characterized by dullness rather than sharpness, by its lack of focus rather than its keen edge; even so, its dissatisfaction with taxonomies and categorizations is driven by an ironic insistence on definition and language's ability to make if not a world then at least a public. Or, increasingly, a counter/public.

Counters and Imbalances: Who's Public in Whose Practice?

> *Without a faith—justified or not—in self-organized publics, organically linked to our activity in their very existence, capable of being addressed, and capable of action, we would be nothing but the peasants of capital— which of course we might be, and some of us more than others.*
> Michael Warner, "Publics and Counterpublics"

Elaine Scarry's proposal that pain is a defining feature of the structure of belief and that its modulation of material makes people visible and invisible brings us decisively to the idea of the counter/public. Or does it? Michael Warner defines a public as "theatrical" in that it is "a crowd witnessing itself in visible space,"[15] to which we would have to add ourselves as part of the crowds of "friends" or "followers" who can now witness ourselves—and others—in the differently visible space of social media. To perceive oneself as part of an identifiable crowd may indeed grant a "sense of totality" to the person in question, but Warner cautions that transpositions between publics have "important social effects" in that a public (say, a *poetic public*) is autotelic, "organized by discourse itself."[16] Such a public not only "exists by virtue of being addressed" but also, in Warner's words, exists as "an addressable object...conjured into being in order to enable the very discourse that gives it existence."[17] Like Scarry's proposition that "the consent to be perceived is the consent to be described,"[18] and my subsequent proposition that the consent granted by self-description is the consent to be perceived and subsequently historicized, Warner's autotelic publics cannot dodge the idea that perception and inclusion assume consent, and tend to exclude histories or politics that operate outside the political and cultural boundaries of the dominant perception.

The role of desultory pain in such a system is significant; it lives on in Warner's caveat against how people that are de-energized through a lack of connection, or through a lack of opportunity to witness the visible and inclusive space of a community or otherwise lose their "faith in self-organized publics," risk becoming "the peasants of capital."[19] Certainly this statement calls for a more thorough Marxist analysis; the Conservative government's drastic reduction of services to Library and Archives Canada and the drastic cuts in arts funding across Canada are evidence of the need for publics to be self-organized. I am not enough of a Marxist critic to proceed much beyond these markers, but I will declare myself— for perception and historicization—enough of a Canadian poet to say that when we lose faith in self-organized publics, when we do not perceive them as "organically linked to our activity in their very existence, capable of being addressed and capable of action,"[20] we also risk becoming peasants of nationalism. We could then be free from the desultory pain of both admiring work and not fully focusing on its aesthetic parameters, but subsumed to the "disintegration of politics towards isolation, frustration, anomie, forgetfulness."[21] There is a vital difference between the restless movement of desultory pain and the stasis of isolation and forgetfulness. While desultory pain is neither enlivening nor energizing, its combination of restlessness and identification coalesces in its intent on making visible that "sense of totality" that Warner claims is necessary to a public. The meandering quality of desultory pain is productive in that it has faith in "how much ordinary belonging" and, I will add, ordinary acknowledgement "requires confidence in a public."[22] This is different, Warner is careful to say, than "the kind of public that comes into being only in relation to texts and their circulation," and he notes that, since publics "exist by virtue of being addressed," there is no public unless we talk about it; there is no public without addressing it as an object we conjure into being with our discourse. Desultory pain, on the other hand, exists in individuals and in the public sphere and is not autotelic, although it does the work of a public when addressed in public space.

The public space of this contribution to *Public Poetics* is in some ways a conversation begun by poetic and critical colleagues, but it also builds on a fundamental component of a public as "a relation among strangers" that relies on the "embodied creativity and world-making of publicness."[23] As social media throw the idea of friendship into sharp relief, we can think of a public as a relation among familiar strangers: blithe commenters, perpetual jokesters, lurkers, trolls, ranters, people who comment very little but avidly spread the opinions and postings of others, and everyone in-between. In *Prismatic Publics*, Kate Eichhorn and Heather Milne make the excellent points that "publics are always works in progress" and that publics must take note of how "bodies *in context* become bodies *as context*," especially when in texts, or in public discourse, "figures have a tendency to lose identitary markers and bleed into their surroundings" becoming "subjects...mysteriously reconstituted as the surfaces upon which a surrounding environment's objects are reflected."[24] These surfaces may be texts, of course, but they also include regions, institutions, publishers, funding applications, grants, reading series, Twitter and Facebook accounts, blogs, reviews (and reviewers), and performances, to suggest just a few possibilities.

So who then, in this welter of media and textual choices, is the counter/public in Canadian poetry? One answer could be those who are not addressed, and those who do not have a sense of belonging to this specified public: people whose unequal power relationship with an acknowledged public, or several overlapping or intersecting publics, means that those writers remain "invisible to us" in the ways that Brandt and Godard, Betts, and Clarke illustrate in their aforementioned studies. It could also mean people who do not predicate themselves as countable, visible, addressable: people who have given up identitary markers or cannot claim them for a variety of reasons. The postmodern slash in counter/public is intended to suggest, among other things, the counter that publics itself and the public that counters itself. The term implies opposition about who makes up a public, who gets to be public, whose voice is the counterforce or the counterweight to a public voice, and even the basic question of who counts in Canadian poetry, and who takes it up, notes it, and writes the article on the poet's work, the entry in the *Canadian Literary Encyclopedia*, the Wikipedia entry, the review, the seminal article, even the counterargument that such a poet is overrated or under-studied. I used to think these questions were about canonicity; now I think they are about community. I used think these questions were about poetic quality; now I think they are about predicated visibility.

Constraint and Its Desultory Discontents
It is usual in Canadian criticism to speak of antipathy between avant-garde and lyric poetics, or to distinguish between radical and more conventional poetic practices, but in the addressable, flawed, contextual, and shifting publics of Canadian poetry, beleaguered as we are by desultory pain, the more we position these ways of proceeding as competing or oppositional, the more we lose. Every time I write poetry, every time I teach it, every time I begin a conversation in any kind of public forum, be it academic, literary, or among people who do not read poetry, I feel radical, no matter what poetry I am talking about and no matter what my method. Marjorie Perloff, in her illuminating book *Unoriginal Genius: Poetry by Other Means in the New Century*, quotes Roland Barthes: "To be avant-garde is to know that which has died. To be arrière-garde is to continue to love it."[25] Perloff reads the arrière-garde as something other than "a throwback to traditional forms," and rather as a revival of the avant-garde model that is in a position to save postmodernism from the debilitating sense of being "finished" not only with modernism and discourse, but with life itself.[26] She notes that "citational and constraint-bound poetry" has paradoxically "turned once more to the literary and artistic tradition" in its allusiveness and use of intertexts,[27] and indeed, constraint and citation seem apt metaphors for the non-cathartic movement of desultory pain as it stubbornly drifts through Canadian poetic publics, noting alliances and rifts, charting influences, and constraining histories while citing other histories. If we consider constraint and citation as the public tools of desultory pain, then we can think about not only how we address Canadian poetics but also how we are addressed by it.

Those moments of desultory pain that haunt the counterpublics of Canadian poetry, while they are not clarifying, remind us—uncomfortably—of what is unfinished and what may always be unfinished: a way to think about exchange in discourse, and even reciprocity between poets, between poetics and politics, between institutions and people, and a chance to consider what exactly that groggy, restless refusal to knuckle under to any simple definition of national literature has to be restless about. It is not that reciprocity cannot be a problem unto itself; it can be abused and turned into a minefield of unequal power dynamics and canted privilege. But if a public, even the shifting and dissatisfied publics of Canadian poetry, cannot find generosity or engagement within its consent to be described, then we risk not only becoming peasants of capital, but also becoming serfs of alienation rather than the usefully distracted wranglers of the relentless drift of desultory pain.

Notes

1. Adorno, *Aesthetic Theory*, 81.
2. Scott and Smith, "Introduction," xvii.
3. MacDonald, *The Daughter's Way*.
4. Scarry, *The Body in Pain*, 22 (italics in original).
5. Scarry, *The Body in Pain*, 22.
6. Smith, "A Rejected Preface," 39.
7. Sutherland, "Review of Poems by Robert Finch," 107.
8. Dudek and Gnarowski, *The Making of Modern Poetry in Canada*, 26.
9. Scarry, *The Body in Pain*, 217.
10. Ngai, *Ugly Feelings*, 3.
11. Ngai, *Ugly Feelings*, 270–71.
12. Ngai, *Ugly Feelings*, 7.
13. Ngai, *Ugly Feelings*, 5.
14. Ngai, *Ugly Feelings*, 3.
15. Warner, "Publics and Counterpublics," 50.
16. Warner, "Publics and Counterpublics," 50–51.
17. Warner, "Publics and Counterpublics," 51.
18. Scarry, *The Body in Pain*, 217.
19. Warner, "Publics and Counterpublics," 51.
20. Warner, "Publics and Counterpublics," 51.
21. Warner, "Publics and Counterpublics," 52.
22. Warner, "Publics and Counterpublics," 51.
23. Warner, "Publics and Counterpublics," 52.
24. Eichhorn and Milne, "Introduction," 12.
25. Perloff, *Unoriginal Genius*, 177.
26. Perloff, *Unoriginal Genius*, 58–67.
27. Perloff, *Unoriginal Genius*, xi.

Bibliography

Adorno, Theodor. *Aesthetic Theory*, edited by Gretel Adorno and Rolf Tiedemann, Translated by Robert Hullot-Kentor. London: Continuum, 2002.

Betts, Gregory. *Avant-Garde Canadian Literature: The Early Manifestations*. Toronto: University of Toronto Press, 2013.

Brandt, Di, and Barbara Godard, eds. *Wider Boundaries of Daring: The Modernist Impulse in Canadian Women's Poetry*. Waterloo: Wilfrid Laurier University Press, 2009.

Campbell, W.W., Archibald Lampman, and Duncan Campbell Scott. *At the Mermaid Inn*. 1958. Toronto: University of Toronto Press, 1979.

Clarke, George Elliott. *Odysseys Home: Mapping African-Canadian Literature*. Toronto: University of Toronto Press, 2002.

Dudek, Louis, and Michael Gnarowski. *The Making of Modern Poetry in Canada: Essential Articles on Contemporary Canadian Poetry in English*. Toronto: Ryerson Press, 1967.

Eichhorn, Kate, and Heather Milne. "Introduction." In *Prismatic Publics: Innovative Canadian Women's Poetry and Poetics*. 9–16. Toronto: Coach House Press, 2009.

Jasper, Adam. "Our Aesthetic Categories: An Interview with Sianne Ngai." *Cabinet* 43 (2011). Accessed 6 March 2013 at http://www.cabinetmagazine.org/issues/43/jasper_ngai.php.

MacDonald, Tanis. *The Daughter's Way: Canadian Women's Paternal Elegies*. Waterloo: Wilfrid Laurier University Press, 2012.

Ngai, Sianne. *Ugly Feelings*. Cambridge, MA: Harvard University Press, 2005.

Perloff, Marjorie. *Unoriginal Genius: Poetry by Other Means in the New Century*. Chicago: University of Chicago Press, 2010.

Scarry, Elaine. *The Body in Pain: The Making and Unmaking of the World*. New York: Oxford University Press, 1985.

Scott, F.R., and A.J.M. Smith. "Introduction." In *The Blasted Pine: An Anthology of Satire, Invective. and Disrespectful Verse, Chiefly by Canadian writers*. xvii–xx. Toronto: Macmillan, 1957.

Smith, A.J.M. "A Rejected Preface." *Canadian Literature* 24 (1965). Reprint, *The Making of Modern Poetry in Canada*, edited by Dudek and Gnarowski, 38–41.

Sutherland, John. "Review of *Poems* by Robert Finch." *Northern Review* 1, no. 6 (1947). Reprint, *The Making of Modern Poetry in Canada*, edited by Dudek and Gnarowski, 107–9.

Warner, Michael. "Publics and Counterpublics." *Public Culture* 14, no. 1 (2002): 49–90.

4

Writing the Body Politic: Feminist Poetics in the Twenty-First Century

Heather Milne

In a 2009 issue of *Open Letter* titled "Feminist Poetics: Beyond Stasis?," editors Barbara Godard and Kate Eichhorn claim that at least two generations of feminist poets writing since the early 1990s have been critically overlooked in Canada.[1] While this may have held true in 2009, in 2015 we can arguably risk removing the question mark and declare feminist poetics in Canada to have moved "beyond stasis." After all, many of the writers featured in that special issue—Margaret Christakos, Sina Queyras, Rita Wong, and Rachel Zolf, for example—have received a considerable degree of recognition both in the field of Canadian literary criticism and in the study of North American innovative poetics. But in spite of the increased critical and poetic currency of these writers, their work signals a significant yet underexamined departure from the established frameworks through which feminist poetics tends to be read in Canada.

Feminist literary criticism in Canada has tended to represent feminist poetics as nearly synonymous with a body of writing produced during the 1980s and early 1990s and in particular with writers like Nicole Brossard, Daphne Marlatt, Gail Scott, and Lola Lemire Tostevin. Although feminist poetics during this period was diverse in its aesthetics and its aims, much of it developed a poetics of writing in the feminine that extended lines of inquiry from French Feminist theory and engaged in what Barbara Godard terms "fiction theory," or "writing that embraced a new critical posture, a writing with the text rather than a magisterial critique on the text."[2] The writing was also energized by collaboration and exchange between Québécois and English Canadian writers and theorists. This agenda of cross-cultural exchange can be traced to 1981, when Barbara Godard organized the Dialogue Conference at York University to bring together Québécoise and English Canadian women writers.[3] Out of the Dialogue Conference emerged the Women and Words Conference, which was held in Vancouver in 1983, and shortly thereafter, the bilingual feminist journal *Tessera*, founded by Barbara Godard, Daphne Marlatt, Kathy Mezei, and Gail Scott.[4] Because *Tessera* was so instrumental in the development of feminist poetics in Canada in the 1980s and 1990s, Canadian feminist poetics became almost synonymous with cross-cultural collaboration and exchange between writers from Quebec and English Canada, as well as with translation and innovative "fiction theory" that was heavily influenced by French feminism.[5]

In more recent years, a poetics of bicultural exchange has largely given way to a poetics of global exchange that transcends the borders of the nation, reflecting instead the conditions of global capitalism and its attendant patterns of migration and consumption as well as the role of technology and cyberspace in creating new affinities and alliances. Place is an important theme in this work, but instead of exploring a politics of location in relation to the nation, these writers tend to focus on specific urban spaces and seek to explore the relationship between the local or the intimate and the global. Rather than exploring a poetics of embodied female subjectivity and a mode of writing in the feminine that draws from French Feminist frameworks, these poets conceptualize the embodied subject as always already fractured and fragmented by technology, globalization, and capitalism. Gender does not emerge as a singular concern in this writing but as an implicit and ongoing one, or an "already present jumping-off point,"[6] exemplifying what Rosi Braidotti refers to in a discussion of twenty-first-century feminist thought as "an opening outwards of the process of redefining female subjectivity...that calls for a broadening of the traditional feminist political agenda to include, as well as the issue of women's social rights, a larger spectrum of options that range from cultural concerns related to writing and creativity, to issues that at first seem to have little to do specifically with women."[7] Although the broadened political scope of feminist poetics is in keeping with shifts that have occurred in feminist thinking in general, it arguably renders the work of these poets less easily read through the critical frameworks by which feminist poetics in Canada has largely come to be understood.

The goal of this essay is to orient contemporary innovative feminist poetics in relation to the political concerns that are at the crux of current feminist thought, and to show how the poetic strategies developed and deployed by these writers contribute to a shared and ongoing conversation regarding the relationships between gender, technology, late capitalism, and globalization. In exploring critical, aesthetic, political, and theoretical frameworks through which we might read early-twenty-first-century feminist poetics, I ground my analysis in a brief examination of three texts published over the past decade: Rita Wong's *forage*, Rachel Zolf's *Human Resources*, and Sina Queyras's *Lemon Hound*. It is not my intention to impose a narrative of progress on feminist poetics, nor is it to overdetermine a generational schism or exaggerate the differences between work produced over the past decade and work produced twenty years earlier (there are as many lines of continuity as there are differences, and there is much diversity among feminist poets of all generations). Rather, I wish to posit feminist poetics as a changeable, diverse, dynamic, and rhizomatic political and aesthetic practice that is attuned to the pressing social, political, and theoretical concerns of the cultural and historical context in which it is produced and to show how feminist poets have developed compositional strategies that critically respond to a changing socio-political and technological climate.[8]

Much of this writing is characterized by an embracing of materialist poetics coupled with proceduralist and conceptualist compositional methods, leading somewhat paradoxically to poems that are socially and materially situated yet not always referential in the ways they convey meaning. Many of these writers work with found texts, choosing to modify existing writing in addition to—and sometimes instead of—composing from scratch. In addition to drawing on philosophical, theoretical, and literary texts as source material, they draw on websites, advertisements, newspapers, and scientific discourses, making poetry out of the raw material of contemporary culture. Implicit in this strategy is a questioning of poetic genius and inspiration and the humanist underpinnings of the lyric subject; at the same time, this poetry reflects a generalized anxiety regarding the unprecedented mass of information available in the context of the Internet and the twenty-four-hour news channel. Recycling found discursive materials might also be read in relation to the strong environmental ethic underscoring much of this writing, raising issues regarding the scale of human consumption and waste, issues explored not only through the content of the poetry but also at the level of poetic procedure and form. Much of this poetry is also strongly oriented in opposition to neoliberalism and draws attention to the androcentric and imperialist underpinnings of free market economies, which value profit above all else. While these political and aesthetic concerns are consistent with aspects of contemporary conceptual and innovative poetries in general and specifically with the politics and poetics of groups like the Vancouver-based Kootenay School of Writing, feminist writers have developed a poetics that advances and explores a politicized inquiry into the specific effects of contemporary politics on female subjects. I turn now to a brief examination of texts by Rita Wong, Rachel Zolf, and Sina Queyras to explore some of the ways in which these writers advance a politicized, feminist poetics attuned to the specific social, political, technological, and economic forces of the early twenty-first century.

Poetic Ecologies in Rita Wong's *forage*
In *forage*, Rita Wong develops a process-based poetics that queries the lived effects of globalization, colonialism, and advanced capitalism and posits a close connection among all three terms insofar as they involve the exploitation of people, animals, and the environment in the interest of generating wealth. Although many of the political concerns of this book are not at first glance feminist issues, as Christine Kim observes, "the speaker [of these poems] underscores the need to examine different kinds of violence and complicity, some of which, like the international traffic in wombs encouraged to bear 'emotional crops,' are specific to women."[9] The speaker of Wong's poem forages through the textual, scientific, linguistic, social, and political fragments of a late-capitalist globalized culture and asks ethical and political questions about the land, water, and lives that have been sacrificed for the sake of capital, and the global and national structures of power that persistently devalue the lives of women of colour and Aboriginal women.

Wong explores the history of Chinese immigration to western Canada as well as the present-day effects of globalization on China and its relationship to the West. She writes of her own personal relationship to both of these dimensions of Chinese identity, writing as a Chinese Canadian woman living in a province with a history of racist policies against its Chinese residents that dates back to the nineteenth century while also addressing her own complicity in unequal relations of global power. She makes reference to "the military industrial complex embedded in [her] imported electronics"[10] and the harmful toxins leaching into the groundwater in China, where obsolete computers from all over the world are shipped and dismantled. In a poem called "*sort by day, burn by night,*" she asks, "what if your Pentium got dumped in guiyu village? / your garbage someone else's cancer? economy of scale / shrinks us all / global whether / here or there."[11]

The specificity of place is not absent from Wong's writing, but rather than writing about Canada as a nation-state, she focuses on the social and geographic history of Vancouver and British Columbia, concentrating specifically on the region's legacy of colonial domination and racial oppression and its role in relation to free market global economies. In "reverb," Wong writes, "i counted sweatshops in vancouver's eastside until I got dizzy and / fainted."[12] In "snipstream," she describes Vancouver as a "city of mass condo construction" in which a "social housing shortage continue[s]."[13] Inspired by Aboriginal writers like Lee Maracle and Jeanette Armstrong, she examines the relationships between colonization, language, and place, reflecting on the loss of Aboriginal languages by having Halkomelem words "cracked into or sprouting from" poems in a gesture of remembrance for the languages lost through colonization."[14] In so doing, she aims to "giv[e] back to the languages and cultures invoked," and to explore the intimate connection between language and the geographies from which they emerge."[15]

Underlying Wong's poetics is an ongoing attempt to displace the humanist subject central to conventional lyric poetry in order to see the world through a "less human-centric lens"; in this, she is trying instead to think from the perspectives of land, air, and water.[16] Displacing the humanist viewpoint is a political and ethical act that resonates with her commitment to environmentalist, anti-colonial, and anti-capitalist practices. Wong urges us to re-evaluate our relationship to the land and to living organisms by working against colonial patterns of domination, exploitation, capitalism, and resource extraction. Instead of seeing natural resources as a source of capital, she urges us to radically rethink this relationship as one not of dominance over but rather of coexistence with the land. Such an epistemological shift draws inspiration from Aboriginal and Indigenous frameworks and challenges the anthropocentrism of Western culture. At the same time as it actively attempts to displace the humanist subject, Wong's poetry addresses, and arguably laments, the ways in which technology, globalization, and capitalism have irrevocably altered the self. In "value chain," she reflects on how the self in late capitalism is increasingly delineated through and identified by what people buy: "the internal frontier: my consumer patterns."[17]

Wong develops an ecopoetics that answers Marcella Durand's call for poetry to take ecological processes into itself, "a confluence of matter with perception, observation with process, concentration to transmission, that would most decisively turn what can seem nostalgic remnants of nature poetry into a more dynamic, affective, and pertinent poetry."[18] Wong treats language as a system akin to an ecology that she pollutes and modifies in order to reflect her ecopoetic and ecopolitical concerns. As with all systems, the import or redaction of compounds affects flow and meaning and opens up new political and aesthetic possibilities. Her poems are especially attuned to the issue of genetic modification. In "Nervous Organism," she splices words like a scientist splices genes, resulting in a linguistically playful critique of genetic modification, transgenic experimentation, and globalization: "jellyfish potato / jellypo-fishtato / glow in the pork toys / nab your crisco while it's genetically cloudy boys."[19] Genetic modification turns jellyfish into potatoes, lettuces into basketballs, and avocados into bullets. The "science lab in [her] esophagus" turns the speaker against her will into a site of scientific experimentation and monstrous becomings that "yields slugfish arteries brain murmurs tumour precipitation whack."[20] A "po little jelly-kneed deomonstrator" hurls "flounder-crossed tomatoes" as she protests the North American Free Trade Agreement, suggesting that rather than eating these mutant vegetables, one might use them as tools of resistance.[21] The poem is framed by a handwritten quotation from Northrop Frye's *The Anatomy of Criticism* that reads:

> Some philosophers who assume that all meaning is descriptive meaning tell us that, as a poem does not describe things rationally, it must be a description of emotion. According to this, the literal core of poetry would be a *cri de coeur*, to use the elegant expression, the direct statement of a nervous organism confronted with something that seems to demand an emotional response, like a dog howling at the moon.[22]

Wong builds on Frye's idea to offer a poetic utterance, the emotional response of a "nervous" not to mention "monstrous" organism that moves beyond humanist understandings of the subject and also romantic notions of poetry as a pure emotional expression since expression happens here, at least in part, through a poetics of splicing and experimentation. This speaker is a hybrid experiment, and her "direct statement of emotion" is itself mutated and modified rather than pure.[23]

Although transgenic modification might, on the surface, hold the promise to displace the humanist subject and break down boundaries between species, such activities are, as Vandana Shiva reminds us, an extension of colonialism: "The land, the forests, the rivers, the oceans, and the atmosphere have all been colonized, eroded, and polluted. Capital now has to look for new colonies to invade and exploit for its further accumulation—the interior spaces of the bodies of women, plants, and animals."[24] As such, genetic modification reifies rather than dismantles dominant structures of power. In "Chaos feary," Wong develops a process-based poetics directly inspired by Vandana Shiva's *Biopiracy:*

> pyre in pirate
> mono in poly breeder in
> womb pull of landrace allo
> me poietic auto me diverse
> trans over genic harassment
> over seas genetic as pathetic
> as engine of disease socio
> me catastrophe political and
> eugenic organ as an ism[25]

Wong, following Shiva, develops a poetic biopiracy through playful but politically pointed language in order to draw attention to the colonization of living organisms occurring in the context of genetic engineering. "Chaos feary" enacts a poetics of splicing in order to critique the acts of biopiracy that increasingly characterize the relationships between industry, capitalism, and nature. Wong's process-based poetics enacts "a lucid yet *wild* fusion of structure of poem with structure of matter/energy—*things*."[26] Form and content work together as Wong forages through the fragments of contemporary culture to advance a poetics that is attuned to the ways in which colonialism lives on in current economic and scientific policies and practices.

Poetic Economies in Rachel Zolf's *Human Resources*
While Wong's *forage* explores the radical potential of poetic ecologies, Rachel Zolf's *Human Resources* explores the radical potential of poetic economies. In some respects, Wong's and Zolf's poetics are starkly divergent. Wong urges us to slow down to pay attention to the rhythms of the body and the environment rather than giving in to the demands of a hypercapitalist speed culture. In contrast, Zolf's poetics are frenetic, a point emphasized by the breakneck speed with which she reads these poems aloud at poetry readings. However, both writers develop poetics that are especially useful for thinking through the complexities of embodied, materially grounded subjectivity in the context of advanced capitalist global cultures. Both let go of the humanist subject; Wong through a poetic becoming world, and Zolf through a poetic becoming machine. Wong infects and mutates language. Zolf gleans dirty, discarded devalued fragments of language. Wong's poetics are grounded in ecologies, Zolf's in economies; however, both ecologies and economies favour flux and process over fixed meaning, open texts over closed texts, and mutations and transformations over stasis.

Zolf plays with libidinal, financial, linguistic, and gift economies, creating hybrid poetic economies that implicitly call into question the commodification of identities, politics, sexualities, bodies, and words. Like Wong, Zolf challenges humanist understandings of subjectivity, but she does so through the use of computerized search engines and poetry generators to aid in the composition of her poetry, challenging the equation of poetry with creative inspiration and calling into question notions of poetic value. *Human Resources* answers American poet Laura Elrick's call for a poetics that "bring[s] about new ways of engaging in the practice of poetry, a poetics, in short, that points less toward a fetishistic valorization of 'the text' as object (form & content) and more toward an investigation of mediated textualities that intervene in (and experiment through) the mode of production, circulation, and exchange."[27] Zolf is interested in reclaiming linguistic waste—the banal, the obscene, and the ugly—as part of her poetic practice, disrupting the association of poetic language with beauty. She composes virtually unreadable poems out of material gleaned from a range of sources, including Powerpoint presentations from a continuing education course she took at the University of Toronto, Zolf's own freelance corporate communications for banks and insurance companies, websites, literary theory, and philosophy. Language ceases to function referentially and becomes, instead, a kind of raw material or commodity. These poems investigate the excess of text available through platforms like the Internet, advertising, and corporate communications and further consider how words are both commodified and wasted in these contexts. Zolf sees herself as a gleaner, reclaiming words that have been devalued through excessive use and circulation.[28] She does not evoke a nostalgia for a mythical time when words were valued. Rather, she plunders waste for its poetic possibilities, positing the poet as a "writing machine" that can "spew about anything: private jets, exquisite gardens, offshore banking havens, the Great Ephemeral Skin."[29] Zolf's gleaning is parallel to Wong's foraging; both entail sifting through the fragments of contemporary culture to map "cartographies of the present."[30] Arguably, both are also traditionally female forms of work. *Human Resources* serves as an example of what Marjorie Perloff has termed "unoriginal genius" and Kenneth Goldsmith has termed "uncreative writing." Faced with an unprecedented amount of available text in our contemporary moment, many writers negotiate this excess not by creating more text but by manipulating what already exists, doing so with both aesthetic and political intent.[31]

Human Resources is composed with the help of WordCount (a searchable Internet database of the most frequently used words in the English language), QueryCount (a searchable list of the words most often queried in WordCount), and Gematria of Nothing (a search engine that applies Hebrew numerology to English words). She also uses" Lewis LaCook's Markov chain-based Flash poetry generators" to compose a handful of the poems in the collection.[32] The use of WordCount, QueryCount, and Gematria of Nothing are sometimes indicated in the poems by the inclusion of a "w," "q," or "g" and a number that corresponds to the word's rank or value in the given database at the time the poem was composed (these ranking are constantly shifting since language use is dynamic rather than static). Many of the poems in the collection are so fragmented and disrupted by the letters and numbers that indicate the database values that they are virtually unreadable. Meaning is to be found instead in an understanding of the conceptual and procedural methods informing the composition of these poems.

Perhaps not surprisingly, the highest-ranked words in WordCount are among the most banal (a, the, and) while the most queried words are generally those related to sex, religion, and war (also high in the rankings are certain common men's names, reflecting, perhaps, the fact that men occupy public spaces—including the space of the Internet—more than women). In using WordCount and QueryCount, Zolf draws attention to the hierarchies implicit in how we engage with language and conceptualizes language as an economy in which words circulate with assigned yet ever-shifting values. One poem is comprised mainly of the one hundred highest-ranked words in QueryCount:

> Mass affluent consumers' key satisfaction drivers aspirational by most common queries of most-common-English-words engine: fuck Q1 sex Q2 love the shit god i penis cunt a ass jesus dog Q13 pussy hate bush john me hello vagina america bitch cat dick you war yes she like and cock no damn david gay man computer money word mother michael poop Q42 happy mom asshole orgasm he mike apple peace help one hi car bob fart cool it chris microsoft crap woman what good is death hell conquistador iraq james house mark butt porn cum girl paul home dad work but of beer nigger Andrew tom tit tits usa anal baby stupid boy joe father kill mary school sarah smith Q100 re-scoped the guestimate—the generic one month is longer than 30 days. You can control the reader's reaction without changing the facts[33]

The poem reads like a list of obscenities juxtaposed with numbers, religious references, and men's names, reflecting the ugliness of a patriarchal linguistic economy in which women are objects rather than subjects and militaristic and pornographic discourses are prized above most others. Zolf is not attempting to hold up a moralistic mirror to provoke our horror or contempt over how our culture uses or values language; rather, she is making poetry out of conventionally unpoetic language, reclaiming and defamiliarizing the obscene and the ugly. Zolf recontextualizes sexually explicit language, racist and violent language, clichés, colloquialisms, and the language of corporate capital, building poems that become part of a critical commentary on language and culture. I read this as a politicized, feminist reclamation of language that is at once ironic and irreverent and that speaks back to a cultural discourse rife with sexism and homophobia. Zolf is a queer-identified feminist; her engagement with sexist and homophobic language subverts this language at its very core.

Human Resources is a feminist and queer text that constantly draws attention to the ways in which female bodies, especially queer female bodies, are valued and devalued. It is also a profoundly anti-capitalist project that seeks to interrogate notions of value, commodity, and exchange. Much of the language Zolf uses in this book is gleaned directly from the world of finance, business, and marketing. She skilfully oversees the collision of monetary, libidinal, and poetic economies, as is evident in the following passage:

> You know the drill, there is no writing that is not in economic W383 love W384 with commodity form, and there's stuff coming at me from all directions. Not the downward spiral of deferred want, not tied to lack or cost but generative and regenerative with the lesbian body, compound interest and the juice, the spittle the fluids the fluxes the excrements the flatulence, the nerves. I was pretty sure she and I were on sync [sic], but nothing is not painful. Let's just use the void to think the full. Key her life positions that discovery of subject can be identity plentiful only while one never never never never never need old look home.[34]

Part of this poem is lifted from Monique Wittig's *The Lesbian Body (Le corps lesbien)*, an experimental French novel written in the 1970s. Wittig's novel develops a language through which to write about lesbian desire that subverts and exceeds the limitations imposed on women's bodies by heterosexist articulations of corporeality and desire. Wittig configures the lesbian body through and in relation to a proliferation of erotogenic zones. Mixing language from Wittig's novel with textual fragments culled from other sources—namely, the language of monetary economies and also popular idioms—Zolf meditates on the relationship between economies of desire, language, and finance in late-capitalist culture. It is worth noting that "economic" ranks as the 383rd most frequently used word in English and that "love" ranks one behind it at 384; Zolf invites the reader to reflect upon the implications of both their proximity in WordCount rankings and the fact that "economic" beats out "love" by one point.

In spite of its engagement with cyberdiscourses and virtual communication, the body is undeniably present in *Human Resources* even if the theoretical, conceptual, and poetic frameworks Zolf uses to "write the body" are markedly different from the French-feminist-inspired *écriture féminine* practised by a previous generation of feminist poets. In one poem in *Human Resources*, Zolf makes direct reference to the feminist writing of a previous generation, specifically noting these writers' interest in post-structuralist and French feminist theoretical frameworks, and posits her own engagement with theory and her own participation in feminist poetics as somewhat belated. She writes:

> ...on our 35th birthday, in fact, the *New York Times Magazine* declared theory was dead—just when you'd gotten around to reading it. Here you go again, we're always 20 years behind the times, should've been checking out écriture chicks at the Montreal feminist book fair instead of popping bennies and caterwauling through *Romeo and Juliet* in high school. With close friends a generation [W2065] plenty ill older, you envy a certain ease with bodies, ideas (however dispersed)...Maybe if you'd come to writing through sex (or the other way 'round), she wouldn't feel so blocked about libidinal farodnj [W54051])urng sitcoms economies, tackling *Desire in Language* or *Dissemination* for that matter. Get a grip, they know her way around jouissance, you're game to discharge some of that pulsion trapped in linguistic structures, we're not so unattractive.[35]

With the wry humour that punctuates so many of the poems in *Human Resources*, Zolf addresses a sense of belatedness in having come to feminist poetics after the 1980s. Zolf was "caterwauling" through high school English instead of engaging in the heady and libidinally charged discussions of feminist writing that were occurring at the International Feminist Book Fair held in Montreal in the 1980s. She invokes the close alignment of writing with desire in much of the French-feminist-inspired poetry of that time period, but posits her own approach to writing as more cerebral than libidinal and more prone to blockage than playful slippage: "Maybe if you'd come to writing through sex (or the other way 'round), she wouldn't feel so blocked...you envy a certain ease with bodies, ideas." However, the poem ends with a push beyond stasis: "Get a grip, they know her way around jouissance, you're game to discharge some of that pulsion trapped in linguistic structures, we're not so unattractive."[36] Indeed, Zolf develops her own conceptual poetics that hold the potential to explore new forms of feminist subjectivity, embodied and otherwise. In her case, this involves a critical examination of the ways in which online environments and market logic dictate language, bodies, and desires.

Vanessa Place and Robert Fitterman point out that conceptual writing has flourished in the context of a repressive market economy in spite of the fact that there seems to be no escaping this economy as discourses of resistance are quickly subsumed and commodified by the capitalist regime itself.[37] Neither feminism nor experimental poetry is immune to becoming a commodity in this context. The poems in *Human Resources* display a canny awareness of capitalism's long reach into the affective and political registers of human experience. Herein lies one of the conundrums of contemporary feminist poetics: constructing a liberatory discourse that is immune to commodification is next to impossible. Consequently, one of the characteristics of recent feminist poetries is a move away from discourses of liberation and utopia towards a meditation on the tendency of neoliberalism to appropriate and commodify forms of political activism and resistance. Sina Queyras's *Lemon Hound*, the third and final text I examine in this essay, explores the contradictions presented when free market capitalism appropriates a feminist rhetoric of liberation.

Feminism and Capitalism in Sina Queyras's *Lemon Hound*

Lemon Hound is a meditation on the lives of contemporary women that shares elements of Wong's ecopoetic vision and Zolf's engagement with the effects of technology on bodies and identities. Like Wong and Zolf, Queyras develops a poetics rooted in the language of late-capitalist culture in order to explore the affective, corporeal, and political dimensions of contemporary female subjectivity. *Lemon Hound* draws on both lyric and conceptual poetic traditions and is intertextually engaged with a female modernist literary tradition through a sustained conversation with the work of Virginia Woolf and Gertrude Stein. One section of *Lemon Hound* "unmakes" Woolf's novel *The Waves*, reimagining Woolf's characters as twenty-first-century Torontonians. Queyras's engagement with Stein occurs in part on a formal level, as Queyras "appropriate[s] the tension Stein creates between the borders of poetry and prose...and conveys a poet's understanding of Stein's project of rhythm, insistence and repetition."[38] When asked about her interest in locating this work in relation to Stein and Woolf, Queyras explains:

There was this sense of both of them moving through the city as a way of working things out. And that's what I tried to do with *Lemon Hound*, it was a kind of walking through all the things I had been reading and trying to make sense of. One of the questions I had for myself was: are the lives of women today any different from the questions and concerns Woolf and Stein would have been walking through Paris and London with in the 20s and 30s?[39]

Queyras develops the figure of the Lemon Hound, a *flâneuse* who walks the streets of twenty-first-century New York and Toronto relaying her observations. The Lemon Hound is not so much an embodied speaker or tangible figure as she is a "conceptual lens" through which the reader views a kind of montage of contemporary female subjectivity.[40] Through this figure, Queyras challenges the masculinism implicit in the modernist trope of the *flâneur*. As Griselda Pollock has argued, the *flâneur* has historically represented the "privilege or freedom to move about the public areas of the city, observing but never interacting, consuming the sights through a controlling but rarely acknowledged gaze...the *flâneur* embodies the gaze of modernity, which is both covetous and erotic."[41] Women, as sexualized objects of scrutiny and subject to strict rules of social decorum, were not free to inhabit public space in the same way, making the existence of the *flâneuse*, at least in the nineteenth and early twentieth centuries, an impossibility.[42] Queyras's *flâneuse* not only occupies public space but also records and relays the activities of other women who also occupy this space. In doing so, she writes back to a tradition from which women were largely excluded.

Like Zolf and Wong, Queyras problematizes the humanist subject and its dualisms of nature/culture, human/animal, and human/machine. In this respect, *Lemon Hound* echoes Donna Haraway's call for a cyborg subjectivity that rejoices "in the illegitimate fusions of animal and machine."[43] The women in Queyras's poems are "more engine than mother,"[44] "carry toxins in their fat," and "fold the new into [their] ovaries."[45] The female body in these poems is marked by internal contradictions; it is not the organic body, nor is it the modernist machinic body. The poems are attuned to the ways in which selfhood is irrevocably mediated by technology, media, and advertising. Queyras develops metaphors that liken bodies and affects to machines and technology: "How can she describe the windmill of her aorta? How tibia is her confusion? How like the Microsoft song her frustration flits and crescendos. How like the blue of the XP screen her mood flickers in the traffic-jam hour."[46] These poems do not lament a bygone era, nor do they uncritically celebrate the present. Rather, they offer a series of glimpses into the affective and embodied registers of contemporary female subjectivity and show how technocapitalism shapes ontology and epistemology: "She can name a thousand corporate logos. Her hands and feet are not easily disassembled. She knows fear. She understands Internet wallpaper, Happy Meals and smart bombs. She doesn't worry about cyborg subjectivity. She is a fully unlicensed florist. She is a hothouse."[47]

Empowerment and disempowerment are intertwined in *Lemon Hound*, and many of the poems draw attention to the ways in which liberatory rhetorics have, under neoliberalism, become detached from the collective politics of feminism and aligned instead with notions of individual freedom that are closely tied to consumerism. In the words of Wendy Brown, "the body politic ceases to be a body but is rather a group of individual entrepreneurs and consumers."[48] These dynamics are particularly present in "A River by the Moment" and "On the Scent," the first two sections of the book. The fourteen numbered poems that comprise "On the Scent" track multiple and often contradictory dimensions of female subjectivity. The section is prefaced with an epigraph by Lisa Robertson that reads: "It is too late to be simple," which can be understood as a statement about the complexity of subjectivity, affect, and embodiment in a late-capitalist culture, in which discourses of empowerment are quickly commodified and depoliticized. The women in "On the Scent" are citizen-consumers who both engage in and defy stereotypes. They are caught in a network of contradictions as they attempt to navigate through a culture in which the self is increasingly defined through acts of consumption, and the marketing of individuality and desire under the guise of consumer choice serves to mask underlying forces of homogenization and normalization.

Queyras creates rhythmic, anaphoric, rhizomatic poetic explorations of contemporary female subjectivity through a careful balance of repetition and variation; repetition provides structure, rhythm, and continuity, while variation allows for gradual but significant shifts in perspective that underscore the multidimensionality and mutability of identity and set up a play of contrasts. For example, the fifth poem in "On the Scent" plays with repetition and variation to present a range of political, social, economic, and affective dynamics underscoring late-twentieth-century motherhood:

The mothers were feminists. The mothers marched. The mothers wore purple and read Betty Friedan. The mother listened to Janis Ian and Ferron. The mothers dropped out. The mothers went to Michigan and danced topless... The mothers wore Birkenstocks and dreamed of living in Vermont or Saltspring. The mothers ate dried fruit and brown rice. The mothers lived in the suburbs and shopped. They fought to build credit ratings. The mothers wore sweater sets. The mothers knew nothing of feminism. The mothers ran off to Los Angeles. The mothers liked to sunbathe. The mothers went to Holt's; they discussed Bloomingdale's and Saks. The mothers went to the opera. The mothers had good educations. The mothers had nothing to say. The mothers voted for Regan and Mulroney. The mothers read *Newsweek* and *Cosmo*.[49]

Queyras de-essentializes motherhood by attributing a wide spectrum of activities and convictions to the mothers; notably, none of the actions ascribed to the mothers directly involve childrearing. Queyras defines motherhood in part in relation to political convictions—both left and right—but also though acts of consumption and lifestyle choice: what one eats, where one shops, which pharmaceuticals one ingests, what one buys, what one reads, and the kind of culture one consumes. Irony emerges through the juxtaposition of opposing activities, tastes, and beliefs.

Queyras constructs a similar set of ironic juxtapositions in the fourth poem of "On the Scent," which catalogues the wide-ranging activities of a group of women:

The women are blue. They consider heels an option. They have unplugged Ani and plugged in Radiohead. They are amused. They toast veggie dogs and buy organic; some of them embrace beef. They wear Birkenstocks, they smoke cigars, they wear their hair long or they shave it. They find time. They buy soy. They surf. They bookmark Bitch, Slut, Whore. They are sworn to transgress. They diss meatloaf and socks with sandals. They buy appliances. Everyone is witty. They blend fabrics. They make their own porn. They know the eighteenth century.[50]

Again Queyras plays with oppositions—heels and Birkenstocks, veggie dogs and beef, Ani Difranco and Radiohead, long hair and shaved heads. The catalogue of activities, habits, tastes, and opinions coheres to construct a portrait of the women as having choice and autonomy; however, agency is once again circumscribed by a capitalist logic and a neoliberal individualism that posits the women as individual consumers rather than a collective political entity. Choice, as Inderpal Grewal reminds us, is a "central ethical framework for feminist as well as neoliberal consumer practices and the imbrication of feminism within consumer culture," but choice in these contexts does not always disrupt the status quo.[51]

It is worth noting, however, the points at which Queyras complicates attempts to locate contemporary understandings of female subjectivity simply in relation to consumption and individualism. After spending several paragraphs documenting habits and activities that firmly locate the women in this poem in relation to the marketplace and acts of consumption, she shifts to a more abstract, metaphoric register in the poem's concluding lines: "They are full bodied, they are sweltering, they are rock and graphite, purloined and vegan, heavy-hipped and encyclopedic. They are annotated. They invite the optic. They embrace titanium. They shed their skin daily. Others gather it. There are bags of us in a basement. Earth is there too, aluminum and feather."[52] "Full bodied," "rock and graphite," "heavy-hipped," and "earth" create a kind of weighty groundedness and provide a space outside the registers of popular culture explored elsewhere in the poem. "Encyclopedic" and "annotated" suggest complexity and scope. The reptilian image of shedding skins might be read as a manifestation of a Deleuzian notion of becoming-animal, which, as Suzanne Zelazo suggests, offers a rich framework through which to make sense of Queyras's rhizomatic poetic collages;[53] it might also evoke the constantly shifting identities these women assume as they navigate a culture driven by the fickle whim of the consumer. In such a culture, feminism is often depoliticized through its presentation as a consumer choice or rejected as a relic of the past, the "bags of us in the basement" left and forgotten in a "post-feminist" world.

Lemon Hound is not a post-feminist work; however, it does explore the implications of a post-feminism that, in the words of Angela McRobbie, "positively draws on and invokes feminism as that which can be taken into account, to suggest that equality is achieved in order to install a whole repertoire of new meanings which emphasize that it is no longer needed, it is a spent force."[54] The "Tummy Flat Girls" in the concluding poem of "On the Scent" embody the very post-feminist spirit that McRobbie identifies. These girls "will not embrace feminism. Will not consider ecology or philosophy anything more than a brand name... They are so done with all that. They are so over it. They are so *Whatever*. They are so *Yeah, yeah, yeah*... They are so done with political messages. They are so past any need to protest."[55] Post-feminism relegates feminism to the past, suggesting it is no longer necessary and associating it with older women. Sexual desirability in this framework is linked to youth and a repudiation of feminism,[56] a sentiment echoed by the Tummy Flat Girls in the poem's concluding line: "They are so *Anger is so uncool*. They are so *Move out of the way, rigid one, and let the beautiful one sing*."[57] Empowerment might be found in distancing oneself from feminism in an effort to locate oneself as youthful and desirable, but this empowerment rings hollow, especially when the one-dimensional voices of the Tummy Flat Girls are read against the densely textured explorations of women's lives that comprise *Lemon Hound*. The individualism of the Tummy Flat Girls, and indeed the individualism of the neoliberal consumer-citizen who appears in several of the poems in *Lemon Hound*, is ultimately countered by book's ongoing project of collecting and, indeed, collectivizing dimensions of female subjectivity. In this respect, *Lemon Hound* works against the individualizing tendencies of neoliberalism even as it seeks to articulate their role in the construction of contemporary female subjectivity.

Those looking for narratives of feminist empowerment will not find them in *Lemon Hound*. What they *will* find is a series of provocative meditations on what it means—politically, affectively, economically, and technologically—to occupy a female body in North America in the late twentieth and early twenty-first centuries. The book's politics are located in the irreconcilable contradictions that emerge through these meditations. As Donna Haraway reminds us in "A Cyborg Manifesto," "irony is about contradictions that do not resolve into larger wholes, even dialectically, about the tension of holding incompatible things together because both or all are necessary and true."[58] Irony, central to Haraway's manifesto, is also central to *Lemon Hound*, and like Haraway, Queyras attempts to "build an ironic political myth" that is faithful to feminism and that does not attempt to reconcile contradictions but instead lets the contradictions speak for themselves. The fragments of Queyras's montage-like book speak to, past, and against one another and in the process reveal that, indeed, it is "too late to be simple."

These three writers develop feminist poetics that facilitate complex engagements with contemporary politics: Wong's poetic splicing and foraging allow her to explore the implications of genetic modification and globalization; Zolf's engagement with online search engines advances a feminist, anti-capitalist meditation on the ways in which notions of economy structure our lives; and Queyras's invention of a feminist *flâneuse* allows her to construct a complex montage of contemporary female subjectivity that reflects upon and also subverts the individualizing tendencies of neoliberalism. In each case, poetic form enables a complex engagement with contemporary politics, gender, and public life. This is a poetics that is materialist *and* conceptual.

The work is also marked by a lack of geographical specificity, a moving out into the deterritorialized space of the Internet and global capital. While many of Wong's poems are set in Vancouver and many of Queyras's are set in Toronto, the poems are also set in cyberspace, the global marketplace, the genome, the PowerPoint slide, which makes it a challenge to situate this writing in relation to a national poetry. However, I would hesitate to refer to any of these writers as purely "post-national," since they all participate actively in local and national writing communities both on and off the page. Nevertheless, their work is less concerned with articulating a Canadian imaginary than it is with exploring other dimensions of identity and subjectivity, and in the three texts examined here, in enacting a critical examination of the impact of late capitalism on women in the early years of the twenty-first century. This poetry reflects a turn towards conceptual and procedural writing that is currently occurring within the work of many feminist poets not only within Canada but also elsewhere.[59] These writers work with the raw linguistic excess of technocapitalist, patriarchal culture by redeploying this excess subversively and politically.

Feminist poetics is diverse in its aesthetics and its aims, and it is not my intention in this contribution to *Public Poetics* to suggest that all recent Canadian feminist poetry is marked by a conceptual turn or engages with the themes of technology, neoliberalism, and capitalism. However, a significant number of poets are grappling with the affective and political complexities of female subjectivity in a historical moment that has undergone swift and rapid change in the context of economic restructuring, technological innovation, and the rise of global capitalism. These factors have cohered over the past two decades to advance sweeping social and cultural changes that have necessitated a perceptible turn in feminist poetics away from writing the body towards writing the body politic,[60] or perhaps more accurately, a feminist poetics that explores the interface between body and body politic as a site mediated by technology and the marketplace.

Notes
1   Eichhorn, "Beyond Stasis," 8.
2   Barbara Godard and Smaro Kamboureli, "The Critic, Institutional Culture, and Canadian Literature: Barbara Godard in Conversation with Smaro Kamboureli," in Godard, *Canadian Literature,* 35.
3   The Dialogue conference has been cited by critics as a pivotal moment in Anglo/Franco feminist collaboration in Canada. The proceedings of the conference were published under the title *Gynocritics/La Gynocritique* (1987).
4   Godard and Kamboureli, "The Critic," 35.
5   While there were other strands of feminist poetics, most notably, a West Coast strand associated with the Kootenay School of Writing and the journal

Raddle Moon, this work tends to be "categorized unevenly in relation to feminist writing" (Capperdoni, "Feminist Poetics," 34). While Lisa Robertson has received widespread critical recognition, writers like Dorothy Trujillo Lusk, Nancy Shaw, and Catriona Strang have been largely neglected by feminist critics in Canada.

6 Rankine and Sewell, "Introduction," 5.
7 Braidotti, *Metamorphoses*, 83.
8 Some of my earlier thinking on this topic, specifically in relation to the work of Rita Wong and Rachel Zolf, appeared in *Topia* 25 (Spring 2011): 182–89.
9 Kim, "Resuscitations," 167.
10 Wong, *forage*, 11.
11 Wong, *forage*, 47.
12 Wong, *forage*, 60.
13 Wong, *forage*, 40.
14 Wong, "Interview," 347.
15 Wong, "Interview," 347.
16 Wong, "Interview," 351.
17 Wong, *forage*, 11.
18 Durand, "The Ecology of Poetry," 117.
19 Wong, *forage*, 20.
20 Wong, *forage*, 20.
21 Wong, *forage*, 20.
22 Wong, *forage*, 20.
23 Several of the poems in *forage* are framed by handwritten texts from secondary sources. Wong includes a list of references at the back of the book and encourages her reader to seek out these sources.
24 Shiva, *Biopiracy*, 45.
25 Wong, *forage*, 37.
26 Durand, "The Ecology of Poetry," 118.
27 Elrick, "Poetry," 190.
28 Zolf was influenced by Agnes Varda's documentary, *Les glaneurs et la glaneuze (The Gleaners and I)* in her development of a poetics and politics of gleaning. Zolf, "Interview," 191.
29 Zolf, *Human Resources*, 6.
30 Braidotti, *Metamorphoses*, 11.
31 Goldsmith, *Uncreative Writing*, 1.
32 Zolf, *Human Resources*, 93.
33 Zolf, *Human Resources*, 36.
34 Zolf, *Human Resources*, 70.
35 Zolf, *Human Resources*, 16.
36 Ibid.
37 Fitterman and Place, *Notes on Conceptualisms*, 30.
38 Zelazo, "Slipping Teeth into Lemon," 197.

39 Queyras, "Interview," 316–17.
40 Zelazo, "Slipping Teeth into Lemon," 201.
41 Pollock, *Vision & Difference*, 67.
42 Wolff, "The Invisible Flaneuse," 41.
43 Haraway, *Simians, Cyborgs, and Women*, 176.
44 Queyras, *Lemon Hound*, 16.
45 Queyras, *Lemon Hound*, 19.
46 Queyras, *Lemon Hound*, 25.
47 Queyras, *Lemon Hound*, 16.
48 Brown, *Edgework*, 43.
49 Brown, *Edgework*.
50 Queyras, *Lemon Hound*, 28.
51 Grewal, *Transnational America*, 3.
52 Queyras, *Lemon Hound*, 30–31.
53 Zelazo sees *Lemon Hound* as "depicting the perfect liminality of Gilles Deleuze and Félix Guattari's 'becoming-woman,'" (195) and further understands the persona of the Hound as a manifestation of "becoming-animal" (196).
54 McRobbie, "Post-Feminism," 255.
55 Queyras, *Lemon Hound*, 45.
56 McRobbie, "Post-Feminism," 255.
57 Queyras, *Lemon Hound*, 45.
58 Haraway, *Simians, Cyborgs, and Women*, 149.
59 American poets like Laura Elrick and Jennifer Scappettone and European poets like Caroline Bergvall are engaging with similar issues in their work.
60 I borrow this turn of phrase from Kristin Prevallet, who, in a review of Laura Elrick's sKincerity, describes the work as articulating a new dimension of feminist poetics and argues that Elrick's language "is not of the body but of the body politic" (http://www.kayvallet.com/?page_id=171).

Bibliography

Braidotti, Rosi. *Metamorphoses: Towards a Materialist Theory of Becoming*. London: Polity, 2002.

Brown, Wendy. *Edgework: Critical Essays on Knowledge and Politics*. Princeton: Princeton University Press, 2005.

Capperdoni, Alessandra. "Feminist Poetics as Avant-Garde Poetics." *Open Letter*. Spec. Issue. Kootenay School of Writing. (Summer 2010): 33–51.

Durand, Marcella. "The Ecology of Poetry." *((Eco (Lang) (Uage (Reader))*, edited by Brenda Ijima. 114–124. New York: Portable Press at Yo-Yo Labs, 2010.

Eichhorn, Kate. "Beyond Stasis: Proceedings of an Unrealized Conference." *Open Letter*. Spec. Issue. Beyond Stasis: Poetics and Feminism Today (Summer 2009): 7–10.

Elrick, Laura. "Poetry, Ecology, and the Production of Lived Space." *((Eco (Lang) (Uage (Reader))*, edited by Brenda Ijima. 186–99. New York: Portable Press at Yo-Yo Labs, 2010.

Fitterman, Robert, and Vanessa Place. *Notes on Conceptualisms*. Brooklyn: Ugly Duckling Presse, 2009.

Godard, Barbara. *Canadian Literature at the Crossroads of Language and Culture: Selected Essays by Barbara Godard*, edited by Smaro Kamboureli. Edmonton: NeWest Press, 2008.

Goldsmith, Kenneth. *Uncreative Writing*. New York: Columbia University Press, 2011.

Grewal, Inderpal. *Transnational America: Feminisms, Diasporas, Neoliberalisms*. Durham: Duke University Press, 2005.

Haraway, Donna. *Simians, Cyborgs, and Women: The Reinvention of Nature*. New York: Routledge, 1991.

Kim, Christine. "Resuscitations in Rita Wong's *forage*: Globalization, Ecologies, and Value Chains." *Open Letter*, Spec. Issue. Beyond Stasis: Poetics and Feminism Today (Summer 2009): 166–73.

McRobbie, Angela. "Post-Feminism and Popular Culture." *Feminist Media Studies* 4, no. 3 (2004): 255–64. Accessed 16 August 2011 at DOI 10.1080/1468077042000309937.

Milne, Heather. "Feminist Cultural Studies and Innovative Poetics: Disciplinary Dislocations." *Topia* (Spring 2011): 182–89.

Perloff, Marjorie. *Unoriginal Genius*. Chicago: University of Chicago Press, 2010.

Pollock, Griselda. *Vision & Difference: Femininity, Feminism, and the Histories of Art*. London: Routledge, 1988.

Prevallet, Kristin. Rev. of Laura Elrick's *sKincerity*. Accessed 13 February 2013 at http://www.kayvallet.com/?page_id=171.

Queyras, Sina. "Interview." *Prismatic Publics: Innovative Canadian Women's Poetry and Poetics*, edited by Kate Eichhorn and Heather Milne. 316–28. Toronto: Coach House, 2009.

———. *Lemon Hound*. Toronto: Coach House, 2006.

Rankine, Claudia, and Lisa Sewell. "Introduction." In *Eleven More American Women Poets in the 21st Century: Poets across North America*, edited by Claudia Rankine and Lisa Sewell. Middletown: Wesleyan University Press, 2012.

Shiva, Vandana. *Biopiracy: The Plunder of Nature and Knowledge*. Boston: South End Press, 1997.

Wolff, Janet. "The Invisible Flaneuse: Women and the Literature of Modernity." *Theory, Culture, Society* 2, no. 37 (1985). Accessed 1 May 2013 at DOI 10.1177/0263276485002003005.

Wong, Rita. "Interview." *Prismatic Publics: Innovative Canadian Women's Poetry and Poetics*, edited by Kate Eichhorn and Heather Milne. 344–53. Toronto: Coach House 2009.

Wong, Rita. *forage*. Gibsons Landing: Nightwood Editions, 2007.
Zelazo, Suzanne. "Slipping Teeth into Lemon: Reading Sina Queyras Reading." *Open Letter*, Spec. Issue. Beyond Stasis: Feminism and Poetics Today (Summer 2009): 195–204.
Zolf, Rachel. "Interview." *Prismatic Publics: Innovative Canadian Women's Poetry and Poetics,* edited by Kate Eichhorn and Heather Milne. Toronto: Coach House, 2009. 186–97.
Zolf, Rachel. *Human Resources.* Toronto: Coach House, 2008.

5

Rewriting and Postmodern Poetics in Canada: Neo-Haikus, Neo-Sonnets, Neo-Lullabies, Manifestos

John Stout

For several decades now, experimental poetry in Canada has been associated with bold creative energy and a desire to change language. For the major experimental poets of the 1960s and 1970s—I am thinking especially of bill bissett, bpNichol, Steve McCaffery, and Nicole Brossard—the push for social change and the foregrounding of linguistic and formal change in poetry went hand in hand. For example, bissett's use of phonetic spellings in his poetry works to "liberate" language. As Len Early explains, bissett's "revolutionary" spelling is conceived as a political act: "'Correct' expression is in his view elitist, one more self-perpetuating device of the privileged classes, and one more restriction on the creative spirit."[1] Similarly, in her 1990 essay "Poetic Politics," Brossard writes that "as a woman, I am left with a language that has either erased or marginalized women as subjects. Therefore in my poetic I perform what is necessary to make space for a positive image of women. This task engages me to question language."[2]

Canadian experimental poets of the twenty-first century have inherited this legacy of politically charged writing. Fully aware of its importance, they nonetheless may choose to approach the issue of poetic politics more obliquely. For the poets whose work I will be discussing in this chapter, the rewriting of a traditional genre or text becomes the vehicle for asserting change implicitly rather than explicitly. Their poetry is more quietly subversive. Still, as we shall see, their practices of rewriting perform a fundamental questioning and renewal of literature through institutional critique.

Why has rewriting become such a useful and recurrent strategy in postmodern Canadian poetry? Pauline Butling offers some compelling thoughts on why rewriting matters and on potential consequences in her book, co-authored with Susan Rudy, *Writing in Our Time: Canada's Radical Poetries in English (1957–2003)*. Butling appeals to Fred Wah's notion of "*re* poetics," expanding on that term as follows: "*Re* posits lateral, spiral, and/or reverse movements rather than the single line and forward thrust of avant-gardism... A *re* poetics involves rewriting cultural scripts and reconfiguring literary/social formations. The goal is to *change*, not conserve, past and present constructions."[3] Via a *re* poetics, notions of meaning and authorship become fluid. When a later poet appropriates a canonical text or genre in order to alter it beyond recognition, this act of rewriting carries political force.

A postmodern questioning of genre characterizes each of these works. By appealing to the term "postmodern," I do not mainly intend it to mean "following after modernism" in a linear sequence. Instead, I want to use the term as Gregory Betts does in his essay "Postmodern Decadence in Canadian Sound and Visual Poetry," where he observes that "a generation of postmodern writers and theorists" has "challenge[d] the whole notion of linear, progressive time and literary influence."[4] Betts argues that "postmodernism in general opens texts forward and backward in time rather than working toward closures or teleologies of any kind."[5]

The postmodern transformations and deformations of the haiku, the sonnet, and the lullaby that I will be studying here may also be read more specifically as examples of conceptualism. During the last decade, conceptual poetry has been increasingly recognized as a dominant trend in American experimental poetry—and in Canadian experimental poetry as well, given the general acknowledgement of the importance of texts like Christian Bök's *Eunoia* and Darren Wershler and Bill Kennedy's *Apostrophe*. The recent anthology *Against Expression*, edited by Kenneth Goldsmith and Craig Dworkin, demonstrates that a wide array of practices of what Goldsmith calls "uncreative writing" are now occurring. In conceptual poetry, genres and texts of the past are recycled, either verbatim or in altered form, and published as one's own (new) work. Through this type of writing the entire institution of literature is changed and its authority is challenged. It is becoming clear that "uncreative writing," as practised by the authors featured in *Against Expression* and by the five Canadian poets I will discuss (two of whom also appear in the Goldsmith/Dworkin anthology), is much more than a fad or a gimmick. In conceptual writing, the meaning of a poem is not to be found in its lyricism or subject matter but in the poet's particular eccentric use of a source text.

Rewriting the Haiku: Barwin and Beaulieu and Sherwin Tjia

Contemporary Canadian poets have discovered a valuable resource for experimental writing in the haiku. Steve McCaffery, Gary Barwin, derek beaulieu, and Sherwin Tjia have all developed startling new approaches to haiku. A classic poetic form perfected by Matsuo Bashō (1644–1694), haiku has afforded these Canadian poets a malleable and effective tool for interrogating language, for playing with the possibilities of form, and for taking lyric poetry into new territory.

Haiku is attractive to poets for a number of reasons. It is an apparently simple poetic form. Classic Japanese haiku consist of seventeen syllables divided into three lines of verse: 5–7–5. It is organized into two images, juxtaposed without further commentary. Despite this deceptive simplicity, an individual poet can bring potentially infinite variations to the form. A haiku focuses on what is seen, leaving the lyrical subject—the speaking, feeling "I"—a marginal and implicit presence in the poem. In haiku, an object seen in a particular moment in time shocks the perceiver into a new awareness of life's mystery and strangeness. Yet the poem achieves its aesthetic effects in a humble way. As Hiag Akmakjian explains, "haiku shuns the poetic and tries to sound spontaneous and thoroughly mundane. The best haiku have an impersonal tone while conveying a feeling about a small, freshly perceived truth."[6] Akmakjian outlines the characteristic features of a good haiku, according to its systematization within Japanese culture: "A haiku has *shiori*, a 'tender feeling,' and *hosomi*, a 'slenderness in its expression'—nothing excessive. It has *sabi*—'dry hard-ness.' *Sabi* derives from *sabishi*, which means 'lonely' or 'solitary.' A haiku also has what Daisetz T. Suzuki called *wabi*, a taste for the quiet and homely."[7]

Akmakjian notes that a haiku is more than just a description of a thing within a landscape or scene; it aims at a merging of the perceiver with the thing perceived: "A haiku poet gets inside a piece of wood, feels its 'woodness.' The poet 'becomes' a flower, a tree, water. A haiku does not describe. Description introduces a division between poet and experience...In a haiku, poet and experience become one."[8]

The haiku became an important influence on Western poetics early in the twentieth century when the Imagists found in it a strong formal precursor for their own spare, objective, impersonal poetry. Ezra Pound's famous "In a Station of the Metro" reflects this encounter with haiku. By contrast, in the haiku-inspired postmodern poetry of today's Canadian experimentalists, a much bolder, irreverent approach is evident. beaulieu, Barwin, Tjia, and McCaffery stretch the haiku well beyond its traditional limits, turn it inside out, and reimagine it in fundamental ways. Humour and parody are omnipresent in Tjia's *The World Is a Heartbreaker* and in Barwin and beaulieu's *frogments from the frag pool*. However, despite this emphasis on humour, it would be a mistake to read these works primarily as a joke or a put-on. The authors' approach to language and to poetic renewal is serious and complex. They are having fun with haiku, but they are also working to push poetry in unexplored directions. Their engagement with aesthetic strategy and the politics of writing poetry is profound, as two recent statements on poetics published by beaulieu and Barwin indicate. First, in the "Manifestoes Now!" issue of the *Capilano Review*, beaulieu presents "26 Statements on Poetry." A sampling of those "26 Statements" reflects beaulieu's radical and uncompromising stance on poetics:

> Poetry is the last refuge of the unimaginative.
> Poetry has little to offer outside of poetry itself.
> Writing—on the other hand—is a much more dynamic space.
> Poets chose to be poets because they do not have the drive to become
> something better.
> All bad poetry springs from genuine feeling
> . . . .
> In poetry we applaud mediocrity and ignore radicality.
> Poetry has more to learn from graphic design, engineering, architecture, cartography, automotive design, or any other subject, than it does from poetry itself.
> . . . .
> Please, no more poetry.[9]

Gary Barwin published a short text in *Filling Station* 52 (2012) that offers a critique of the lyric similar in thrust to beaulieu's "26 Statements." Barwin's text, "Words Cannot Express," presents pseudo-Wittgensteinian reflections on language. Through these reflections, he artfully expresses his scorn for lyricism, for the idea that poetry is meant to convey emotion:

> How emotion or the self (or selves)—the lyric, the
> semi-lyric, or the illyric, the lyrictus—appears in writing
> varies. Is TBA. The N/A may be. Or not.

Self-expression may be shelf-expression. Shelf-centred. Shell-
fish centred. Self-centaured.

They said my work was emotionally one-dimensional.

It hurt my feeling.
. . . .
The self and its effluvia—emotion—need not be present
in writing. Possible but not necessary. The effluvia of some
writing is the self, the way the broken mirror or the empty window are effulgentia of light. There may be emotion without the
self. Or vice versa (I know about this—I once had a girlfriend...)[10]

In these comments by Barwin and beaulieu, both writers deliver their critique of lyric poetry in the form of a manifesto (explicitly in beaulieu's case, implicitly in Barwin's). By their choice of the manifesto, they link their position as experimental poets to the twentieth-century gesture of the public manifesto that began with F.T. Marinetti's 1909 Italian *Futurist Manifesto*. In her introduction to her edited collection *Manifesto: A Century of Isms*, Mary Ann Caws notes that

> originally, a "manifesto" was a piece of evidence in a court of law, put on show to catch the eye, "A public declaration by a sovereign prince or state, or by an individual or body of individuals whose proceedings are of public importance, making known past actions and explaining the motives for actions announced as forthcoming."[11]

She underscores the manifesto's political thrust:

> The manifesto was from the beginning, and has remained, a deliberate manipulation of the public view. Setting out the terms of the faith toward which the listening public is to be swayed, it is a document of an ideology, crafted to convince and convert... The *Communist Manifesto* of Friedrich Engels and Karl Marx in 1848 is the original model, of immense influence and historical importance for later aesthetic proclamations and political statements."[12]

Caws characterizes the modern aesthetic manifesto as

> by nature a loud genre, unlike the essay... The manifesto is an act of *démesure*, going past what is thought of as proper, sane, and literary.[13]

Clearly, beaulieu's "26 Statements" and Barwin's "Words Cannot Express" fully replicate the key features of the manifesto as a genre. Through an exaggerated condemnation of lyric poetry, both writers aim to convert readers to a radically different understanding of poetry. Their very public stance in their manifestos echoes the examples of bissett and Brossard discussed above. As Caws, again, states,

> the manifesto is immodest and forceful, exuberant and vivid, attention-grabbing. Immediate and urgent, it never mumbles, is always in overdose and overdrive.[14]

As its title suggests, Barwin and beaulieu's *frogments from the frag pool* is an extended homage to Bashō, as well as a book-length parody of his most famous poem. In that poem, Bashō offers a single image, which is both banal and oddly cryptic: the image of a frog jumping into an old pond:

An old pond
A frog jumping—
Sound of water[15]

To alert the reader to the subversively postmodern approaches they will be using to rewrite, unmake, and revitalize Bashō's poem, Barwin and beaulieu preface their text with a sort of "enter at your own risk" warning:

> This water-sound is intended for the haiku-master or entity to which it is addressed, and may contain confidential and/or privileged material. If you are not the intended recipient of this water-sound, you are hereby notified that any use, review, retransmission, dissemination, distribution, reproduction, or any action taken on reliance upon this water-sound is prohibited. If you received this water-sound in error, please contact the leaper and delete the material from any poem. Any views expressed in this water-sound are those of the individual frog and may not necessarily reflect the views of the pond.[16]

Bashō's frog poem has often been translated, leading to a surprising number of variations. (The collection *One Hundred Frogs* actually reproduces a hundred different versions of this simple three-line poem!) It is crucial to point out, then, that *frogments from the frag pool* in no way represents a conventional translation of Bashō's poem. Barwin and beaulieu's poem belongs, instead, to the (non-)genre of "transtranslation." A transtranslation deliberately alters, distorts, and reimagines its source text. Rejecting the (conservative) notion of a "faithful" translation, a transtranslation purposefully takes liberties with its source text by making a lack of respect for faithful reproduction of pre-existing meanings and forms into a productive aesthetic strategy. Transtranslation has arguably become a notable trend in Canadian poetry ever since bpNichol published his text *Translating Translating Apollinaire. frogments from the frag pool* can be considered a major contribution to this eccentric genre.

In transtranslating Bashō's frog poem, beaulieu and Barwin make it perform clever and amusing tricks for the reader:

Old pond leaping
into mind of frog

old pond leaping—
the mind of frog[17]

old pond
it's a good thing it wasn't
a rhinoceros[18]

basho
frog in the throat
leaps in the mind[19]

tadpold
tadpond
tadplop
tadpole[20]

frog
despondent

pond
respondent

pond
frog resplendent[21]

other pond
other frog
same plop[22]

In certain instances, the two poets show their awareness of the possible connections between haiku and Zen Buddhism. Some interpreters of haiku contend that haiku poems exemplify Zen concepts such as egolessness and non-attachment. However, Barwin and beaulieu's approach to this Zen-oriented view of the haiku is determinedly playful:

water-shaped hole in silence
frog-shaped hole in pond

poem shaped hole in mind[23]

```
    old (            )
        (            ) pond
        (            )
    water (          )
        (            )
        (            ) sound

    (frog)[24]
```

A significant number of the pieces in *frogments from the frag pool* are written as concrete poems and sound poems. Barwin and beaulieu's text is thus as much an homage to the work of the avant-garde Canadian poetry of bpNichol and Steve McCaffery from the 1960s and 1970s as it is an homage to Bashō; indeed, McCaffery's *The Basho Variations*, republished by Book-Thug in 2007, is arguably the real model for the two contemporary poets' "frogments". The rise of concrete and sound poetry effected a sea change in Canadian poetry by challenging traditional verse-lyricism's emphasis on meaning and subjectivity. As Brian Henderson explains, in the concrete poetry of McCaffery and Nichol, "signs are 'events' we are to experience rather than traditionally read. In short, it is a transformation of what reading is that such poetry demands."[25] Through the heightened emphasis on the visual and the aural in this poetry, "reading becomes an exploration of possibilities—sonic, lexic and/or iconic," Henderson asserts.[26] At least twenty-two of the poems in *frogments from the frag pool* are "drawings." Moreover, the visual style of these drawings will immediately remind a reader who knows Nichol's concrete poetry of Nichol's own idiosyncratic drawing techniques. In Nichol's work an individual letter can fill an entire page as it is pulled and contorted into odd but revealing shapes by the poet. In extending the linguistic experiments of an earlier generation of Canadian poets into the present moment, Barwin and beaulieu have shown the lasting legacy of this earlier work.

Sherwin Tjia's use of the haiku is quite different from Barwin's and beaulieu's, although equally eccentric. In a review of *The World Is a Heartbreaker*, Lorianne Garrison describes Tjia's poetry as follows: "Punchy, postmodern, irreverent, surreal, somehow flirtatious and occasionally just plain weird."[27] She adds that "Tjia is…a pop culture poet who likes to make his poetry 'immediate,' he says, imbuing it with a sense of the fragmentary moments that filter in and out of people's everyday lives."[28] At first glance, Tjia's poems remain close to the original haiku form: three short lines placed together on the page to represent a small moment in time. Nonetheless, by their content and tone, his poems diverge entirely from their classical Japanese model. *The World Is a Heartbreaker* is one hundred sixty-nine pages long. On each page, about ten separate haikus are arranged at intervals from one another. Tjia generates jarring challenges to interpretation via the possible connections and disjunctions he suggests among the various poems brought together on each page. On the back cover of his book, the little poems that make up the book's content are described as "pseudohaikus":

This collection of 1600 pseudohaikus goes down like
potato chips.

What's a pseudohaiku? It's a poem of pure indulgence,
a three-liner without the constraint, the pretension or the
5/7/5 form. The subject matter? Relationships, cats, insecurities—
themes that recur and build into a pulsing non-linear narrative.

Easily digestible yet remarkably acute, *The World Is a Heartbreaker* is a catalogue of shotgunned emotions and pointed
bite-sized observations.

Sometimes sexy, sometimes scandalous, but always three lines
long.

There are no pleasures like the guilty ones.[29]

Reading this collection of "pseudohaikus," one quickly becomes aware of the fundamental ambiguity and strangeness of Tjia's project. He is, in effect, offering us a familiar poetic form yet substituting an inappropriate, unsettling content for its expected themes of nature, impersonality, solitude, and tranquility. Here is a page from *The World Is a Heartbreaker*, chosen more or less at random:

> looking
> pretty was
> the project

> life as a
> cranky
> romantic

> idling
> in her
> underwear

> my throat is
> squeezed because it
> was really touching

> the whole
> sixth grade
> agrees and all

> watering
> my
> grudges

> she's probably
> interested in boys
> who aren't me

> hair
> barrette
> boy

> the
> ninja
> pirates

> people date
> people who
> look like them[30]

Like classic haiku, these tiny poems foreground events and thoughts that are apparently banal. These are unadorned moments pulled from everyday life. However, whereas Zen spirituality is discernible beneath the surface of the haiku of Bashō and his followers and contemporaries, Tjia's poems evoke a world that is ambiguous and difficult to grasp. In his pseudo-haikus an overall air of irony and bemusement is undercut by references to war and death. Tjia's poems focus on sex, interpersonal relationships, and daily life, yet a disturbing apprehension of violence and mortality mars or complicates their bland surface. Traditional haiku lead the reader to a sense of the hidden serenity in everyday reality. Tjia's haikus generate an atmosphere of uncertainty, even anxiety, as many of the poems contradict the impression created by others on the same page: "burn / again / christian," "fighting / depression / with both feet," "a painting so / big you can't see / it all at once," "come / come, new / clear bomb," "she was / conspiring / to steal him," "you deserve / a happy / ending."[31] Most of these little poems could be either humorous or serious or an odd mix of the two. In any case, one feels that Tjia is not subverting the haiku merely as a game or a writing exercise. He is using it as a sort of mask to allow him to evoke contemporary anxieties indirectly.

Re/Undoing the Sonnet: Gregory Betts's *The Others Raisd In Me*

There has been a noteworthy revival of interest in the sonnet in recent Canadian poetry. Many poets today have tried their hand at writing sonnets, as the recent anthology *Jailbreaks: 99 Canadian Sonnets*, edited by Zachariah Wells, shows. What makes the sonnet so fascinating to these poets? Perhaps it is the form's unique marriage of freedom and constraints that appeals. The sonnet offers challenges and rewards comparable to those of the haiku. It must contain fourteen lines, usually arranged into two quatrains and two tercets, and must include a definite thematic movement across those four stanzas. It is traditionally restricted to a fairly narrow range of subject matter, with the love sonnet being most representative of its thematics. Although the sonnet is a rule-bound genre, it still, paradoxically, allows poets the freedom to display their own individual talents.

To rehearse the well-trod history of the form, we can simply state that English poets produced an important body of sonnets in the sixteenth century, following the model developed by Petrarch in his fourteenth-century *Canzoniere*. It is well known that Shakespeare created *the* model for the sonnet that would be most influential for later English-language poets. Shakespeare's sonnets represent the expression of a specifically modern consciousness, in the view of most critics. In his book *The Birth of the Modern Mind: Self, Consciousness, and the Invention of the Sonnet*, Paul Oppenheimer states that "the new form [i.e., the sonnet] was quickly understood as a new way of thinking about mankind," adding that "the invention of the sonnet did not, of course, 'create' self-consciousness...It led to a fashion in self-conscious, silent, and meditative literature that continues into our own day."[32] Oppenheimer observes that "the sonnet remains to this day the oldest poetic form still in wide popular use."[33] He argues that the intricacies of the sonnet's language made, and make, it an attractive vehicle for representing, and even resolving, problems and conflicts within the self: "Emotional problems, especially problems in love, needed no longer merely be expressed or performed: they might now actually be resolved, or provisionally resolved, through the logic of a form that turned expression inward, to a resolution in the abiding peace of the soul itself, or if one were not so certain of the existence of the soul, in reason."[34]

Shakespeare wrote his sonnets between 1593 and 1597. Since their first publication in 1609, they have been objects of fascination for generations of readers. In undertaking an extended rewriting of one of these poems, Sonnet 150, Gregory Betts assumes a huge challenge. For a poet of a later century to dare to rewrite Shakespeare must be the ultimate literary risk.

Much of Gregory Betts's work relies on an audacious borrowing or "plundering" from others' texts. The SUNY–Buffalo Electronic Poetry Centre has an author's page on Betts stating that his first published poem was an anagrammatical translation of a short poem by bp Nichol. Betts's work has consistently troubled individual authorship through such mechanisms as anagrams, collaboration, response-text writing. Each of Betts's "plunderverse" projects, including *The Others Raisd in Me*, constitutes an open, public challenge to traditional notions of authorship and originality, following the model of uncreative writing championed by Kenneth Goldsmith and other contemporary conceptual poets. In the prefatory note to what he calls his "plunderverse project," Betts links his eccentric and bold remakings of Shakespeare's Sonnet 150 into 150 new poems to the notion of paradigm shifts and to the technological reinvention of the human in our age:

> This book, appearing exactly four hundred years after the publication of Shakespeare's infamous sonnets, creatively misreads his Sonnet 150 as a prophetic program for the centuries of Western culture from his time through to our future doom. The rise of modern individualism in the sixteenth century has provoked a rush of arts, science and technology; consecutive waves of idealistic revolutions that pushed humanity beyond the limits of the body. The mechanical evolution of the human experience builds from the "I" within us to its projection and animation in cybernetic form. The Others that rise are the self and its metal shadow.[35]

In this passage, Betts begins by reiterating the standard literary historical equation of Shakespeare's development of the English sonnet with the rise of a modern self-consciousness. He then extends the discussion of the sonnets' (and the self's) broader historical significance to include the rise of a digital and cyborg subjectivity now in a postmodern fusion of human and machine: "The Others that rise are the self and its metal shadow."[36]

This argument regarding subjectivity, which Betts introduces in the prefatory note, is echoed and extended in a series of quotations that precede each of the fourteen sections of *The Others Raisd in Me*. Two or three quotations from famous thinkers and writers are placed in dialogue with Betts's own poems in each of the book's sections. The poet presents these quotations in chronological order, moving from statements by Elizabeth I and Francis Bacon, through the seventeenth, eighteenth, nineteenth, and twentieth centuries, to end with quotes from twenty-first-century figures like Donna Haraway and Darren Wershler-Henry. This long parade or historical pageant of quotations constitutes a sort of parallel text reminding the reader of changing attitudes towards the body and consciousness from Shakespeare's time to our own. Betts's truncated and fragmentary versions of Shakespeare's Sonnet 150 thus repeatedly come into contact and dialogue with a broad range of voices of historical authority. Betts has set himself ambitious goals for his plunderverse project.

To begin to gauge the significance of this project, let us look, first, at Shakespeare's Sonnet 150:

> O from what power hast thou this powerful might,
> With insufficiency my heart to sway,
> To make me give the lie to my true sight,
> And swear that brightness doth not grace the day?
> Whence hast thou this becoming of things ill,
> That in the very refuse of thy deeds,
> There is such strength and warrantise of skill,
> That in my mind thy worst all best exceeds?
> Who taught thee how to make me love thee more,
> The more I hear and see just cause of hate?
> O though I love what others do abhor,
> With others thou shouldst not abhor my state.
> If thy unworthiness raised love in me,
> More worthy I to be beloved of thee.[37]

This sonnet presents a complete thought using the resources of classical rhetoric. Shakespeare begins the first and eleventh lines of the poem with an apostrophe: "O from what power [...]" and "O though I love [...]." The object of the speaker's desire is directly addressed. The poem features a series of rhetorical questions evoking the speaker's sense that he must yield to the power of love, even though reason would convince him that love is deceptive. Even as he realizes that he is being tricked into overlooking the beloved's flaws, he cannot deny or alter the strong feelings of love to which the poem bears witness. This carefully and artfully constructed sonnet presents a rational statement acknowledging that its speaker cannot escape the irrational hold that love now has upon him. Shakespeare's poem relies in part on the use of decasyllables to achieve its effects of musicality; the rhythms created by the use of ten syllables per line reinforce the argument made by the speaker to and about the beloved.

In appropriating Shakespeare's poem, Betts pursues a strategy of radical reduction, cutting the poem down to a few very short lines per page in each of his 150 plunderverse poems. American poet Jen Bervin has undertaken a project similar to Betts's in her brilliant work *Nets*, where she employs erasures to remove words from Shakespeare's sonnets in order to create a new text. The poems in *Nets* read like a ghostly echo of Shakespeare's sonnets. Betts accomplishes an equally daring rewriting of the sonnets, selecting only a few words from Sonnet 150 for each of his poems. These new poems are odd, minimalist, and puzzling. Here are a few examples:

what is
missing
when this
becoming

thinks,
      exceeds

who taught
me to see
hidden

this word[38]
we are not
made of words
tho we is[39]

might
make me

my mind
make
me more

more my
me more[40]

this is not
all we are

we evolve
with Others[41]

Whereas Shakespeare's poem strives to make its meaning clear, in Betts's poems ellipsis and silence are paramount. He underscores what remains unsaid or half-said. Betts's poems read like riddles, yet they are not merely playful. They address some of the same concerns (like love, time, and the self) that recur in Shakespeare's sonnets, but they approach these themes indirectly, through humour and ambiguity. Unlike Bervin's poems in *Nets*, which adhere closely to their source text, Betts's *The Others Raisd in Me* gradually moves away from a strict transcription of words from Shakespeare's text. Echoes of Nichol emerge in Betts's poems. Like the intertextuality with McCaffery in *Frogments in the frag pool*, these Nichol intertexts again remind us of the crucial influence of Canadian experimental poetry of the 1960s and 1970s for the current generation of practitioners.

Although Betts's poems in *The Others Raisd in Me* seem to bear no real similarity to Shakespeare's original sonnets, one can still speculate on possible ways in which Shakespeare's aesthetics may have links to Betts's work. In his study of the *Sonnets,* John Blades draws attention to the subtleties and artfulness of Shakespeare's poetic techniques:

> The poet/speaker's vexations are inevitably paralleled in Shakespeare's language and poetic technique. The themes of the Sonnets are mobilised by ambiguity and, consistent with the themes of dissembling and deception, its language is in general terms epitomised by supersubtlety, duplicity, ellipsis, equivocation, evasion, unsettled and open syntax, and unstable punctuation. By the same token we should not overlook the role played in the creation of uncertainty by Shakespeare's cunning and deep-reaching ironies.[42]

Different as the two poets' approaches to language are, Shakespeare and Betts both practise an artfulness that is distinctive. If Shakespeare's sonnets have often been equated with the rise of a peculiarly modern consciousness, Betts's discontinuous, fragmentary poems exemplify a postmodern stance towards language and subjectivity in peforming a recycling of earlier poems.

Margaret Christakos's Lulls and the Lullaby

Margaret Christakos has long been active in writing and promoting poetry in Canada, and her Influency Salon has become famous. She has taught and facilitated the Influency Salon course through Continuing Education at the University of Toronto for the past several years. In each iteration of Influency, Christakos has invited eight poets to attend the class and assigned a recent book of the poets' work as reading for the students. Each week the course includes a guest lecture by a poet focusing on the work of the featured poet for that evening, followed by a reading by the featured poet and a discussion period. Via these classes and via the online journal *Influencysalon.com,* which makes available a rich sampling of work from the course, Christakos's Influency Salon has contributed significantly to the recognition of poetry and poetics in public space in this country.

This attentiveness to poetry and publics is traceable in Christakos's own poetic production. In her 2002 book of poems *Excessive Love Prostheses*, she presents an alphabetically sequenced series of poems centred mainly on maternal subjectivity. Writing as the mother of three small children in 2002, Christakos uses an experimental approach to representing a kind of subjectivity—female, maternal, bisexual—largely absent from literature. In an interview with Heather Milne published in 2009 in *Prismatic Publics*, Christakos discusses the challenges and pleasures of this project:

> [C]onfessionality has actually been an important engine of the work I've done around maternal subjectivity. I have been writing about extremes of psychological and emotional experience that have occurred in the context of raising babies and children in a way that is perhaps different than how they've been written about, even within feminist poetries... I've encountered extreme states in myself and observed them in other mothers of my generation. And at the same time adding that reality to the utopian tales of motherhood. And then playing and using some of it, ironically, using some of it in terms of looking at what's there and then again manipulating and intentionally altering those narratives so they're not pure or not reifying the pure authentic emotion once again.[43]

To create *Excessive Love Prostheses*, while drawing upon her own experience as a mother, Christakos also appropriates a classic literary genre: children's literature. As she notes in the acknowledgements at the end of the book, the cover image for *Excessive Love Prostheses*, which shows two frightened small children in the woods, is taken "from *The Babes in the Wood*, one of Randolph Cadecott's Picture Books... 'No burial these prettye babes / of any man receives, / Till Robin-redbreast painfully / Did cover them with leaves.'"[44] Throughout her text Christakos is deconstructing, perverting, and playing with children's literature in multiple ways. Her ironic reproduction of the image from *The Babes in the Wood* suggests from the outset that her use of the genre will be parodic, skewed, not "straight."

Despite the liminal presence of children's literature as catalyst, most of the poems in *Excessive Love Prostheses* focus on the adult worlds of work and sexuality. Experience, rather than a clichéd innocence, is foregrounded in this citation. The opening sections, "A Repetitive Strain" and "B-G Career Paths," feature fragmentary monologues by people working in a series of different professions: "A1. Accountant," "A2. Streetcleaner,"

"A3. Director," and so on. A sense of alienation, confusion, and ironic distance characterizes most of these poems. Then, in Section "H-K Journal Notes," Christakos assumes a confessional or mock-confessional stance. Her poems "Heterosexual Affair Journal Notes," "Homosexual Journal Notes," and "Bisexual Journal Notes" explore the complexities of sexuality through extravagant and lush experimental writing.

The middle section of *Excessive Love Prostheses*, "L: Mother's Lessons," is set apart from the rest of the poems. "Mother's Lessons" is printed on a light-brown paper and, thus, given a special importance in this project. In this segment the poet offers "six and twenty lessons" to small children. The archaic "six and twenty," in place of "twenty-six," is a reference to the source text Christakos has used for this section: "The source text for 'Six and Twenty Lessons' is Leonard de Vries, *Flowers of Delight: an agreeable Garland of Prose and Poetry*, 'a unique book containing hundreds of the best poems, nursery rhymes, chapbooks and stories written between 1765 and 1830' [front cover overleaf note]."[45] The poet then gives a sobering twist to the traditional cautionary tale for children by quoting in section M. from a newspaper story concerning toxic chemicals found in mothers' milk in Britain. Again, harsh contemporary reality intrudes into the "innocent" realm of children's poetry.

Christakos ends *Excessive Love Prostheses* with section "S-Z: Lulls." In these final poems, she adapts the lullaby in surprising ways. Coming at the end of the book, the lulls correspond to the moment in the day when, after Mother has told her children a bedtime story, she is singing them a lullaby.

The traditional lullaby is a fairly limited genre. In her "lulls," Christakos takes it in a number of unexpected directions. For her, the lullaby becomes a catalyst for freely exploring the possibilities of language. "Lull One" presents rows of lower-case vowels: "aaaaaaaa...," "eeeeeeeee...," and so on.[46] The poem references the importance of learning the alphabet (the ABCs are, of course, another genre in children's literature). The poem also recalls the work of sound poets, like Canada's Four Horsemen, who play with vowels and consonants to create sound environments. "Lull Two" is a sort of stream-of-consciousness passage in verse: "child in this cotton chasm we will make of birth press through the / cushions crown through and you shall become cradle pretend like it was / new and rare time sparse abdomen has that pancake swing from tree / limbs and over onto sleeve and motion rushing incautious movement upon chest / surged out of light and arm / going over and meaning and there / is my mommy my is there and meaning and over going arms [...]"[47] The poet shares with the child the freedom to play (with language).

"Lulls" ends with long horizontal rows of "Zs" covering the page.[48] These rows of "Zs" indicate that the lull(abies)s have achieved their aim of putting the children to sleep. They also show Christakos completing her text with a metalinguistic flourish, as the alphabetical series of poem cycles that began with "A. Repetitive Strain" now ends with "Zs." Beginning, then, with stereotypical images of mother and children, the poet subjects those images to postmodern techniques of decontextualization and fragmentation. Through her parodic mash-ups of existing children's poems, combined with early-twenty-first-century images of the alienated worker and an eroticized image of the mother, she radically alters children's literature.

Christakos's "Lulls," like the neo-haikus and neo-sonnets of Betts, Barwin, beaulieu, and Tjia, enact the potential of experimental poetry to extend and renew existing poetic traditions. All of these poems showcase Canadian poets' explorations of the *strangeness* of language. Given the striking number of examples of this kind of rewriting of others' texts happening in Canadian poetry today, I am tempted to call the early twenty-first century the age of "re" poetics. However, it is probably wise to leave to future critics the task of how best to designate our present age.

Notes

1 Early, "bill bissett," 5.
2 Brossard, "Poetic Politics," in *Selections*, 190.
3 Butling and Rudy, *Writing in Our Time*, 21.
4 Betts, "Postmodern Decadence," 155.
5 Betts, "Postmodern Decadence," 155.
6 Akmakjian, *Snow Falling*, 14.
7 Akmakjian, *Snow Falling*, 15.
8 Akmakjian, *Snow Falling*, 16.
9 beaulieu, "26 Statements," 123–24.
10 Barwin, "Words Cannot Express," 5–6.
11 Caws, ed., *Manifesto*, xix.
12 Caws, ed., *Manifesto*, xix.
13 Caws, ed., *Manifesto*, xx.
14 Caws, ed., *Manifesto*, xxi.
15 Basho, *On Love and Barley*, 58.
16 Barwin and beaulieu, *frogments*, 5.
17 Barwin and beaulieu, *frogments*, 12.
18 Barwin and beaulieu, *frogments*, 18.
19 Barwin and beaulieu, *frogments*, 19.

20 Barwin and beaulieu, *frogments*, 36.
21 Barwin and beaulieu, *frogments*, 39.
22 Barwin and beaulieu, *frogments*, 39.
23 Barwin and beaulieu, *frogments*, 22.
24 Barwin and beaulieu, *frogments*, 23.
25 Henderson, "New Syntax," 1–2.
26 Henderson, "New Syntax," 1.
27 Garrison, "Sherwin Tjia."
28 Garrison, "Sherwin Tjia."
29 Tjia, *The World*, back cover.
30 Tjia, *The World*, 154.
31 Tjia, *The World*, 14.
32 Oppenheimer, *The Birth*, 27.
33 Oppenheimer, *The Birth*, 3.
34 Oppenheimer, *The Birth*, 3.
35 Betts, *The Others*, 7.
36 Betts, *The Others*, 7.
37 Shakespeare, "Sonnet 150."
38 Betts, *The Others*, 20.
39 Betts, *The Others*, 27.
40 Betts, *The Others*, 47.
41 Betts, *The Others*, 192.
42 Blades, *Shakespeare*, 29.
43 "Interview," in Eichhorn and Milne, eds., *Prismatic Publics*, 112.
44 Christakos, *Excessive*, 107.
45 Christakos, *Excessive*, 106.
46 Christakos, *Excessive*, 92.
47 Christakos, *Excessive*, 93.
48 Christakos, *Excessive*, 100–101.

Bibliography

Akmakjian, Hiag. *Snow Falling from a Bamboo Leaf: The Art of Haiku*. Santa Barbara: Capra Press, 1979.

Barwin, Gary. "Words Cannot Express." *filling station* 52 (2012): 5–6.

Barwin, Gary, and derek beaulieu. *frogments from the frag pool: Haiku after Bashō*. Toronto: Mercury Press, 2005.

Basho, Matsuo. *On Love and Barley: Haiku of Basho*. Lucien Stryk, trans. Harmondsworth, UK: Penguin, 1985.

beaulieu, derek. "26 Statements on Poetry." *Capilano Review* 3, no. 13 (2011): 123–24.

Betts, Gregory. *The Others Raisd in Me*. Toronto: Pedlar Press, 2009.

———. "Postmodern Decadence in Canadian Sound and Visual Poetry." In *RE: Reading the Postmodern: Canadian Literature and Criticism after Modernism*, edited by Robert David Stacey. 151–79. Ottawa: University of Ottawa Press, 2010.

Blades, John. *Shakespeare: The Sonnets*. Houndmills: Palgrave, 2007.

Brossard, Nicole. *Selections*. Berkeley: University of California Press, 2010.

Butling, Pauline, and Susan Rudy. *Writing in Our Time: Canada's Radical Poetries in English (1957–2003)*. Waterloo: Wilfrid Laurier University Press, 2005.

Caws, Mary Ann, ed. *Manifesto: A Century of Isms*. Lincoln: University of Nebraska Press, 2001.

Christakos, Margaret. *Excessive Love Prostheses*. Toronto: Coach House Press, 2002.

Early, Len. "bill bissett/Poetics, Politics & Vision." *Essays on Canadian Writing* 5 (1976): 4–24.

Eichhorn, Kate, and Heather Milne, eds. *Prismatic Publics: Innovative Canadian Women's Poetry and Poetics*. Toronto: Coach House, 2009.

Garrison, Lorraine. "Artist, Organizer & Pop-Culture Addict Sherwin Tjia." *Daily Xtra* 15 April 2009.

Henderson, Brian. "New Syntax in McCaffery and Nichol: Emptiness, Transformation, Serenity." *Essays on Canadian Writing* 37 (Spring 1989): 1–29.

Levack, Chandler. "Sherwin Tjia pushes Toronto out of its comfort zone." Accessed 9 September 2014 at www.blogto.com/arts/2011/11/sherwin_tjia_pushes_toronto_out_of_its_comfort_zone.

McCaffery, Steve. *The Basho Variations*. Toronto: Book Thug, 2008.

nichol, bp. *As Elected: Selected Writing*. Vancouver: Talonbooks, 1980.

Oppenheimer, Paul. *The Birth of the Modern Mind: Self, Consciousness, and the Invention of the Sonnet*. New York: Oxford University Press, 1989.

Shakespeare, William. *The Sonnets*. G. Blakemore Evans, ed. Cambridge: Cambridge University Press, 1966.

Tjia, Sherwin. *The World Is a Heartbreaker*. Toronto: Coach House Press, 2005.

Poetry I

The Sturdiness

by Sina Queyras

For a long time I was thinking that I had to do more.

The way a dancer looks away from the camera.

I want to be a direct leap, not a hesitation.

I like the sturdiness of gladioli. As flowers go, they are a good investment.

Ironically, many people who are protesting the tar sands have investments in them.

The postmodern moment is not to take delight in one's own destruction, but to unconsciously facilitate it.

When I think of Gary Cooper I think of socks.

I probably would have fallen for a young Pound.

I have no idea why so many intelligent people choose to devote their lives to poetry so early and so exclusively.

Not all joy is simplistic.

If Pound were a contemporary I might have asked him for some sperm.

I would rather have asked Gertrude Stein but I don't believe she had any sperm.

There are always things to worry about: not being the next big thing is far down the list.

I think of Lisa sleeping in my small office in Philly, worrying all night that the bookshelves would fall on her head.

Later I thought my books were probably up all night too, rigid with anticipation as to whom she chose to read.

I don't mean to animate my library, I just do.

The first book I owned I stole from the Hudson's Bay at Portage and Main. I walked across the river with it under my parka.

The covers of a book feel differently after being read by others, more open.

The scents that linger are too intimate.

My skill as a thief is entirely wasted on me. I still regret that book. I suppose I didn't really own it.

I let myself worry about being followed and caught out but the truth is I am a terrific thief.

The Sexual Politics of Bluestockings

by Tanis MacDonald

It is a truth universally acknowledged that a department in possession of a tenured position must be in want of a bluestocking.

She tolerates no drive-by quoting.

She lets her blues do the stalking.

She pulls herself up by her bluestraps.

If the bluestocking fits, she wears it.

Every bluestocking learns how to run.

All happy bluestockings are alike, but she doesn't know many.

Routine

by Amanda Jernigan

for Tim and Elke Inkster

"The world of publishing," you told
me on my first day on the job, "is mad.
Well—what did you expect?
There is no money in it: what we've sold
this summer wouldn't buy you lunch,
which is what editors are out to—in both senses.
Authors? Unavoidable expenses.
Printers? An eccentric bunch,
but mostly daft (myself excepted).
One more thing: the public doesn't read."

All this no doubt intended to dissuade.
Instead, intrigued (and obstinate) I stayed—
and saw, against the fickle post,
which might bring money or disaster,
there was coffee at exactly ten o'clock,
the local gossip at the dairy, toasted
sandwiches in paper bags, and last
year's bulbs reliably emerging. And though
we were behind, the press would slow
unfailingly at four, for Simba's walk.

You've been typecast (excuse the pun)
quixotically: on pressback, Zephyr

Antique laying waste forever
to shoddy bindings, box-stores, bills.
Yet I have seen this battle done
with neither swords nor slings—nor quills.

On Friday nights you swept the shopfloor clean.
Against the wrack of publishing, the sanity of routine.

(First published in *All the Daylight Hours: poems* [Cormorant Books, 2013])

Volume

by Shannon Maguire

asleep, astronomers observe her
ignored wife

awake, she is a transmission grid
delivering hidden worlds

to the unemployed playground repair workers'
incarcerated children, she turns

twenty-five years of union membership
into particles of light with a key-twist

* * *

awake, discrete physicists flatten out
air mattresses, tuck into slight drops

roads shoot their hungers up towards
her syntactic six turns more abundant

to observe properties that go beyond
the end of the muddy bush

Beau Mournful trots on collapsed pump
fetishizes her light imprint on decaying sofa

* * *

she turns her wife on
the centers of galaxies

ethicists and the law became frozen in
small unexplained time

animals, toys, and babies
observe the uninhabited playground

every five-year body acclimatized to
silkworms with semiconductors, hidden light

September Still

by Rob Winger

Across the erstwhile diary duck-fog,
we're still. Stairs spin into long-lost
slingback benches, our lit, backdeck
hibachi, rusted through to dreck.

They say the emerald-headed ducks are migratory,
which means they depart and arrive responsibly,
cutting into weeks of still water as though
moored in deep hypnosis psychotherapy.

Beyond our proletariat essays, vines still ripen and pop.
All the stones become blackbirds.
We stop-down so light can flood our frames
with the greatest possible depth of field.

No river stays as frozen as these ducks do.
The water beneath the steeples in that photo
you took on the park boardwalk, still using film,
fifteen, maybe twenty years ago,

greedily young, all our grandparents still alive,
our hairlines and budgets not yet receding.
The past is a country closed by revolution,
entered only by sunset, every staid September.

(First published in *Old Hat* [Nightwood Editions, 2014])

The inevitability of gravity on glass

by Vanessa Lent

The earthquake-interrupted argument
remained unresolved.

Usually when arguing
each graciously alternated victory
and it was a matter of pride
that their relationship could sustain
such an architecture.

Plaster dust clotted with sweat
as they clung to each other;
        anticipating aftershocks.
And the only sound they bothered to hear
was the tinkling of glass falling
                  down down
from windowpanes.

Everything dark
        and altered.
Only the faint light of stars
blinked in at them.

They feared to stand and walk
in the new landscape.
But to crawl would be to
risk cutting palms on the still-falling glass.

"Where is it coming from?" Peter anguished.
"Don't move so," Sasha whispered back.

They spent the night on the floor
waiting for the thin light of morning.

Section II
[The Embedded Field]

6

The Ingeminate Eye: Peter Sanger's Public Poetics

Amanda Jernigan

The poet and critic Peter Sanger has always seemed to me a private man: he lives with his wife and dog in a farmhouse in South Maitland, Nova Scotia, at the end of a long driveway. They have made friends, of the "good fences" sort, among their neighbours, but their house is pleasantly enclaved by gardens and trees. Though Sanger is a man of letters, he keeps out of the way of literary "scenes"; his correspondents are far-flung and are astonishingly various in terms of their literary personalities.

I once believed that Sanger was a private *poet*, too. In a 2003 article, I quoted his remark that he considered his collection *Ironworks* (a collaboration with the photographer Thaddeus Holownia) to be "a private book."[1] I took this to mean the book was wilfully hermetic: closed to all but the most diligent readers (although not without its rewards, I argued, for those willing to do the work). This characterization of Sanger's poetry has come back to haunt me. Zachariah Wells cites it in his 2007 article on Sanger and goes on to take Sanger to task for "privileging one sort of poet (a *poeta doctus* who writes uncompromisingly dense and allusive verse) and one sort of reader (a cryptographer scarcely distinguishable from the poet she reads)."[2] Yet Wells knows that things are not so simple: "there is far too much conflict, contradiction and ambiguity in the public ethics of [Sanger's] poetics to reductively portray him as a snobby elitist or aesthetic solipsist," Wells writes.[3] And I have come, over the years, to see the "privacy" of Sanger's poems—in a later letter to me Sanger used the word "decorum"—as a kind of forbearance. Its motive is generosity, not stinginess; it respects the privacy of his subjects and his readers, even as he reaches out to them ("good fences make..."). In that sense, the privacy of Sanger's work is very much a part of its "public ethics" (and Wells's phrase seems to me exactly right, there). At the same time, Sanger's decorum is motivated by honesty. It is a function of his scrupulous observation of the *gaps* that are part of our experience: gaps between one person and another, or between two aspects of ourselves; between artifice and nature; between the imagined and the real; between saying and doing. Ironically, it is precisely by being a scrupulous observer of these gaps that Sanger manages occasionally, almost magically, to leap over them.

In his essay "Our Word Is Our Bond," the poet and critic Geoffrey Hill writes: "Modern poetry... yearns for this sense of identity between saying and doing... but to [the poet's] embarrassment and ours it discovers itself to possess no equivalent for 'hereby'"[4]—that magic word that might make an utterance *performative*, in J.L. Austin's sense. The gap between saying and doing remains. Austin's classic example of the performative utterance is the marriage ceremony: I [hereby] pronounce you man and wife. The saying *does:* the words make it so. Yet the nominal union of the marriage ceremony can be (to quote the poet Richard Outram) "something very much other than conjoined loves."[5] In order for the ceremony to work, as a ceremony, one must marry one's heart to the words: only then can one's words ("I thee wed") be effective in marrying one to another. As readers and writers, we also have the option of marrying hearts to words and thereby "mak[ing] truth," as Sanger puts it.[6] Love is involved (of which more, below). And also a sense of culpability.

In the poetic sequence *Abatos*, published in *Aiken Drum* (2006), Sanger casts the reader, or the reader-aspect of himself, as lawman to the poet's outlaw. He found his outlaw and lawman roles in a script from life: the 1817 account, by Walter Bates, Esquire, Sheriff of Kings County, New Brunswick, of his encounters with a con man and horse thief known variously as Henry More Smith, Frederick H. More, William Newman, and Henry J. Moon. Moon and Bates—who is at once Moon's legal conscience and his biographer—have a symbiotic relationship (in a 2006 letter to Wells, Sanger calls it "co-inherence").[7] "As a thief, I'm out after justice / not truth,"[8] Sanger's Moon-figure says: "Caught, I am caught so that / all I've stolen may turn into gold."[9] Yet despite Bates's best efforts, despite the reiterated bonds of iron and language in which Moon is confined, Moon escapes. Like the historical con man, he is pardoned: "Why?" he asks.

"Sanity, / madness? A left-handed thief / has been forgiven." And then, perhaps sadly, "All the crimes / I'll commit can only be ordinary."[10] In his afterword to *Aiken Drum*, Sanger writes that Moon is "the inner breath of language, whose power wanes if pardoned."[11] Poet and outlaw alike, it seems, must be apprehended in order to survive.

The relationship between the outlaw and the poet, or maker, is underscored in the Moon story by the fact that the historical Moon was a maker of puppets: "God made man out of dust of earth," Sanger's Moon-figure says; "I must make man from wood."[12] The historical Moon feigned insanity in part through affecting belief in the reality of his creations: he called his marionettes his family, and he fretted over their comfort and amusement.[13] Yet the sort of belief the con man feigns is exactly the sort of belief that poets ask of their readers—and of the reader-aspect of themselves; it is what brings our words to life.

The identity of poet and outlaw is played out on another level in *Abatos*. I'll quote from the sequence's first section:

Some time in the month
of July 1812 he turned
up in Nova Scotia at the prosperous
port of Windsor. He pretended

he'd come quite lately from England.
When asked for his occupation
he answered, tailor, but
could turn his hand

to any mechanical business
or country employment. Genteel,
prepossessed, he seemed
to know himself well.[14]

Sanger goes on to give us the outline of Moon's story, from his initial employment by "a respectable farmer of Rawdon,"[15] whose daughter he marries, through a mysterious series of petty thefts perpetrated while on so-called business trips to Halifax, to his culminating theft of a horse, in that day a capital crime, and his subsequent apprehension. Wells has objected to the "prosy" nature of this preamble.[16] He's right: it is prosy. Not only that, it's filched: much of it is stolen, taken word for word from Bates's historical account. Here is Bates's opening paragraph:

> Henry More Smith, the noted individual who forms the subject of this narrative, made his first appearance among us in the year 1812. Previous to this, we have no information concerning him. Some time in the month of July, in that year, he appeared at Windsor, in Nova Scotia, looking for employment, and pretended to have emigrated lately from England. On being asked what his occupation was, he stated that he was a tailor; but could turn his hand to any kind of mechanical business or country employment. He was decently clothed, genteel in his appearance, and prepossessing in his manner, and seemed to understand himself very well.[17]

The similarities between the two passages are too great to be accidental; indeed, Sanger calls it "intentional plagiarism" in his 2006 letter to Wells.[18] But Sanger is no simple plagiarist (cf. Wells's remarks on Sanger's poem "Plagiarist" in *Earth Moth*).[19] Horses can stand for both word and world in Sanger's work (more on this below): word-stealer, world-stealer, Sanger is playing the horse thief here, as much an outlaw as is the stranger he describes. When we attempt to hold him culpable, we become the pursuing sheriff: we apprehend him; he escapes. In the sixth section of *Abatos*, his verse leaps free of its prosy incipit and, at the same time, sheds Bates's language:

> At Kingston, a jail between rivers,
> where the salt of the lower Saint John
> meets the iron of Kennebecasis,
> I enter anti-asphyxis.
>
> Am I you, I, Smith (Henry More),
> Frederick H. More, Newman (William),
> or all the selected Henrys (Bond, Preston or
> Hopkins) each a name
>
> given by ultimate Smith
> who spoke at a confounding moment
> as Henry J. Moon, moonman, moonsmith?[20]

The language is mercurial, the imagery alchemical; yet the section ends with the words "I can't take history for life."[21] It is the first in a series of leaps and returns, escapes and reapprehensions, the poet speaking sometimes as Moon, sometimes as Bates, constructing bonds (in the sense of fetters) and bonds (in the sense of promises) out of language.

I borrow the "bond" pun from Hill, from the same essay of his that I quoted above. It is from Hill's collection *The Lords of Limit*, which Sanger reviewed at attentive length in the *Antigonish Review* when the book came out in the late 1980s. Here is another section from *Abatos*. I hear Hill's bond-puns in the background.

> On his legs, a pair of steel
> fetters, case-hardened, ten
> inches long, with a chain
> from the middle
>
> seven feet long stapled
> into the floor. On his neck
> an iron collar with hinge
> and clasp, grappled
>
> by chain and padlock. Of iron
> there was forty-six pounds.
> Tormentors of man, tear up this place,
> turn it upside down.[22]

The bonds in this section are made out of language. They are as easy and as difficult to break as a vow. The closing lines ("Tormentors of man," etc.)— which I take to be in Moon's voice—are made of language, too: a command that we may or may not choose to obey. To go back to the terms of Hill's essay, there is a gap between saying and doing. Or, as Hill writes elsewhere, quoting Coleridge, "Our chains rattle, even while we are complaining of them."[23] And yet: when we obey a command (not least a command issued by ourselves to ourselves), when we keep a promise, when we allow ourselves to be *bound* by the bonds of language, we leap (Sanger's word) across that gap between saying and doing.

Henry J. Moon is a horse thief, as I have said. Both his name and his vocation resonate with Sanger's later work, in which gaps continue to figure. In the title sequence from his 2012 collection *John Stokes' Horse*, a little boy—who may be a boy-version of Sanger—says, "Come on Mummy, let's cross the road": these are his first words, the speaker tells us—indeed, his first sentence, all puns intended. "And there," the grown-up poet writes,

> …on the other side
> of the street of a village in England,

bay-coloured and glistening,
trotting a tightrope of muscle
in sunlight, that great bay horse
carried its noble rider...[24]

Sanger describes this formative memory in terms that recall Wallace Stevens's "Noble Rider and the Sound of Words." We might think also of Pegasus, emblem of poetry, who—along with other legendary horses—is mentioned by name elsewhere in the sequence. But there is another, archetypal child-and-horse encounter, lurking in the background here:

Ride a cock-horse to Banbury Cross,
To see a fine lady upon a white horse;
Rings on her fingers and bells on her toes,
And she shall have music wherever she goes.

The rhyme is a touchstone for Sanger—not only in this sequence, but in *Aiken Drum,* the volume in which *Abatos* appears. ("I'll ride a cock-horse / through the world," says Moon.)[25]

Ride a cock-horse to Banbury Cross,
To see a fine lady upon a white horse...

There are *two* horses in these lines: the cock-horse and the white horse. Across the road's gap—which is also, here, the white space between one line and another—the imagined regards the real: the cock-horse regards its real-world double, just as the child-speaker of the nursery rhyme regards that enigmatic "fine lady," and just as the child in Sanger's poem regards the noble rider of the glistening bay. The child may grow up to be a rider of horses, or so we tell ourselves—but the cock-horse will never grow up to be the glistening bay. Or so we tell ourselves: there is an insuperable gap between the actual world and the work of art and craft that represents it, between doing and saying, to use Hill's dichotomy. Yet art and craft continue to represent: "she shall have music," the rhyme tells us—*even as,* to quote from a later poem in Sanger's sequence, "she goes, she goes, she goes."[26]

The child may grow up to be a rider of horses, I said. But do children ever really grow up to be adults? In Sanger's work, we can't be sure: children disappear, and adults appear in their places, but the transition is as mysterious as that between life and art, between doing and saying. In his discussion of metaphor in *Anatomy of Criticism,* Northrop Frye gives the identity of child and man as an example of the likewise mysterious identity, in radical metaphor, of "independent forms."[27] In "Leaping Time," the essay that forms an afterword to *John Stokes' Horse*, Sanger recounts the story of "Ivan and the Chestnut Horse," which he recalls having had read to him in childhood. In the story, a young boy becomes an adult by passing through the head of a magical horse—in one ear and out the other. Sanger's sense of his own transformation, from listening child into the speaking adult who repeats the story, is equally mysterious. "Ivan enters the head of the chestnut horse," he writes:

> If that is so, the child I have been writing about is myself. Or perhaps I am a variation on the theme of the man he might have become living in another country, during a time which can only become less and less his own. Or perhaps my relationship with the child is not that of a variation on a theme but that of the theme itself played by two flutes, one of them me, two flutes waving out and away towards some other minute particular as yet unborn.[28]

Child and adult are both identical and dissimilar: like saying and doing, the cock-horse and the glistening bay, they may be in accord, but the gap between them never quite closes.

In other poems of Sanger's, the cock-horse and the white horse become the moon and the sun. "We live by empirical / sounds," he writes in "The Earrings":

> ...empirical
> sounds, like those which make
> Latin, a little old puzzle
>
> whose pieces must
> parse together
> or else even simplest
>
> things become at last
> incommunicate. These earrings,
> as instance, are *diamond*, Sanskrit
>
> for *luminous being*, conjunction
> of sun and moon
> where words might begin

> to yield lightly again
> some sense
> of the given.²⁹

In the notes to *Aiken Drum,* Sanger writes of the moon: "The moon of [Dante's] *Paradiso* is occupied by those who have paid less than they vowed" (that is, they have refused to allow themselves to be bound by the bonds of language). He continues: "In the medieval scholastic scheme, the moon also corresponds to grammar. It reflects a certain splendour."³⁰ The moon reflects the sun, as the word reflects the world. Reflecting, the poet is both moonman (that is, a mountebank, like Henry Moon) and moonsmith (a creator); he is both certain, in the sense of partial, and certain, in the sense of sure. Sometimes he is Aiken Drum, the hero of the Scottish nursery rhyme, who lives in the moon and plays upon a ladle: a figure for imaginative exuberance and comic immortality. At other times he is Willy Wood, Aiken Drum's nursery-rhyme double, who plays upon a razor, and meets a tragic end. Sanger writes:

> The traditional Scottish nursery rhyme...is polyphonic with possible meaning, although as far as I know it has never been suggested that Aiken Drum and Willy Wood enact a ritual pattern of immortality and mortality, or that in alchemical language Aiken Drum is mercury, Willy Wood the sacrificial king. At another level, the pair are twins, the dioscuri, the lords of limit.³¹

The lords of limit come from Auden, among other sources. Here is the third stanza of his poem "The Watchers":

> O Lords of Limit, training dark and light
> And setting a tabu 'twixt left and right,
> The influential quiet twins
> From whom all property begins,
> Look leniently upon us all to-night.³²

Hill uses the first of these lines as an epigraph to *The Lords of Limit*. In Sanger's 1989 review, he cites this epigraph, and here his review takes a personal turn (more on this below): "Some of us have seen these lords of limit in dreams," he says.³³ It seems to me that for Sanger, these Lords of Limit, "from whom all property begins," preside over the gap between saying and doing—the gap that separates the cock-horse from the bay, the child from the adult. To bridge this gap—to ride a cock-horse, "hoofed with psalms, / beyond the equivocal moon," as Sanger puts it in the *John Stokes'*

Horse sequence[34]—requires magic, or, failing that, sleight-of-hand: hence the importance of the trickster figure, like Henry Moon, in Sanger's work. The trickster/poet needs someone to trick, however, if his ruse is to succeed: hence the equal importance of the credulous straight-man/reader—that is, of the one who believes. For belief itself has a kind of magic, transforming illusion into reality. Writing of Bates's account of his interactions with Henry Moon, Sanger says, "We have two choices: either Bates's account is factual, or Alias-Moon had the ability to transmute illusion into the semblance of reality by the force of his character";[35] that is to say, Moon was the sort of man who compelled belief.

What Sanger does on the level of the sequence in *Abatos*—dramatizing the relationship between a poet and his public, between writer and reader—he has done on a larger scale in each of his recent collections, not only of poetry, but of prose. In each of these books, poetry (that writerly language) and prose commentary (that readerly language) weave around each other in concentric loops, never quite touching. I think of the two strands of the helical necklace in Sanger's poem "Necklace"—"Doubled, they're one"[36]—and also of those two flutes, in the passage from "Leaping Time" quoted above. Thus, his essay-collection *Spar: Words in Place* ends with a poem; his book-length study of the poet Richard Outram begins with a poem; and his essay-collection *White Salt Mountain: Words in Time* has poems as both beginning and ending. At the same time, his poetry collections *Arborealis*, *Aiken Drum*, *John Stokes' Horse*, and *Fireship* (a recently published selection of early work) feature essays at or near their endings. Poetry and prose chase each other through these books, as do Moon and Bates in the *Abatos* sequence, or the "rocking-horse" spaniel and the stag of the world in another Sanger poem, "The Fifth Day": "pursued, pursuing pursuit, / a chase caught by chase with no / beast in view."[37]

If we increase our focus, so as to take in life as well as letters, we see this chase recapitulated on still a larger scale: it characterizes the relationship between Sanger, as critic, and the poets he has studied—particularly Outram, who, Sanger has told me, was in his mind as something of a Moon figure when Sanger was working on *Aiken Drum*. (The story of the Sanger–Outram friendship could form the subject for a study in itself. The correspondence between the poets occupies two thick folders at the Thomas Fisher Rare Book Library in Toronto, where Outram's papers are kept, and evidence of the friendship is in both poets' published writings.) It also characterizes the relationship between Sanger, as poet, and certain of his readers, myself among them.

This chapter began with a discussion of culpability, and it comes now to a confession. In 2006 I was living in St. John's, Newfoundland, working as a freelance editor for Gaspereau Press, and I was assigned to serve as editor of

Aiken Drum. Bowled over by the brilliance of the collection, its intellectual scope, its care of construction, I nonetheless suggested that certain of the poems could benefit from "an elaborative note or an epigraph"—by more in the way of critical context.[38] In his review of *Aiken Drum*, Wells wrote, "Sanger seems concerned that his readers won't 'get it' without this help";[39] in fact, that concern was mine, not Sanger's. The surficial evidence is that Sanger cheerfully complied with my request: *Aiken Drum* comes with an afterword and a small raft of annotations. Even the *afterword* comes with an annotation—a seeming excess that should warn us that parody is at play. For on closer inspection, I see that Sanger has outfoxed me: the voice we hear speaking in these notes is that of the poet in critic's guise. The note to the afterword ends: "And now, to quote from the last poem by Zen nun Ryonen, 'I have said enough about moonlight.'"[40] The effect is of the mountebank winking beneath a judge's wig. We might think, also, of the historical Henry Moon, who, at one point in Bates's account, eludes his pursuers by disguising himself as one of his pursuers.[41]

In his review, Wells accuses "Sanger the critic and professor" of making "periodic intrusions into the territory of Sanger the poet" in *Aiken Drum*.[42] He's right, but it seems to me he only tells half the story: for the poet makes intrusions into the territory of the critic and professor, too. Sanger is a writer whose poetics are sustained by the interplay (the "co-inherence," as he would say) of writerly and readerly sensibilities. In *Abatos*, he keeps these sensibilities in careful balance: if the writer's power wanes when pardoned, the reader's power wanes when he gets his man.

"Abatos" is the name of one of the horses that pull Pluto's chariot: the word means "inaccessible." For Sanger, it seems that the purchase of language on the world depends, ironically, on the world's inaccessibility to language. As in the transmission of nerve impulses, there is a gap that connects. I think of the writings of ecologist Gregory Bateson, whose work Sanger has studied in connection with Outram's poetry: "*Noncommunication* of certain sorts is needed if we are to maintain the 'sacred.'"[43] When the gap disappears, language disappears as well: "at the end of the world / will be sounds of furious riding," Sanger writes in *John Stokes' Horse*. "Its muzzle will dip, drink."[44]

Language disappears. Yet again, we're only telling half the story. For the world disappears, too—or, rather, word and world become one: like the plaited strands in "Necklace," "they are a unity in which duality continues to exist."[45] Such moments are rare—but at its best, Sanger's work enacts them. Occasionally, it also speaks about them: "I hear / the waterfall falling, / word of the waterfall / falling," he writes in *Abatos*.[46] Or, in *John Stokes' Horse*, "Not mimesis, but moments / the world is beside itself, / the dove whose call / is elsewhere and here."⁴⁷ Often, such moments show up in Sanger's work as dance, that art expressed in the medium of the human body, in which, accordingly, the boundaries between art and life break down: "Let knife leave the wood. Let / wood be this wooden man / dancing," he writes, in the final poem in *John Stokes' Horse*, the sole poem to follow the (otherwise) concluding essay.⁴⁸

At the beginning of this essay, I said that readers can bridge the gap between word and world by marrying their hearts to language: by obeying a command, by keeping a vow, by taking a poet at his word. I have talked about the sense of culpability that is involved here. But I also mentioned love, and I want to return to that now. Bates's pursuit of Moon begins in blame; it ends in love. Long after Moon has left his jurisdiction, long after Moon has dropped the name Moon, the enamoured Bates tails him, and *tells* him. So the critic's pursuit of a poet can begin in scholarship and end in love. Love, too, can join a poet to his language, his language to the world. Near the middle of *Aiken Drum*, we find two epithalamiums: wedding poems, poems located at that traditional cite of performative language. Here, we find love, art, and life dancing close circles:

> *From dance to dance the air*
> *of life goes on.*
> . . . .
> *From air to air the dance*
> *of love goes on.*
> . . . .
> *From life to love the dance*
> *of air goes on.*
> . . . .
> *With dancing life the air*
> *of love goes on.*⁴⁹

Love, art, and life are plaited together: like the strands of that helical necklace—its own shape reminiscent of our DNA, or the spine of Wolverine from which the world can be remade⁵⁰—they go round and round, making and remaking.⁵¹

I have moved from the literary implications of Sanger's poetics to its linguistic and ontological implications. I want to return to the literary, however, before chapter's end. In his book *Lazy Bastardism: Essays & Reviews on Contemporary Poetry*, Carmine Starnino includes an excerpt from a panel discussion in which the poet Patrick Warner says to him: "A lot of poets out there don't seem to respond to criticism. In fact, I've talked to quite a few who just despise any kind of criticism. I was wondering if any of you have any idea of why that is?" Starnino answers:

> People believe you have this thing called *movements, schools, controversies* and *debates*. Then you have this whole other thing called *the poem*. The small, perfect lyric. And the poem defeats that other thing. It always trumps that mess of opinions—that foment of intellectualizing and disagreement. The problem is that this humble lyric would never exist without all that intellectualizing and disagreement. To despise criticism, in other words, is to despise one of the forces that makes poetry possible. Poems, after all, emerge out of our ideas about poems.[52]

Starnino and Sanger are radically different thinkers. I can imagine Sanger substituting "scholarship"—or even, simply, "reading"—for Starnino's catalogue ("movements, schools," etc.) above. And I can imagine him saying, what should go unsaid but often doesn't, that our ideas about poems emerge from poems, and woe betide a critic who forgets that. Yet I can't think of another poet working in Canada whose oeuvre so convincingly argues for the interpenetration of poetic and critical modes, as does Sanger's. This brings us back to Wells's remark about the "public ethics" of Sanger's poetics. Sanger's oeuvre, taken as a whole—and including, alongside his published works of poetry and prose, his letters, thus far uncollected—suggests new ways for us to speak about writing and reading, about the relationships between poetry and the public: ways of speaking in which writer and critic, maker and scholar, poet and (sometime hapless) editor, are brought into conversation as two aspects of the creative impulse rather than as antagonized forces. It's a way of frankly acknowledging the readerly context in which a work is published (a context too often covered up in a literary culture in which poets are critics, critics are editors, and editors are poets—*mea maxima culpa,* here) without at the same time denying, in Foucauldian fashion, the author's shaping role.

Sanger's poetics show us that the poet–critic distinction is in some ways a red herring: it stands in for a still more important gap, that between language and listener, word and world—thus, the literary shades into the linguistic and the ontological, overriding (all puns intended) my earlier distinction. Once the poem is made, poet and critic stand together, outside of it, as readers and listeners (take Sanger's rereading of his own early work, depicted in the afterword to *Fireship*,[53] as example); either one of them can attempt, to his gain or to his peril, to ride the poem "beyond the equivocal moon." In his article on Sanger, Wells portrays him as, at times, a kind of anxious meddler: the writer attempting to mediate readers' experience of his poetry. I see Sanger in a different light: as critic and correspondent, he is a reader among readers, attempting to *track* the poet who is never quite himself yet who, the signs tell us, he has been. The penultimate poem of *John Stokes' Horse* takes up the language of tracking, alongside the language of versification:

> Other signs I know:
> the ermine's ghazals, the ptarmigan's
> feathered triads, the hare's
> discursive quatrains. Not the trackless
>
> child who once kept watch
> by his window, then secretly
> mounting his steed ran off
> into snow and evergreen darkness.[54]

True poetry can be a sign: a mark left by the world in the medium of words, even while the child (who both is and is not the poet) runs off "into...evergreen darkness," the mystery that surrounds our experience, perennially renewed.

In the afterword to *Fireship*, Sanger represents the world of signs as a "*mare sonans*, the sounding sea surrounding this world with the voices of animals, birds, insects, trees, grasses, winds, waterfalls, glaciers, rivers and other ardours, including those of humans."[55] It is the domain of the "true sounds": those which descend to "fetch...back" buried Eurydice in Sanger's poem "After Monteverdi";[56] these are sounds quite other than the ditty sung "mutely" by a narcissistic Orpheus, yet they do not exclude the poems a true poet—or even a false poet, truly listening—might write.

After I presented an earlier version of this paper, in September 2012, I wrote to Sanger: Bates, still tailing Moon, even after the trial. I was hoping he would remind me of some details in that letter to Wells, a copy of which he had sent me years before. I had drawn on that letter, from memory, in my presentation, but I wanted to do better than that here. Sanger confirmed, in essence, what I remembered—but he also told me something new. It is a personal detail: the sort of thing that Sanger the poet is known for "repress[ing],"[57] that Sanger the scholar is known for uncovering (see, for instance, the final chapter of *Through Darkling Air*). It is the sort of thing that his poems both conceal *and* reveal:

> I was born in May, a Gemini. I was an "only child." Actually, I had a
> half sister I didn't really know about until my father died—although

I met her when I was a baby and did have an unconscious and scarifying memory of her. This "only child" made language his missing twin.[58]

He continued: "In the Gemini myth, one twin is mortal and the other immortal. Prose and poetry in my mind."[59] I thought about the Heraclitean aphorism "Immortals become mortals, mortals become immortals, they live in each other's death and die in each other's life."[60] And I went back again to that poem "Necklace":

Mocking, demanding continuous
miracle, makes little difference

in towers where gold is spun.
Strands which turn while they turn,

coils woven under or
over in constant ravels of either

still plait their helical
concourse, whatever we will.

Doubled, they're one.
Once upon time after Eden,

when earth was the centre,
sun wheeled its circle

above as if light could be left,
and our eyes still glisten ingeminate.[61]

Ingeminate means redoubled; it comes from Latin *geminus,* twin. In Sanger's work, poetry and prose, writing and reading, afford a binocular view. If we ask ourselves what they afford a view *of,* we encounter that larger ingemination, in which word and world afford a binocular view. And if we ask ourselves what *they* afford a view of, well, we move, as the critics love to say (winking at the poets), beyond the scope of this paper.[62]

Notes

1. Jernigan, "Ironworks," 30.
2. Wells, "Responsibilities," 40. This essay was subsequently republished in Wells's essay collection, *Career Limiting Moves*.
3. Wells, "Responsibilities," 40.
4. Hill, *The Lords of Limit*, 154.
5. Outram, letter to the author, n.pag.
6. Sanger, *John Stokes' Horse*, 114.
7. Sanger, letter to Zachariah Wells, 6.
8. Sanger, *Aiken Drum*, 60.
9. Sanger, *Aiken Drum*, 58.
10. Sanger, *Aiken Drum*, 68.
11. Sanger, *Aiken Drum*, 131.
12. Sanger, *Aiken Drum*, 58.
13. Bates, *The Mysterious Stranger*, 97–123.
14. Sanger, *Aiken Drum*, 51.
15. Sanger, *Aiken Drum*, 52.
16. Wells, review of *Aiken Drum*, 52.
17. Bates, *The Mysterious Stranger*, 9.
18. Sanger, letter to Zachariah Wells, 4.
19. Wells, "Responsibilities," 43–44.
20. Sanger, *Aiken Drum*, 56.
21. Sanger, *Aiken Drum*, 56.
22. Sanger, *Aiken Drum*, 63.
23. Hill, *The Lords of Limit*, 142.
24. Sanger, *John Stokes' Horse*, 77.
25. Sanger, *Aiken Drum*, 58.
26. Sanger, *Aiken Drum*, 86.
27. Frye, *Anatomy of Criticism*, 124–25.
28. Sanger, *John Stokes' Horse*, 114.
29. Sanger, *Aiken Drum*, 39–40.
30. Sanger, *Aiken Drum*, 133–34.
31. Sanger, *Aiken Drum*, 133.
32. Auden, "The Watchers," 63–64.
33. Sanger, "'Some Kind of Revelation,'" 144.
34. Sanger, *John Stokes' Horse*, 86.
35. Sanger, *Aiken Drum*, 128.
36. Sanger, *Aiken Drum*, 45.
37. Sanger, *Aiken Drum*, 97.
38. Jernigan, letter to Peter Sanger, 2–3.
39. Wells, review, 52.
40. Sanger, *Aiken Drum*, 136.
41. Bates, *The Mysterious Stranger*, 51.

42 Wells, review, 52.
43 Qtd. in Harries-Jones, *A Recursive Vision*, 222.
44 Sanger, *John Stokes' Horse*, 76. On the relation between limit and apocalypse, see Sanger, "'Some Kind of Revelation,'" 143–45. I should emphasize that in Sanger, as in Auden and Hill, the lords of limit exist as "balancers between opposites": as definers, without whom life ceases to exist. So the leaping of limits (or gaps, as I've been calling them here), in Sanger, never annihilates them: it is an act that unifies *and* defines.
45 I quote from Sanger's description, in *The Stone Canoe,* of the Wolverine figure from Mi'kmaq mythology, another embodiment of unity-in-distinction. Sanger, *The Stone Canoe,* 180.
46 Sanger, *Aiken Drum*, 59.
47 Sanger, *John Stokes' Horse*, 90.
48 Sanger, *John Stokes' Horse*, 117.
49 Sanger, *Aiken Drum*, 88–89.
50 Cf. Sanger, *The Stone Canoe,* 178.
51 For more on dance as theme and form in Sanger's oeuvre, see my essay *Living in the Orchard*.
52 Starnino, *Lazy Bastardism,* 11.
53 Sanger, *Fireship*, 179.
54 Sanger, *John Stokes' Horse*, 101.
55 Sanger, *Fireship*, 179.
56 Sanger, *Aiken Drum*, 77–78.
57 Cf. Wells, "Responsibilities," 47.
58 Sanger, email to the author, n.pag.
59 Sanger, email to the author, n.pag.
60 This translation is the one that appears, uncredited, at the end of Richard Outram's *Brief Immortals* (2003)—an important text for Sanger—although Sanger must have known the aphorism from other reading.
61 Sanger, *Aiken Drum*, 45.
62 I am grateful to Peter Sanger for his permission to quote his letters. Thanks, too, to the organizers of the *Public Poetics* conference, where this chapter was first aired.

Bibliography

Auden, W.H. "The Watchers." *Collected Poems*, edited by Edward Mendelson. New York: Vintage, 1991.

Bates, Walter. *The Mysterious Stranger*. 1910. Fredericton: Non Entity Press, 1979.

Frye, Northrop. *Anatomy of Criticism: Four Essays*. Princeton: Princeton University Press, 1957.

Harries-Jones, Peter. *A Recursive Vision: Ecological Understanding and Gregory Bateson.* Toronto: University of Toronto Press, 1995.

Hill, Geoffrey. *The Lords of Limit: Essays on Literature and Ideas.* New York: Oxford University Press, 1984.

Jernigan, Amanda. "Ironworks: The Art of Collaboration." *Canadian Notes & Queries* 64 (2003): 26–32.

———. Letter to Peter Sanger. 12 September 2005. TS. Private collection.

———. *Living in the Orchard: The Poetry of Peter Sanger*, illustrated by John Haney. Literary Criticism Monograph no. 4. Victoria: Frog Hollow Press, 2014.

Outram, Richard. Letter to the author. 26 April 2003. TS. Private collection.

Sanger, Peter. *Aiken Drum.* Kentville: Gaspereau Press, 2006.

———. Email to the author. 22 February 2013. TS. Private collection.

———. *Fireship: Early Poems 1964–1991.* Kentville: Gaspereau Press, 2013.

———. *John Stokes' Horse.* Kentville: Gaspereau Press, 2012.

———. Letter to Zachariah Wells. 17 June 2006. Photocopied MS. Private collection.

———. "'Some Kind of Relevation': Geoffrey Hill's *The Lords of Limit*." *Antigonish Review* 79 (1989): 137–46.

———. *Spar: Words in Place.* Kentville: Gaspereau Press, 2002.

———. *The Stone Canoe: Two Lost Mi'kmaq Texts.* Kentville: Gaspereau Press, 2007.

———. *Through Darkling Air: The Poetry of Richard Outram.* Kentville: Gaspereau Press, 2010.

———. *White Salt Mountain: Words in Time.* Kentville: Gaspereau Press, 2005.

Starnino, Carmine. *Lazy Bastardism: Essays & Reviews on Contemporary Poetry.* Kentville: Gaspereau Press, 2012.

Wells, Zachariah. *Career Limiting Moves: Interviews, Rejoinders, Essays, Reviews.* Windsor: Biblioasis, 2013.

———. Review of *Aiken Drum* by Peter Sanger. *Quill & Quire,* May 2006, 52.

———. "Responsibilities and Obligations, Masks and Alterities: On the Poetry and Prose of Peter Sanger." *Canadian Notes & Queries* 71 (2007): 39–48.

7

Reading for a Civic Public Poetic: Toronto in Raymond Souster's "Ten Elephants on Yonge Street" and Dennis Lee's *Civil Elegies*

Will Smith

Raymond Souster and Dennis Lee have both written poetry engaged with Toronto, with its peoples, its sense of history, and its built environment. Both poets have also received national acclaim, winning the Governor General's Award for Poetry. Canadian literary critical opinion of their writing is split, however; to many, Souster is both the essence of a local poet and a former national poet writ large from an era of a smaller national literary marketplace. Lee's *Civil Elegies* (1968/72), meanwhile, have been prominent in the literary critical re-examination of the relations between local, national, and global discourses, demonstrating the transnational at work during a period of heightened cultural nationalism. The recent adaptation of *Civil Elegies* for the stage indicates a continuing sense of the work's local relevance. Ongoing local recognition for Souster's and Lee's poetry has operated with ambivalence to any national critical narrative. Both have been viewed as Toronto's poet laureate: Lee as the city's first official laureate and Souster as a popular, if unofficial, laureate. The role of a city's poet laureate is a nexus of civic public poetic concerns, drawing on the complex work of representation and recognition, alongside wider questions surrounding the audience for poetry in and about the city. Such questions are complicated by the agents who positioned the poets into the role of Toronto laureate. If a laureate is a position in the sense that it is a job title, where a municipal council commissions work and poetic activity more broadly, how might the essential qualities of the laureate role exist outside of employment, or more pointedly outside a level of government sponsorship? Unpacking these concerns, this chapter will examine what such questions mean when we read Souster's and Lee's poetry about Toronto. Although civic public claims can be made in terms of the extratextual encounters with poetry in the city space, poetry itself can also be seen to do the work of a civic public poetics. At stake in both approaches is the question of how poetry engages a civic public. To begin to answer such a question requires some understanding of what critical framework we use to examine the poetry itself and how understandings of the civic and public might be conceived and reformed through the process of reading.

By focusing on the work of Souster and Lee, this case study is necessarily about Toronto, but the questions of public poetics it raises are multivalent. The increasing number of appointed poets laureate across Canada, at local, regional, and national levels, speaks to a particular movement towards arts engagement in the Canadian literary landscape. Internationally, the role of laureates—and, one might add, of place-based poet-in-residence positions—reflects a concern with creating a public poetic engagement with concepts of place on multiple levels. To glean how a public is shaped in relationship to poetics of place requires a more thorough understanding of the spatial dimensions of a poetic public. Kate Eichhorn and Heather Milne have emphasized the diversity of public membership and the plurality of any such groupings with the concept of "prismatic publics."[1] Within this diversity of fractured affinities, Eichhorn and Milne recognize that literary texts have a compelling creative function in creating and engaging publics: "Under modernity the concept of 'public' has always recognized that the circulation of texts, be they literary, journalistic or judicial, is important not because texts hold the potential to mirror the world but rather because they are actively engaged in making social worlds by fostering dialogues, bridging, assimilating and reifying differences, and authorizing and delegitimizing ways of speaking, knowing and being."[2]

Within Eichhorn and Milne's definition, the literary public is conceived via the very circulation of texts and the engagements created by these texts. While a physical public audience for the literary text might be traceable, in the text's potential circulation and aesthetic engagement the spatial dimensions of all publics involved in the text are themselves complex and prismatic. Nonetheless, there are spatial concerns in this description that need attending. For Eichhorn and Milne the literary text constructs a social world, which inhabits a push-and-pull affinity with what we might call the embodied experience of everyday life. The recognition that the text is a centre of its own social world is indicative of a generative literary public space. Such conceptions echo the terms by which Michael Warner begins to define a public. Warner's seminal discussion of how publics function draws on similar spatial rhetoric: "A public is a space of discourse organized by nothing other than discourse itself."[3] Within this formulation the text's coherent social world is available and inhabited by a public simply by virtue of the crafted discourse. In terms of poetic engagement, instability arises when considered in light of an independent conception of the public, those everyday people who might not be reading the text. The bridging work of the literary text is to draw linkages between these two domains.

Literary geography, as a broader interdisciplinary exchange between spatial theory, cultural geography, and literature, has also sought to reconcile the spatial dimensions bound up in poetic publics. As a working methodology for rigorous literary geography, Andrew Thacker posits four basic foundations that resonate with Eichhorn and Milne's understanding of poetic publics as those which are both formed by and engaged with through crafted poetic texts. These foundations can be summarized as an attention to spatial metaphor, representational space, textual space, and literary maps.[4] The first three terms serve here as the basic tools of inquiry into the poetry of Lee and Souster. In discussing spatial metaphor, Thacker emphasizes that texts "creat[e] metaphorical spaces that try to make sense of... material spaces."[5] Spatial metaphor is one way through which literary texts construct a social world and perpetuate or revise multiple public conceptions of imagining space. Thacker is keen to highlight the potential for critical work on such texts to further engage in a process of making sense, identifying the metaphorical and material implications of critical texts. This may therefore serve as a reminder to be reflexive, given that critical work on public and poetic spaces, when considered in light of the critical boundaries negotiated, is also an actively shaping voice.

Thacker's thought is influenced by the French urban theorist Henri Lefebvre. Lefebvre's conception of space as necessarily produced informs much of the critical methodology set out here and none more so than Thacker's second critical term, "representational space." Thacker follows Lefebvre in distinguishing the cultural depiction of "official organizations of space" from the aesthetics of space.[6] As with Lefebvre's conceptions of spatial terminology, such opposing forms are part of a tripartite dialogic when taken alongside the embodied experience of everyday life.[7] Separating official narratives of space from the aesthetic productions of space is a provisional move, but one that remains attentive to the multiple levels of power that attempt to sanction public narratives. Such analysis can be practised only in terms of the third element of Thacker's scheme, which readdresses the contextual meeting of poetic work and these multiple senses of space. Thacker's conceptualizing of this meeting may be seen as defining the literary text's public, pushing past the model of text as mirror to the social worlding of the text described by Eichhorn and Milne. Thacker proposes that the term "textual space" describes the meeting of the material space of the page with the social space of the lived environment: "We should reconnect the formal properties of literary and cultural texts not only to the material spaces they depict, but also reverse the movement, and understand how social spaces dialogically help fashion the literary *forms* of texts...Literary texts represent social spaces, but social space shapes literary forms."[8]

Thacker attempts to move literary analysis of texts past considerations of how a familiar place may be revised or directly depicted within the text. Without this complexity of understanding, such analyses too often disregard a public for a reiteration of what Leon Surette once derided as "topocentric" analysis.[9] Taking the fluidity of place and the social engagement of the text in dialogue, Thacker suggests that language and literary structure are at once influenced by and part of Lefebvre's conception of "social space." Such a view emphasizes the experiential space in which a creative work comes to fruition, whether by direct representation or by artistic location. It understand texts as *located* both in creation and publication, and perhaps also in their mutual construction of and by civic publics.

Understanding a poem's publics as overlapping, as both discourse affiliation and engaged in civic narratives, requires further clarification of the term civic. Interpreted as meaning "of the city," a civic public would seem all-consuming and arbitrarily bounded. In turn, scholarly discussions on the scope of the city might struggle to come to a consensus about its very limits, perhaps settling on a sensed shift in land use between one set of social spaces and another. When speaking about Toronto, there are practical legislative considerations imposed on discourse by municipal and provincial history. The city proper might mean the old City of Toronto, more popularly called downtown Toronto, which was governed until 1998 by Toronto City Council, or it might mean the sprawling megacity that has since absorbed previously distinct cities. Given the time period of Lee's and Souster's poetry, a civic reading of 1960s Toronto would carry differing mental boundaries. Civic is clearly a more connotative term, however, often used as a catch-all for a variety of urban narratives. Ben Berger has untangled these uses and their corresponding notions of engagement. His attempt to reorient scholarly discussion of civic engagement notes that "civic simply means that a subject pertains to citizenship or a city, so it can easily be subsumed under the rubric of political without any loss of conceptual clarity. In fact, clarity prevails when we stop stretching civic to mean sociable, helpful, or trusting, as so often happens in civic engagement scholarship."[10]

Berger's definition of civic helpfully illustrates the word's easy alignment of city and citizenship. It is this relationship, made emblematic in the word civic, that is so enticing for scholarship on specific notions of urban publics. The corresponding senses of sociability are difficult to dispel, however, perhaps because it is hard to think of a sense of the civic that is not engaged with constructions of social spaces and of publics. The commitments to the city or to citizenship involved in the civic, while fluid and shifting, are still bound up in discourses of recognition and representation.

Two considerations of Canadian critical usage help us explore the valence of the "civic." Michael McKinnie highlights the enticement of the term in a study of Toronto's theatre culture. McKinnie's study uses the term civic to define a narrative of urban development in downtown Toronto, aligning the term both with the municipal council's funding of theatres and with a broader indication of located public provision. In spite of this, in a notable moment of reflection, McKinnie expands the term: "Does the 'civic' in 'civic theatre' signify a theatrical intervention in Toronto's urban development?"[11] While it may be easy to suggest that the "theatre" of "civic theatre" is the theatrical agent here, it is worth considering the notion that the civic alludes to a performative role. In the slippage between city and citizenship, the civic is both a demonstrable quality and a kind of public, necessitating participants but potentially self-organizing. The civic is therefore bound up in the performative work of representation. As such it is important to consider how open the civic can be or if it is indeed a neutral category.

Analyzing the expression of a civic Toronto, or a civic subject within Toronto, requires attention to potential inclusions and exclusions. Daniel Coleman's work illustrates the close proximity of the civic and the civil with the shared Latin root of the word in "citizen," grounding a sense of required behaviour and exclusionary norms. In his study *White Civility*, Coleman is concerned with the "conflation of whiteness with civility" in English Canadian literature.[12] Such concerns cannot be overlooked when we seek to use the civic as a methodological term. To be aware of this tension in the civic, and to avoid the reinscription of preformed values, requires an element of Coleman's suggested practice of "wry civility": "'civil'...– the contradictory or ambivalent project that purports to provide a public space of equality and liberty for all at the same time as it attempts to protect this freedom and equality from threats within and without—and 'wry' in the sense of being critically self-conscious of this very ambivalence and of the contradictions it involves."[13]

Coleman's approach to critical self-consciousness is useful in forming a sense of the civic as a similarly helpful critical term.[14] While there are clear parallels between the ideal public space suggested by the civil and the civic, a key difference is the association of the civic with the city. Given the instability of the concept of the city, any deployment of the civic might be seen as harbouring a self-conscious element. This is relevant, as contemporary urban development is seen as spatially incoherent and unstable.[15] At the same time, it is possible to conceive of the civic against a purely "civil" public space, given the always traceable spatial demands of the civic and the tendency towards boundless idealism in the presentation of civil public space. Mark Kingwell highlights how such clashes over spaces deemed, or imagined, to be public spaces are always in tension with public and private interests, noting that we "enter into the so-called public space as floating bubbles of private space, suspicious of intrusion by strangers and jealous of their interests."[16] Attention to civic publics allow for conflicting interests to be explored. Using such terms in conjunction with poetry that is engaged with a particular city attends to both aesthetic and material geographies in preference to idealized philosophical conversations about public space. The civic publics constructed in the poetry and the poetic engagements of Lee and Souster reveal powerful attachments and models of creative participation.

Raymond Souster and "Ten Elephants on Yonge Street"
Although Raymond Souster has not achieved governmental recognition in the form of an official laureateship, many have highlighted his poetic engagement with Toronto. Stephen Cain notes how "long before Lee was officially made the poet laureate of Toronto, Raymond Souster was the acknowledged poetic chronicler of Toronto."[17] Responding to the League of Canadian Poets' decision to bestow an annual prize in Souster's name, the writer and journalist Joe Fiorito adds to a public mythology where Souster is "this city's life-long laureate and the reason why so many people, including those who don't read poetry, smile if you mention these words: 'Ten Elephants on Yonge St.'"[18] Fiorito honours Souster by drawing attention to a multitude of unacknowledged local readers, and indeed non-readers. Cain's recognition of Souster is also premised on local acknowledgement and on the authority of a long engagement with place. Formal literary critical opinions on Souster's work have differed greatly, although the most insightful point out its sense of lived engagement with place. Tom Marshall describes Souster

as "probably Canada's most successful imagist, the equivalent of William Carlos Williams" and one of a number of Canadian "social poets."[19] John Sutherland discerns a definite political stance in Souster's work, believing that "Souster is the first poet in Canada who has tried to give voice to the man in the mass."[20] Souster himself notes an affinity with Charles Olson as a "poet of place,"[21] and in the preamble to the 1965 collection *Ten Elephants on Yonge Street* he describes himself as "an unrepentant regionalist."[22] Northrop Frye remarked that the "essential, or creative, candour in Mr. Souster is that of the candid camera."[23] Given the amount of footage required to produce a candid camera moment, Frye's judgment is perhaps the most telling here. To describe Souster as prolific is to underestimate him. As of 2004, Souster's collected poems with Oberon Press stretched to ten volumes. Following *Uptown Downtown* in 2006, Souster authored eighteen further collections of poetry, each published by Battered Silicon Dispatch Box press.[24] The sheer volume of his work impacts any attempt to engage with Souster's poetry itself. In Cain's article, this fruitful publication record produces a unique analytic method: "While reading ... four volumes I prepared a concordance of his references to Toronto and its specific landmarks. Rather than seeking a general impression of Toronto as a monolithic entity, this concordance uncovers a textual map of Souster's Toronto and thus identifies specific sites of aesthetic representation."[25]

Cain's concordance presents an enticing angle of approach to Souster's poetry and has much in common with Franco Moretti's theorization of distant reading approaches.[26] To uncover a particular civic public poetic in the present analysis, however, I will focus on close reading, and on one poem in particular—"Ten Elephants on Yonge Street." This is the poem mentioned by Fiorito as significant even to those who do not read poetry, which seems all the more important in the construction of poetic publics. This is in effect a poem by an "unofficial laureate" for an "unpoetic public." The title poem of Souster's *Ten Elephants on Yonge Street* (1965) sees the speaker evoking a localized sense of place by acknowledging the histories of one street in Toronto. In doing so, the poem invokes multiple senses of space, revealing the street's complicity with different spatial discourses. The choice of Yonge Street as the poem's setting is justified by its sense of witness. It is the street where "just about everything / or everyone / has passed up or down" (135). Setting up a list of significant figures who have inhabited the street, the poem confers an unstable value to each figure's sense of witness. The idiomatic expression of passing up conveys an inattention to the street. In its possible derision, this line unsettles the values at stake in traversing the street. As one of the oldest streets in the city, and a direct route to Northern Ontario, the road serves a literal and symbolic function in bridging notions of the city/non-city boundary. In attitude and setting, the poem emphasizes a precarious attachment to stable notions of Toronto.

The first significant figure invoked in the poem gestures to the history of Yonge Street road, taking up its role in the staging of the Upper Canada Rebellion of 1837. The poem's description is pared down and brief, compressing the references to the time, the participants, and the location:

> William Lyon Mackenzie's boys
> on the quick way down
> from Montgomery's Tavern,
> Year of Tyrants
> 1837.[27]

This stanza generates multiple links. First, it underscores the geographic proximity of the events, which are only a "quick way down" from the site of the original tavern. The outskirts of the city in early-nineteenth-century Toronto now appear on maps as Midtown Toronto, measuring the cognitive shift that accompanies urban development. Next, the figure of Mackenzie himself, the city's first mayor, is a resonant historical symbol. As Edward Keenan has noted in his recent study of Toronto's political history, Mackenzie is an "all-purpose civic hero today."[28] Both a rebel and a populist, his encounter with Yonge Street symbolizes his failure to retaliate against a colonising force. His "quick" retreat emphasizes the inattention he too would have paid to Yonge Street, as the stage for ideological protest remained long after his failure. The poem's reference to tyrant-rulers hints at Mackenzie's distaste for colonial rule and the Family Compact. In its pared-down language, the stanza resembles the layout of a heritage plaque, echoing the National Heritage sign at the site of the original Montgomery's Tavern.[29] As such, the poem plays with a particular kind of public language of commemoration, crafting unexpected judgments from a discourse more used to passive and bland consensus terminology. Remembering a "Year of Tyrants" is pointed in this respect, and collides with official narratives of space.

The poem's next stanza recalls the reception in Toronto in March 1941 of the former US Republican presidential nominee, Wendell Willkie "smiling / his 1940 smile." The hint of retrospect in the poem is illuminating, tacking the fixity of the moment of the visit to an earlier image of the politician. As with the poem's treatment of Mackenzie, the concern here is for what images and senses of the historical moment are both co-present and omnipresent in an image of the street's history. When *Life* magazine reported Willkie's visit, it too placed the visit in the context of the street, emphasizing that this was "the most tumultuous welcome any personage had received since the royal visit in 1939" and drawing the reader's attention to how the "ticker tape showers [the] Willkie retinue as it rolls north along Toronto's venerable Yonge Street" ("Canada Gives" 30). Souster situates this visit to the wartime city by mentioning "planes overhead" before noting the warm reception with "the crowds gone crazy." The image represents a way in which the street space of Toronto is caught up in transnational spaces of political theatre, signifying local, national, and global concerns. Willkie's early advocacy of the war in Europe found support in the city. Souster applies a synecdochic relationship of the nation to this street space, suggesting that this was "the year he could have made / Prime Minister!"

The Yonge Street of Souster's poem bears witness to a chain of experiences distinctive for their interest in US–Canadian relations. The figure of Mackenzie, having gained American support for the Upper Canada Rebellion and working towards a republic, resonates in juxtaposition with the image of a visiting American Republican supporting intervention in a war in Europe. The use of the Republican mascot, the Elephant, in the final stanzas echoes this comparison in a surreal and sardonic manner. Souster's description, which refers to a recent procession of elephants down Yonge Street, is full of mock-respect for the "ten grey eminences moving / with the daintiest of steps." Their presence in the poem invites some reflection on the nature of past promenading figures, but it also converts the streetscape into a natural landscape where the elephants move with "the greatest unconcern / up the canyon." The elephants not only display total indifference to the street but also lead the reader to see the concrete and stone tower blocks of the street as a steep-sided gorge. As if this surreal denial of the urban is not disruption enough, jarring against the staid notions of civility in the roles of Mackenzie and Willkie, the poem comically shifts in the final lines:

> they slowly twist their trunks
> and empty their bowels
> at a pace which keeps the two men following
> with shovels and hand-cart
> almost swearingly busy.

From a poem that begins on a trajectory of wry political commentary and local staging, the final scene introduces the confrontation of aesthetic performance and practical lived experience. These are aligned in a parody whereby the fine art of the parading elephant cannot be perceived without acknowledging those who must clean up behind in. The reader's sympathies are drawn to those cleaners, who are both local and universal in their social status as street-level labourers. The delight is conjured by fond recollection of historical figures and their subsequent dismissal in the knowledge that the city continues to surprise and require maintenance no matter who is walking down Yonge Street. This allows the civic public the role to simply look at famous figures and reflect on their historical position and how they rely on a civic public. There can be few celebratory civic poems that so happily bask in elephants defecating on the road. It is this image more than the roll call of political events that ties the poem to a public imagination. Indeed, it was this image that struck a chord when Souster's collection was reviewed by George Bowering in *Canadian Literature* at the time of publication: "The opening title poem ends with the elephants emptying their bowels on one of Toronto's main thoroughfares, with men following with shovels, and already we know that these will be Souster poems, not the metrical artichokes of academy. Souster poems show a great sureness of the poet's measure, along with an eye's view that seems to be growing steadily more wry."[30]

Bowering's suggestion that Souster's poetic view is wry underscores the inclusive civic public created in the poem. The poetics on display resist formal and perhaps implicitly European literary tendencies. Souster's poem is crafted into short lines that resemble a processing column on the page and that reflect the narrative preoccupation, as if the street is on the page. After the more sophisticated sarcasm aimed at local history, the lingering humour is bodily and crass. Yet both attitudes ensure that the patriarchal historical narrative of famous names and dates does not exclude the poem's public. This inclusiveness leads Cain to posit "Ten Elephants" as one of Souster's carnivalesque poems.[31] The iconic image of those elephants on Yonge Street is positioned into a similar historical literary trajectory by virtue of its title as that of the collection. Souster's public role might then be read as twofold—as wryly and affectionately lampooning both symbolic cityspace and the literary landscape at large.

Dennis Lee's *Civil Elegies*

Dennis Lee's production of a civic public poetic is invested both in his work and in its biographical context, given his position as Toronto's first official poet laureate. Although exploring the laureate position brings a sociological dimension to civic public analysis, it also shows that such frameworks of localized power are collaboratively authored methods of situating poetry. Lee's position as the city's inaugural laureate from 2001 to 2004 warrants examining. In title, the stipendiary role parallels that of the many poet laureate positions that have sprung up across Canada, from the parliamentary poet laureate to multiple provincial and municipal poets laureate. Each of these positions receives cultural capital from the recollection of historical poets laureate in Ancient Greece and latterly in British literature. Historically, the position is meant as an acknowledgement of authority in poetics by the state. The continuing located nature of each position creates a curious geography of public poetry, a map of those places where poetry is being promoted and authorized through a particular agent. There is no transferrable theory of how being a laureate frames poetry, and the insistent cultural terrain attached to the poet laureate and *where* the laureate "rules" invites a consideration of place and of the domain of poetic publics.

The officially legislated Toronto poet laureate is selected by City Council's "culture" department. That department's description of the role, publicized on the official web page, designates duties of diplomacy, lobbying, cultural continuity, and place:

> Toronto's Poet Laureate serves as the City's literary ambassador. As an advocate for poetry, language and the arts, the Poet Laureate attends events across the city to promote and attract people to the literary world. The Poet Laureate's mandate also includes the creation of a legacy project that will be unique to the individual.
>
> The position of the Poet Laureate honours a Toronto poet whose work displays excellence and has written on themes that are of relevance to Torontonians.[32]

The description outlines a somewhat vague and hard-to-quantify position for the poet laureate. This was not the reason for Marni Soupcoff's critique of the position in the *National Post* when Dionne Brand became Toronto's third poet laureate in 2009.[33] Soupcoff's criticism focused on two central issues: the city's taxes being spent on such a nebulous position, and the unhealthy imbrication of presumed political art with political power. The first point may be dismissed by the city clerk's report that "funding for the Poet Laureate honorarium is provided by a $5,000.00 allocation from funds donated to the Public Art Reserve Fund and a $5,000.00 grant from the Canada Council for the Arts."[34] While funding is at arm's length, City Council still administers the position, and this is not without political impact. While Soupcoff's criticism drew on perceptions of identity politics, denying the public appeal and public resonance of one of Canada's best poets working today, it did raise the question of what authority is conferred on this public engagement with poetry.[35]

The most visible contribution to the city from the four Toronto poets laureate to date is the "legacy project on which they decide. Lee's legacy project aims at a physical inscription in material space, primarily in the form of the names of Toronto's artists and thinkers on the city's streets, squares, parks and other public places ('Toronto's First Poet Laureate: Dennis Lee 2001–2004'). The Bloor-Spadina Parkette, for example, has been renamed the Matt Cohen Park."[36] Brand's poet laureate legacy project is to reclaim physical public space in Toronto for the inscription of poetry itself. The first example is the entrance to the newly refurbished Cedarbrae Public Library, where verse from Toronto poet Rosemary Sullivan is embedded in bronze lettering in the walkway to the library.[37]

Early council briefing documents demonstrate how the definition of the laureate position became bound up in the city's sense of representation. In 2000, Joe Halstead, the Commissioner for Economic Development in Culture and Tourism, articulated the Council position as follows: "In order to establish a poet laureate for the City, consistent with Toronto's status as a 'world class city,' it is important to ensure that community partners and professional organizations be included in any discussions surrounding the development of a process for selecting an appropriate individual to occupy the position."[38]

Halstead emphasizes a careful council arts advocacy in line with established arts and business authorities. The documents finalizing Dennis Lee's appointment suggested that it was "Council's wish that the Poet Laureate help bring poetry to the public."[39] This would appear to be a relatively direct wish, by which the poet laureate would carry forth relevant poetry to a prefigured civic audience. This conception of a civic audience, however, is very much framed by the matrices of local government power. It is therefore useful to consider how such an aim, and the potential social worlding of poetry, might jar with the coucil's role in perpetuating official spatial narratives. While Lee was chosen by a panel of experts, themselves defined in council documents, the official acceptance required a committee comment on Lee's suitability for the role of poet laureate. The critical judgment on Lee's work was as follows: "In much of his work, he uses Canadian place-names, local cultural idiosyncrasies, and environmental issues to try to communicate a sense of national identity, but his poems have proven popular among English-speaking audiences all over the world."[40] This judgment makes surprisingly little of the civic qualities of Lee's poetry and is silent on the aptness of the author of *Civil Elegies*, poems set in Nathan Phillips Square, being approved by a council that meets inside that very building on the square.

Lee's *Civil Elegies*, first published in 1968 and redrafted for 1972 publication, becomes in retrospect the work of a poet laureate for the city of

Toronto. The elegies' intense engagement in civic public poetics draws out the complicity of city spaces in multiple discourses of empire, nationalism, and morality. Lee's poetry, like Souster's, turns to local histories of place, using the lived ancestry of the city as a way to appreciate dwelling in place. As the Council judgment above indicates, however, Lee's *Civil Elegies* have been read more broadly in terms of their national and transnational meanings than for their local civic sensibility. Kit Dobson's attentive discussion of the elegies identifies this as the major theme: "*Civil Elegies* is of interest primarily because of the ways in which it attempts to work out problems of nation and space within its poetic form."[41] Admitting the locale of Toronto to discussion, Dobson suggests that Lee's speaker "sits in Toronto's Nathan Phillips Square, which is used as a synecdoche for Canada."[42] Although there are national dimensions to such moves, one might also consider how the elegies and their criticism just as fluidly use Canada as a synecdoche for Toronto and how conflating social spaces changes the conception of the poetic public engaged.

There is also a search for municipal identity in exploring the city's local social spaces through Lee's elegies. Priscilla Uppal's focus on the elegiac and mourning in Canadian poetry identifies Lee's summoning of ancestral figures as a way of "advocating the formation of a local identity." However, Uppal's work goes on to express the complexity of Lee's civic dimension, given the nationalist reading. The "overt nationalist agenda," Uppal writes, "is perhaps also indicative of the possibility that the Toronto-based poet may not be able to claim a regional identity for himself."[43] The nationalist symbolic usage of Toronto as a centre of Canadian power, in literature, politics, and economics, overshadows the resonance of the everyday space. The locality sought in the elegies may not resound with a sense of a region, but it provides a strong model for Toronto's ongoing spatial definition among multiple negotiating spatial claims. This is demonstrated in the first elegy through the use of the nickname for Toronto: "you would not expect / the furies assembled in hogtown."[44] Toronto's nickname, Hogtown, has been attributed to Toronto's local meat-packing industries during the 1940s, but it has also been read in the media in the literal sense of the city's greed, "where the word 'Hogtown' has been used to identify Canada's greediest and snootiest urban centre."[45] The poem's use of the nickname reflects on the colloquial and linguistic construction of social space. The poetic public constructed by *Civil Elegies* forms from the mythic dimension of the wraith-like furies and their explicit location in hogtown. This discord establishes the tenor of Lee's investigation. There is a deferential element here, too, in the suggestion that the city's square is too unremarkable for such a fantastic scene. The everyday lives of those criss-crossing the square are observed by Lee's speaker, who establishes the square as a locale for the temporary construction of a "passionate civil man" amidst "the men and women [who] moved in their own space."[46] Like Kingwell with his comments on the conflicts of public space, Lee gestures towards those individual private spheres that dominate the lives of the civic public. Citizens are set in a local historical context, mimicking the selfishness of the "patricians in muddy York"[47] and establishing "their compact together against the gangs of the new."[48] This history is a trigger for an uncanny view that projects alternative bodies as located markings, the "lives we had not lived in phalanx invisibly staining / the square."[49] Attending to the bearing of these bodies in an officially sanctioned public space, Lee begins to imagine alternative underpinnings for civic identity.

The square's proximity to Yonge Street allows Lee to tap into the same historical memory as Souster, tracing Mackenzie's rebellion of 1837. Before expanding his commentary to a national and global level, Lee hones in on the participants of the rebellion, described as "plain men much / goaded by privilege—our other origin."[50] In a comment on the heritage of a privileged elite and its complicity with colonial power, these origins are further fragmented by the language that introduces the rebellion's outcome. The plain men are perceived by Lee's speaker to have "cried / 'Mackenzie knows a word, Mackenzie / knows a meaning!' but it was not true."[51] Mackenzie's false words foreshadow Lee's struggle to find words for an experience bound up in colonization. The hope and failure bound up in the words' local deployment are echoed by the elegies' greater aim for civility. The speaker is described as a "passionate civil man" in search of a "civil habitation."[52] Ironically, these words are located in a public square that has since been governed by a great number of civic bylaws. Mariana Valverde has highlighted how, due to these laws, "we find that it is...forbidden to 'present or take part in any dramatic, musical, artistic or other performance' [in Nathan Phillips Square]. Curiously, however, poetry reading is said not to be a performance, which means one can recite poetry in the square, but not sing."[53] Poetry is exempted from practical concerns about the potential for civic squares to host contentious behaviours. While the notion that an artistic sense of governance may have made a "Dennis Lee exemption" for the square is entertaining, it is more interesting to consider the exemption as acknowledging poetry as a civic public necessity. Seen as idealized speech, poetry is aligned with the ideal of free and open public discourse.

The social concerns surrounding public performance of poetry within city bylaws are pre-empted by Lee's first elegy, where the speaker reflects on the official structures that shape his environment: "I know / the dead persist in / buildings, by-laws, porticos—the city I live in is clogged with their presence."[54] These haunting presences are still enacted and acted upon in

Lee's incomplete city. Porticos become the city's language of design, representing another small way in which private spaces might masquerade as open public spaces, resisting a full embrace of alterity and diversity for a set of restrictive boundaries. Nevertheless, within the speaker's construction of a poetic social world, Toronto is home to self-reflection and to the creation of "a space in which / the full desires of those that begot them, great animating desires / that shrank and grew hectic as the land pre-empted their lives / might still take root."[55] In this compulsion, historical antecedents might be reclaimed to fulfill their unbuilt and uncompleted local projects. The attention to historic incompletion resists the claim for the great men of patriarchal historical lineage, looking instead to the fractures and discontinuities where contemporary creativity might foster a civic public poetic to textual or material response.

Lee and Souster are mutually attentive to histories that undercut any grandly defined public heroic narrative. In "Ten Elephants," Souster positions us alongside the minor players in a historical parade, while allowing us agency to acquire credit for any parade and to choose who might be celebrated. The ironic acquisition of elephant dung, and the lack of glamour in such a role, acknowledges the sometimes uncomfortable clash of the private and public in civic performance. Engagement with local geography and history is an open form of civic public. Similarly in Lee's elegies, the emphasis is on recognition and contestation. The eighth elegy demonstrates how the idea of the civic square acknowledges a tension between local poetic voice and multiple open connections of lives that constitute a civic public: "not as a / lyric self in a skin but divided, spinning off many selves to attend each."[56] The return to the square draws attention to the length and breadth of Lee's elegies. Long lines and stanzas that stretch reflection and recurrent theoretical diversions demonstrate how Lee's elegies echo Souster's lifelong chronicling project. Both poets' works embody Eichhorn and Milne's conception of prismatic publics engendered through notions of the civic and demonstrate poetry "actively engaged in making social worlds."[57] Lee and Souster pay attention to everyday Toronto life and to the larger literary and civic publics who act in material creation and representation. Their attention to Toronto's city spaces and to the creative performance of civic public work is amplified by both poets' association with the role of laureate. By engaging with the social space of Toronto, inhabited by multiple literary, historical, and everyday citizens, Lee and Souster move past any simple mirroring of local detail. In so doing, they resist prescriptive senses of the local, or the civic, developing an open sense of a civic public poetics.

Notes

1 Eichhorn and Milne, *Prismatic Publics*, 12.
2 Eichhorn and Milne, *Prismatic Publics*.
3 Warner, "Publics and Counterpublics," 49–90.
4 The last of these terms is suggested to address both critical and creative texts that make creative use of maps themselves. While not relevant in the poetry examined here, this is an active field of research in and of itself. See Huggan, 1994; Moretti, 2005; Bushell, 2012.
5 Thacker, *Moving Through Modernity*, 53.
6 Thacker, "The Idea."
7 Lefebvre is at pains to point out that such experience should only be seen alone as "cohesive" rather than "coherent." For more on this and the tripartite dialectic, see his *The Production of Space*, 38–41.
8 Thacker, "The Idea," 63.
9 Surette, "Here Is Us."
10 Berger, *Attention Deficit Democracy*, 3.
11 McKinnie, *City Stages*, 53.
12 Coleman, *White Civility*, 5.
13 Coleman, *White Civility*, 55.
14 It is notable that Coleman's analysis here is built on an understanding that Lee's *Civil Elegies* are "the most articulate expression of this condition of elegiac, even ironical, White self-consciousness in English Canada." *White Civility*, 42.
15 For a more in-depth view of urban theory's problems in determining a coherent understanding of urbanization and the boundaries of the city, see Neil Brenner, "Theses on Urbanization."
16 Kingwell, "Masters of Chancery," 3.
17 Cain, "Mapping Raymond Souster's Toronto," 10.
18 Fiorito, "Happy Birthday, Raymond Souster."
19 Marshall, *Harsh and Lovely Land*, 79, 52.
20 Sutherland, *Essays, Controversies, and Poems*, 79.
21 Souster, "The Heart Still Singing," 186.
22 Souster, *The Colour of the Times*, n.pag.
23 Frye, *The Bush Garden*, 69.
24 Since presenting a conference paper version of this chapter at the Public Poetics conference at Mount Allison in September 2012, more has been written on Souster, sadly in the form of obituaries. The obituary form does not often provide the most insightful critical eye, but in this case more than one obituary highlighted the importance of Souster's literary career. Russell Smith in *The Globe and Mail* reiterated the critical ambivalence in which Souster's poetry is held while acknowledging his wider poetic labour: "Souster should be remembered not for his somewhat sentimental and craft-free poetry. He should be remembered for what he did as an editor and

critic" (Smith, 2012). While Souster's editorial role with the mid-century Contact Press is hugely important in the story of Canadian literary production, dismissals of Souster's poetry overlook the craft involved in writing the city and writing for a reading public.

25 Cain, "Mapping," 61.
26 See Moretti, "Conjectures on World Literature," for more on this unorthodox literary approach.
27 Souster, *The Colour*, 135.
28 Keenan, *Some Great Idea*, 53.
29 The heritage designation acknowledges that the real-life site has no obvious structural remains of the tavern, but might still have some below ground.
30 Bowering, "Sun, Seasons, City," 79.
31 Cain, "Mapping," 67.
32 "Toronto's Current Poet Laureate."
33 Soupcoff, "A Job."
34 Toronto City Council, "Appointment."
35 Political clashes were barely present during Lee's tenure as laureate. Much more might be said about how Dionne Brand's public poetic engagement contrasted starkly with the shifting language of the Council administration under the mayoralty of Rob Ford, as well as during George Elliott Clarke's current laureateship.
36 Cohen himself has emphasized that the wider notion of Toronto as a material and lived space has not been a beneficiary of its national cultural and economic power. See Cohen, "Realism."
37 Rosemary Sullivan, "Poetry Is Public Is Poetry." *poetryispublic.ca*. Accessed 14 May 2013. http://www.poetryispublic.ca/about.php.
38 Halstead, *Poet Laureate*.
39 Halstead, *Poet Laureate*, 3.
40 Halstead, *Poet Laureate*, 3.
41 Dobson, *Transnational Canadas*, 42.
42 Dobson, *Transnational Canadas*, 43.
43 Uppal, *We Are What We Mourn*, 125.
44 Lee, *Civil Elegies*, 42.
45 Rayburn, *Naming Canada*, 47.
46 Lee, *Civil Elegies*, 33.
47 Lee, *Civil Elegies*, 33.
48 Lee, *Civil Elegies*, 33.
49 Lee, *Civil Elegies*, 33.
50 Lee, *Civil Elegies*, 34.
51 Lee, *Civil Elegies*, 34.
52 Lee, *Civil Elegies*, 33, 36.
53 Valverde, "Taking 'Land Use' Seriously," 52.
54 Lee, *Civil Elegies*, 34.

55 Lee, *Civil Elegies*, 35.
56 Lee, *Civil Elegies*, 52.
57 Eichhorn and Milne, *Prismatic*, 12.

Bibliography

Berger, Ben. *Attention Deficit Democracy: The Paradox of Civic Engagement*. Princeton: Princeton University Press, 2011.

Bowering, George. "Sun, Seasons, City." Review of *Ten Elephants on Yonge Street* by Raymond Souster. *Canadian Literature* 28 (Spring 1966): 79–80.

Brenner, Neil. "Theses on Urbanization." *Public Culture* 25, no. 1 (Winter 2013): 85–114.

Bushell, Sally. "The Slipperiness of Literary Maps: Critical Cartography and Literary Cartography." *Cartographica* 47, no. 3 (2012): 149–60.

Cain, Stephen. "Mapping Raymond Souster's Toronto." In *The Canadian Modernists Meet*, edited by Dean Irvine. 59–78. Ottawa: University of Ottawa Press, 2005.

"Canada Gives Willkie Its Biggest Show since Visit of King & Queen." *Life*, 7 April 1941, 30–31.

Cohen, Matt. "Realism in Modern English Canadian Fiction." In *A Sense of Place: Essays in Post-Colonial Literatures*, edited by Britta Olinder. 57–63. Gothenburg University Commonwealth Studies. Göteborg: Gothenburg University English Department, 1984.

Coleman, Daniel. *White Civility: The Literary Project of English Canada*. Reappraisals Series. Toronto: University of Toronto Press, 2008.

Dobson, Kit. *Transnational Canadas: Anglo-Canadian Literature and Globalization*. TransCanada Series. Waterloo: Wilfrid Laurier University Press, 2009.

Eichhorn, Kate, and Heather Milne, eds. *Prismatic Publics: Innovative Canadian Women's Poetry and Poetics*. Toronto: Coach House Books, 2009.

Fiorito, Joe. "Happy Birthday, Raymond Souster." *Toronto Star*, 13 January 2012. Accessed 28 February 2013 at http://www.thestar.com/news/gta/2012/01/13/fiorito_happy_birthday_raymond_souster.html

Frye, Northrop. *The Bush Garden: Essays on the Canadian Imagination*. Toronto: House of Anansi, 1971.

Halstead, Joe. Economic Development and Parks Committee. *Poet Laureate for the City of Toronto*. Toronto Staff Report. 29 May 2000. Toronto: Toronto City Council, 2000. Accessed 28 February 2013 at http://www.toronto.ca/legdocs/2000/agendas/committees/edp/edp000619/it018.pdf.

Huggan, Graham. *Territorial Disputes: Maps and Mapping Strategies in Contemporary Canadian and Australian Fiction*. Toronto: University of Toronto Press, 1994.

Keenan, Edward. *Some Great Idea*. Toronto: Coach House, 2013.

Kingwell, Mark. "Masters of Chancery." In *Rites of Way: The Politics and Poetics of Public Space*, edited by Mark Kingwell and Patrick Turmel. 3–22. Waterloo: Wilfrid Laurier University Press, 2009.

Lecker, Robert. *The Cadence of Civil Elegies*. Toronto: Cormorant Books, 2006.

Lee, Dennis. *Civil Elegies and Other Poems*. 1968. Toronto: House of Anansi, 1972.

Lefebvre, Henri. *The Production of Space*. 1974. Translated by Donald Nicholson-Smith. Oxford: Blackwell, 1991.

McKinnie, Michael. *City Stages: Theatre and Urban Space in a Global City*. Toronto: University of Toronto Press, 2007.

Marshall, Tom. *Harsh and Lovely Land: The Major Canadian Poets and the Making of a Canadian Tradition*. Vancouver: UBC Press, 1979.

Moretti, Franco. "Conjectures on World Literature." *New Left Review* 2, no. 1 (2000): 54–68.

———. *Graphs, Maps, Trees: Abstract Models for Literary History*. London: Verso, 2005.

"Poetry Is Public Is Poetry." *poetryispublic.ca*. Accessed 14 May 2013 at http://www.poetryispublic.ca/about.php.

Rayburn, Alan. *Naming Canada: Stories about Canadian Place Names*. Toronto: University of Toronto Press, 2001.

Smith, Russell. "Raymond Souster: A Great of CanLit When CanLit Was Great." *Globe and Mail*, 24 October 2012. Accessed 28 February 2013 at http://www.theglobeandmail.com/arts/books-and-mediaraymond-souster-a-great-of-canlit-when-canlit-was-great/article4639517.

Soupcoff, Marni. "A Job No Outspoken Poet Would Want." *National Post Online*. Accessed 28 February 2013 at http://www.nationalpost.com/opinion/columnists/story.html?id=529add79-1708-4fa3-be70-5df981e4c2c8. Originally published in "Dionne Brand, Agitator Laureate." *National Post–Posted Toronto Online*, October 8, 2009. http://network.nationalpost.com/np/blogs/toronto/archive/2009/10/08/dionne-brand-agitator-laureate.aspx#ixzz1SpmuYzLm.

Souster, Raymond. *The Colour of the Times/Ten Elephants on Yonge Street*. Toronto: McGraw-Hill Ryerson, 1973.

———. "The Heart Still Singing: Raymond Souster at 82." Interview with Tony Tremblay. *Studies in Canadian Literature* 27, no. 2 (2002): 183–201.

Sullivan, Rosemary. "Poetry Is Public Is Poetry." *poetryispublic.ca*. Accessed 14 May 2013. http://www.poetryispublic.ca/about.php.

Surette, Leon. "Here Is Us: The Topocentrism of Canadian Literary Criticism." *Canadian Poetry* 10 (1982): 44–57.

Sutherland, John. *Essays, Controversies, and Poems*, edited by Miriam Waddington. Toronto: McClelland and Stewart, 1972.

Thacker, Andrew. *Moving Through Modernity*. Manchester: Manchester University Press, 2003.

———. "The Idea of a Critical Literary Geography." *New Formations* 57 (2005): 56–73.
"Toronto's Current Poet Laureate." *City of Toronto, Arts Heritage & Culture*. City of Toronto. Accessed 28 February 2013 at http://www.toronto.ca/culture/poet_laureate.htm.
Toronto City Council. Economic Development and Parks Committee. "Appointment of the City of Toronto Poet Laureate (All Wards)." Rept. 3 Clause 16. April/May, 2001. Toronto: Toronto City Council, 2001. Accessed 28 February 2013 at http://www.toronto.ca/legdocs/2001/agendas/council/cc010424/edp3rpt/cl016.pdf.
Uppal, Priscila. *We Are What We Mourn*. Montreal and Kingston: McGill-Queen's University Press, 2008.
Valverde, Mariana. "Taking 'Land Use' Seriously: Toward an Ontology of Municipal Law." *Law Text Culture* 9, no. 1 (2005): 34–59. Accessed on 9 September 2014 at http://ro.uow.edu.au/ltc/vol9/iss1/3.
Warner, Michael. "Publics and Counterpublics." *Public Culture* 14, no. 1 (2002): 49–90.

8

To the Bone: The Instrumental Activism of Dionne Brand's *Ossuaries*

Geordie Miller

> *Plato ordered us cast out*
> *of the City where Wisdom reigns.*
> *In a new Ivory Tower made of (human) bones.*
>   Aleksander Wat, "Dark Light" (1968)

In early 2012, municipal councils across Canada were encouraged to get into the spirit of the upcoming National Poetry Month. April was to be less "cruel" than T.S. Eliot had envisioned: Regina Mayor Pat Fiacco, the Saskatchewan Writers' Guild, and the League of Canadian Poets planned to "breed" poetry and politics.[1] Specifically, poets were invited to read one of their poems at a local council meeting and have it included in the minutes. More than twenty towns and cities participated in what came to be known as "The Mayor's Poetry City Challenge."[2] Toronto was not among them; Dionne Brand, the city's Poet Laureate, reportedly refused.[3] Certainly it is the Laureate's prerogative how she wishes "to promote and attract people to the literary world," to borrow the phrasing from the "Culture" section of the City of Toronto's website;[4] nevertheless, the council's invitation must have seemed strikingly contradictory to Brand. After all, it was the same council whose proposed cuts to libraries and other social services "challenged" the idea that public interests could be measured without a balance sheet. "Who's afraid of the city?" asks Brand in a July 2011 *rabble* blog entry.[5] "City council," she answers. "It's not capable of imagining us, of expressing our ambitions, so it has brought a consultancy firm in to stifle them."[6] The council's desire to celebrate poetry while systematically dismantling the spaces that make literacy possible is a typical example of neoliberal doublethink. Despite its commendable aim of raising poetry's public profile, the Poetry City Challenge implies that verse is an ornament of *realpolitik*. Poets could momentarily occupy council agendas before the business of running the cities resumed. The juxtaposition of the Poetry City Challenge and Brand's critique of the council raises the broader issue of the extent to which poetry "express[es] our ambitions" outside the chambers of political and corporate elites. How do poets call (out) the public?[7] How might poetry be understood as a form of political activism?

All too easily, according to Susan Buck-Morss, whose "The Second Time as Farce...Historical Pragmatics and the Untimely Present" (2010) detects "current pressure on artists to *do* the work of politics for us."[8] She avers that this "pressure" is a symptom of an identitarian strain of theorizing that privileges narratives of cultural authenticity at the expense of recognizing the "fact [that] people today are living culturally porous lives under the far more universal subjective conditions of capitalism, urbanism and hybridity."[9] Brand addresses this "universal" subjugation throughout her *rabble* post on the proposed library cuts; for example, she ventriloquizes the council's ideological investment in enclosure: "they say, it is not public space it is real estate, we are not citizens we are stakeholders or customers."[10] Her antagonistic stance towards an economic model of civic engagement and other products of neoliberal doctrine is widely rewarded when she incorporates it into her poetry.[11] Her latest long poem, *Ossuaries* (2010), was feted with Canada's Griffin Prize, the nation's most lucrative award for a volume of poetry written in English. *Ossuaries* is a repository for hard truths about social injustice and ecological catastrophe. Its absorption into relatively mainstream Canadian culture through such traditional tributaries of public acclaim as the literary prize[12] merits skepticism about the work's activist potential. Namely, might praising the poem, as the quotation from the *Toronto Star* on the back of the book does of Brand more generally, for "chronicl[ing] the ache in our body politic," only help prolong the agony? Such a hostile question stems from Buck-Morss's sense that art about politics is a type of resistance tolerated by those, like the Toronto City Council, with a vested interest in manufacturing and protecting the status quo. Brand's long poem is *about* politics insofar as its speaker and protagonist, Yasmine, recalls her years of activist training and underground asylum. She goes into hiding during the 1970s after taking part in a bank heist in upstate New York and eventually flees to Canada. In what follows, I respond to Buck-Morss's charge by identifying how *Ossuaries* can be considered political.

Brand distances herself from conventional political lexicon in a *rabble* entry from April 2011, "Reckless coalition: Of language and politics." The occasion was Stephen Harper's late-March election announcement, when he summoned the spectre of a "reckless coalition" made up of the Liberals, the NDP, and the Bloc Québécois.[13] He opposed this "reckless coalition" to the "stable, national majority" offered by his party, the Conservatives.[14] Harper's speech demonstrates the typical obfuscations of political discourse, in which words "are completely incomprehensible and have no relation to their meaning."[15] Brand wonders how, exactly, a democratically elected coalition could be *a priori* characterized as "reckless": "I take language too seriously," Brand writes, and therefore "won't call [Harper's speech] language."[16] In her self-professed bewilderment about the grammar of politicians, she touches on something that is especially germane to the aesthetic of *Ossuaries*. For Brand, Harper's doomsday narrative of a coalition of "arch-centralists and Quebec sovereigntists" is unconvincing because "the sky has already fallen—at least a hundred times."[17] *Ossuaries* indirectly reinforces that we are "already" situated in the economic collapse that Harper's policies, among others in what is truly a "reckless coalition" (the G20), insistently advance, and the planetary collapse that they just as consistently deny.

Ossuaries neither conceals nor minimizes the details about the latest tears in the fabric of capitalism and liberal democracy; however, its content does not suffice as a measure of its oppositional politics. In Brand's poem, the form radicalizes the familiar leftist message that "the sky has already fallen." To develop this position, I foreground four formal features in my analysis: the tercet stanzas, enjambment, sparse punctuation, and incessant repetition. These features intersect with the poem's instrumental motif, its allusions to Afro-Latin and African American jazz artists, various lexical inflections of instruments and instrumentality, and Brand's signature lyricism. I argue that reading the formal elements in the context of this motif harmonizes poetics and activism. My reading of the poem implicitly recognizes the distinction that Smaro Kamboureli makes between "the body literary" and "the body politic" in her "Preface" to *Trans.Can.Lit* (2007). However, while Kamboureli praises the fact that "the body literary does not always have a symmetrical relationship to the body politic," *Ossuaries* suggests that such "symmetry" does not necessarily limit the work's power to disturb totemic narratives.[18] Kamboureli posits the exceptionality of the literary body as a possible site of resistance to the body politic, whereas I instrumentalize the literary body to highlight how it can reinvigorate the body politic by rendering as co-extensive the political responsibility of poets and their public(s). As I hear it, instruments and instrumentality stand in for the body literary in Brand's poem.

Brand organizes the poem into fifteen ossuaries, which alternate between lyric and narrative—first- and third-person—address. The movement within each ossuary is subtler but equally significant. "Ossuary I" establishes a pattern whereby commonsense phrases like "some might say" and "of course" are mobilized in order to express weariness with what we all purportedly know already. For example, the opening tercet, "I lived and loved, some might say, / in momentous times / looking back, my dreams were full of prisons" is rearticulated in the second line of the following stanza as "so many dreams of course were full of prisons."[19] Here we have not only the journey from the particular ("my dreams") to the more universal ("so many dreams"), which mirrors the structural oscillation between first- and third-person address, but also the idea that there is something unremarkable about "dreams...full of prisons." "So what," as another popular refrain in the poem puts it.[20] Of course there is no escaping the epistemic tragedy of modern life. Of course "we are speeding on / our atrocious axis."[21] These consensual phrases challenge readers not to indulge in laments for the "fatal future"—to not dwell on our "insatiable forecasts."[22] For such gestures reify Enlightenment thought's problematic link between knowledge and action.[23] Instrumental reason, as the poem suggests, is a broken chorus. The phatic quality of the poem's language—its "of courses," "some might says," and "so whats"—shows that knowledge is too often inert. Our mutual awareness of the global death drive secures its inevitable outcome.

The tercet stanza structure intervenes in this gap between knowledge and action, with the third line disrupting the potential unity of the couplet. There are only two stanzas in the poem that are not tercets. The first occurs when Yasmine contemplates her lover's "motionless face, redundantly handsome, condescending, / as if this truth should give her comfort."[24] Here the missing line strengthens her sense of the incompleteness of her account of him. A catalogic stanza towards the end of the poem includes

tumours of sightlines, readjusted

ankles, fenced mouths,
mechanic vulva, plastic toenails
pincered knee, nib of palms, wire
lifelines, elongated radius, cellular

disintegration,[25]

Coupled with the use of enjambment, the presence of the fourth line supplements the disorder inherent in the techno-dystopian posture of these stanzas. The tercets that dominate the rest of the poem operate dialectically[26]—they represent thought-in-motion, signalling a way beyond the Enlightenment dead end of instrumental reason. This third way promises no simple synthesis of knowledge and action. And it is more complex than the resolution of opposites that characterizes the textbook misreading of Hegelian dialectics.[27] Yasmine's beliefs about her militancy are constantly changing; in turn, the very process of thinking changes her. One stanza midway through the poem nicely encapsulates this dynamic: "Yasmine knows in her hardest heart, / that truth is worked and organized by some, / and she's on the wrong side always."[28] The truism from the first two lines—history ("truth") is made ("worked and organized") by the few (the "some")—does not settle comfortably into the third line ("she's on the wrong side always"). To put it bluntly, if a select subset gets to define the events that negatively affect the entire species, then "the wrong side" is really the *right* one to be on. The point, though, is that Yasmine cannot *know* that her side is the "wrong" one; she is never directly confronted with the choice: either wrong or right. She can only act with the hope that what is "wrong" with regard to existing conditions is *right* in the long run—that out of her failure to imagine revolutionary alternatives will arise new ones. The third line is there to remind readers that such choices are both necessary and always already rendered partial by whatever comes next.

The third line or term can also serve to implicate the speaker in the existing conditions. Take the superficial inarticulateness and isolation voiced in "Ossuary I": "what to say / life went on around me."[29] The cliché of having nothing "to say" while "life [goes] on [all] around [her]" is compromised in the third line: "I laughed, I had drinks, I gathered with friends."[30] These three activities may be empty in light of the more serious matter of civilization's discontents, but she cannot justify separating herself from the violence of the surrounding world. Nevertheless, her guilt has a radical dimension. She does not acknowledge her responsibility because this violence constitutes, rather than distorts, the current order. Near the beginning of "Ossuary III," she catalogues a series of crimes in the first two lines of a stanza—"larcenies, robberies, trespassing, / loitering, intimidation, resisting arrest, vagrancy"—before unifying them with a coordinating conjunction in the third: "but fundamentally existence."[31] The list cannot go on. In its very universality, the "fundamental" violation ("existence") indicts the law's regulatory pretensions. Laws are part of a criminal whole. So-called liberal guilt is limited to temporary recognitions of subjective interpellation by this whole, which explains why Yasmine expands the horizon of her violence beyond the subjectivist one. The transgression of civilized life itself, though, is more permanent, as is underscored in one of the poem's numerous triplet lines: "being alive, being human, its monotony."[32] "Monotony" normalizes the daily operation of systemic violence. At the end of the stanza, Yasmine tallies the sum of this sameness, "the awareness, at its primal core, of nothing";[33] exceeding pathetic nihilism, Yasmine's "awareness" also amounts *to* "nothing."

Yasmine does, at last, do something. Along with her "comrades," she robs a bank. She assaults a guard during the holdup. Her act is sudden and shocking, with the guard's "face crushed into gristle / by the butt of her avenging gyre."[34] Displaying the naive homeopathy of countering systemic with subjective violence, Yasmine's "vengeance" is ethically indefensible. Most troublesomely, perhaps, Yasmine rationalizes the assault in the vocabulary of vulgar Marxism. To her, the victim "betray[s] his class / by putting up a fight."[35] We should certainly be critical of Yasmine's matter-of-fact translation of the guard into an "incidental" figure.[36] The use of enjambment in the subsequent escape scene underscores the insufficiency of such crude translations. On the surface, enjambment heightens the tension in this cinematic scene:

> before the bank door erupts,
> or the supplicants of its
> marble floor rise from their prayers, or sirens mewl
>
> their syrup song,
> they drive, drive, drive, drive, drive,[37]

Beneath the surface contradiction between the fraught event (a bank heist) and the enjambed, saccharine words ("sirens mewl / their syrupy song") lies a deeper structural point. Enjambment conveys that reality is inadequately captured in Yasmine's convictions, not to mention in the tercets I had previously associated with dialectical progression. The authoritarian "song" spills over into the next stanza, as does the robbers' retreat. Both are unending: the robbery invites perpetual pursuit. Yasmine is "driven" underground into an indefinite life sentence. The fugitives are no longer "angels," as they were described while inside the bank. Instead, the holy accent has shifted to their victims, "supplicants" whose "prayers" undoubtedly command mercy.[38] Insofar as their music is a feeble cry ("mewl"), the police are included in this collective.

The poem's onward orientation is not confined to instances of enjambment, nor is music sole property of the police. Without full stops, the entire poem tilts forward, and the absence of periods connotes an absence of boundaries between the poem's intellectual and musical heritage. The "Acknowledgements" section lays bare this duel ancestry. It lists a series of works as "instrumental during the writing of [*Ossuaries*]," such as Karl Marx's *The Eighteenth Brumaire of Louis Bonaparte* (1852) and Charlie "Bird" Parker's "Ornithology" (1946). These influences are weaved throughout the poem in direct citations and explicit allusions. Listening to Charlie Parker delivers Yasmine the moments of transcendence promised in his nickname. Her identification with Parker plays out while she is in Havana, where "one night she walks fully clothed, like Bird, / into the oily pearl of the sea's surface, / coral and cartilage, bone and air, infrangible."[39] Afro-Latin and African American jazz provides an antidote to her "intuitions of gloom" through "the beacon of the record player."[40] She has discerning taste, though. Her lover and co-conspirator, Owusu, worships Miles Davis. To her, Parker's occasional bandmate embodies a flawed model of cynical engagement, with his "who gives a fuck trumpet."[41] As she says to Owusu, "Miles kept living, till life was rancid, Bird flew off."[42] The difference between the two takes on added importance, since the previous stanza features partial quotations from Friedrich Engels's *The Origin of the Family, Private Property, and the State* (1884): "when these people are in the world…" and "…that will be the end of it…"[43] The ellipses draw attention to excision; the full passage from Engels reads:

> What we can now conjecture about the way in which sexual relations will be ordered after the impending overthrow of capitalist production is mainly of a negative character, limited for the most part to what will disappear. But what will there be new? That will be answered when a new generation has grown up: a generation of men who never in their lives have known what it is to buy a woman's surrender with money or any other social instrument of power; a generation of women who have never known what it is to give themselves to a man from any other considerations than real love or to refuse to give themselves to their lover from fear of the economic consequences. *When these people are in the world*, they will care precious little what anybody today thinks they ought to do; they will make their own practice and their corresponding public opinion about the practice of each individual—and *that will be the end of it*.[44]

The passage is worth quoting in full because it gleans the possibility that the end of capitalism will mark the beginning of an equitable allotment of social power. The "these people" phrasing makes existing gender differences secondary to new systems of value that might prohibit any objectification and thus render these differences benign. Owusu's commitment to Davis communicates a commitment to the present, in which he treats Yasmine as "some receptacle for his spit, his sperm, his combed-out / hair, the shavings of his fingernails, each liquid phrase."[45]

The distinction between the successive allusions to Engels and Parker collapses in the absence of periods. Political theory and music are combined as ingredients for praxis. Yasmine cannot seem to tell where each begins and ends. She can, however, be selective about the musical and political traditions she invokes and aligns. At the opening of "Ossuary VI," these choices and their pairings are striking: "Engels plaited to Bird, Claudia Jones edgestitched / to Monk, Rosa Luxemburg braids Coltrane."[46] To follow through on the example from my preceding paragraph, with Engels "plaited to [him]," Parker's promise of romantic escapism assumes critical substance. It awakens Yasmine to the utopian possibility, that of the not-yet-become. Conversely, Parker enables a becoming not presaged in the bleak passage that she includes from the work of Engels's collaborator: "'The tradition of all / dead generations weighs like a nightmare on the brains of / the living...'"[47] Parker's bebop improvisation resonates with the call to action expressed later on in Marx's *Eighteenth Brumaire* (1852), "The social revolution of the nineteenth century cannot draw its poetry from the past, but only from the future."[48] Activist interventions, like bebop, require spontaneous action. The poem rushes ahead.

Without periods, though, the formal space for symbolizing revolutionary irruption is foreclosed. Brand's 2006 long poem, *Inventory*, likewise has no periods. The effect is to formally register the indistinction between bodies (of thought; human bodies) and the surrounding world. In *Inventory*, the downside is that without periods, there is little room to extendedly pause, to reflect; the threat in *Ossuaries* is parallel: barbarity is even in Yasmine's organs. "Grenades took root / in my uterus," she attests.[49] She cannot disentangle herself from "dead generations," past, present, and future. Homi Bhabha's interpretation of Frantz Fanon's "The Fact of Blackness" (1952) posits the caesura as critical to Fanon's razing of "the binary structure of power and identity."[50] Fanon critiques the "Other"-orientation of blackness "from the signifying time-lag of cultural difference" that Bhabha also refers to as a "temporal caesura."[51] Lily Cho concludes that for Bhabha, a caesura indicates "a break in the rhythm of history that allows for a different story."[52] Yasmine alludes to Fanon on these "temporal" grounds. He becomes "like a double-edged knife in her teeth" because Yasmine discovers no such "break," nor does the poem.[53] Like the speaker in *Inventory*, Yasmine is too caught up in history to change its course. *Inven-*

tory's speaker cannot complete the task of accounting for all of the ills of contemporary end times;[54] Yasmine cannot carry her oppositional tune.

Instruments offer a means of interrupting history's brutal metre, but they do not possess an entirely positive valence in the poem. Escaping from the United States into Canada, Yasmine spends the final two ossuaries working in a factory farm owned by the conglomerate Maple Leaf Foods.[55] On the killing floor, Yasmine's tools are described as "sharp instruments for butchering / to appease which rain god, / which government god / which engine god."[56] The thrice-repeated "god" represents the sacrifice that is packaged to "appease" those whose only exposure to meat may be as a palatable source of protein—one that is allegedly natural as "rain," "government"-approved—and delivered through the capitalist "engine" of mass distribution.[57] Repetition is the poem's instrument for highlighting the persistence of large-scale problems, such as the routine elevation of consumptive desire over animal welfare. To take another example, Yasmine is attuned to environmental eschaton in "Ossuary VII," purporting to "hear the crackle of the oceanic crust, / the fracture of extraterrestrial plains."[58] She responds, "I've got no time, no time, this epistrophe, no time / wind's coming, no time, / one sunrise to the next is too long, no time."[59] In her urgency, she conspicuously repeats things—"history" emerges from losses that are "long, long," "humanity" is a "fragile, fragile promise," and "spiked municipalities" make assurances of "free, free, absolutely free freeness."[60] Yasmine has "no time" to refine her diction; moreover, repetition consciously rejects the notion that her primary job—as poet, speaker, activist—is to manage the information she encounters. Language is by nature unable to do so, as the speaker frequently insists: "adjectives" are "insentient," "prepositions are irrelevant," first-person pronouns are "slippery," and "verbs are a tragedy."[61] These pre-existing associations weigh on the skeleton of every new utterance, which is partly why form is so significant. Words alone cannot perform activism; "it's always in the lyric," since this form invests her failures with symbolic force.[62] The lyric energy of *Ossuaries* ultimately combats Yasmine's "moral exhaust[ion]."[63] Words do not weigh on Yasmine because her bones are declared "untranslatable."[64] Since the poem characterizes the "big world" as "our ossuary," the broader implication—again and again in Brand's work—is that language, and especially poetic language, is not interested in recording reality;[65] instead, it fleshes out what bears repeating. In other words, the poem seeks a common language to structure its depiction of struggle in these "momentous, ravenous, ugly times."[66]

To conclude, I want to return to the uneasy relationship between the "ugly times" of outright cuts to heretofore basic social provisions (like library access) and the promotional duties of Poet Laureates. For Brand, these duties include serving on advisory committees, such as the one for the recent *Poetry Is Public Is Poetry* installation at the Cedarbrae branch of the Toronto Public Library. She helped select three lines from Rosemary Sullivan's "Exile" (1991) to be emblazoned on the entrance walkway. The quotation that dominates the press release for the installation is not from Sullivan's poem, but rather from Brand. It serves as the press release's epigraph: "Poetry beautifies public space, pays respect to the intelligence of the citizenry, gives respite from the grind of daily living and engages the city's humanistic ideals."[67] Compare this statement to Sullivan's lines, "'a man packed a country / in a suitcase with his shoes / and left.'"[68] The civic function Brand invokes relies on a notion of citizenship that is challenged in Sullivan's rendering of the portability of belonging. Additionally, poetry's rootedness for Brand ("the city") contradicts the shifting, and indefinite sense of place in Sullivan's lines ("a country"). The tension does not hold insofar as placelessness and exile are well-founded topics in discussions of Brand's work. But Brand's claim that poetry "beautifies public space" gives voice to those commercial delivery mechanisms that celebritize her and celebrate her activist poetics as "beautiful."

Brand does have her detractors, which illustrates that the public her poetry reaches is heterogeneous. A caustic opinion piece in the *National Post* assessing her appointment as Toronto's poet laureate expresses skepticism about the wider appeal of her language. Its author, Marni Soupcoff, claims that Brand "fulfills every stereotype of the identity-obsessed activist insider who turns normal workaday people of all races and genders off of poetry in the first place."[69] She then quotes a snippet of Brand's response to the appointment: "Ms. Brand said, that the city 'in its multiplicity...is constantly rich and surprising. I've written this about it in *thirsty*—that wild waiting at traffic lights off the end of the world, where nothing is simple, nothing, in the city there is no simple love or simple fidelity, the heart is slippery.'"[70] Soupcoff proudly confesses that "I can't tell you what she's talking about because I have no idea."[71] Brand is "talking about" how the complexity of the city demands that her love for it have a critical capacity. Soupcoff "ha[s] no idea" because her vision of the city is more pragmatic: "I'd feel a little less bitter about the idea of an official Toronto poet if I felt my city government were taking care of the basics and not over-taxing me."[72] In a single breath, Soupcoff petitions for essential social provisions ("the basics") and critiques their economic basis (taxation). The more disturbing subtext is the Platonic one addressed in my epigraph from Aleksander Wat. Poetry is frivolous, but dangerous; therefore, poets should be expelled from the city or, more applicable to the *National Post*'s case, left out of the calculus of urban governance. Soupcoff intimates the public risk posed by poetry through her reference to the example of one-time New Jersey poet laureate Amiri Baraka, particularly his poem "'Somebody Blew Up America,' in which he contended that Israel was involved in the World Trade Center Attacks."[73] Of course, nowadays political authorities do manage to find uses for poets, as my opening reference to the "Poetry City Challenge" showed.[74] Brand's reported refusal to participate finds a somewhat curious point of connection to Soupcoff's headline: "A job no outspoken poet would want." Soupcoff never develops this conjecture that Brand is compromised by her co-option, that she cannot simultaneously be "outspoken" and "want" the position. "Outspokenness" is instead dubiously established as her main credential; she is chastised for "focusing on predictable lefty favourite themes."[75] This statement brings us back to Buck-Morss. Soupcoff may be right to imply that commentators are sometimes prepared to let Brand's poetry "do the work of politics for us," as Buck-Morss claimed. However, as I have argued from the outset, such affirmations focus purely on the content of the diagnosis, and—in the case of the *Post* piece—underestimate the form. When we explore the form of *Ossuaries*, we can discover an instrumental poetics that negates the apparent opposition between commercial viability and structural critique, thus cutting to the bone.

Notes

1 Eliot mocks academic footnotes such as this one in his *magnum opus*, but rather than presume I will acknowledge that the quoted words are borrowed from the opening line of *The Waste Land* (1922): "April is the cruellest month, breeding" (1).
2 "Guelph Takes Up Mayor's Poetry Challenge."
3 I am indebted to Tanis MacDonald for relaying this detail to me.
4 "Toronto's Poet Laureate."
5 Brand, "Public Libraries."
6 Brand, "Public Libraries."
7 This question adopts the title of the panel I was on at the Public Poetics conference, "Voices Calling (Out) the Public." I was fortunate to have Erín Moure and Karis Shearer as my co-panelists. Their paper, "Poetry Reading: Call for a New Paradigm," advocated for more experimental approaches to the live performance of poetry. We shared an interest in the evolving ways that publics can be engaged. Their focus was on the medium of exchange between poet and audience, while mine was on how form shapes the political potential of this exchange.
8 Buck-Morss, "The Second Time as Farce," 70 (emphasis in original).

9 Buck-Morss, "The Second Time as Farce."
10 Brand, "Public Libraries."
11 Leslie C. Sanders elegantly ties together Brand's poetic and civic projects at the close of her introduction to *Fierce Departures: The Poetry of Dionne Brand* (2009): "The helplessness and despair so frequent in Brand's work arise out of the demands the poet makes first and foremost of herself, as citizen 'like any other' in both the place and the wider world in which she lives" (xv). I locate these "demands" on a formal level in my discussion of *Ossuaries*.
12 For a sustained discussion of the agents and emblems of global prize culture, see James English, *The Economy of Prestige* (2005). English focuses on the "middle-zone of cultural space" occupied by the numerous "instruments" that negotiate cultural value (27). He endeavours to understand "the collective ambivalence or uncertainty" about prizes as well as "the deeper equivocality of all such prizes" (1, 7); more broadly, he locates his analysis in a global framework wherein "relationships [across lines of state or nation] have been [in some part] produced and facilitated through the agency of the cultural prize" (320). I do not further develop my claim about how prizes function because I am not wary of "anticommercial critique" (306). In the case of *Ossuaries*, its Griffin Prize *does* reflect the widespread commercial appeal of poems with political topics and themes. This appeal is negative insofar as in celebrating the poem's apparent message, we risk overlooking the radical aspects of the medium. The prize thus "inoculates," in Roland Barthes's sense of the term, wherein "a little 'confessed' evil saves one from admitting a lot of hidden evil" (42).
13 Brand, "Reckless coalition."
14 Brand, "Reckless coalition."
15 Brand, "Reckless coalition."
16 Brand, "Reckless coalition."
17 Brand, "Reckless coalition."
18 Kamboureli, "Preface," viii.
19 Brand, *Ossuaries*, 9, 10. Fredric Jameson would agree with Yasmine's sentiment. According to his appropriation of Aphorism 522 in Friedrich Nietzsche's *The Will to Power* (1901), language itself is a "prisonhouse." As a consequence, the very act of describing one's dreams is imprisoning. In their 1968 edition of *The Will to Power*, Walter Kaufmann and R.J. Hollingdale translate Nietzsche more literally than Jameson's *The Prison House of Language* (1972) version. They substitute "constraint" for "prisonhouse" (283). Here I should also note that I am citing the page numbers, as opposed to the line numbers, from *Ossuaries*.
20 Another example is "Her whole existence was mourning, so what?" (30). This question echoes the following lines from *thirsty* (2002): "even these confessions of failure so unreliable, / hardly matter" (52).

21 Brand, *Ossuaries*, 109.
22 Brand, *Ossuaries*, 27, 89.
23 *Inventory* (2006) succinctly addresses this problematic link: "full knowing, there's something wrong / with this" (7). The supposed link between knowledge and action is between the lines of the "motto" that Immanuel Kant, borrowing a Horatian epistle, makes famous in "An Answer to the Question: 'What Is Enlightenment?'" (1784): "Sapere aude!" [Dare to know!] (54). A "dare to know" is implicitly a dare to do something.
24 Brand, *Ossuaries*, *Ossuaries*, 41.
25 Brand, *Ossuaries*, 111.
26 Paul Barrett pairs, but does not develop his point concerning, dialectics and poetic form in his insightful analysis of *Inventory*. He notes that the poem obeys a "dialectical form" (101).
27 Slavoj Žižek glances at this tendency to misread Hegel in *Less Than Nothing* (2012): "What makes [Hegel] a Christian philosopher and a philosopher of love is the fact that, contrary to the common misunderstanding, in the arena of dialectical struggle there is no Third which unites and reconciles the two struggling opposites" (112).
28 Brand, *Ossuaries*, 53.
29 Brand, *Ossuaries*, 11.
30 Brand, *Ossuaries*, 11.
31 Brand, *Ossuaries*, 33.
32 Brand, *Ossuaries*, 63.
33 Brand, *Ossuaries*, 63.
34 Brand, *Ossuaries*, 77.
35 Brand, *Ossuaries*, 76.
36 Brand, *Ossuaries*, 77.
37 Brand, *Ossuaries*, 78.
38 Brand, *Ossuaries*, 76, 77.
39 Brand, *Ossuaries*, 67.
40 Brand, *Ossuaries*, 43.
41 Brand, *Ossuaries*, 44.
42 Brand, *Ossuaries*, 45.
43 Quoted in Brand, *Ossuaries*, 45.
44 Engels, *The Origin*, 145 (emphasis mine).
45 Brand, *Ossuaries*, 57.
46 Brand, *Ossuaries*, 52. Like Luxemburg, Yasmine knows that revolution does not come to those who wait. In *The Sublime Object of Ideology* (1989), Žižek substantiates this idea vis-à-vis Luxemburg's "description of the dialectics of the revolutionary process" (59). He "allud[es] to [Luxemburg's] argument against Eduard Bernstein, against his revisionist fear of seizing power 'too soon,' 'prematurely,' before the so-called 'objective conditions' had ripened—this was, as is well known, Bernstein's main reproach to the

revolutionary wing of social democracy: they are too impatient, they want to hasten, to outrun the logic of historical development. Rosa Luxemburg's answer is that the first seizures of power *are necessarily 'premature'*: the only way for the working class to reach its 'maturity,' to await the arrival of the 'appropriate moment' for the seizure of power, is to form itself, to educate itself for this act of seizure, and the only possible way of achieving this education is precisely the 'premature' attempts... If we merely wait for the 'appropriate moment' we will never live to see it, because this 'appropriate moment' cannot arrive without the subjective conditions of the maturity of the revolutionary force (subject) being fulfilled—that is, it can only arrive after a series of 'premature,' failed attempts" (59, emphasis in original). *Ossuaries* leaves open the question of whether, not to mention what, Yasmine learns from her "failed attempts." At minimum, the reference to Luxemburg challenges us, as readers, to learn or resist the lesson(s) of Yasmine's "failures."

47 Quoted in Brand, *Ossuaries*, 40.
48 Marx, *The Eighteenth Brumaire*, 18.
49 Brand, *Ossuaries*, 11.
50 Bhabha, "'Race,'" 237.
51 Bhabha, "'Race,'" 237.
52 Cho, *Eating Chinese* (2010), 160.
53 Brand, *Ossuaries*, 44.
54 My pessimistic reading of *Inventory* disputes the compelling interpretation that Katherine McKittrick offered at a recent plenary talk, "Plantation Futures" (2012), where she argued that Brand's poem "recasts knowledge" in order to imagine an alternative future, moving past a static Us/Them paradigm ("Plantation Futures"). Such recasting requires the reader to "acknowledge the data," notably the civilian body counts from the US-led invasion and occupation of Iraq. I am not convinced that the "recasting" is achieved in *Inventory*, given its titular nod to Antonio Gramsci. Diana Brydon persuasively draws attention to the influence of Gramsci's idea of the inventory on the composition of Brand's *Inventory*. Brydon credits Edward Said for having "revived" this Gramscian concept in the introductory chapter of *Orientalism* (1978), in which Said quotes from Gramsci's *The Prison Notebooks* (1929–1935): 'The starting-point of critical elaboration is the consciousness of what one really is, and is 'knowing thyself' as a product of the historical process to date, which has deposited in you an infinity of traces, without leaving an inventory... therefore it is imperative at the outset to compile an inventory'" (994). The corporeality of the poet, in whom the "traces" are "deposited," is connected to her creative labour of "compiling." Brydon writes that "Brand has told [her] that she kept this excerpt from Said pinned above her desk as she wrote this poem" (994). For Gramsci, the inventory is "imperative" for establishing the grounds of one's own critical position. I would argue that

unlike in Gramsci, the speaker's inventorying does not beget critical independence from its object, the "infinity of traces" that constitutes the world. Rather, these "traces" become indistinguishable from the speaker.
55 The same Maple Leaf Foods whose Toronto-based plant was traced to an outbreak of listeria in 2008. Thank you to Deborah Wills for drawing my attention to this connection.
56 Brand, *Ossuaries*, 123.
57 The trebled "god" also glimpses the "privatiz[ation] [of] the spiritual" by "different social forces," which M. Jacqui Alexander views as an obstacle to "taking the Sacred seriously" in discourses of "transnational feminism and related radical projects" (295, 326).
58 Brand, *Ossuaries*, 61.
59 Brand, *Ossuaries*, 61.
60 Brand, *Ossuaries*, 102, 83, 32.
61 Brand, *Ossuaries*, 14, 26, 22, 14.
62 Brand, *Ossuaries*, 108.
63 Brand, *Ossuaries*, 108.
64 Brand, *Ossuaries*, 50.
65 Brand, *Ossuaries*, 82.
66 Brand, *Ossuaries*, 33.
67 "Poetry Is Public Is Poetry."
68 Quoted in "Poetry Is Public Is Poetry."
69 Soupcoff, "A Job."
70 Soupcoff, "A Job."
71 Soupcoff, "A Job."
72 Soupcoff, "A Job."
73 Soupcoff, "A Job."
74 That said, I would definitely hesitate to label Toronto Mayor Rob Ford a "philosopher king."
75 Soupcoff, "A Job."

Bibliography

Alexander, M. Jacqui. *Pedagogies of Crossing: Meditations on Feminism, Sexual Politics, Memory, and the Sacred*. Durham: Duke University Press, 2005.

Barrett, Paul. "'there are atomic openings in my chest / to hold the wounded': Intimacy, the Body, and Transnational Solidarity in Dionne Brand's *Inventory*." *Canadian Woman Studies* 27.2/3 (2009): 100–106.

Barthes, Roland. *Mythologies*. 1957. Translated by Annette Lavers. New York: Farrar, Straus and Giroux, 1972.

Bhabha, Homi K. "'Race,' Time, and the Revision of Modernity." *The Location of Culture*. 236–56. London and New York: Routledge, 1994.

Brand, Dionne. *Inventory*. Toronto: McClelland and Stewart, 2006.

———. *Ossuaries*. Toronto: McClelland and Stewart, 2010.

———. "Public Libraries, gravy and Tim Hortons." *rabble.ca*. 28 July 2011. Web. 5 Nov. 2012.

———. "Reckless coalition: Of language and politics." *rabble.ca*. 4 April 2011. Web. 9 September 2012.

———. *thirsty*. Toronto: McClelland and Stewart, 2002.

Brydon, Diana. "Dionne Brand's Global Intimacies: Practising Affective Citizenship." *University of Toronto Quarterly* 76, no. 3 (2007): 990–1006.

Buck-Morss, Susan. "The Second Time as Farce…Historical Pragmatics and the Untimely Present." *The Idea of Communism*. Edited by Costas Douzinas and Slavoj Žižek. 67-80. London and New York: Verso, 2010.

Cho, Lily. *Eating Chinese: Culture on the Menu in Small Town Canada*. Toronto: University of Toronto Press, 2010.

Eliot, T.S. "The Wasteland." 1922. *Selected Poems*. 51–74. London: Faber and Faber, 1967.

Engels, Friedrich. *The Origin of the Family, Private Property, and the State*. 1884. Translated by Alec West. New York: International Publishers, 1978.

English, James. *The Economy of Prestige: Prizes, Awards, and the Circulation of Cultural Value*. Cambridge: Harvard University Press, 2005.

"Guelph Takes Up Mayor's Poetry Challenge." *Guelph.ca*. 19 April 2012. Accessed on 11 September 2014 at http://guelph.ca/2014/04/guelph-takes-mayors-poetry-challenge.

Kamboureli, Smaro. "Preface." *Trans.Can.Lit: Resituating the Study of Canadian Literature*. Edited by Smaro Kamboureli and Roy Miki. vii–xv. Waterloo: Wilfrid Laurier University Press, 2007.

Kant, Immanuel. "An Answer to the Question: 'What Is Enlightenment?'" 1784. *Kant: Political Writings*. Edited by H.S. Reiss. Translated by H.B. Nisbet. 54–60.Cambridge: Cambridge University Press, 2003.

Marx, Karl. *The Eighteenth Brumaire of Louis Bonaparte*. 1852. New York: International Publishers, 1975.

McKittrick, Katherine. "Plantation Futures." 2012 Canadian Association of American Studies Conference Keynote. Munk School of Global Affairs, Toronto. 27 October 2012.

Nietzsche, Friedrich. *The Will to Power*. 1901. Translated by Walter Kaufmann and R.J. Hollingdale. New York: Vintage, 1968.

"Poetry Is Public Is Poetry." *poetryispublic.ca*. Accessed 14 May 2013 at http://www.poetryispublic.ca/about.php.

Sanders, Leslie C. "Introduction." *Fierce Departures: The Poetry of Dionne Brand*. ix–xv. Waterloo: Wilfrid Laurier University Press, 2009. ix–xv. Print.

Soupcoff, Marni. "A Job No Outspoken Poet Would Want." *National Post*. 8 October 2009. Accessed 11 September 2014 at http://www.nationalpost.com/opinion/columnists/story.html?id=529add79-1708-4fa3-be70-5df981e4c2c8.

"Toronto's Poet Laureate." *Toronto.ca*. 3 September 2012. Accessed on 11 September 2014 at http://www.toronto.ca/culture/poet_laureate.htm.

Wat, Aleksander. "Dark Light." Translated by Clare Cavanagh. *Ciemne s′wiecidlo*. 11. Paris: Libella, 1968.

Žižek, Slavoj. *Less Than Nothing: Hegel and the Shadow of Dialectical Materialism*. London: Verso, 2012.

———. *The Sublime Object of Ideology*. London: Verso, 1989.

9

Rearticulate, Renovate, *Rebuild:* Sachiko Murakami's Architectural Poetics of Community

Emily Ballantyne

> *Vancouver exemplifies the city as [a] space of flows and recurrent restructuring, rather than as a durable construct of stable identities, labour, social class and communities.*
> Thomas Hutton, qtd. in "The Future of Vancouver's Economy"

> *In Vancouver, at least, opposing constituencies in the gentrification 'wars' have a very different reading of real property. This does not only entail different renderings of what property is... it also leads to struggles over what property* ought to be.[1]
> Nicholas B. Blamley, *Unsettling the City*

Real estate—and architecture more generally—acts as the central mode through which Sachiko Murakami's 2011 collection *Rebuild* structures and explores her response to Vancouver as a domestic urban space, as a home, and as a site for community development. Taking up the architectural phrasing of "rebuilding," Murakami creates a text that is constantly reconstructing itself, exploring the gaps and fissures that open up when the poem itself is treated as a renovatable or "rented" object, susceptible to structural and content changes, improvements, and revisions represented by multiple versions of a poem in Murakami's collection. In her companion project, Project Rebuild, an interactive website, Murakami extends the invitation to explore poetry as a community-oriented building project by offering a neighbourhood of interconnected poetry that can be "moved into," "rented," and "rebuilt" to be placed in conversation with previous poems in a connected but differentiated context of shared space and experience.

Murakami uses building metaphors in her poetry to articulate the political and affective effects that Vancouver's severely unaffordable[2] housing market has on the way she responds to domestic places of living and dwelling in the city. In this chapter, I explore Murakami's use of building metaphors as an extended commentary on the complex relations of production both in her poetry and in the cityscape to which she responds. I argue that Murakami develops an architectural poetics of community, one that emphasizes rebuilding as a rhizomatic[3] process that has the power to undermine and reimagine the concept of home and home ownership in Vancouver. I explore how the cultural values of renovation can be rearticulated through examining "home" as a spatialized and commodified affective ideology that dialectically reorients the seeming dichotomies of public and private, or home and community.

This chapter will first examine Murakami's renovation of her own poetry in the *Rebuild* collection and then explore how her poetic engagement is extended and mobilized on the digital community website Project Rebuild. I will suggest that the privacy of a poem, or a home, and its singular ownership, becomes public when it is treated as a commodity for exchange and is examined not stagnantly, as owned by one person, but instead as property that any number of people may be able to temporarily occupy. When the focus is on the fluid movement of exchange associated with renting a space only for a limited time, occupation overrides ownership as a primary way of understanding domestic and poetic environments. Property and poetry are rearticulated based on social occupation and inhabiting a space, undermining the political value of private ownership as a concept that inhibits community. By exploring the three separate but related concepts of rearticulation, renovation, and rebuilding in Murakami's poetics, this chapter will explore the political possibilities of a rigorous poetic engagement with the hegemonic neoliberal[4] values that structure and define this particular geopolitical moment in urban Vancouver.

I. Rearticulate

Murakami's architectural poetics respond directly to late capitalism as it is represented through the physical structures in the built environment of Vancouver and the affective and ideological linguistic structures that make the asymmetrical power relations of home ownership so rhizomatic. Her poem "Ocean Views" illustrates this series of neoliberal interconnections between the condo and affect:

> It's hard to imagine the condos
> as unintentional. I can't see myself in one.
> I can't afford the view. I can't help.
> I can't help wanting to.[5]

Here the poem relies on enjambment and repetition to show the complex linkages between desire for and the inevitability of the condo as a commodity, and the financial impossibility of realizing this exchange for the speaker. The condo is not a neutral or "unintentional" dwelling. Instead, it is contingent social space that marks an insurmountable financial barrier for its viewer without removing her compulsion to desire the commodity. The speaker's reflection on the condo's "unintentionality" ascribes a kind of affective power to the condo, personifying the place as being able to both have intentions, and perhaps generate or condition intentions (to want, to buy) in its viewer. The speaker's reaction to the condo seems to disable resistance. While initially the speaker asserts "I can't see myself" in the condo, she also "can't help wanting to." In between these lines, the speaker reflects that she "can't help"; that is, she is unable to fully participate in or resist this process. She is paralyzed between her inability to conceptualize herself within the condo and her guilty desire to be implicated in the system that created the conditions for her exclusion. This moment captures the central dilemma that Murakami is grappling with in *Rebuild:* How do you resist a political system you are *always already* a participant within? In a collection that harshly critiques the condo as the "ultimate fetish object, especially in Vancouver,"[6] it remains just that: an object of desire that Murakami's speaker "can't help" but want. The condo and the conditioned affective response of the speaker are two avenues through which neoliberalism asserts its control over the subjectivity of the individual.

As "Ocean Views" suggests, Murakami places herself firmly within, not outside of, her particular geopolitical moment and its reigning desires. Her poetics are decidedly political, and as she looks for ways to resist and respond to the valuation of Vancouver's skyrocketing real estate, she finds herself implicated within this system. Murakami's engagement with globalization's impact on urban subjectivity can be usefully informed by theoretical models for understanding the spatialized politics of late capitalism. Globalization has fundamentally shifted the scale at which individual subjectivities are constructed, and thus the urban that Murakami is responding to cannot be singularly located at the level of the local. Instead, the urban must be examined as a site of power that negotiates across the local, national, and transnational simultaneously. Michael Hardt and Antonio Negri's conceptual framing of Empire usefully articulates the asymmetrical power relations of global capitalism in a way that resonates with Murakami's divided response to the condo. Empire is "a *decentred* and *deterritorializing* apparatus of rule that progressively incorporates the entire global realm within its open, expanding frontiers."[7] Hardt and Negri describe deterritorialization and decentring as mobile tools that undo previously defined borders and boundaries. Deterritorialization is more than just a method for maintaining power; it also creates the conditions through which Empire can be resisted. It can reclaim space, like the condo, and write over the previous markers of territory, to allow for new occupants. Deterritorialization and reterritorialization are part of a process of circulation, where power is asserted by making claims on physical, conceptual, and affective spaces. Murakami's poetics are necessarily deterritorial as she carefully manipulates the conventional building blocks of poetry in the politicized arena of the printed page and computer screen.

While Murakami's project engages with these theoretical discussions of globalization more broadly, she also operates in a specific political avant-garde writing tradition that more directly addresses her approach to resisting neoliberalism. Her poetics have their roots in collaboration and active discussion, first as a member of a strong writing community in Montreal associated with her M.A. in English literature and creative writing at Concordia University (and the writing of her first book of poetry, *The Invisibility Exhibit*)[8] and subsequently as a member of the writers' cooperative, the Kootenay School of Writing (KSW) in Vancouver, where she returned after graduation.[9] Both environments facilitated her development as a community-oriented poet with a highly politicized poetics, although of particular interest here is her relation to the shared political project of writing with the KSW. The KSW describes its communal identity as stemming "not [from] a specific aesthetic vision, but rather [from] a politicized understanding of how art and literary production often contributed to the ruling class's hegemonic influence over society."[10] The KSW defines itself politically in opposition to hegemonic processes, while asserting that writing, art, and literary production can also play a formative role in resisting these influences. The KSW denies that writing is inevitably just a way to reproduce contemporary ideology, and instead explores its possibilities for resistance and rearticulation.

KSW poet Jeff Derksen is perhaps the most vocal about how his poetics engage in a political project of rearticulation. Derksen defines rearticulation in contradistinction to opposition and resistance. He suggests that his poetics reframe and respatialize the links between the local and the transnational while still operating within established structures of power. He describes the need to

> mov[e] away from the idea of opposition and resistance to an idea of rearticulation...Opposition and resistance have imagined itself as being outside of the debilitating structures of power, and has been critical from the exterior, whereas rearticulation is about disarticulating and rearticulating linkages within systems, somehow rearrang[ing] structures from within it. To be critical of a world system, you have to somehow imagine yourself within it, as opposed to barking at it from a local position.[11]

Like Murakami's speaker, who "can't help wanting to," Derksen presents a poetics that allows for articulation of the neoliberal ideology while still making room for countering it. Rearticulation is still articulation, but with room for dissent or contradiction so that it better acknowledges the gaps, fissures, and discontinuities that riddle the neoliberal ideology. Because of the poet's inability to step outside the rhizomatic, deterritorialized system of power, rearticulation better reflects his role in countering from within. The poet is *always already* implicated within the system of power; he cannot rally from outside. The local and the global cannot and should not be bifurcated, as this false division fails to acknowledge the structural role each plays in the building of global capitalism.

Derksen further develops this perspective in his book of criticism *Annihilated Time*, in which he offers an excellent overview of the potential for politically engaged poetry to serve as a forum for developing strategies that counter and resist hegemony. He emphasizes the spatial capabilities of poetry and links them to the development of alternative publics:

> Critical strategies have an urgency then to address the ways in which neoliberalism has moved, has spread across spatial scales, for space and the idea of solidarities through and across space counter a neoliberal imagination of the competition between places and people. Space is a weak concept in neoliberalism for it imagines space only

being produced from above, by the forces of the market, and it tends to only police the production of space from below, to use these terms from Henri Lefebvre. But poetry and other cultural practices can also be imagined to cross scales, to link people, and struggles, and to produce space. One of the ways poetry has historically done this is through an avant-garde engagement with the public space and notions of publicness.[12]

Derksen's argument emphasizes the importance of new concepts of space and new sites of community as two important elements in poetry that counter neoliberal ideology. In the following two sections of this chapter, I have chosen to separate the spatialized "renovations" of language in *Rebuild* from the creation of a counterpublic in Project Rebuild. These two processes in Murakami's work are separate but connected engagements with countering and politicizing language as a site both for rearticulation and for community formation. There is room for reversal and alternative spatial configurations in language, instead of language being produced from above and policed from below. The spatialized language of making space to counter the conditions that reinforce neoliberal values, and the inhabiting of physical places with new forms of public connection and congregation, come together to form Murakami's architectural poetics of community.

II. Renovate

Murakami adopts the tactic of revision to identify gaps and inconsistencies that rearticulate neoliberal values. Revision is perhaps most famously conceptualized by Adrienne Rich as "re-vision," a process she defines as "the act of looking back, of seeing with fresh eyes, of entering an old text from a new critical direction."[13] Her approach, like Murakami's, disrupts hegemonic systems of power. Rich seeks to undercut patriarchal definitions of literature in order to create space for the female voice and perspective; Murakami's reframing of revision as renovation extends this argument, productively placing it in conversation with spatial theorists such as Henri Lefebvre. Lefebvre argues that space is socially constructed and imbricated in power relations: "Space...serves as a tool of thought and of action...In addition to being a means of production it is also a means of control, and hence of domination, of power; yet that, as such, it escapes in part from those who would make use of it."[14] Lefebrve describes space as linked to systems of power, yet through its linkages to thought and action, space also simultaneously offers a way to resist power through its ability to resist its user's intentions. I see Murakami's poetics as productively engaging in a process of revision that is highly attuned to the spatial practices of neoliberal hegemony; as such, her project of revision seeks to make change from within, literally renovating the home as a decentring site of ideological power.

Murakami chooses to mobilize revision as renovation in order to spatialize the editing process along the lines of architecture. Renovation is a rearticulation of revision that combines her writing process with her theoretical praxis:

> Editing is just a process of renovation, and I wanted to make that process visible. Often the renovated poems use very different methods—I knock out nouns and strip off letters; I flip one poem on its head; sometimes I just rewrite it leaving the "spirit" of the original intact, etc. It's this idea that every poem needs to be a perfectly arranged little room—those white rooms my friends' parents had, the ones kids weren't allowed in. I wanted to mess things up.[15]

A major part of the process of rearticulation is the making strange of something that otherwise is treated as a constant, as a "little white room." This disrupts the cycle of circulation, using the language of the writing against itself. By letting things stay "messy," and by showing various stages of process, integration, and disintegration, the *Rebuild* collection acts as a kind of representation of urban Vancouver, revealing many half-finished, uncertain and incomplete "renovations" that deny the stable exterior of a high-rise condo building or a sprawling suburb.

Rebuild uses renovation as a way to return to poems and open them up to new forms of meaning. The collection includes series of paired poems, often with similar titles and usually exploring a similar concept or using a similar structure or scheme. The first two poems in the collection, "The Form of a City" and "The Form of a" chart a progression from a localized conception of the city using Vancouver-based signifiers in the first poem to a structural abstraction through a series of deletions in the second poem. We can read the second poem as a renovation of the first. "The Form of a City" is highly descriptive, identifying the "condo," "pajamas," and the "mountain and citizen" as key components of "here," which the title suggests is the city. However, to problematize these descriptions, Murakami simultaneously questions these as components of the city, asking "would you call this 'metropolis'? // Or 'New World'? Or 'Pacific Rim'? / The living, 'inhabitants'? 'Tenants'? Citizens'?"[16] It is not clear on which scale the city belongs and which geographic markers are most relevant. The city seems to encompass all and none of these cultural quotations.[17] Murakami's use of quotation marks here distinguishes the separate discourses implicit in the various terms, contrasting the regional "Pacific Rim" with the transnational and historicized "New World" and placing the people of the city into geographic ("inhabitants"), economic ("tenant") and political/legal ("citizens") contexts.

The second poem, "The Form of a," includes various deletions of many of these markers, leaving gaps and empty quotations that emphasize the structure of the poem, now devoid of much of its content. "The Form of a" reveals the building blocks of the poem, empty quotations and hanging punctuation in space that define the outline of the poem but leave it wanting meaning. In "The Form of a City," the first couplet offers a descriptive passage about life in Vancouver. The speaker states:

> Here, one can walk out the condo door
> Dressed in "clothes" known elsewhere as "pyjamas."[18]

Murakami makes a subjective statement about life and attitudes in Vancouver through dress, making a small dig at comfort over function and style in a citizen's public wardrobe. She cheekily generalizes her subject in order to characterize the city based on its inhabitants. In "The Form of a," all of the cultural context of these details is stripped away, as is the humour:

>   ,   can walk out the
> dressed in "   " known elsewhere as "   ."[19]

The time, the subject, and the two descriptive nouns have been removed. The verbs *walked* and *dressed* remain, but without the context necessary to decode their meaning in the new poem. Attempts to decode are almost anthropological, as we are asked to perform a comparison between two missing terms. Similarly, the list questions posed in "The Form of a City" are also renovated to really emphasize the uncertainty of the question mark itself. Here is a comparison of the second and third couplets of the two poems:

> Cash, no cash. Village, no village. Or village,
> to village, to village, would you call this "metropolis"?
>
> Or "New World"? Or "Pacific Rim"?
> The living, "inhabitants"? "Tenants"? "Citizens?"[20]

REARTICULATE, RENOVATE, *REBUILD* 185

```
            , no      .        no         . Or      ,
    to        , to        , would     call    "         "?

Or "New        "? Or "Pacific       "?
The living, "            "? "           "? "          "?²¹
```

Like a Mad Libs word game, the remaining words in the second poem may suggest some meaning or way of reading, but ultimately they provide only a generic structure. The key nouns and signifiers are only empty space. What remains is largely negation and questions, quotation marks attributed to no one, with no actual content. The words have "moved out" of the previous poem, creating a kind of uninhabited structure. "The Form of a" is the structure of a poem, its external blocks of a poem—building with only minimal signifying contents. Yet the second poem is quite affective, with only negations and questions. This is not a new start, a clean page, but obviously a renovation and reinvention of something that is now no longer accessible.

When the two poems are read together, the nouns in the first pop out even more starkly as signifiers for the discourses and ideologies that underwrite our cities. Even the ability to fill-in-the-blank suggests a familiarity with the structuring tendencies of language and capital that allow the reader to be interpellated in ideology even without clearly stating its buzzwords. However, it is the force of the second poem, without ideological occupants, that allows for new concepts, new occupants or inhabitants of the poem. Murakami does not suggest what these new occupants might be but instead provides the structure for others to create meaning. These first poems set the tone for the rest of the collection, establishing relationships between the texts as buildings but denying their stability or security by offering alternative renovations to their implications and discourses.

Murakami frequently returns throughout her collection to the home as a central place for individual self-definition, as a space linked with commodity fetishization and accumulation to determine subjectivity. The home can be read as both a concept and a concrete location. It is both a literal place and an ideological one. "Homeowning," the second section of *Rebuild*, engages in a renovation of the concept of home, exploring the affective connotations of the house as something publicly driven by marketing and ownership. This section takes as its central image the Vancouver Special, a style of blocky two-storey home that was representative of a trend in suburban architecture in the 1970s.[22] Known for its economic use of space and reviled for its ugly, boxy shape, the Vancouver Special is described by Murakami as a "creeping advancement" into most neighbourhoods in Vancouver, where it was met with great resistance but continues to persist.[23] In the poem "Let the Home," the speaker asks, "Is there anything wrong with letting our homes stand for us?," a question that Murakami meditates on particularly in relation to the trend towards reproducibility and the mobile quality of this undesired but recurring image of urban Vancouver.[24]

Illustrating a process of renovation, Murakami presents four different versions of the poem "Vancouver Special."[25] She begins with the architectural foundation of a single poem titled "Vancouver Special," which does not appear in *Rebuild*. Then she engages in a process of defamiliarizing her own language through adopting a procedural technique to create the four different versions of the poem.[26] On the Project Rebuild website, she clearly outlines her process for creating these four versions: "I ran the poem through Google Translate and back again through four languages of people I have known who have lived in Vancouver Specials—Cantonese, Italian, Portuguese, and Serbian—and back into English again."[27] By engaging in this process to provide a uniform structure for the produced poems, Murakami engages in an architectural rearticulation that stabilizes the form of the poem in order to emphasize the disparities in each poem's signifying contents. Each language constructs the contents based on its own grammar and syntax, usurping the role that Murakami played as initial author. The procedural principle she uses takes power away from the author as the holder of meaning and owner of the poem, and temporarily places that authority in the hands of a computerized system.

Once more, Murakami works within a hegemonic system, here represented by the massive corporation Google's translation software. She has replaced the human translator and author with a "statistical machine translation."[28] She *chooses* to submit her writing to a process of deterritorialization by Empire, relinquishing her control over the work to explore the complexities of ownership as it relates to poetry as a form of property. Like an architect who has sold her concept to a developer and relinquished rights over the drawing, she has created the plans for the poem but is allowing a machine to determine the final language product. But this is not simply a one-way sales transaction; ownership here reverts to the architect, who engages in a process of reterritorializing the deterritorialized poem. While Murakami has separated herself from the final language of these poems, it is she who serves as the poems's procedural author. Murakami's procedures deny the stability of language ownership, rearticulating neoliberalism by using the tools it provides.

The "Vancouver Special" poems rearticulate poetic ownership at the level of structure and procedure, but they also demand a close reading of the linguistic limitations of Empire. Unlike the stark deletions of "The Form of a," these four poems' revisions present much more subtle structural and linguistic changes that challenge the idea of one central or universal meaning. The gaps in translation, the untranslatable elements, defamiliarize the Vancouver Special by denying its universality and blocked sameness. While the poems should offer uniformity, semantics change across language, and Murakami's poems develop unique tones and subjective points of view. These changes are both simple and complex. For example, three of the poems use the first person,[29] while the fourth uses a male pronoun.[30] Some poems depend on enjambment for every single line, while others provide punctuation that distinguishes almost every line.[31] These poetic choices stretch and make room for multiple interpretations, as the poem rearticulates itself differently each time it is presented in the text.

The varying translations of each "Vancouver Special" poem reveal unique concerns about the relationship between self and home. All four poems ask important questions about subjectivity and self-definition, but their ontological interests ultimately vary. While I can't explicate all four poems in detail here, I want to trace one example that addresses the relationship between the subject and the home as a commodified space. One speaker is interested in finding ways to concretize identity, asking the question, "How do I make myself less / abstracted? In the house but not of it"; another speaker phrases a similar question, "How do I make *me* / less abstract? Home, but not of it."[32] The first speaker seems to resist close definition with his or her living space, wanting to retain a sense of self that has not been abstracted into the house and the commodities that fill it. In contrast, the second speaker invokes the home (not the house), and seems to have a more difficult time separating "me"[33] from "home," although she is also interested in becoming "less abstract." In the second instance it is possible to read the home as the space through which identity can become concretized, tied to material objects, as opposed to being abstracted by them. A tension exists between the two versions as the connotations shift from a negative to a positive conception of identity-as-commodity. These poems, with similar content, can be read directly against one another as competing perspectives of home as a form of subjective definition.

The other two poems do not have this shared vocabulary but do invoke a similar concern with the self. One poem simply repeats the phrase "To be. To be. To be. To be.",[34] seemingly obsessively reflecting on the nature or being, or perhaps placing things in a future context, waiting for something that hasn't yet been experienced. The other poem collapses this idea with the previous one, making the statement: "How to emulate the look of elsewhere, to be *of*."[35] Here, identity is linked to place, to a relational understanding of the self that is rooted in the image of elsewhere, of appearing to be linked to something definitional. Each of the four poems conceptualizes the home as a form of being with varying degrees of directness. "Vancouver Special" is not a united body or statement about these relations; rather, it is a contradictory, rhizomatic set of poems that rebuilds and rearticulates the same image through distinctive vocabularies and modes of understanding that simultaneously contradict and echo one another.

The four versions of "Vancouver Special" presented in *Rebuild* have no demarcations to show which poem was translated through which language, nor does Murakami offer an original poem against which the others can be read as derivative. There is no hierarchy among the poems, except perhaps one determined by placement, which moves the texts away from a straightforward genetic revision history of the text and enforces her concept of a constantly evolving renovation. Murakami's *Rebuild* project respatializes the home as a commodified extension of the self. By engaging in a practice of renovating ideology through renovating language, Murakami creates the necessary conditions for contesting neoliberal conceptions of subjectivity and its links to the built environment.

III. Rebuild

While *Rebuild* engages in a politics of dismantling and renovating, making space for dissent and rearticulation, Murakami's Project Rebuild works in conjunction with these aims to create alternative, language-based communities. This movement takes place through a revaluation of renting in the move from the Vancouver Special on the page in *Rebuild* to the Vancouver Special on the screen in Project Rebuild. While Murakami begins by defamiliarizing her poetry when she engages in procedural poetic techniques, in her online project she relinquishes all control of her work when she places her poems on the rental market. Denying a stable definition of ownership over language, Murakami reframes authorship when she asks on her website, "What is a poem but a rental unit of language?"[36] Poetry is a type of cultural production, implicated in the discourses of power and ideology as a commodity for circulation and exchange in the global marketplace. Poets make and sell their creative works, and market them, branding them with their authorship, which is part and parcel of the commodity being sold. Project Rebuild destabilizes these ownership conventions by "renting out" Murakami's poems and creating a neighbourhood of poems that stem from the four versions of "Vancouver Special" included in *Rebuild*. Unlike the transaction of buying and selling real estate, renting recognizes the shared history of a poem with multiple types of dwelling, rather than attributing a poem to a single author or creator. The space of the "rental" creates a shared sense of community, a shared sense of ownership, because the owner does not have control over the space although he or she may choose to renovate and occupy it.

The Project Rebuild website reconceptualizes poetry from an individual pursuit into a communal and collaborative process. Each poem is visibly represented on the website as a drawing of the Vancouver Special, with the name of the author indicated below. When you click on each version, a tab presents itself with the option to renovate, which places the poem in an editable field so that its text can be completely deleted, manipulated, or rewritten at will. A user has the ability to participate instantaneously, becoming connected to the conversation because the links among various poems are maintained. Below each poem is a house representing any renovated versions of that poem, which can be selected individually, as well as a bar on the left that allows users to view "previous tenants," placing each poem in a genetic sequence that also links users to the other members of this community.

Writing process and publishing history are made visible in the move to an online medium. Because the user of the website can renovate any poem however he or she likes, the result is collaboratively, and not individually, determined and controlled. In an interview with Natalie Zina Walschots, Murakami describes Project Rebuild as an "unedited anthology, but one that is constantly being edited by the participants every time they respond."[37] Unlike a print anthology, which marks a particular moment in time determined by its various social collaborators (printers, editors, writers, publishers), this type of online anthology is always in process, generating a constantly evolving text that defers the finality of ownership by constantly leaving space for new participants.

This community-based poetic model is invested in creating alternative discourses that bring to light the limitations of so-called totalizing systems of power. The movement from individual authorship to community and collaborative-based projects creates an important counterdiscourse based in dialectic and polyphony. Project Rebuild's users can be read productively as a counterpublic for both traditional print publishers and the real estate market. Michael Warner conceptualizes the kind of publics that form around dissenting or alternative discursive communities as counterpublics.[38] These groups are formed dialectically in opposition to dominant publics created by systems of power. Warner briefly defines the counterpublic: "Counterpublics are 'counter' to the extent to which they try to supply different ways of imagining stranger sociability and its reflexivity; as publics, they remain oriented to stranger circulation in a way that is not just strategic but constitutive of membership and its affects."[39]

Counterpublics are built upon communication networks among disparate strangers, who are organized in ways that resist hegemony through participation and engagement. Unlike dominant publics, who simply seek to replicate ideology in their communication, a counterpublic is invested in transforming cultural geography. Each author on Project Rebuild is able to literally change the shape and content of the poetic communication to respond to and reimagine the poems that came before. This process is both collective, when the poems are read together as a neighbourhood, and individual, as disparate friends and strangers come together to read and respond to the work that came before.[40]

The *Rebuild* collection identifies the neighbourhood as an important site for dominant publics to circulate their ideologies. Murakami presents the concept of individual ownership as a neoliberal tool meant to divide and discourage community formation outside of the reach and control of economy. She describes the commoditization of the home as "tumors in a neighbourhood organism,"[41] or as a kind of competitive assimilation process: "See the patterns we set: can you follow them? Are you willing / to civilize your differences?"[42] Home ownership in dominant publics collapses difference and asserts conformity, largely based on physical appearance and commodity. The speaker describes ownership as a plague or disease that has infected communities and public discourse and that has turned individuals against collective identification. In stark contrast to these processes is the counterpublic space created by Project Rebuild, which is based on affiliation without a necessary shared identification. Unlike homeowners, whose economic status and ability to consume create the conditions for neighbourhood publics, renters, who use but do not own space, have no equivalent shared identity. What is common to them is their choice to participate in and shape the shared public space of the website. While Murakami does not foreground the website as a political space, her assertions about poetics are decidedly transformative. She states that "poetry is a community project in which we are all participants: poems are written in context and in conversation."[43] Her statements retain the quality of a manifesto, although without the clear politics of *Rebuild*. Murakami has opened up her poetry to erasure and revision. With this decision, she has allowed for the specific contexts of her own writing to become one part of a larger dialogue about language and poetics and their ability to rearticulate and transform the contexts that surround them.

Because Murakami defers her own poetic ownership to her collaborators, it is useful to trace the complex way power is decentralized on the website. The poems presented on Project Rebuild do not have a linear progression. Any poem is available for revision, so navigating the website itself becomes a complex engagement with online structures of meaning. Some poems have four or five distinctive revisions, each of which can have any number of revisions of its own. The poems also vary in terms of their interpretation of what constitutes a poem. Because the houses on the opening page are updated and moved around, it is not possible to locate a poem simply because it was first found it in a particular place on the page during a previous visit to the website. Without a fixed location to "house" a poem, inhabitation or rental is foregrounded as a place of movement and change, circulation and dislocation. The uniform houses representing the poems in part mask this disorientation; it is not until you scroll over a particular house you realize that its occupant has changed. The website itself provides an important visual testimony to the ways power is hidden in the movement and circulation of people across urban environments.

Murakami is the originator of Project Rebuild, but the poetic sequences and conversations that form around the website extend beyond her influence to create an architectural poetics that becomes grounded in community. While initially Murakami invited other Vancouver-based writers to be the first new inhabitants of her poetry, the site has expanded to offer commentary by writers across the country with various attachments to writing communities, from classrooms to freelance writers, professional poets, bloggers, and literary scholars. The poems themselves offer many fascinating perspectives on the way one inhabits a space in language. For example, Darren Werschler creates a "housing boom" of ASCII art "_[^]_ [^]_[^]_[^]_[^]_[^]_[^]_[^]_" that builds over a terrain intentionally left blank by a previous poet.[44] The blank space, represented by a "blank" or underline "_____," suddenly becomes a suburb, breaking the lines and reconstituting the way the space is seen and used.[45] Another poet, Ray Hsu, interprets renovation as a kind of dubbing, choosing to rewrite the Vancouver Special as a video poem. In "Ray Hsu vs. Sachiko Murakami: Vancouver Specials," Hsu creates his own video featuring news footage of skating from the Vancouver Olympics with an oral poem recited by text-to-speech software.[46] As the computer repeats lines of poems, often seeming to stumble in its reading, the skaters perform fluid movements that are then themselves cut up with interview footage and news scenes. The website also leaves room for dissent: "Just a student" includes a poem that asks "When you pay so much to learn and dream / should something not be more practical?"[47] This poet challenges the value of this kind of community collaboration, although she does choose to participate in the process and does enter the counterpublic. Her poem has yet to be renovated.[48] These poems renovate space and simultaneously extend the definition of poetry, pushing its limits to include multiple competing forms at the same time that it creates the conditions for multiple viewpoints and responses to the project itself.

While it is productive to read across various poems on the website, I think it is also useful to trace a genetic progression forward and backward through one particular building or poetic sequence to suggest the ways the poems specifically speak to one another beyond their original text. One poet rewrites "Vancouver Special" as an eviction notice, attributing authorship to Henri Lefebvre.[49] A subsequent poem, written by ryan fitzpatrick, renovates the poem by stating that he lived with his parents for the months of May and June, the time frame of unpaid rent that is connected to the eviction notice attributed to Lefebvre.[50] This sequence is then responded to by another poem attributed to Lefebvre, which repeats "Rent is owed" on each line, spacing out the letters on each line to take up more and more space on the screen until all that is left is the onomatopoeia "ow   ow   ow".[51] Here the space of owed rent is visually represented as increasingly weighing on the reader and suggesting some real physical harm. The poem is affected by the unexchanged money, by the renter's inability to pay what is owed, which then is internalized as a source of pain and irresolution. This connection to the body, to its affective response to the money owed, is temporalized in another renovation, this time by Nanci Lee, who frames the final "ow" with backslashes and n's, invoking the word now while retaining the slash, the broken or fragmented space created by the unpaid rent.[52] This poetic sequence's rhizomatic evolution across various authors allows for a more varied conceptual approach to inhabitation of place, as well as eviction from it. When a place is not owned, renting can lead to eviction, a process that identifies a corruption in an economic system of exchange that foregrounds the sometimes impossible requirements necessary to live in a place where the cost of living is not determined by wage. By reading through a specific progression, it is possible to trace how a specific concept or idea can morph into a new conversation that refracts, reflects, and repositions the poetic ideas that were constructed in the original poem.

Rebuilding is a constant, a process and not a product. In a desire to rearticulate urban Vancouver, Murakami develops an architectural poetics that inflects this process through renovations, which eventually multiply to the point of complete rebuilding. Her choice to revise and renovate her own poetry gives it mobility and allows her ideas and techniques to become conversational and dialectic. Even on the static page, the poetry of *Rebuild* constantly moves backward and forward, denying a linear progression as the poems refract upon, rewrite, and revise one another. Bringing this process to a new level, Project Rebuild takes an individual, politicized poetics and gives it a community in which to congregate. There, the multiple voices of the individual speaker give way to the polyphony of voices of many speakers recirculating and building upon one another's communication. By using these spatialized practices, Murakami explores the possibility of using poetry to radically reframe and revise the neoliberal systems of power that have made homeowning and dwelling in Vancouver two very different lived experiences. Creating a counterpublic through Project Rebuild, Murakami is able to facilitate a new form of writing community that is determined only by choosing to participate. Through this community, she is able to extend the scope of her project; poetry that began as an examination of urban domesticity in Vancouver has now been mobilized to explore representations of the urban in an unbound, digital context.

Notes
1 My emphasis.
2 Demographia, "9th Annual [...] Survey 2013," see esp. 2, 47. This survey ranks Vancouver as the second most severely unaffordable city worldwide, between Hong Kong and Sydney, Australia. The median price of a home in Vancouver in October 2012 was $621,300, while the median income was $65,200.
3 For Deleuze and Guattari on rhizomatic power relations, see *A Thousand Plateaus*.
4 I am interested in defining neoliberalism as a hegemonic system of values that reflects contemporary global capitalism, its practices and products. David Harvey, "Neoliberalism as Creative Destruction," provides a succinct definition of neoliberalism as "a theory of political economic practices proposing that human well-being can be advanced by the maximization of entrepreneurial freedoms within an institutional framework characterized by private property rights, individual liberty, unencumbered markets, and free trade" (22).
5 Murakami, *Rebuild*, 38.
6 Queyras, "Sachiko Murakami's *Rebuild*."
7 Hardt and Negri, *Empire*, xii. Their emphasis. Hardt and Negri borrow from Deleuze and Guattari's conception of deterritorialization and reterritorialization to describe the processes of becoming and resistance through which power is circulated in a rhizomatic structure.
8 *The Invisibility Exhibit* (2008) is also a highly politicized poetic examination of the City of Vancouver. This project was fuelled by the lack of investigation into the "Missing Women" in the Downtown Eastside neighbourhood. The text investigates the subjects who are missing or made invisible in the urban environment, particularly due to gender and class biases structured into the neighbourhood stratifications of the city. Murakami explores the

city's indifferent affective response to the abduction and death of its own inhabitants and the ways in which news media and journalism both inform and remove dominant publics from communities on the periphery.
9 Latosik, "Make It New."
10 Klobucar and Barnholden, "Introduction," 2.
11 Derksen, "A Conversation," 130–31.
12 Derksen, "A Conversation," 253.
13 Rich, "When We Dead Awaken," 35.
14 Lefebvre, *The Production of Space*, 26.
15 Wilson, "In Conversation With."
16 Murakami, *Rebuild*, 13.
17 Blair's article "Ambling in the Streets of Affect" offers an extended treatment on the cultural quotation as a proximity technique that emphasizes Derksen's project of rearticulating neoliberal affects. See especially 86–87.
18 Murakami, *Rebuild*, 13.
19 Murakami, *Rebuild*, 14.
20 Murakami, *Rebuild*, 13.
21 Murakami, *Rebuild*, 14.
22 See also Keith Higgins's art project vancouverspecial.com. It depicts 1,241 individual houses that fall into the category of the Vancouver Special. This project provides an alternative interpretation of the Vancouver Special's role within the urban space that speaks productively in conversation with Project Rebuild. The website identifies key features of the individual houses and their geographic location; in this way, it maps the proliferation of the Vancouver Special along both aesthetic and spatial lines.
23 Murakami, Sachiko. "About." *ProjectRebuild.ca*. n.d. 8 February 2012. http://projectrebuild.ca/about.php.
24 Murakami, *Rebuild*, 52.
25 Murakami, *Rebuild*, 51, 53, 57, 64.
26 Marjorie Perloff helpfully describes the procedural poem as operating in the tradition of the group of mathematical poets Oulipo, leading to the creation of the Oulip law, where "a text written according to a constraint describes the constraint" (n.p.). The procedural poem offers a self-reflexive examination of the constraints under which it is created. In simple terms, Murakami's use of translation software reveals the untranslatable nature of lyric poetry and thus the limitations of the technology even as she uses its products.
27 Murakami, "About."
28 Google, "What Is Google Translate?"
29 Murakami, *Rebuild*, 51, 53, 57.
30 Murakami, *Rebuild*, 64.
31 Murakami, *Rebuild*, 57, 51.
32 Murakami, *Rebuild*, 51, 57. Her italics.

33 The second poem's invocation of the word "me" has a further link to identification as commodity. The baby boomers have often been called the first self-indulgent "Me Generation," a term that originated with Tom Wolfe's description of the 1970s as the "Me Decade." "Me Generation" has had a resurgence as "Generation Me" since the publication of Twenge's *Generation Me*. This term has been co-opted to describe the way Generation Y's self-conception has become tied to the economic and commodified ideals of money, fame, and (perhaps most important to the home) image.
34 Murakami, *Rebuild*, 64.
35 Murakami, *Rebuild*. Her italics.
36 Murakami, "About."
37 Walschots, "Natalie Zina Walschots Talks to Sachiko Murakami."
38 I have chosen to ground this section in the public sphere tradition Warner participates within. Here he writes in response to the shift in the role of the public sphere as a place of dissent and criticism as described by Jürgen Habermas and elaborated upon by Nancy Fraser, who uses the term counterpublics to refer to those who are not included in public discussion. Another possible way to conceive of this is by applying the multitude model of Hardt and Negri. This, briefly, is their definition: "The multitude, designates an active social subject, which acts on the basis of what the singularities share in common. The multitude is an internally different, multiple social subject whose constitution and action is based not on identity or unity (or, much less, indifference) but on what it has in common" (*Multitude* 100). I have chosen Warner over Hardt and Negri because of the way they problematically reduce the multitude to a single "active social subject," even though they acknowledge the rhizomatic quality of that subject. Publics retain a stronger sense of individuation and a broader range of commitment; one can choose to participate in a public for any amount of time, and these publics are grounded in particular communications being circulated within them, as opposed to just in general opposition to Empire.
39 Warner, *Publics and Counterpublics*, 122.
40 According to the Project Rebuild website, initially the poems were opened up only to other poets in Vancouver to renovate. The site is now fully accessible for anyone to complete a renovation to any of the available poems.
41 Murakami, *Rebuild*, 52.
42 Murakami, *Rebuild*, 59.
43 Murakami, "About." ProjectRebuild.ca.
44 Wershler, "Vancouver Special."
45 rawlings, "Vancouver Special."
46 Hsu, "Ray Hsu vs. Sachiko Murakami."
47 Just a student, "Vancouver Special."
48 As of 18 May 2013.

49 I note this here as "attributed to" Lefebvre as opposed to penned by him because of his death in 1991 (not to mention his publication only in the French language). This attribution should be read to evoke the politics involved in the expulsion from place associated with the evacuation notice, instead of simply as a marker of authorship.
50 fitzpatrick, "Vancouver Special"; Lefebvre, "Vancouver Special."
51 Lefebvre, "Vancouver Special."
52 Lee, "Vancouver Special."

Bibliography

Bourdieu, Pierre. *The Field of Cultural Production*. Translated by Randal Johnson. New York: Columbia University Press, 1993.

Blair, Jennifer. "Ambling in the Streets of Affect: Jeff Derksen's 'Happy Locally, Sad Geopolitically.'" *Open Letter* 14, no. 3 (Spring 2011): 74–91.

Blamley, Nicholas B. *Unsettling the City: Urban Land and the Politics of Property*. New York: Routledge, 2004.

Bula, Frances. "The Future of Vancouver's Economy." *Vancouver Magazine*. 2 October 2011. Accessed 12 March 2012 at http://www.vanmag.com/News_and_Features/The_Future_of_Vancouvers_Economy.

Demographia. "9th Annual Demographia International Housing Affordability Survey 2013." *Performance Urban Planning*. Intro. Bill English. October 2012. Accessed 11 September 2014 at http://www.demographia.com/dhi.pdf.

Deleuze, Gilles, and Félix Guattari. *A Thousand Plateaus: Capitalism and Schizophrenia*. Translated by Brian Massumi. Minneapolis: University of Minnesota Press, 1987.

Derksen, Jeff. "A Conversation on Cultural Poetics." Interview by Pauline Butling and Susan Rudy. *Poets Talk*. 115–42. Edmonton: University of Alberta Press, 2005.

———. *Annihilated Time: Poetry and Other Politics*. Vancouver: Talonbooks, 2009.

fitzpatrick, ryan. "Vancouver Special." n.d. *ProjectRebuild.ca*. Accessed 11 September 2014 at http://projectrebuild.ca/poem.php?id=98.

Google. "What Is Google Translate?" *Google Translate*. Accessed 11 September 2014 at http://translate.google.com/about.

Hardt, Michael, and Antonio Negri. *Empire*. Cambridge, MA: Harvard University Press, 2000.

———. *Multitude: War and Democracy in the Age of Empire*. New York: Penguin, 2004.

Harvey, David. "Neoliberalism as Creative Destruction." *The ANNALS of the American Academy of Political and Social Science* 610, no. 1 (March 2007): 21–44. doi: 10.1177/0002716206296780.

Higgins, Keith. "Vancouver Special." *VancouverSpecial.com.* 2009. Accessed 11 September 2014 at http://www.vancouverspecial.com.
Hsu, Ray. "Ray Hsu vs. Sachiko Murakami: Vancouver Specials." *ProjectRebuild.ca.* n.d. Accessed 11 September 2014 at http://projectrebuild.ca/poem.php?id=14.
Just a student. "Vancouver Special." *ProjectRebuild.ca.* n.d. Accessed 11 September 2014 at http://projectrebuild.ca/poem.php?id=425.
Klobucar, Andrew, and Michael Barnholden. "Introduction." *Writing Class: The Kootenay School of Writing Anthology.* Vancouver: New Star Books, 1999.
Latosik, Jeff. "Make It New: An Interview with Sachiko Murakami." *Open Book Toronto.* 17 March 2011. Accessed 11 September 2014 at http://www.openbooktoronto.com/jeff_latosik/blog/make_it_new_interview_with_sachiko_murakami.
Lee, Nanci. "Vancouver Special." *ProjectRebuild.ca.* n.d. Accessed 11 September 2014 at http://projectrebuild.ca/poem.php?id=136.
Lefebvre, Henri. *The Production of Space.* Translated by Donald Nicholson-Smith. London and New York: Wiley-Blackwell, 1991.
———. "Vancouver Special." *ProjectRebuild.ca.* n.d. Accessed 11 September 2014 at http://projectrebuild.ca/poem.php?id=91.
———. "Vancouver Special." *ProjectRebuild.ca.* n.d. http://projectrebuild.ca/poem.php?id=121.
Murakami, Sachiko. *Rebuild.* Vancouver: Talonbooks, 2011.
———. "About." *ProjectRebuild.ca.* n.d. Accessed 11 September 2014 at http://projectrebuild.ca/about.php.
Perloff, Marjorie. "The Oulipo Factor: The Procedural Poetics of Christian Bök and Caroline Bergvall." *Jacket* 23 (August 2003): n.p. Accessed 11 September 2014 at http://jacketmagazine.com/23/perlof-oulip.html.
Queyras, Sina. "Sachiko Murakami's *Rebuild.*" *Lemon Hound.* 18 July 2011. Accessed 11 September 2014 at http://lemonhound.blogspot.ca/2011/07/sachiko-murakamis-rebuild.html.
rawlings, a. "Vancouver Special." *ProjectRebuild.ca.* n.d. Accessed 11 September 2014 at http://www.projectrebuild.ca/poem.php?id=78.
Rich, Adrienne. "When We Dead Awaken: Writing as Re-Vision." *On Lies, Secrets, and Silence: Selected Prose 1966–1978.* 33–50. New York: W.W. Norton, 1979.
Twenge, Jean M. *Generation Me: Why Today's Young Americans Are More Confident, Assertive, Entitled—and More Miserable Than Ever Before.* New York: Free Press, 2007.
Walschots, Natalie Zina. "Natalie Zina Walschots Talks to Sachiko Murakami." *Lemon Hound.* 22 November 2011. Accessed 11 September 2014 at http://lemonhound.blogspot.ca/2011/11/natalie-zina-walschots-talks-to-sachiko.html.
Warner, Michael. *Publics and Counterpublics.* Cambridge: Zone Books, 2002.

Wershler, Darren. "Vancouver Special." *ProjectRebuild.ca*. n.d. Accessed 11 September 2014 at http://projectrebuild.ca/poem.php?id=100.

Wilson, Julie. "In Conversation With: Sachiko Murakami on Community Poetry Renos and ProjectRebuild.ca." *49th Shelf*. 3 August 2011. Accessed 11 September 2014 at http://49thshelf.com/Blog/2011/08/03/In-Conversation-With-Sachiko-Murakami-on-Community-Poetry-Renos-and-ProjectRebuild.ca.

Wolfe, Tom. "The 'Me' Decade and the Third Great Awakening." *New York Magazine*. 23 August 1976. Accessed 11 September 2014 at http://nymag.com/news/features/45938/index12.html.

10

"We jimmied the radio": Gillian Jerome, Brad Cran, and the Lyric in Public

Kevin McNeilly

In this essay, I want to interrogate critically the intersection of the lyric and its publics, focusing especially on the writing of two emerging poets from the City of Vancouver on the Canadian West Coast: Brad Cran and Gillian Jerome. Both Cran and Jerome understand their poetry as essentially civically engaged but also as essentially lyrical in form and conception. Taking a cue from Michael Warner, I want to argue that in these poets' interrelated, contemporary work, a reflexive verbal attentiveness that informs their lyric poems also lays the groundwork—or better, opens up the possibility—for engaged public discourse, for viable public address.

1.
I'm going to declare, publicly and in print, that lyric poems want an audience: even here at the margin of the north Pacific Ocean, even now in this late and scattered age. That is, not only do poems still ask to be published, read, and heard, but they also tend both to enact and to interrogate specific practices of audition, of listening, of attentiveness. Lyric thought, Jan Zwicky claims, "bespeaks an awareness that is vulnerable to the world. Open."[1] That openness isn't necessarily all sweetness and light, and a tangible risk—of bathos, of anachrony, of the abstruse—persists into the present as lyric vulnerability. But it also persists, nonetheless, as the stuff of

verbal melody, as a palpable melopoeia. The lyric continues to define itself, for me, in the essence of such contemporary risk.

If the contemporary lyric is marked by word-music, its current and various manifestations aren't signalled so much by particular stylistic or formal characteristics as by a conflicted modality of language, a conflict that hinges on collisions of the public with the subjective. For example, Robert von Hallberg privileges an orphic persistence—or perhaps, a remainder—in the poem's heightened language, while still admitting its enmeshment in public speech, in rhetoric: "What I am calling the authority of the lyric derives more from orphic, than from rhetorical, poetics, even when a rhetorical ambition generates orphic achievements, or when rhetorical tools, such as syntax, sustain a poet's authority."[2] Von Hallberg frames this tension, in part, as what, after Aristotle, he calls a "civic poetics," a writing practice that both fulfills and exceeds its social imperatives: "The language of our time might be transformed into something consistent with but greater than its established civic uses."[3] Theorizing the contemporary lyric a year or two before von Hallberg, Mutlu Blasing suggests a strikingly similar conjunction of engagement and withdrawal, maintaining a privileged aesthetic purview for the lyric while also asserting its historical and social connectedness: "Lyric language is a radically public language, but it will not submit to treatment as a social document—of a certain stage of capitalism, for example—because there is no 'individual' in the lyric in any ordinary sense of the term."[4] Addressing the formal and material practices of the lyric as civic poetry—making a convincing critical case, that is, for its contemporary relevance—impels both Blasing and von Hallberg to contend with Theodor Adorno's "On Lyric Poetry and Society," a lecture that defines the terms and the terrain for thinking about the persistent value of poetry in recent history.

The fraught figure of the expressive individual, on which the lyric appears so deeply to depend, inhabits for Adorno an agonistic, antagonistic (and antithetical) conceptual and social space: "the lyric work is always the subjective expression of a social antagonism. But since the objective world that produces the lyric is an inherently antagonistic world, the concept of the lyric is not simply that of the expression of a subjectivity to which language grants objectivity."[5] The elitist privilege that enables lyric expression—the leisure to think and to write, a version of a "room of one's own"—is not, for Adorno, a depoliticized sinecure, but mirrors instead the antagonism to individual expression that characterizes the contemporary human world, its pervasively oppressive and suppressive character. If anything, Adorno argues for a recovery of that privilege, a politicizing at the level of form of the lyric poem:

> Poetic subjectivity is...indebted to privilege: the pressures of the struggle for survival allow only a few human beings to grasp the universal through immersion in the self or to develop as autonomous subjects capable of freely expressing themselves. The others, however, those who not only stand alienated, as though they were objects, facing the disconcerted poetic subject but who have also literally been degraded to objects of history, have the same right, or a greater right, to grope for the sounds in which sufferings and dreams are welded. This inalienable right has asserted itself again and again, in forms however impure, mutilated, fragmentary and intermittent—the only forms possible for those who have to bear the burden.[6]

The melopoeia that Adorno wants to recover from the lyric is exactly this groping for sounds, an agonistic collision of "suffering and dreams" not merely on behalf of a broken, inexpressive public but also with and through their voices.

In a review of Lisa Robertson's *The Weather* (published prior to both von Hallberg and Blasing), Sina Queryas argues for Robertson's recovery of lyric as a means of overcoming the cynicism surrounding genuinely engaged poetry in a media-dense and alienated present:

> As [Claudia] Rankine and [Juliana] Spahr point out, much of the interesting work of the day is concerned with the question of lyric—whether it is in connection with the relationship to prose, or an investigation of what I term our "lyraphobic" tendency toward positioning one's self as the center of a fashionably ordered, and limited world complete with unscorched language and mail order "otherness." (In other words, life experienced through internet trolling, or observed, chardonnay in hand, from the delicate frontier of a front porch.)[7]

Queyras's frame of reference remains, in this particular review, American L=A=N=G=U=A=G=E poetry, which she rightly suggests maintained a stolid resistance to expressive poeticism, favouring a presentation of subjectivity that rendered the humanistic "self" both ontologically untenable and politically suspect. But Robertson, she asserts, has found a formal and stylistic means to embrace the lyric again, to produce what Queyras calls a language of "intoxication" that, in its tangible and vital otherness, uncovers the means to make poetry worldly again. For me, what Queyras rediscovers is not so much a style as a modality of language, albeit a modality that can locate itself only in poetic particulars, in particular facets of poetic language. In the cosmopolitan, multicultural, and polyphonic Canadian contexts from which both Robertson and Queyras emerge, the lyric has in recent decades reappeared in a variety of sometimes incommensurate poetics: the "lyric philosophy" of Jan Zwicky, Robert Bringhurst, and Tim Lilburn; the media-savvy, abstracted lyricism of Karen Solie, Ken Babstock, or Suzanne Buffam; the recursive nature poetry emerging around Don McKay; the plainspoken working-world poetry of Tom Wayman; the L=A=N=G=U=A=G=E–influenced work of the Kootenay School of Writing. But in each of these contexts, the intersection of the orphic and the rhetorical, of the public and the private, of the social and the subjective, plays out its disconcerted music; and it is into this welter of latter-day lyric that both Cran and Jerome deliberately venture.

Teasing out the slippages between "an audience" and "a public," Michael Warner distinguishes between a material, "concrete audience, a crowd witnessing itself in visible space, as with a theatrical public" (or, I'd say, as with book-buying attendees at a poetry reading) and a textual or discursive public, a notional construct not so far removed from rhetorical conceptions of audience: situated, plural, contingent, addressed.[8] Warner maintains the empirical tangibility of any such public, but also insists on its autotelic textuality, its reflexive circularity; like an autopoetic ecology, a public creates and sustains itself as discursive affect: "A public might be real and efficacious, but its reality lies in just this reflexivity by which an addressable object is conjured into being in order to enable the very discourse that gives it existence."[9] While Warner makes the self-made and self-making public sound, in the abstract, as if it emerges from aesthetic sleight of hand, a discursive conjuring trick, I'd suggest that the linguistic reflex onto which he maps the gesture from language outward—its worldliness—is encountered radically and intensively in the reflexive opening up of the lyric poem, and more so than in any rhetorical genre. Lyric occurs as vulnerability in language, in text, at the momentary inception of a public, of publics.

Rather than simply let this declaration stand, however, I need to situate my claim in specific, contemporary poetic practices. So let me open this essay with a reading of a particular poem, "Midsummer" by Gillian Jerome, a brief meditative lyric from her 2009 collection *Red Nest*. In the poem, Jerome describes a picnic "out at Trout Lake" near Commercial Drive in East Vancouver; she situates herself in a lived and living urban context, in what she calls elsewhere in the collection "neighbourhood":[10] not just a proximity of houses, but a variegated collation of lives and voices, people and animals. She positions herself off centre: "remote" in the park, even as she finds herself amid a cluster of children and pets as some kind of parental supervisor, "wondering with all these children at my feet / where the peace went," but hesitant to intervene, merely watching and listening. She records the inception of a discursive counterpublic (to borrow Warner's terminology) as she copies out fragments of the "dirty words" the kids she's been observing are mouthing off, and teaching themselves to say, like parrots:

> But parrots have been welcomed
> into the noses, ears, armpits, hearts of the children
> where they never hasten to repeat
>
> the dirty words they teach them. Nobody hears
> their curses but me and so I say them softly back to myself—
>   Fuckhead. Shitballs. Gaylord.[11]

This last line is hardly what we might expect for melopoeic lyricism, but I think that's exactly what it might be. The lyric marginality of the observer-poet is a skewed echo of Keats—"Darkling I listen..."—but nightingales (whether Keats's or Shelley's) have degraded into crass parrots, and the solipsistic egotism of the lonely voice ("So remote is the island / of myself from my self") is self-consciously parodied, but also parodies its own saccharine privation. Still, instead of withdrawal, the listener seeks genuine entry into a contingent, local, familial scene. The repetition that the poem both remarks upon and enacts offers a definitive instance of the reflexive circularity that Warner describes, what the poem calls "the circuitous circus / of the heart" that comes temporarily to rest "in the grass" nearby. The harsh fricatives, dentals, and plosives of those "dirty words" soften into lyric not by being thinned out or cleaned up into flowing lines, but by having their small fractures, an inappropriately public–private cursing (that nobody else "but me"—the lyric subject—hears), carried intact over into the private but open visceral space—the wet interior—of the poet's mouth, up till then missing from her partial list of sensitive body parts, those noses, ears, armpits, and hearts. Appropriated by the poem as raw language, they resist being sweetened or smoothed over, instead remaining (in fact, as discursive remainders) not hypostatized but suspended within becoming, held on a trajectory towards some state of heightened language that, arrested typographically on the page, they can now never reach. To borrow a term from another poem in Jerome's collection, those words—now neither theirs nor hers, but held scintillant between testimony and poem—have been jimmied. And that suspension marks the lyric vulnerability at which a public—their shared commonality—finds its contingent purchase.

2.

To come at the question of a lyric public or of a public lyric from another angle, Gerald Bruns repurposes a key question from Martin Heidegger, who had swiped it in his turn from Friedrich Hölderlin: "And what are poets for in a destitute time?"[12] Heidegger has poets pursuing the traces of fugitive gods, but for Bruns, the question becomes more pressing and immediate—transplanted to our own times and places, our own anthropologies—because that destitution, for which the loss of poetry itself as a largely public, expressive genre is symptomatic, has produced a fractured and uncertain plurality of voices, voices that can only be engaged, for Bruns, in an answerable critical style that remains situated, local, and contingent itself: "For if there is no one thing that can be called poetry—if it is made of anomalies... then one's study must proceed, like an anthropologist's progress through an alien culture, at ground level, from one local practice or artifact to another, without subsuming things into a system."[13] Put another way, a responsive and responsible criticism, one that seeks to assess how poetry can matter, what it can be for, needs to start at "ground level," mindful still of the inexpressible abyss, the *Abgrund*, that poetic practice inevitably confronts in and through formalized—or, better, formational—language: saying what you mean and making it heard.

For the better part of the last decade, Brad Cran and Gillian Jerome have been working, both separately and collaboratively, often in and around Vancouver, to produce a decidedly urban, public poetry and to make that work heard: their writing practices, as crafted amalgams of social commitment and oblique lyricism, often engage with the urban particulars of the Vancouver cityscape and of city life, particularly those of the disenfranchised populations of the city's Downtown Eastside. Jerome and Cran, it's fair to say, tend to seek in their poems and in their documentary works various means of advocating for and of conversing with the living, speaking inhabitants of their "wild sprawling city," but they also want to do so in ways that remain both aesthetically rigorous and ethically attentive. Their intersecting poetic projects aim to produce, and at the same time critically to interrogate the possibility of, what might be called the civic lyric: a tactical verbal compromising of the phenomenological rarefication of the poem—what Yeats might have called the "perfection of the art"—by the prehensile tug of public voices, of the speaking, teeming world in which we find ourselves inexorably and daily thrown, and to which we are, whether we like to hear it or not, called upon to respond.

I want to use the poetries of Cran and Jerome as exemplary moments of this effort to, in a sense, compromise without compromising. When

I interviewed her informally earlier this year, for example, Jerome said she wanted to write poetry that her grandmothers—the dedicatees of *Red Nest*—could respond to and not be alienated by. Her aim wasn't condescension—never to patronize readers who might not be party to hermetic trade secrets or arcane formal alchemies—but to communicate clearly and directly while still attending with exacting care to the material demands of words. The goal, as Cran puts it at the close of "Today After Rain," is to become "common."[14] There are issues of class mobility and social privilege that have ghosted themselves into this language and that ought to be attended to more critically, but for the moment I want to recognize a pluralistic imperative in both of their poetries that inheres in a specific conception of the common, of some set of language partials that can be held in common, of the nature and limits of shared words. Whenever they have been asked about the demands and the potential challenges of finding a public lyric voice—some sort of functional poetic *vox pop* that might account for and enact such a sharing—both Jerome and Cran have tended to resist generalizing about particular styles, genres, or even poetics: not to be coy or cagey, but to recognize, I think, the inherent multiplicity of any public sphere, the fact, plainly put, that people talk and think in different ways. Striving for public engagement through a poem or poems means, to both of them, not ventriloquizing advocacy, not speaking on behalf of others or subsuming subject positions they don't necessarily share or know, but addressing, poetically and lyrically, the phenomenology of engagement itself. The poems, that is, are for me not only efforts at engagement with others but also inquiries into what it is to engage.

Both of them thematize this inquiry as a practice of listening, of an auditory verbal attention. Listening—as physiological, as phenomenological, and as technological—comes for Cran and Jerome, at least insofar as their social documentary work is concerned, to demand not only a disavowal of lyric subjectivity, but also a verbal practice that exceeds—albeit respectfully, as they put it—the constraints and pitfalls of ethnographic detachment. I think they would deny that their award-winning anthology of voices from Vancouver's Downtown Eastside, *Hope in Shadows*, is a book of poetry, and might point instead to Elee Kraljii Gardiner's recent *V6A*, a gathering of poems from the Carnegie Centre's Thursday Writing Collective, as something closer to a public representation of Downtown Eastside poetry and poetics. Jerome and Cran's collaborative introduction to *Hope in Shadows* nonetheless offers a provocation and an intervention into the debate over the possibility of engaged public lyric, as they describe their efforts to keep their own voices out of the way:

It became clear to us as we progressed that our job was not an academic one and certainly not a journalistic one. At its easiest, our job was to turn on the microphone and make the contributors feel comfortable enough to discuss personal matters that were important to them. At its hardest, our job was to engage with participants in an empathetic way while preserving our position as unbiased recorders of their stories.[15]

The thing is, if it isn't ethnographic and it isn't journalistic, what is it? It might be easy to charge them with descriptive naïveté: nobody can keep themselves entirely objective, and somebody's doing the choosing, the shaping, the editing here, right? Cran and Jerome acknowledge as much, while still deferring to the many mouths other than their own: "As writers, we strove to keep ourselves out of the project as much as possible; we wanted to lend our skill and not our voices. This project was about making connections with people."[16] I'm sure it's possible to find traces of their politics and their interests lightly overlaid onto the many accounts they collect here, but I'm not sure how critically productive that might be in the end. What I do want to stress here is how the fraught articulation of the poetic in public, its inherent and troubling egocentricity, is put at issue whenever one tries to listen carefully and respectfully to a cityscape, to its untempered sprawl.

3.
Brad Cran's collection *The Good Life* (2001) offers up a set of early career maps that collide the urban and the lyrical. By that I mean that the book presents both a personal, poetic topography—an overview of tactics and preoccupations to come in his writing—and what Cran names in its core sequence a cityscape. The concept of the "-scape" comes from the aesthetics of eighteenth-century Dutch painting, and denotes both a technique of physiographic pictorial realism and, significantly, the human intervention in demarcating and reshaping property: landscape and landscaping. That is, the term indicates both detached description and subjective intervention. Urban space is hardly given or natural, but the poems in *The Good Life* treat Vancouver streets and architecture as analogous to a naturalistic given: whatever is there to meet the eye and the ear. You can hear, I think, that I am trying to set up in Cran's cityscape poems a tension, around the question of aesthetics, closely akin to the problematic of respectful attentiveness that emerges around *Hope in Shadows*. To show more closely how this tension plays out, I want to look at the last poem in the book, "Today after Rain." The book is dedicated to Lorna Crozier, who along with Patrick Lane would help introduce Cran's (and Jerome's) poetry to a wider audience

in *Breathing Fire 2* (2004); but the descriptive tenor of Cran's work is much less whimsical and much more blunt, at least on first pass, than Crozier's, as the opening tercet of the poem epitomizes: "Today after rain / the streets are bare / and smell only of dust."[17] Complexity and lyric density are eschewed in favour of Hammett-like directness, a bare minimum. The agency of any perceptual apparatus—the eye, the ear—is muted, restrained.

Within a few lines, however, that restraint gives way to metaphoric and melopoeic descriptive thickening:

> The sky opens like a cabinet
> and inside there is a blue
> but then quickly
> clouds move and the door
> slams shut. A collapse
> of black on the ground
> and down each street
> there is no sound
> or movement at all.[18]

The inexorable, entropic collapse of this urban world, washed away and washed clean by rainfall, is countered by the elaborating assemblage of a furniture conceit: an unruly sky, contingently overlaid with human carpentry, remains forbidding and forbidden, even if it appears more closely knowable. The insurgent rhyme (ground / down / sound) answers a wordless and inhuman—dehumanizing—stillness, and voice becomes an effect not merely of listening but of deliberate and crafted response, of a bit of backtalk. The subtle move from the light rush of an anapestic cadence ("A collapse of black on the ground") to blunt trisyllabic clusters ("down each street"; "is no sound") suggests a voice seeking an acoustic agency, defining itself, provisionally, aloud. Cran's poem, as if self-aware of what must be both an ethical and an aesthetic quandary here (selfish assertion over alienated, descriptive detachment), falls back on the abstracted language of aesthetic commentary:

> Somewhere this is art.
>
> Somewhere a place like this
> opens and an eye peers in.
>
> Somewhere this is a collection
> worth polishing.[19]

Cynical about its own attraction to poetic possibility—the ripeness of a situation for artistic exploitation, for grabbing the lyric "moment"—the poem turns those suspicions, vestigially I'd say, into a form of lyrical hope. Simile takes on a vagueness ("like this") and a rather romanticized topographical uncertainty (not here, but "somewhere"), which both disavows the agency of the lyric subject—refusing to force-fit situation to poem—while making a poem of that moment nonetheless, making it sing. "For a moment," the poem asserts as it closes on itself, "we are common." Collective belonging—the only first person in the poem is plural, a significant alteration of the lyric "I"—manifests itself not as claims of solidarity or similitude, but in the identification of commonality in shared aspiration: the work of trying to make human sense, rather than in any particular meaning or ideological position.

The Good Life is also dedicated—in the acknowledgements—"to Gillian and Rory: this theme, this love, as much as we can, the good life."[20] The "we" of the poem doesn't necessarily pertain to hazy social bonds with other inhabitants of a sprawling city, but can also mark an assertion of the *eros* of family, the small social collective of spouse and child. "Apiary of Underclothes," from Jerome's *Red Nest*, reciprocates. Her book, like Cran's, offers up a set of sequences addressing Vancouver's cityscape, what she calls, with deceptive directness, its "neighbourhood." "Apiary of Underclothes" stands apart, a little, from the city poems, but I want to pay it some readerly attention because it negotiates self-consciously between lyric intimacy and public chatter and because it revisits and reshapes, with an eye and an ear to networked urbanism, the kind of nature lyric that Russell Smith among others seems so keen to dismiss. The poem is dedicated to Brad Cran and sounds like an oblique confession of a first erotic encounter, beginning love:

> After the beer parlour we set off for the islands
> drinking whiskey from Tupperware cups. We jimmied
> the radio for baseball—Expos were up.
> I didn't know what day it was, or the year.[21]

Jerome jimmies a common language rife with brand names and slang, turning it with slightly fey anachrony (who says "jimmied" or "beer parlour" any more?) and accreted internal rhyme (parlour / Tupperware cups / were up) into gently compelling verbal music; rhythmically, these first lines drift around the hexameter, clipping a syllable with a dash or tacking on a weak beat to skew the inherent symmetries of a twelve-syllable line into odd, prime-number quantities and lightly fractious run-ons. The effect, for me, is to disrupt any technically knowing verbal certainties while at the same time hinting at the discovery of similitudes and contingent closures.

The "I" describes the encounter ("Finally, I thought, a good sized man...") in what feels like direct, savvy terms, but also holds off being explicit: we never really do know what happens between them, but hear instead echoes and reiterations of radio noise and small talk, as fireflies and June bugs flit past the moving cars, images in a slipstream only fleeting enough "to whet our eyeballs":

> Have you heard so-and-so's having a baby? Well no.
> Well yes. I hummed my favourite Bo Diddleys,
> rattled off some names of local birds.[22]

The highly mediated languages of gossip and mass culture mix here with a hint of the descriptive precision of Roger Tory Peterson, rattled off. The Canadian nature poem becomes one among many available languages that deflect and even cover over confessional directness, but Jerome's poem doesn't give up on personal, lyric intimacy so much as displace it, as one generic code among many, into the overdetermined swells of radio language, all that talk.

The poem closes by turning its gaze demurely aside, as the prospective lovers head into the landscape, presumably to find someplace where they can be alone:

> When the car stopped
> furs of dandelions flew around us
> & we hastened like they did
> into that broom.[23]

The shortening lines suggest a diminution of the capacity of the voice to declare that likeness, as well as a retreat from the knowing, prying eye into the private space of darkness. The subtly awkward hint of poeticism here ("hastened") isn't anything like a technical error, but reminds us, texturally, of the lyrical effort at stake in trying to take hold of an alterity, to say "we." The local idiomatic character of Jerome's diction—"broom" refers to Scotch broom, *Cytisus scoparius*, an invasive species of weed on Vancouver Island—only heightens this texture of uncertainty. The poem closes, I'd say, by refusing us any closeness; this is, I think, a disavowal akin to Cran's becoming common—a reminder that the lyric consists not in the melopoeic assertion of subjective will, but rather in a music that both promises and refrains from asserting what it knows. Desire jimmies its language, at once saying and unsaying itself. In a blurb for the book, Suzanne Buffam calls Jerome's poetry "deeply political...without the cant." A politics, I want to claim, isn't so much thematized in the poems as enacted by and through their lyric self-awareness, their civics.

4.
The civic practice of poetry foregrounds itself in several different registers in Brad Cran's "civic poems,"[24] which appear in his 2013 collection *Ink on Paper*. Cran served as Vancouver's second poet laureate (after George McWhirter, and preceding Evelyn Lau) from 2009 to 2011, and in those two and a half years he used his largely honorary position to bring poetry into grade schools, to introduce poetry reading into civic events and celebrations, and to compose a number of civic-minded poems that appeared in venues such as *Geist* and, significantly, the *Globe and Mail*—although it's pretty clear that a poem like his "Fun-Loving Nickelback Policy Machine (with Kittens)" has little to do with the discursive excesses of official apostrophe, a genre it more or less satirizes.

"Thirteen Ways of Looking at a Gray Whale" initially appeared in a 2011 issue of *Geist*, as one of Cran's laureate poems, and it offers a reassessment of poetic response and responsibility, of how to collide the civic and the aesthetic. Like Wallace Stevens's "Thirteen Ways of Looking at a Blackbird," which serves as a loose formal scaffolding for Cran's piece, the poem maps out brief perspectival shifts as it passes through an unresolved set of discursive and generic registers. While Stevens's haiku- and tanka-like fragments maintain a certain standoffishness, signalled formally by their "noble accents / And lucid, inescapable rhythms,"[25] Cran's slightly more elaborated takes (or looks) tend to transition among, and even meld, disparate idioms, from the figural ("An armoured lung, / a living castle of barnacle)"[26] through the quasi-empirical ("an ocean cave / populated by sea otters")[27] to the colloquial ("No I didn't see the whale but / the man behind me at Starbucks did.")[28] Rather than the rarefied hypersensitivity of Stevens, however, for whom those "thirteen ways" present different aspects of a unified and singular sensibility, Cran offers a prismatic public, a constellation of responses from a small crowd of spectators overheard in and culled from Vancouver's urban soundscape.

The poem was occasioned, Cran admits in a note, "by two gray whales that swam into the harbour in downtown Vancouver in 2010, one in May and one in August."[29] As with the public-radio-informed language of Jerome's "Apiary of Underclothes," the diction and pitch of the Canadian nature poem become in Cran's sequence one of many viable descriptive genres; the poem's two-line fifth section succinctly collides Wordsworthian pretense—capital-n Nature as object of serious meditative tranquility—with the parodically inflated heft of the King James Genesis: "And the whale said / Behold the natural world."[30] "Nature" becomes a decidedly cultural production, the name of a particular brand of poetic discourse. Wordsworth's "Intimations" ode, arguably the *sine qua non* of encounters with a Romantic natural sublime, is directly echoed in the second section, when Cran notes how "The child knows more / about the gray whale / than the adult."[31] Compare, for example, "The child is father to the man..." The poem skirts around a nostalgia for transcendent innocence that clearly recasts Wordsworth, for whom a decrepit adulthood requires replenishment in childlike wonder. Or, as Cran frames things, "When given crayons / the adult says he does / not know how to draw."[32] But just as complex self-awareness of metaphor making is reduced, in the poem, to a child's random and offhand creative excess, using whatever crayons happen to be to hand ("The child is already drawing / the gray whale / with blue and pink"),[33] so too is the romantic sublime not so much rejected as reduced to one banal and incomplete verbal register among many. The whales—as incursions of an oversized and unknowable nature, self-evidently out of place in the urban harbour—each carry an *aporia* into public view; the body of a gray whale offers a mobile abyss around which discourse gathers, out of doors, but which no single description, and especially no romantic lyric, can hope to capture. One can claim to see but can never represent the plenitude of that visual experience: "I did, he kept saying. I did. / I saw the whale."[34] The point of Cran's multi-perspectival takes on the event of a gray whale happening into the harbour isn't a levelling relativism, nor is it a deprivileging of the poetic, rather it is a poetry of differential plurality, a succession—or better, a set—of perceptual openings.

This shared encounter with the aporetic produces what Cran calls the "common." The point isn't to collapse different perspectives into one another to find commonalities as similitude, so much as it is understand difference as a kind of bonding itself, the means by which we start to talk:

> The thing is, my dad doesn't like people much.
> We saw the whale on the pier outside the market.
> Even after the whale had gone, my dad wanted to stay
> and talk to everyone else who had seen it.[35]

A public forms not in the closure of a site-specific moment of shared talk, but in the ways in which that talk refuses to close, even despite itself, but keeps going. People keep talking. That talk, for Cran, takes on a specifically lyric quality inasmuch as it invites a renovation—that is, both a renewal and a disruption—of our perceptual securities: "Do not live in habit. Do not take the most / basic assumptions for granted."³⁶ While such lines sound closer to imperative than to invitation, it's important to recognize that talk can only open up a space for intersubjective response; it can't impel an answer, which is always the provenance of another, of an interlocutor.

I want to call this opening lyrical because of the last line of Cran's sequence, an imperative purloined from Rilke's sonnet "Archaic Torso of Apollo": "You must change your life."³⁷ Contemplating the inscrutable alterity of an ancient fragmented sculpture, Rilke asserts that the work of art requires of observers, and even of onlookers, a moment of self-revision: *Du mußt dein Leben ändern*.³⁸ (P.K. Page repurposes this same line, as a convocational charge, in her 1990 "Address at Simon Fraser": "Art and the planet tell us. Change your life.")³⁹ The German suggests not only change but also that life needs to be lived differently, or otherwise (*anderer*), and I think that, rather than the presumption of imperative, it is this sense of opening oneself up to what is other than oneself that better catches the sense of nascent public, and even of counterpublic, that Cran understands as common: "I've stopped believing / in loneliness. Here we are."⁴⁰ The poem acknowledges in its penultimate section the irresolution of shared perspectives, but it also seems to reinvoke a mystical knowingness that sounds like the provenance of an enlightened few (poets?): "Some were trying to decipher what the whale / was telling us. Others already knew."⁴¹ Read back through the filter of Rilke's sonnet, however, these lines also suggest that what can be fully known is otherness itself, an unknowing that persists in the uncertainty of what the disturbing presence of a whale, or what the whale itself, might actually tell, or say. That unreadable music, at which the poem gestures, is the stuff of lyric.

5.

The situated and parochial specifics of Gillian Jerome's or Brad Cran's politics might differ, just as the particulars of their contingent and prismatic publics do, and I don't want to suggest that their ideologies—while no doubt coincidental and connected—are necessarily ever identical. But what they do share in their poetic projects, work unfolding in a common urban space and a common public sphere, is an address to the lyrical inception of a public, of publics. The printed lyric page incepts a public space. Jerome's "Tenement Song"—the first poem in her collection—foregrounds the character of this inception, an opening out rather than a solitary ingestion, in the syntactical and spatial arrangement of its last lines:

Sing the song of Cecil nailing the shingles to the roof
Sing the song of mist hovering in the button trees
                              of Caesarian sunset
The song of hydro bills, of snow storms
The song of bottles, of algae, of billy goats

Sing the song of Mars, of Mercury, of the Americas
The song of our finger bones tapping the locks
The song of the pale bow of the moon, the sun
Slipping into our song:
                              Dear Landlord,[42]

Like Cran's "Thirteen Ways," Jerome's poem condenses and constellates various discursive registers into the raw matter of song, although here even the banal or the colloquial is melopoeically intensified. The poem offers a litany of culture trash, of ugly beauty, but also stirs an incantation from those layers—like those heard over the car radio in "Apiary of Underclothes"—by jimmying the language; notice how, for instance, the lines are more widely prised apart, and the lack of any end-stopped punctuation. There are no periods in the poem, and the only line that closes with any punctuation mark is the last one, and it's a comma. The end of the poem, that is, seeks a beginning, voicing the lyric *ur*-text out of which an appeal to a landlord (for apartment repairs? for rent relief?) might emerge. Nominally plain public writing, signalled by legalistic apostrophe, is shaped and informed by the poetically variegated lives and voices of her neighbourhood. I think Jerome might be echoing a poem by Jan Zwicky, "Brahms Clarinet Quintet in B Minor, Op. 115," which finds lyric music in the unrequited love letters of Johannes Brahms to Clara Schumann, and which ends with a similar address: "That a letter might honestly / begin, *Dear beloved.*"[43] But whereas the lyric vitality of Zwicky's poem and the honesty it seeks depend on a specifically aesthetic experience, an intensity suspended in the more definitively closed syntax of her lyric, Jerome wants to hear behind something as uncomfortable as a letter to a landlord the vitality of a common plurality, to start to recover what might remain of something close to love.

Both Cran and Jerome are committed to an active cultural politics, a politics that had circulated and continues to circulate around and through their writing practices. Among Cran's efforts during his term as poet laureate, two high-profile interventions merit remarking: first, his public refusal to participate in the opening ceremonies of the 2010 Winter Olympics, on the grounds that a muzzle clause in VANOC documents would rein in free expression. The second was his organizing of the Vancouver 125 Poetry Conference in October 2011, in part as a response to the apparent narrowness of the Cultural Olympiad, and as a way of using his increased civic profile and the city's interest in funding cultural events for its 125th anniversary to increase the public profile and the public engagement of many poets of his own generation. "You have to go out and be active in the world," he says, "and use poetry."[44] Jerome was an organizer and a key participant in the 125 conference, but as of May 2012 has also been instrumental in founding CWILA (Canadian Women in the Literary Arts), a grassroots advocacy organization focused on the public profile of writing, and writing reviews, by women. In an interview with Kim Minkus that summer, she offers up a powerful and necessary critique of the antagonistic public ethos surrounding the reception of women's writing in North America, but goes on to make a case for the entwining, at least in her own work, of the aesthetic and the critical—I want to say the lyric and the political, but I won't at this moment, because she doesn't. Negotiating the complexities and contradictions in the amalgamated writing practices of poet and critic, Jerome refuses to close off the play, the resistances inherent in, conceptual differences: "Critical work is fundamental to my artistic practice. I resist the idea that my artistic practice is somehow separate from my critical and/or political work. but I am the first to admit that they require very different energies from me, very different ways of being."[45]

What I have hoped to do here is to show how Jerome's and Cran's artistic practices take up those tensions, and make them speak.

Notes

1. Zwicky, *Lyric Philosophy*, 130.
2. Von Hallberg, *Lyric Powers*, 35.
3. Von Hallberg, *Lyric Powers*, 233.
4. Blasing, *Lyric Poetry*, 4.
5. Adorno, *Notes to Literature*, Vol. 1, 45.
6. Adorno, *Notes to Literature*, Vol. 1, 45.
7. Queyras, "Lines Composed Indoors."
8. Warner, "Publics and Counterpublics," 50–51.
9. Warner, "Publics and Counterpublics," 51.
10. Jerome, *Red Nest*, 17.
11. Jerome, *Red Nest*, 37.
12. Heidegger, *Poetry, Language, Thought*, 91.
13. Bruns, *What Are Poets For?*, x.
14. Cran, *The Good Life*, 75.
15. Cran and Jerome, *Hope in Shadows*, 16.

16 Cran and Jerome, *Hope in Shadows*, 17.
17 Cran, *The Good Life*, 74.
18 Cran, *The Good Life*, 74.
19 Cran, *The Good Life*, 74–75.
20 Cran, *The Good Life*, 79.
21 Jerome, *Red Nest*, 31.
22 Jerome, *Red Nest*, 31.
23 Jerome, *Red Nest*, 31.
24 Brad Cran, *Ink on Paper*, 9.
25 Wallace Stevens, *The Palm at the End of the* Mind, ed. Holly Stevens (New York: Vintage, 1971), 21.
26 Cran, *Ink on Paper*, 11.
27 Cran, *Ink on Paper*, 11.
28 Cran, *Ink on Paper*, 11.
29 Cran, *Ink on Paper*, 11.
30 Cran, *Ink on Paper*, 12.
31 Cran, *Ink on Paper*, 11.
32 Cran, *Ink on Paper*, 11.
33 Cran, *Ink on Paper*, 11.
34 Cran, *Ink on Paper*, 11.
35 Cran, *Ink on Paper*, 12.
36 Cran, *Ink on Paper*, 13.
37 Rilke, *New Poems*, 183.
38 Rilke, *New Poems*, 182.
39 Page, *Planet Earth*, 87.
40 Cran, *Ink on Paper*, 13.
41 Cran, *Ink on Paper*, 13.
42 Jerome, *Red Nest*, 13.
43 Zwicky, *Songs*, 13.
44 Lederman, "Brad Cran."
45 Minkus, "4/4."

Bibliography

Adorno, Theodor. *Notes to Literature*, Edited by Rolf Tiedemann. Translated by Shierry Weber Nicholsen. New York: Columbia University Press, 1991.

Blasing, Mutlu Konuk. *Lyric Poetry: The Pain and the Pleasure of Words*. Princeton: Princeton University Press, 2006.

Bruns, Gerald R. *What Are Poets For?: An Anthropology of Contemporary Poetry and Poetics*. Iowa City: University of Iowa Press, 2012.

Cran, Brad. *The Good Life*. Gibsons: Nightwood Editions, 2001.

———. *Ink on Paper*. Gibsons: Nightwood Editions, 2013.

———. "Thirteen Ways of Looking at a Gray Whale, After Wallace Stevens and Ending with a Line from Rilke." *Geist.* Accessed 11 September 2014 at http://www.geist.com/articles/thirteen-ways-looking-gray-whale-after-wallace-stevens-and-ending-line-rilke.

Cran, Brad, and Gillian Jerome. *Hope in Shadows.* Vancouver: Arsenal Pulp Press and Pivot Legal Society, 2008.

Heidegger, Martin. *Poetry, Language, Thought.* Translated by Albert Hofstadter. New York: Harper, 1971.

Jerome, Gillian. *Red Nest.* Gibsons: Nightwood Editions, 2009.

Lederman, Marsha. "Brad Cran: A Poet Laureate Pens Those Tricky Last Stanzas." *Globe and Mail,* 18 October 2011. Accessed 11 September 2014 at http://m.theglobeandmail.com/arts/books-and-media/brad-cran-a-poet-laureate-pens-those-tricky-last-stanzas/article557881/?service=mobile.

Minkus, Kim. "4/4: The Spectacle of Absence—Gillian Jerome on the CWILA Count." *Capilano Review* 3, no. 20 (2013). Accessed 11 September 2014 at http://www.thecapilanoreview.ca/44-the-spectacle-of-absence-gillian-jerome-on-the-cwila-count.

Page, P. K. *Planet Earth: Poems Selected and New.* Erin: Porcupine's Quill, 2002.

Queyras, Sina. "Lines Composed Indoors While Contemplating the Weather." *How2: Contemporary Innovative Writing by Women,* 2 no. 3 (2005). Accessed 11 September 2014 at http://www.asu.edu/pipercwcenter/how2journal/archive/online_archive/v2_3_2005/current/alerts/queyras.htm.

Rilke, Rainer Maria. *New Poems.* Translated by Edward Snow. New York: North Point Press, 2001.

Rowe, Sam. "What Are Poets For?—Gerald L. Bruns." *Fullstop: Reviews, Interviews, Marginalia,* July 27, 2012, Accessed 11 September 2014 at http://www.full-stop.net/2012/07/27/reviews/sam/what-are-poets-for-gerald-l-bruns.

Stevens, Wallace. *The Palm at the End of the Mind.* Edited by Holly Stevens. New York: Vintage, 1971.

von Hallberg, Robert. *Lyric Powers.* Chicago: University of Chicago Press, 2008.

Warner, Michael. "Publics and Counterpublics." *Public Culture* 14, no. 1 (2002): 49–90.

Zwicky, Jan. *Lyric Philosophy.* Toronto: University of Toronto Press, 1992.

———. *Songs for Relinquishing the Earth.* London Ontario: Brick Books, 1998.

Poetry II

Hungry

by Kevin McNeilly

Where some kinds of people come from, you need to learn
another way to talk, the claims and protocols
of subsistence. You need to know what works or else.

You need to learn the politics of not eating
enough, the politics of nothing but fish broth
and bitter tea, the politics of refusing

to eat the words people put in your mouth. Where some
people come from, you need to refuse to settle
for second-hand adhesions and treaties, to know

how not to take or get taken. You need to know
how your gut will start to consume its own linings,
the science of starving yourself. Where some people

come from, you need to learn how to make a treaty
eat itself, how not to get fed more ministered
lines about claims and settlements. You need to learn

not to be told what else you need to learn, what works
or else. Where some kinds of people come from, you need
to know who shares your raw, unbroken politics.

    re Victoria Island, 11 December 2012, and Winisk, 28 July 1930

Potter's Hearing Is Not Khadr's Ruling

By Kathy Mac

Potter's "Disciplinary Hearing into Offences Committed under the Decree for the Reasonable Restriction of Underage Sorcery and the International Statute of Secrecy" (OP 127)
is not
Khadr's "Ruling on Defense Motion for Dismissal Due to Lack of Jurisdiction Under the MCA (Military Commissions Act of 2006) in Regard to Juvenile Crimes of a Child Soldier" (Brownback 2–7).

"You received an official warning from the Ministry for using illegal magic three years ago, did you not?"
   "Yes, but –"

"The defense motion states that Congress did not give the commission 'jurisdiction over juvenile crimes by child soldiers' (Paragraph 5a (1), Defense Motion)."

"And yet you conjured a Patronus on the night of the second of August?" said Fudge.
   "Yes," said Harry, "but –"

"That statement is not legally correct. Congress said nothing about jurisdiction over child soldiers."

"Knowing that you are not permitted to use magic outside school while you are under the age of seventeen?"
   "Yes, but –"

"Reading the statutory provisions together, it is clear that Congress did not, either by implication or otherwise, limit the jurisdiction of a military commission so that persons of a certain age could not be tried thereby."

"Knowing that you were in an area full of Muggles?"
"Yes, but –"

"In pertinent part, 18 USC § 5032 provides:
> A juvenile alleged to have committed an act of juvenile delinquency, other than a violation of law committed within the special maritime and territorial jurisdiction of the United States for which the maximum authorized term of imprisonment does not exceed six months, shall not be proceeded against in any court of the United States…"

"Fully aware that you were in close proximity to a Muggle at the time?"
"Yes," said Harry angrily, "but I only used it because we were…"

"The commission finds that a military commission established pursuant to the MCA is not a 'court of the United States'…"

The witch with the monocle cut across him in a booming voice.
"You produced a fully-fledged Patronus?"
"Yes," said Harry, "because –"

"The commission finds that the provisions of the Juvenile Delinquency Act are not applicable to a military commission established under the MCA."

"A corporeal Patronus?"
"A – what?" said Harry.

"The commission accepts the position of the defense that the 'use and abuse of a juvenile by al Qaeda is a violation of the law of nations.'"

"Your patronus had a clearly defined form? I mean to say, it was more than vapour or smoke?"
"Yes," said Harry, feeling both impatient and slightly desperate, "it's a stag. It's always a stag."

"The commission further accepts the general statements contained within all of the *amicus* briefs which point to many ways in which various nation states and the international community are attempting to limit the recruitment and use of child soldiers."

"Always?" boomed Madam Bones. "You have produced a Patronus before now?"
　"Yes," said Harry. "I've been doing it for over a year."
　"And you are fifteen years old?"
　"Yes, and —"

"Having accepted these matters, the commission does not find them to be germane to the issue before it."

"Impressive," said Madam Bones, staring down at him...
　"It's not a question of how impressive the magic was," said Fudge in a testy voice, "in fact, the more impressive the worse it is, I would have thought."

"The Defense Motion for Dismissal Due to Lack of Jurisdiction Under the MCA in Regard to Juvenile Crimes of a Child Soldier is denied."

Works Cited

Brownback III, Peter E. "D-022." *Ruling on Defense Motion for Dismissal Due to Lack of Jurisdiction Under the MCA in Regard to Juvenile Crimes of a Child Soldier, 30 April 2008.* Accessed July 12, 2008. Web.

Rowling, J. K. *Harry Potter and the Order of the Phoenix.* (OP) Vancouver: Raincoast, 2003. Print.

The House Which Is Not Extension but *Dispositio* Itself

from *Insecession*, by Erín Moure

an echolation of Secession, *by Chus Pato (BookThug, 2014)*

Inventio, dispositio, elocutio. So as to harness electrical impulses in the brain to communicate with one in a vegetative state, investigators ask her to imagine walking in the house for "No" or playing tennis for "Yes" and she answers our questions. Yes, Olexiy is my father's name. *Memoria. Pronunciatio.* The head, chief member of the body. Consciousness as spatiality and motor call. After the accident, Alberta nestled in the glass prism, tubes and wires, her torso and head puffed, the machine breathing outside her body, a pallor pronounced and shiny, halo and plates, painkillers in liquid penetrative form, the hole sawn then sewn with skin, through which her cortex bulges. *Alberta,* I whisper, *it's me.* There is no surface reaction but deep in her body a chemical knowledge shivers. *Alberta.* Land of aspens and her father, the lard pail lunch-bucket of her uncle and the river valley and horses. Or "organized blood." The lump in the leg looks like organized blood, the radiologist tells me; you should get an MRI. *Oh you bet I should,* I said, and did and it was not organized blood.

Converse with silence. Condition upgrade to "hopelessly conscious." EEGs show enhanced motor area activity following a request to imagine playing tennis, and activity in the parahippocampal gyrus, posterior parietal lobe and lateral premotor cortex after a request to imagine walking in the house.[1] Consciousness is awareness of language. Consciousness is language reversible and striated in the cells. A thing removed from its use and brought to its origin—the way forest intends "house." Senses—it's

---

1 Mashour, George A., Michael S. Avidan, *The Lancet* 381, no. 9863, 271–72, January 26, 2013.

now known—can be built atop other senses; touch neurons can act as sight when receiving impulses from infrared beams of light. Touch neurons use the beams of light to touch distant points, and the organism sees. Language is also a prosthetic beam of light. At a poetry reading, extra senses bloom on the participants' skulls. It is an operation of words that touch with voice-beams, enabling new sense capacities. Now, offer listeners three paired stimuli: silence vs. sound, unintelligible noises vs. intelligible speech with low semantic ambiguity, and speech with low vs. high ambiguity (poetry). Activation in the temporal lobe occurs in response to sound/silence pairs and speech/noise pairs. More widespread brain responses are obtained to ambiguous/unambiguous speech pairs. Activation is detected too in the inferior frontal lobe in response to ambiguous speech, in Broca's area and the area for management of risk. The primary auditory cortex responds to a familiar voice calling the listener's name. Higher order temporal areas activate as well. A name, voice. A familiar voice. A poetry reading. Ambiguous speech and the name of the poet = widespread cortical activation.

When awake, we can report that we are conscious.

Poetry mechanism: I report I am conscious.

Alberta's forest? It took a long time to live in the ruined body, its heterogeneous particles. Though Alberta today speaks but few vocables, words still touch her, beams of light.

Imagine yourself, I say to her, *walking through* poetry, *your new home.*

(First published *Insecession* by Erín Moure published in one volume with the Moure translation of *Secession* by Chus Pato [BookThug, 2014])

The Avian Flu

by Brad Cran

My first recollection of the threat of avian flu
was in Tucson in 2002. Some friends
told me of a woman who had dedicated her life
to saving and rehabilitating raptors.
She lived on her own with little human contact
and prophesized a major culling of the human race
through an impending pandemic of avian flu.
It was not a matter of *if*, I was told she said, *but when*.

At times this woman's lack of human contact
became so extreme she'd invented a levered machine
that pressed two mattresses tightly together
so she could stand between them and pull the lever
in an attempt to emulate physical contact.
She had invented an apparatus that would give her a hug.

By all accounts she was not a cold woman:
she built her life on empathy of birds
but for the most part, I was told,
she had given up on humans.

Our daughter Rory turned one that year
and Gillian and I threw her a party
as well as one for ourselves. In the morning
we had her daycare friends to the house
and later in the afternoon we filled
our fridge with beer and hired a mariachi band
to play a set of songs. They gave us a discount
since we agreed to have them come early
in the evening. They arrived in a station wagon

wearing giant hats and matching green
mariachi *trajes*. We lived in a predominately Chicano
neighbourhood. Because of this, the band leader
predicted that when he played his trumpet
our neighbours would almost certainly consider it
an invitation to come over for a drink. Sure enough
he blew his trumpet and that night we met
our neighbours on both sides for the first time.

That was the same fall a disgruntled Gulf War veteran
flunked out of nursing school and walked into
the examination hall during midterm exams,
and in front of the other students he executed
three of his teachers, all of whom were mothers
of young children. He had enough ammunition
to kill hundreds of students but the police happened to
be nearby and arrived immediately, so the disgruntled
veteran turned the gun on himself and committed suicide.

It was days before Halloween. For fun,
some of the students wore costumes.
The shootings took place a few buildings away
from where we taught. For the first few days
no one said much. Gillian asked a friend about it
who said she felt bad for the mothers and their families
but just a year ago she had been living in Manhattan
and personally watched thousands of people die
in the World Trade Center, so it was now hard
to make a big deal out of three deaths
no matter how tragic they were.

It was Gillian who made a big deal about it
in our department. She asked me if she should say
something and I told her it wasn't our country
and nothing would change anyway. Gillian ignored
my advice and wrote an open letter. In it, she simply said
that three women had been killed on our campus
and it was insane no one was talking about it.

The following week the department brought in counsellors
to teach us how to deal with disturbed students,

how to evaluate the risk of violence and to discuss how
the shooting had impacted teachers across the campus.
People didn't know if it was their right to grieve.
They didn't know where to place their fear.

The bombing of Iraq also began that year. Rory went
to daycare at the Jewish Community Center.
When Bush enacted the Orange Alert, the JCC hired
security to monitor the parking lot and protect the daycare.
The guards wore orange t-shirts so people would know
they were there to protect the facility against the threat
of terrorism. Red, white and blue were the colours of
patriotism but orange became the colour of fear.

Fear beat in our chests like second hearts.

Word spread through the media
that the nuclear reactor in Phoenix
could possibly be a terrorist target:
all it would take to cause a meltdown
was one jihadist with a rocket launcher.
It seems silly now, but at the time it was hard not to
imagine the ease with which a nuclear explosion
could happen within a few hundred miles of Tucson.
We vowed not to let the gas tank in the car go below half
in case we needed to race toward California
and back up to Canada to escape the nuclear fallout.

At the JCC there was always one guard in an orange shirt
outside the daycare where a large cement wall separated
the parking lot from the playground. When I asked
about this I was told it was for the children's safety.
Then I was asked, *Do you know how easy
it would be to lob a grenade over that wall?*
By looking at the wall and its proximity to
the parking lot, it was hard to dispute that
yes, it would be easy to lob a grenade over that wall.

We accepted fear into our lives
with the ease of drinking water.

That year we watched news on the war
relentlessly. We followed every nuance
of American politics. When George W. Bush
defeated John Kerry we didn't leave the house
for days on account of a type of depression
I now suppose was really an extended bout of disbelief.
Kerry's concession speech ran on a loop in my mind:
"I wish things had turned out a little differently."

As a Canadian I suppose it is hard to know
if you should believe in bullets, grenades and bombs.
I have every reason not to, even while foreign wars
rage on. The children of those women who were murdered
are now a decade older and motherless.
The avian flu hasn't culled the human population yet but
the swine flu killed a few thousand people in 2009.

I do like plenty of quiet time but I don't care too much
for being alone. I suppose we are built to adapt,
to find ways to accept what we don't want to accept;
to look for comfort in small things, if need be.
A mariachi trumpet on your daughter's first birthday,
the friends who arrive with gifts and guacamole
and later sit down to tell you the story of a woman
who lives alone, rehabilitates birds and has invented
a machine to emulate the human embrace.

Section III
[Expanding the Field]

11

Formal Protest: Reconsidering the Poetics of Canadian Pamphleteering

Andrea Hasenbank

> *Of decisive importance is the struggle both to name the oppressed and oppressors and make the new language of the left something that is spoken throughout civil society. This struggle has invariably meant a determined campaign against older idioms of resistance.*
>
> Ian McKay[1]

The formations of Canadian radicalism, now and through its historical emergence, represent a struggle for and through language. Rhetorically, the writers of 1930s Canada, dwelling on the rupturing events of economic failure, strike suppressions, police raids, show trials, and violent repression, stated and restated moments of refusal against the ruling power while appealing imaginatively to an idealized Canadian people. Refusal, as termed by historian Ian McKay, is a coming to consciousness, an active response to transformative events, those that forever shift "the perceptions of life and the language of politics."[2] Refusal is primal, giving way to a radical shift in the actor's understanding of self and society and prompting a break with old forms and old values. But refusal becomes powerful in the speaking: a new movement crawls up out of the breach in the formation of a new language that makes it intelligible. The viability of a given formation becomes tied to its conceptual system and its ability to construct and reconstruct the new radical understanding. By taking up pamphlet-writing in the process of speaking and codifying refusal, the pamphleteers of 1930s Canada aligned themselves with a deeply rooted Anglo-American tradition of popular (and print) protest. In rejecting the idioms of enlightenment and equality for the language of revolutionary struggle, their texts entered into contested critical ground. The recuperation of this vital form of Canadian writing and political engagement—like that of other modern pamphleteers—requires a shift in its valuation. What has been dismissed as mere propaganda must now be reconsidered in terms of style and strategy.

The resurgence of the pamphlet form in the 1930s within the legal climate of censorship and silence engendered by Section 98 of the Criminal Code of Canada suggests that threatened writers and organizers resorted to the pamphlet to reroute literary response into avenues of praxis. Bart Vautour notes the very limited body of Canadian poetry responding to Section 98; instead, he looks to theatrical traditions to explore the emergence of a new discourse of resistance.[3] Pamphlets, often produced by writers active in both literary and political fields and drawing on complex systems of symbol and address, represent another alternative form of linguistic resistance. I focus their refusal on the emergent shift within a self-conscious poetics, which deliberately structured a new economy of language that reordered literary, political, and legal subjectivity.

The sneering criticism of modern pamphlets rests primarily with George Orwell. As the foremost observer of political language throughout the 1930s and into the Cold War era, Orwell remains a touchstone for the Left in general, as well as a specific reference point for those engaged in critiques of and resistance to state power and control. As a collector of British pamphlets spanning the time of the Diggers to that of the French Revolution, he defined the field of study with a focus on materiality as well as formal structure.[4] His taxonomy is regularly taken up in discussions of pamphleteering, most of which are straight, technologically driven histories of the format as it emerged in parallel with a liberal Anglo-American public life.[5] This narrative, which tends to end at the Age of Enlightenment, leaves the pamphlet form frozen in time. Reflecting on the material surrounding him in wartime London, Orwell found the pamphlets of his own age to be largely inanimate; they flourished in number, he surmised, but had lost their literary vigour.[6]

Orwell's analysis is framed as a rhetorical one, in which the pamphlet's mode of argument "falls" from the imaginative language of public speech to a factional and forensic language; however, his targeting of the "'party line' (any party)"[7] indicates that his criticism of pamphlets in the 1930s and 1940s is made on the grounds of both politics and poetics. This falls under the same precepts by which pamphleteering is treated as a historical form connected to the rise of a liberal public sphere, rather than one responsive to its own reality. The abstract public presupposed by the pamphleteering idealized by Orwell clashes with the materiality of the print object, the conditions of its production and circulation, the climate of its reception, and its ongoing survival. The continued value of pamphleteering can be discovered by following Michael Warner in positing a public beyond the "public sphere," in which the meaning and use of the text are in the hands of an attentive readership for whom self-identification with a rhetorical address is itself a meaningful act. The poetics of the pamphlet form invite an active, politicized version of the reader into the text merely as a prelude to real-world action, as part of a party or otherwise; in this way, the pamphlet participates in its own elision. However, the construction of this conduit to collective action in literary terms is deftly strategic. To recuperate the position of 1930s Canadian pamphlets from their peripheral status and from their association with Orwell's debased party diatribes, we must locate them in a particular context: we must historicize the critique as well as the object of criticism.

A cluster of pamphlets released by the Canadian Labour Defense League (CLDL) in the early 1930s ("Not Guilty!" [1932], "An Indictment of Capitalism" [1932], "Workers' Self-Defense in the Courts" [1933], and "The 'Sedition' of A.E. Smith" [1934]) exemplify the "rubbish"[8] dismissed by Orwell in their connection to Communist Party politics and their deployment of both agitprop techniques and forensic discourse. These characteristics, I would argue, are not symptoms of debasement, but are definitive of Canadian pamphleteering in this period as it works poetically to reorient legal and political subjectivity. The chosen discourse of this set of pamphlets is, in the first place, related to the circumstances of their production. Second, it is purposive, strategically employing the language of the law to build a public and mount a mass protest against legal repression by the state, using Section 98 of the Criminal Code as a central rallying point and positioning the CLDL itself as a core organizer of the revolutionary Left. Finally, it is stylistic, symbolically reversing the power structures of the law and the courts to re-create the courtroom, once the scene of a public authority inaccessible to the working class, as a theatre of protest. These texts work by seizing the pamphlet form to radically alter the meaning of public speech; a proper reconsideration of their worth should accordingly take place on formal grounds.

Seizing Political Ground

The CLDL first appears in the print record in 1927—the same year that Section 98 was officially appended to the Criminal Code—with the publication of its constitution, as noted by bibliographer Peter Weinrich.[9] The organization remained relatively quiet until 1929, when it was taken under the auspices of the Communist Party and began a more direct recruitment campaign, as indicated by the pamphlet "Why There Should Be a Defense League in Canada and Why You Should Join It."[10] Indeed, the declared purpose of the CLDL was to unite a collective membership "for the defense and support of the agricultural workers, regardless of their political and industrial affiliations, race, colour, or nationality, who were persecuted on account of their activity in class interests of the industrial and agricultural workers."[11] The CLDL dramatically increased the number of its publications through the first half of the 1930s, as arrests and prosecutions of Communist Party associates as well as the number of striking and protesting workers jumped under Section 98.[12] Historian Jaroslav Petryshyn notes that between 1931 and 1933, the CLDL distributed five million pieces of literature, pamphlets, and manifestos (211).[13] Following the 1936 repeal of Section 98, the CLDL declined in membership as the CPC was restored to lawful status and moved towards a new focus on Popular Front strategizing.[14] Except for a single wartime pamphlet against the War Measures Act, the CLDL ceased to publish after 1936.[15] Although Petryshyn acknowledges that the CLDL was the Communist Party of Canada's (CPC) "most successful 'front' organization,"[16] whose print tactics reached a "sophisticated level of operation,"[17] it is clear that the existence and work of the league was tied directly to the political and legal challenges to Section 98, reaching its apex of influence in relation to the trial and subsequent public debates of the eight Communist leaders arrested as members of an unlawful association in August 1931.

I have chosen to treat two texts with named authors—Tim Buck's "An Indictment of Capitalism" and Oscar Ryan's "The 'Sedition' of A.E. Smith"—as part of the same group due to the two men's close associations with the league. As leader of the CPC, Buck was *de facto* director of the CLDL; Ryan was its publicity director and took its chief organizer for his titular subject. Both pamphlets were published by the CLDL and were distributed through the same networks; certainly, they were included in the organization's figures. Significantly, the two "authored" pamphlets reflect the same polyvocal assemblage structure as "Not Guilty!" and "Workers' Self-Defense," eschewing first-person argumentation, and may reasonably be considered on the same terms as collective works. Certainly, the "authors" in no way resemble Orwell's Enlightenment pamphleteers.

It is difficult to date this cluster of CLDL pamphlets, making their order of publication uncertain. None of the texts examined here bear a publication date, so we must infer an order of publication from internal and paratextual evidence, such as references to specific events, trials, and citations for republished articles within the pamphlets. Libraries and even bibliographers often date the pamphlets earlier or later than their actual release, in this way shifting their discursive relations with one another. For example, "Workers' Self-Defense in the Courts" is listed as 1930 in the University of Alberta Library catalogue, which would set it before Section 98 was effectively used to target working-class organization, while Weinrich lists it as 1934,[18] which would set it after Tim Buck's second trial and alongside A.E. Smith's sedition case. Based on its contents, this pamphlet can be more accurately dated to around April 1933, after Annie Buller's second trial on 9 March 1933 (recapped in the text)[19] but before the trial of the Kingston Penitentiary rioters in June–July 1933, as evidenced by the comment that "Mr. Sampson knows very well that Tim Buck's case regarding that 'riot' has not come to trial yet."[20] The absence of date information is not an oversight: the CLDL and other radical organizations left out or manipulated dates in their pamphlets as a political strategy. That is, a publication without a date does not appear to be out of date and so can continue to seem timely and to keep major events (especially the trial of the Eight) current in the eyes of readers. Ordinarily, establishing a timeline might offer a sense of exchange, even if that exchange is being imposed retroactively. However, the presumption that pamphleteers participate in a displaced print conversation is bound to bourgeois figurations of the public sphere. Given the desire of the involved organizations to take control of language, this cluster of pamphlets may in fact represent more of a monologue, or a one-way broadcast.

Building a Proletarian Public
Taken together, the pamphlets discussed here represent a developing strategy of agitation and propaganda deployed by the CLDL in the language of the law. These texts reveal a tension between the education and mobilization functions of agitprop, which can be located along a poetic axis.[21] Agitprop, which remakes past and current values into the enemies of the future, operates by invoking a collective imagination. In revolutionary terms, pamphlet readers should spontaneously achieve proletarian consciousness through the text, thus positioning themselves to heed its call to action. In practical terms, pamphleteers must first enact the potential of revolution, making it intelligible to the masses by recasting the received historical narrative in the language of protest. The CLDL, for all its Communist-inflected rhetoric,

had as its primary aim the repeal of Section 98 of the Criminal Code in order to defuse the state's principal legal weapon against working-class organization. To mobilize support on a mass scale, and on class-based terms, a resistant public must be constituted. To that end, first, the pamphlets emphasize that they are chronicling injustice; second, they work to familiarize readers with the language of the law, which is identified with public power; third, they cede the authority of public speech to the readers so that ultimately, the readers become actors speaking back to the law, or to the state, with a collective voice. By setting out the actions involved in constituting a proletarian public as a series of "steps," I do not mean to suggest that this is a strictly linear process. The functions of these pamphlets overlap and often repeat rhetorical moves and tread on one another's propagandistic ground. Considering the various ways in which the texts are oriented towards the ultimate goal of legal protest is valuable for thinking through the poetic strategies that a particular text might apply when addressing a heterogeneous public of uneven attentiveness, disparate literacies, and unequal readiness to engage with the pamphlet's political discourse.

The first stage of the CLDL's print strategy is to make the public, as Orwell puts it, "pamphlet-conscious."[22] Although "The 'Sedition' of A.E. Smith" is chronologically the final pamphlet in this cluster, it typifies the role of publicity in building a public. Rather than focusing on the trial and defence of Smith, the league's leader, who was charged with sedition in January 1934 after publically accusing the prime minister of giving "the order to shoot Buck in his cell in cold blood with intent to murder him,"[23] the pamphlet places Smith's case among thirteen others handled by the CLDL. In less than twenty pages, and in short, telegraphic sentences forming accounts that are often fragmentary, the pamphlet recounts a decade of conflict. The assumption seems to be that the reader can fill in the gaps. Certainly, each of the major events—the 1925 Drumheller mining strike, the 1929 protest and shootings at Estevan, the 1931 arrest and trial of the eight communist leaders, the 1932 Kingston riot and its subsequent trial, the 1933 eviction and killing of Nick Zynchuk, the 1934 crackdown on the play *Eight Men Speak,* the 1934 sedition trial of A.E. Smith, and countless deportation orders—was detailed in the pages of prior CLDL pamphlets as well as in countless newspaper editorials, public addresses, stories, songs, poems, and plays. "The 'Sedition' of A.E. Smith" presents a catalogue of offences, which are connected intertextually to the wealth of CLDL print that precedes it. Although there is some generic variation, including highly fanciful biographies of Smith and Bennett running in parallel[24] and an allegorical conceit linking "Iron Heel" Bennett to Achilles with his fatal flaw,[25] the pamphlet overwhelmingly adopts an elliptical form. None of this material is revelatory; rather, it is a retread of well-known history in the guise of marshalling evidence in opposition to the charges laid against Smith.

The second stage of building a protest lies in making the public legally conscious and familiar with the language of the law, the courts, and civil rights. "Workers' Self-Defense in the Courts" serves as both a polemic and an instructional booklet as it walks readers—presumed to be either facing trial for protest activities, or likely to be arrested in the near future for the offence of being working class—through the Canadian legal process with imperative specificity. This is the only text in this cluster to include a table of contents, which suggests that it was intended for use as reference material. Each stage of the law, from arrest to appeal to possible deportation, is set out in highly adversarial terms and prepares the reader for a defence and interrogation on the scale of *R. v. Buck*. After this, and comprising nearly half of the pamphlet, "Workers' Self-Defense in the Courts" describes the defence of Annie Buller, an organizer tried in 1931 for her role in the fatal Estevan miners' protest.[26] Petryshyn singles out Buller's case as exemplifying the strategic connection between the CPC's revolutionary politics and the CLDL's legal campaigning: "Annie Buller and the Estevan trials personified the League's double-edged role in the thirties. Its 'defender role' was an integral component of the communists' 'agitator-instigator' role. One fed on the other. Taken *in toto*, it represented part of the C.P.C.'s overall strategy for 'revolution' in Canada."[27] Buller's account, which is organized by procedural subheadings, follows every instruction laid out in the first half of the pamphlet and can be read as an extended object lesson in workers' legal self-defence.

Once the discourse and structures of the law have been made intelligible to working-class readers, the pamphlets reverse the power relationships of existing public space within their texts, giving workers a claim to a public voice. Even as it empowers its readers to operate among them, "Workers' Self-Defense in the Courts" interrogates both the authority and the truth-claims of the courts, judges, and legal representatives. The text emphasizes the falseness of the court's "objectivity" and states that "workers should not be deceived by the veneer of 'justice.'"[28] In particular, the pamphlet addresses the soft forms of power codified apart from the law itself—the rituals of court procedure, access to legal resources, and the formal etiquette of dress and custom are methods of denying access to justice and suppressing challenges to existing power just as much as is targeted prosecution under Section 98. The law criminalizes working-class organization and assembly, both physical and imaginative; the court then stamps out subversion by denying workers entry into the public sphere, as represented by linguistic exchange: "The 'dignity' and 'sanctity' of the courts are a means of paralyzing workers' struggles against capitalist institutions. Court language, pomp and ceremony are purposely complicated in order to confuse workers."[29] "An Indictment of Capitalism" takes this critique of exclusionary language and inverts it, ceding the power of definition to the workers. Tim Buck's failed self-defence in the courtroom is re-created as a textual performance, represented as an attempt to teach the "foreign language" of revolution first to the jury, then to the working class at large.[30] As it prepares them for this hitherto closed world, "Workers' Self-Defense in the Courts" encourages workers to represent themselves from an ideological (as well as practical) standpoint: "workers' self-defense plays an important role in exposing the nature of capitalist justice and in bringing out the class implications of the trial before the working class at large."[31] The raising of working-class voices in the courtroom transforms that space into a site of revolutionary uprising, symbolically captured in the cover image of the pamphlet, which shows the giant body of a worker, dressed in ordinary clothes and with clenched fist, rising up in the courtroom and towering over the judge and jury. Rhetorically, this movement to "occupy" is replicated in the abstract public sphere through radical pamphlets like the CLDL cluster. The texts posit a reinscribing of public space and a rewriting of the institutional narrative of power through a new understanding of individual and class potential in legal and poetic terms. This amounts to a reframing of defence as counterpower: if Section 98 can be deployed strategically by the state, then the courts can be seized in a strategic protest by criminalized workers.

Ultimately, the pamphlets address themselves to a politicized public, representing individual experiences before the law as a collective class experience. In pursuit of this strategic aim, the texts employ heavy symbolism and direct modes of address in an increasingly revolutionary stylizing of language. In the CLDL pamphlets, all cases are class action suits. The accused, real or imagined, is always only a witness to an ongoing moral crime, with the court always standing in for capital as a whole: "You are not speaking for yourself alone, but as a representative of your class."[32] Furthermore, this strategy encompasses a silent majority, whose entrance into the court to view the trial aligns them with the accused as additional metaphorical witnesses. The speech of one worker presenting his or her defence thus permits the entrance of other "voices," metonymically connected to the real bodies of workers in the gallery, whose visible mass support turns the courtroom into a scene of mass protest.[33] This class-based reclaiming of public speech is not so much a labouring of cultural language (as in Michael Denning's well-phrased observation)[34] as it is a lawyering of the language of protest.

Speaking a Revolutionary Language

Orwell's critique of modern pamphlets can be read as a desire to preserve public speech from unprecedented and unpredictable uses on the lips of radicals, or from demagogic abuses by totalitarian forces. His is a conservative view, bolstered by what is at core an appeal to the principles of classical rhetoric.[35] Implicitly, Orwell is claiming that the pamphlet is a deliberative genre, properly belonging to the political and the public. It is an incantatory form of writing, invoking a vision of the future in order to persuade its audience in favour of a given course of action. Public speech, in this realm, must make an ethical appeal—the speaker makes a claim for that which is good and tries to persuade his audience to rally behind his path to that good. The so-valued quality of literariness comes in the linguistic gymnastics of exhortation and dehortation: compelling imagery, selective narration, and powerful invective, given moral weight by the argument's ends. The pamphlet, in this sense, is dominated by a singular authorial voice with a personal stake in his words—the rational individual. For Orwell, then, "good" pamphlet writing embraces a literary ethos as a means to asserting the self into society.

The importance of poetics to polemic is emphasized here in the critique of its absence. Orwell explicitly derides pamphlets that take up a forensic approach, that replace the "exuberance of argument" with fact, procedure, and logic.[36] This rhetorical shift is presented as a fall in style. For Orwell, such texts are dry and technocratic rather than rich and imaginative: "A modern political hack, boosting some doubtful cause, would be very unlikely to show the same humour and ingenuity, because he could never allow his imagination to range so freely. Party orthodoxy would not only take all the colour out of his vocabulary, but would dictate the main lines of his argument in advance."[37]

Orwell's criticism misrecognizes the purpose and position of the modern pamphlet. His valuation of public speech is particularly tied to the liberal order as it is manifested in the public sphere of print-capitalism. Canadian pamphleteers of the 1930s were working within an idiom distinctly different from that of the Enlightenment writers of the seventeenth and eighteenth centuries. They were speaking back to the failure of liberal individualism; they were speaking from a place of exclusion but did not see the existing public sphere as a good to be attained. Through a reading of Marx—an analytical path trodden again and again in the writings of Buck and other Canadian leftists—reason was put into action by delineating process as an argument in itself. The narrative of class struggle was set out as historical truth, beyond the realm of argument. This line from the past was used to indict the injustices of the present.

There is historical precedent for questions of law and order being treated in popular forms of text: early pamphlets often featured the "confessions" of infamous criminals or recorded fabricated speeches from the dockets of public executions.[38] The outlaw folk hero of old, however, did not fit into the narrative of refusal; he could be celebrated symbolically, but he could not be made to work schematically and politically. We have seen how, in this cluster of texts produced by the CLDL, 1930s Canadian pamphleteers take up the forensic approach in response to a climate of pervasive, systematic injustice, matching their strategy to its target. These writers marshal facts not for lack of imagination but to press a logic of history in accusation of the capitalist system and in defence of the workers hung high by that system. The textual account is a means to politicize the event, to turn the experience of one single accused into a conscious collective experience. Indeed, the nebulous sense of time within the CLDL pamphlets transposes synchronic and diachronic ordering of the class narrative to emphasize the totality of class conflict: specific events are not just symbolically held up as rallying points for protest; they are also the repetition of an always ongoing refrain of oppression. The set of events recounted in this cluster of pamphlets effectively collapse into a single overwhelming account of class injustice. The old pamphleteers, with their solitary impassioned voices, could not convey the accusations of an entire class. Such a voice must be roared by thousands. In these texts, the individual citizen and subject becomes a self-aware multitude; the pamphlet is rewritten as mass recitation.

The focus of the CLDL pamphlets on claiming public speech connects to Lenin's insistence that agitation operates primarily by means of the spoken word. Indeed, the texts take on their agitprop function in increasingly theatrical terms. Mass recitation represents an attempt to forge a legitimately revolutionary mode of language, particularly one capable of conveying an ideological unity of subject and form. Michael Gold is often credited with introducing mass recitation to North American writing with the 1926 publication of "Strike! A Mass Recitation" in *New Masses*, while Toby Gordon Ryan makes a claim for bringing it to Canada following her encounter with the agitprop troupe Prolet-Bühne in 1931.[39] In Gold's estimation, mass recitation was "one of the most powerful and original forms developed in the struggle for proletarian culture" because of its collectivity and its accessibility to the lives of workers as a group: "It is proletarian; because only revolutionary themes are tense and effective enough to be used; and because only proletarians can deliver a mass recitation: professional actors would seem silly in one."[40] Mass recitation is a performative act that blends terse, rhythmic speech with tightly stylized and choreographed gestures, effective in its multiplication among the bodies of worker-actors; in this it replicates the cadence of the protest march and something of its ominous rumble. Within the minimalist sets of agitprop theatre, mass recitation allows for exaggeration of spoken lines and maximum projection on stage. Modern pamphleteering, read through the CLDL cluster, deploys the same heavy bluntness of language to project its revolutionary aim with maximum force.

The reliance of the pamphlets' form of address on a closed set of stylistic tropes further aligns them with the techniques of agitprop, typified in the language of "Not Guilty!" (1931). Numbers dominate Oscar Ryan's introduction: the Kingston Eight are likened to the Scottsboro Eight, the Haymarket Seven, and the Twenty-Six Soviet Commissars. Victims and heroes are replaced by interchangeable figures, which serve as a means of collective identification, as well as a warning: "Tomorrow it may be another group of eight communists, or a group of eighteen, or of eighty, or even of eight hundred."[41] As the numbers increase, the referent is dropped to increase the power of the text's repetition and the escalating scale of the envisioned threat. Indeed, the term "communists" slips into "workers" to bring the implied working-class reader closer to the Kingston Eight. The eight men stand in for the wider party–audience–proletarian public (the distinction is erased) as leaders; in an image of sacrifice, they "have been selected because they represent the suffering, the desires, the organized action and the hopes of these masses" (5). Not much is left implicit. The text focuses on "representative" characteristics of the Eight; baldly, in their diverse ethnic backgrounds and appropriate occupations, "this group of eight workers is symbolic of the Canadian working class."[42]

The middle section of "Not Guilty!" mirrors the Eight by constructing its central conceit: the "Workers' Jury," an equally representative body tethered to real people only by the slightest bonds. For A.E. Smith, the actual jurors selected for the trial of the Communist leaders proved to be a disappointment, if not wholly antagonistic: "There was not a man on the jury who had any knowledge of what the left-wing labor movement was in Canada. There was not a man who had any idea as to the forces of change that were at work in human society. [They were] ignorant as children."[43] Prior to the trial, a CLDL publicity campaign included selecting a parallel "Workers' Jury": two miners, a lumberjack, a machinist, an auto mechanic, a printer, a carpenter, an ordinary labourer, a (female) laundry worker, a farmer, and an unemployed worker.[44] The workers were instructed to enter the courtroom and hear the evidence; their verdict after the trial was published in "Not Guilty!" By imagining an alternative courtroom scene, and by offering surrogate observers, the text invites the readership into the trial in a way denied to them by the actual event. The re-visioning of the law, first in image and then in substance, takes up the language of mirroring as well: "The Workers' Jury is convinced that this trial is a true reflection of the justice of the working class—the capitalist class,"[45] which is of course a distorted reflection, according to the reality of the workers' account. The verdict of the Workers' Jury is entirely separate from the law under which the accused are charged; it is a verdict based on moral actions and civil rights rather than on fact and argument. This is not to say that the pamphlet avoids forensic language—indeed, it is dominated by that language in the section recounting Buck's speech in his own defence (which *does* address the law directly by setting out the openness of the CPC activities) and in the "demagogic appeal" of the prosecution; both disrupt the account of the Workers' Jury.[46] The section reprinting F.R. Scott's close legal analysis of Section 98's restrictions further emphasizes the technical frame of the pamphlet;[47] the name "F.R. Scott" is equally a marker of the poetic impulse's sublimation to the pamphlet form. Vautour has examined Scott's poetic satire on the social conditions of the 1930s,[48] noting how his role as a jurist rather than a poet dominated his analysis and reponse to Section 98.[49] Indeed, the conceit of the Workers' Jury interrogates the law without engaging with it: it treats Section 98 as the symbol of a distant and repressive force and not as a real and material limit on personal action. This rhetorical image is punctuated at the end of the page with Avrom Yanofsky's actual illustration of a tank bearing the number 98.[50]

The stylization of the pamphlet's language here exceeds that of a symbolic system. The pamphlets in the CLDL cluster are striking for how they hew close to agitprop and for the prevalence in them of metonymic rather than metaphoric structures. For example, the gibbet, the rack, and the electric chair as referenced in "Not Guilty!"[51] offer far more concrete stand-ins for the concept of state repression than a reference to Prime Minister Bennett's iron heel (which is given an origin story in "The 'Sedition' of A.E. Smith").[52] However, they also further distance the relationship between the text and its real-world referent. Indeed, the "ritualistic" feel of heavily symbolic and stylized performances, as identified by leftist critic Candida Rifkind, encapsulates agitprop texts, even when they are written for specific, local conditions.[53] In taking up the form of the mass recitation, these pamphlets follow an avant-garde alignment of moving from realistic to symbolic representations, a line that leads from the CLDL directly to *Eight Men Speak*. Indeed, this cluster of texts repeatedly returns to the courtroom scene, successively reworking Tim Buck's speech, which becomes increasingly dramatic in form, from the block quotation in "Not Guilty!," to the script-style exchange between Buck and Justice Wright in "An Indictment of Capitalism," to the staged scenes of the play.

Caught between the pamphlet tradition and the ultramodern possibilities of agitprop technique, this cluster of pamphlets raises the question of what is at stake in claiming and using a particular form. How can such usage both recognize and subvert formal conventions? Simply taking up an older form and re-creating it is homage at best, and blandly derivative at worst. When formalism is reinvented with irreverence, or even contempt, the disjuncture between form and unanticipated content opens up a discursive space for parody and satire (or, depending on interpretation, scurrilous flippancy). By selecting a particular form, with full awareness of its signification and its limitations, a writer positions him or herself in relationship to the historicity of that form. Formal convention thereby represents a poetic tension between containment and excess that can be generative for those writers who engage with it, whether or not they wish to align themselves with their predecessors. Rifkind, commenting on the challenge of emergent cultural formations in this period, asserts that "one of the most pressing struggles for leftist writers in the 1930s was to dislodge private, atemporal, and disinterested literary forms from their positions of relative dominance and find a place in both English-Canadian literature and socialist politics for public texts that document immediate experiences and are interested in the conditions of their circulation."[54] Effective subversion is predicated on the knowledge of what is being upended. Like its sibling, the manifesto, the pamphlet form works by the seizure and rewriting of historical narrative. In terms of building a movement and forging a public, the restoration of poetic justice can be treated as an actual blow against the injustice of social reality. Aristotle anticipated the revolutionary imagination by acknowledging that "for the purposes of poetry, a convincing impossibility is preferable to an unconvincing possibility."[55] Although a truly radical gesture would be to refuse existing public speech altogether, a revolution must first make its own revolutionaries. On the pages of these pamphlets, deliberately recounting past injustice in a public forum is the first move towards imagining—and raising—an entirely new seat of judgment.

Evaluating a Poetic Legacy

The pamphlets under consideration here rarely merit entry into the records of the Canadian Left; certainly they have never been included among its literary achievements. In part, this is because they deploy their revolutionary language with excessive zeal; when the radical potential of the 1930s did not sustain a reinvention of Canadian society, these potent reminders of revolutionary failure were swept aside. Beneath the veneer of agitprop, however, these texts continue to bear witness to the moment of their production: the party that was, the organization that campaigned, the slogans that circulated, the fears that once pervaded everyday life. They offer material clues to aid us in reconstructing a lost world. The poetic legacy of the pamphlets of the 1930s is a speculative one, which is perhaps appropriate in its reversal of the pamphlets' rhetorical trajectory. Rather than telescoping outward, from immediate experience into the expansive possibility of the future, examining these texts takes us deeply and minutely into historical reality and the historicity of the pamphlet form.

The political value of the CLDL pamphlets is difficult to evaluate, particularly when we measure their success against their texts' own strategic aims. Certainly, Section 98 was repealed in the years following these publications, the law's political costs finally having outstripped its returns amid public disapproval. That Section 98 was able to stand as a galvanizing issue during the first half of the decade was due to the continued attention of an informed public and the pressure it was able to exert on elected representatives. This is not the establishment of a Workers' Tribunal, but it is an indicator of the cumulative currency of such pamphlets, and hundreds more like them. In organizational terms, these pamphlets certainly detail the activities of the CLDL, while suggesting the salient points of intersection with the Communist Party, in Canada and internationally, although they cannot be taken as a wholly reliable record. Notwithstanding the ideological and strategic connection between the CLDL and the Communist Party, it would be a mistake to treat either organization as a monolith. Orwell's criticism of "party literature" has its roots in a fear of totalitarianism. His evaluation of pamphlets, liberal and radical, dates from 1948, expanding on his more cursory 1943 survey of contemporary materials. Orwell's repudiation of party politics, and his excoriation of the Left in the wake of Stalin's brutal dictatorship, strongly inflects his formal meditations. Ian Angus and Ian McKay have both written in great detail about the schisms between the increasingly Stalinist Central Committee of the CPC and its Trotskyite Left Opposition. Indeed, many characteristics of these pamphlets—including named authors, selected reprints, and recurring phrases floating from the writings of one faction to those of the other—speak to an appeal for unity within the party itself as much as to a broader call to action. Angus remains unconvinced even on the importance of the trial of the Eight, which remained at the centre of nearly all CLDL pamphlets from 1931 until its demise. He argues that an effective civil liberties case would have been a significant victory; however,

> the Communist Party utterly failed to organize such a campaign. Its defence in the courtroom was lacklustre; its defence outside of

the courtroom was self-defeating...This was all charade. No-one—certainly not the RCMP—was fooled by the play-acting. Instead of fighting for legality, instead of denying the government's right to drive it underground, the CPC was using its formal illegality to prove its right to the label revolutionary.[56]

Instead of defending its position within the public sphere, the CPC opted out as a gesture of refusal. This move, however, undercut its legally oriented agitprop strategy. Petryshyn echoes this assessment, calling the verdict of the Workers' Jury an "empty gesture."[57]

The single-minded dominance of the class narrative can be taken up as a critical issue as well. For example, opportunities in the pamphlets for a feminist critique seem clear, especially in the account of Annie Buller's speech in her own defence ("Workers' Self-Defense" 19–35) and in the inclusion of a female worker in commentary on the trial of the Eight. But those opportunities are not pursued within the texts. Indeed, the "laundress" selected for participation on the Workers' Jury is noted by Petryshyn[58] and depicted in an image by Avrom Yanofsky accompanying the text of the verdict,[59] but the fact of her presence is not mentioned in the CLDL literature itself. Women were not permitted on Canadian juries until after 1952, and married women were not allowed to serve until 1964.[60] The inclusion of a woman as one among other workers is very forward-looking; this is a lost opportunity to expound on a radical gesture, albeit one based on gender rather than class. Buller's specific role as a female mining union organizer also passes unremarked, as does the opportunity to address the treatment of female prisoners within the legal system. In some ways, this could be read as a signal of equal treatment (i.e., gender is so irrelevant to ability or action that it passes beneath notice), but I remain unconvinced. Even in revolutionary texts, the feminist line is subordinate, in much the same way that Florence Custance's role in the CLDL is effaced by Smith's, and in the way that the contributions of women like Jim Watts or Toby Gordon Ryan in the early stages of the Progressive Arts Club and the staging of *Eight Men Speak* were displaced by the top-down authority of Oscar Ryan and Ed Cecil-Smith as CPC functionaries. There remains a problem with the politicized narratives of this time, when "public" still means "male."

In terms of stylistic "success," some inconsistency remains between rhetoric and form in the pamphlet text. I remain uncertain about how to reconcile a stylized, symbolic approach to language with the appeal to ultra-realism made by structuring arguments forensically, other than to identify agitprop as an inherently unstable form as it oscillates between these two stylistic poles. Most significantly, the material structure of the pamphlet as an assemblage of texts disrupts the focus of the text's rhetorical message with its formal fragmentation. By gathering multiple signed and unsigned texts in a range of genres and creative forms within the pamphlet's frame, the production of these pamphlets reinforces their polyvocality, but this detracts from the focused strategy and ideological unity of agit-prop. "Not Guilty!" strongly exemplifies this characteristic of assemblage, although all of the pamphlets show elements of it in their supplementary illustrations, didactic content, notes, and prefaces. Some of this additional material is indicative of the need to properly situate and polish a given narrative for propaganda purposes. For example, in "An Indictment of Capitalism" and in subsequent accounts of Tim Buck's defence speech, a failed courtroom performance is re-created as a textual performance, several times over. The Introductions, Prefaces, and Comments are all supplementary to the address and in fact are longer than the speech itself. This text shows a need by the CPC, in the person of Buck himself, to restate its ideological commitments and reframe its arguments in order to wrest control of the trial narrative back from the official record. However, the pamphlets in this cluster also show a resistance to ceding that control to a single voice, even that of the party leader; the formal assemblage appends a Greek chorus of commentary and interpreters to Buck's narrative. Even the closest model of Orwell's single pamphleteer is reincorporated into a collective production. The sheer amount of gloss and explanation attached to the revolutionary narrative suggests an anxiety with the message, or with the audience. The texts have a somewhat uneasy relationship with the mass and its ability to rise into class consciousness or to act appropriately as class warriors. Perhaps this mistrust is what underlies Orwell's dissatisfaction with modern pamphlets: they aim not just to convince but also to direct their readers. Ultimately, by displaying the conditions of its production so openly, the assembled modern pamphlet remains extremely relevant to the print historian's meditations on human and material networks of print—particularly the systems of signification and referentiality located within its intertextual and paratextual elements, as well as the collaborative and social character of the labour of print production. Every print object is in fact an assemblage; the pamphlets of the 1930s are just more brazen about it.

In the 1930s, as Orwell tells us, indeed "the pamphlet survives, it even fluorishes," and, yes, "something has happened to it."[61] The rhetorical strategy of modern pamphleteers shows a distinct break with the past. In this shift, the literary qualities of the pamphlet have migrated as poetic resistance flows into it. Orwell's call for a rerecognition of the pamphlet as a literary genre has a kernel of radical possibility, with its plea for imaginative writing over bare diatribe. By reading poetics into the strategic deployment of language into these texts, and into the form of the pamphlet as a whole, we can reframe Orwell's discomfort with the pamphlets of the 1930s as the opening for a radical critical gesture. As an assemblage representing a collective mode of speech, the pamphlet is perhaps a better voice for radical class refusal than more traditional poetic genres. As a material object, the pamphlet represents a network of social relations that is always already public; rhetorically, the pamphlet occupies public space and enacts a narrative that far exceeds the work of a single individual; poetically, the pamphlet's mode of address imagines a vast public on the verge of taking up a new collective subjectivity and being remade. Warner articulates the revolutionary transformation unleashed in the transition from a public sphere occupied by individual subjects to an open public: "The peculiar dynamic of postulation and address by which public speech projects the social worlds has mainly been understood as ideology, domination, exclusion... The projection of a public is a new, creative, and distinctively modern mode of power."[62] In Warner's terms, the pamphlet's potential and its enduring power both lie in the way it continues to construct and invoke new publics. What makes modern pamphleteers so compelling is this move from rhetoric to poetics—leaving behind the world of cold political argument to step into the widening vista of possibility. The moment of refusal so constituted is equally a moment of creation.

By reconsidering pamphlets in the modern era as constituted by poetics as much as by politics, I am invested in how a sense of belonging can be invoked through structures of feeling, and of how a class can be constituted imaginatively long before it begins to act materially. The assertion of a public is a radical gesture, a refusal of existing forms and relationships in favour of those netted from language alone and held together only by possibility. Indeed, the revolutionary vision of the "poetic world" suggested by Canadian pamphleteers continues to fascinate as an image unrealized in its own historical moment, but not yet unrecognizable to our own.

Notes

1 McKay, *Rebels, Reds, Radicals*, 109.
2 McKay, *Rebels, Reds, Radicals*, 96.
3 Vautour, "Writing Left," 122.
4 Orwell, Introduction to *British Pamphleteers*, 7. Orwell's functional definition of the pamphlet as a *form* rather than a strict genre is often cited, and especially facilitates a book history approach to pamphlet production: "A pamphlet is a short piece of polemical writing, printed in the form of a booklet and aimed at a large public... It is written because there is something that

one wants to say now, and because one believes there is no other way of getting a hearing."
5 See, for example, Raymond, *Pamphlets and Pamphleteering*; Halasz, *The Marketplace of Print*; and Warner, *The Letters of the Republic*. Recent work in media studies, typified by Moe, "Everyone a pamphleteer?," incorporates blogging and Web-based communication into the traditional narrative without questioning the construction of the pamphlet form.
6 Orwell, "Pamphlet Literature," 23.
7 Orwell, "Pamphlet Literature," 23.
8 Orwell, "Pamphlet Literature," 23.
9 Weinrich, *Social Protest*, 104. Weinrich notes the variable spelling of the organization's name, which is given inconsistently by historians and in memoirs of the 1930s Canadian Left. In deference to the CLDL's own print material, I will use the spelling "labor" when referring to the organization by name or when quoting CLDL pamphlets, while using "labour" elsewhere.
10 Weinrich, *Social Protest*, 109.
11 Canadian Labor Defense League, "Constitution," Article 2.
12 See Weinrich, *Social Protest*, 113–43.
13 Petryshyn, "A.E. Smith," 211. Petryshyn bases his publication numbers on figures from a CLDL convention report in 1933, which may be inflated.
14 Petryshyn, "A.E. Smith," 248–49.
15 Weinrich, *Social Protest*, 151–52.
16 Petryshyn, "A.E. Smith," 88.
17 Petryshyn, "A.E. Smith," 214.
18 Weinrich, *Social Protest*, 135.
19 For an account of Buller's activity, see Watson, *She Never Was Afraid*, reposted on Ian Angus's *Socialist History Project* website.
20 Canadian Labor Defense League, "Workers' Self-Defense in the Courts," 34.
21 I am here using "agitprop" more or less in the sense taken up by Lenin. In *What Is to Be Done?*, he quotes and approves the formulation of Aleksandr Martynov (who later turned against him): "By *propaganda* we would understand the revolutionary explanation of the present social system, entire or in its partial manifestations, whether that be done in a form intelligible to individuals or to broad masses. By *agitation*, in the strict sense of the word, we would understand the call upon the masses to undertake definite, concrete actions and the promotion of the direct revolutionary intervention of the proletariat in social life" (emphasis mine). See Lenin, "III: Trade-Unionist Politics."
22 Orwell, *British Pamphleteers*, 13.
23 Quoted in Petryshyn, "Class Conflict and Civil Liberties," 10, 54.
24 Ryan, "The 'Sedition' of A.E. Smith," 3–4.
25 Ryan, "The 'Sedition' of A.E. Smith," 19.
26 CLDL, "Workers' Self-Defense," 19.

27 Petryshyn, "The 'Sedition' of A.E. Smith," 162.
28 CLDL, "Workers' Self-Defense," 3.
29 CLDL, "Workers' Self-Defense," 8.
30 Buck, *An Indictment of Capitalism*, 7.
31 CLDL, "Workers' Self-Defense," 3.
32 CLDL, "Workers' Self-Defense," 8.
33 CLDL, "Workers' Self-Defense," 4.
34 See Denning, *The Cultural Front*.
35 See particularly Aristotle's classification of rhetorical genres in the *Poetics*.
36 Orwell, *British Pamphleteers*, 13.
37 Orwell, *British Pamphleteers*, 14.
38 See, for example, Maclean, "Condemned from the dock," an account published in *Western Labor News* (1919) and issued as a separate pamphlet.
39 "I saw Prolet-Bühne, the German agit-prop theatre... This New York appearance by Prolet-Bühne—and several additional performances I saw later—shed light for me on a new and dynamic form of theatre. The experience certainly helped broaden my own view of the stage as a potent instrument for change and a voice through which one could teach and affect people." Ryan, *Stage Left*, 22.
40 Gold, "Foreword" to "Strike! A Mass Recitation," 19.
41 Canadian Labor Defense League, "Not Guilty!," 5.
42 Canadian Labor Defense League, "Not Guilty!," 6.
43 Quoted in Petryshyn, "A.E. Smith," 180.
44 Petryshyn, "A.E. Smith," 180–81.
45 Canadian Labor Defense League, "Not Guilty!," 16.
46 Canadian Labor Defense League, "Not Guilty!," 11–13.
47 Canadian Labor Defense League, "Not Guilty!," 19–25. See also Scott, "Communists, Senators, and All That," 127–29.
48 Vautour, "Writing Left," 97–98.
49 Vautour, "Writing Left," 122.
50 Canadian Labor Defense League, "Not Guilty!," 18.
51 Canadian Labor Defense League, "Not Guilty!," 4.
52 Ryan, "The 'Sedition' of A.E. Smith," 3.
53 Rifkind, *Comrades and Critics*, 133.
54 Rifkind, *Comrades and Critics*, 46.
55 Aristotle, *Poetics*, 1461b.
56 Angus, *Canadian Bolsheviks*, 272.
57 Petryshyn, "A.E. Smith," 181.
58 Petryshyn, "A.E. Smith," 181.
59 Canadian Labor Defense League, "Not Guilty!," 7.
60 "Canadian Women's History."
61 Orwell, *British Pamphleteers*, 11.
62 Warner, *Publics and Counterpublics*, 108.

Bibliography

Angus, Ian. *Canadian Bolsheviks: The Early Years of the Communist Party in Canada*. Montreal: Vanguard Publications, 1981.

Aristotle. *The Rhetoric and the Poetics*. Modern Library College Edition. 1954. New York: Modern Library, 1984.

Buck, Tim. *An Indictment of Capitalism: The Speech of Tim Buck*. Toronto: Canadian Labor Defense League, National Executive Committee, n.d.

Canadian Labor Defense League. "Constitution." Toronto: Canadian Labor Defense League, 1927.

———. "Not Guilty! The Verdict of the Workers' Jury on the Trial and Conviction of the Eight Communist Leaders." Preface by Tim Buck. Introduction by Oscar Ryan. Toronto: Canadian Labor Defense League, National Executive Committee, n.d.

———. "Workers' Self-Defense in the Courts." Toronto: Canadian Labor Defense League, National Executive Committee, n.d.

"Canadian Women's History." *Public Service Alliance of Canada, National Capital Region Website*. 9 January 2013. Accessed 15 March 2013 at http://www.psac-ncr.com/human-rights/canadian-womens-history.

Denning, Michael. *The Cultural Front: The Laboring of American Culture in the Twentieth Century*. New York: Verso, 2010.

Filewod, Alan. *Committing Theatre: Theatre Radicalism and Political Intervention in Canada*. Toronto: Between the Lines, 2011.

Gold, Michael. "Foreword" to "Strike! A Mass Recitation." *New Masses*, July 1926.

Halasz, Alexandra. *The Marketplace of Print: Pamphlets and the Public Sphere in Early Modern England*. New York: Cambridge University Press, 1997.

Lenin, V.I. "III: Trade-Unionist Politics and Social-Democratic Politics," in *What Is to Be Done? Burning Questions of Our Movement*, 1902. Marxists Internet Archive, 2008. Accessed 9 March 2013 at http://www.marxists.org/archive/lenin/works/1901/witbd/iii.htm.

Maclean, John. "Condemned from the dock: a burning indictment of capitalism, being an authorized account of the trial and sentence of John Maclean, M.A., including a verbatim report of his 75 minutes' speech from the dock." Winnipeg: Western Labor News, 1919.

McKay, Ian. *Rebels, Reds, Radicals: Rethinking Canada's Left History*. Toronto: Between the Lines, 2005.

Moe, Hallvard. "Everyone a Pamphleteer? Reconsidering Comparisons of Mediated Public Participation in the Print Age and the Digital Era." *Media, Culture, and Society* 32, no. 4 (2010): 691–700.

Orwell, George. Introduction to *British Pamphleteers, Vol. I: From the Sixteenth Century to the French Revolution*. Edited by George Orwell and Reginald Reynolds. 7–16. London: Wingate, 1948.

———. "Pamphlet Literature." *New Statesman and Nation* (London), 9 January 1943.

Petryshyn, Jaroslav. "A.E. Smith and the Canadian Labour Defense League." Ph.D. diss., University of Western Ontario, 1977.

———. "Class Conflict and Civil Liberties: The Origins and Activities of the Canadian Labour Defense League, 1925–1940." *Labour/Le Travailleur* 10, no. 3 (1982): 39–63.

Raymond, Joad. *Pamphlets and Pamphleteering in Early Modern Britain*. New York: Cambridge University Press, 2003.

Rifkind, Candida. *Comrades and Critics: Women, Literature, and the Left in 1930s Canada*. Toronto: University of Toronto Press, 2009.

Ryan, Oscar. "The 'Sedition' of A.E. Smith." Toronto: Canadian Labor Defense League, n.d.

Ryan, Oscar, E. Cecil-Smith, Frank Love, and Mildred Goldberg. "Eight Men Speak: A Political Play in Six Acts." In *Eight Men Speak and Other Plays from the Canadian Workers' Theatre*. Edited by Richard Wright and Robin Enders. 21–89. Toronto: New Hogtown Press, 1976.

Ryan, Toby Gordon. *Stage Left: Canadian Theatre in the Thirties*. Toronto: CTR Publications, 1981.

Scott, F.R. "Communists, Senators, and All That." *Canadian Forum*, January 1932.

Vautour, Bart. "Writing Left: The Emergence of Modernism in English Canadian Literature." Ph.D. diss., Dalhousie University, 2011.

Warner, Michael. *The Letters of the Republic: Publication and the Public Sphere in Eighteenth-Century America*. Cambridge, MA: Harvard University Press, 1990.

———. *Publics and Counterpublics*. New York: Zone Books, 2005.

Watson, Louise. *She Never Was Afraid: The Biography of Annie Buller*. 1976. Socialist History Project, n.d. Accessed 9 March 2013 at http://www.socialisthistory.ca/Docs/History/Buller/AB01.htm.

Weinrich, Peter. *Social Protest from the Left in Canada 1870–1970: A Bibliography*. Toronto: University of Toronto Press, 1982.

12

Radio Poetics: Publishing and Poetry on CBC's *Anthology*

Katherine McLeod

Poetry readings are events. They are events that involve performances of poetry off the page and out loud for an audience—its public. But do we have the critical language through which to analyze a poetry reading *as* an event? It is with this question in mind that I listen to the audio archive of CBC Radio's literary program *Anthology*. On this program, radio readings of literature offer listeners access to "live" literary performances, even if this liveness is mediated over the distance of airwaves and often over the distance of time in a rebroadcast of a program or an archived recording. In this essay, I examine the complexity of the radio broadcast as a public reading; but rather than analyzing one specific reading, I have selected a broadcast that is a discussion *about* poetry and its publication by Canadian presses in the 1960s. By situating this episode within an awareness of its medium, I argue that radio offers a means to develop critical strategies for engaging with the ephemeral quality of a literary reading (a reading *on air*) and, simultaneously, with its long-lasting impact on readers (as listeners). Importantly, I ask these questions in order posit the notion that radio enables us to think about what poetry readings *do* and how these events can change our own critical practices. By examining the 1968 episode of *Anthology* that focuses on the state of poetry publishing in Canada, I suggest that this program allows us to conceptualize a public poetics enabled by both a discussion of poetry and its publics and the fact that the discussion was disseminated across national airwaves. As Charles Bernstein argues in *Close Listening: Poetry and the Performed Word:* "Readings are the central social activity of poetry. They rival publishing as the most significant method of distribution for poetic works."[1] Building on Bernstein's position, this essay listens to how radio distributes poetry on air and what happens when that very same medium also becomes a forum for discussing the methods through which poetry is distributed across the nation. Informing this essay is the broader methodological question of how radio could provide us with a comparative model for thinking through digital archives of poetry. In other words, how does the radio archive ask us to rethink what constitutes an archive of public poetics? I will argue that the radio archive of *Anthology* asks us to reimagine the airwaves of radio *through* and *as* public poetics. Public poetics as radio. Radio poetics.

The radio archives of *Anthology* (1954–85) document the making of a national literature. Produced by Robert Weaver, *Anthology* was a weekly program that commissioned and broadcast new works of literature by, among others, Irving Layton, Margaret Atwood, Michael Ondaatje, Al Purdy, Gwendolyn MacEwen, and Leonard Cohen. In addition to readings of literature on air, the program offered episodes dedicated to interviews, discussions, and debates about the state of publishing in Canada. That latter function, what might be thought of as radio literary criticism, is the focus of this essay. Even though *Anthology* offered an important discursive forum for Canadian literature, its medium, for today's listeners, poses many challenges, in terms of both our temporal distance from the broadcasts and our physical distance from the recordings (which are not readily accessible online—they are housed in the CBC Radio Archives in Toronto and in Library and Archives Canada in Ottawa). There is also the conceptual challenge of how to listen critically to a radio archive *as* a public archive—one that overflows with performed poetics and discussions about poetics in Canada yet is not often heard by the very public to which it speaks. As an intervention that troubles the "public-ness" of this archive, this essay focuses on a specific episode of *Anthology* broadcast on 21 December 1968, which devoted itself to the emergence of small presses in Canada and which featured Earle Toppings's interviews with Patrick Lane and Seymour Mayne of Very Stone House, Dennis Lee of House of Anansi, and Al Purdy speaking about the publication of his poetry. Having close-listened to this on-air case study, I will argue that radio calls for us to rethink how we critically engage with the recorded archives of public poetry. To make this argument, first I unpack the complexity of radio as a medium with specific implications for the dissemination of public poetics in Canada; then I turn to the episode itself and how it performs a particular staging of public poetics on air.

Radio's Publics
Radio is both public and private. It is public in the sense of its medium—a transmission of sound easily accessible across the airwaves—and in the case of a public broadcaster like the CBC, it is public to the extent that its production receives public funding and has a mandate to promote Canadian arts and culture. Yet within this public-ness, there is the private, be it the private space of individual listening or in the sense of privately funded radio stations. Copyright, which contractually tied broadcast materials to individual authors, is another powerful assertion of the private within the public medium of radio, but also an important assertion of ownership for the writers whose works were read on *Anthology*. Referring to this complex duality of private and public, specifically in the space of listening, American radio studies critic Jason Loviglio refers to radio's audience as an "intimate public"[2]—a term that I would add very much resonates with Michael Warner's characterization of public speech as "both personal and impersonal."[3] As Loviglio argues in the case of radio, "the terms 'public' and 'private' came to represent a complex web of social performances perpetually in play rather than distinct and immutable categories."[4] Although Loviglio is speaking of American radio, this notion of "a complex web of social performances" equally resonates with a negotiation of the public and private vis-à-vis cultural production on Canadian airwaves. The notion that public and private are construed through a web of social performances speaks to the degree to which these public and private audiences understand themselves—or, rather, to the degree that these audiences remain unknowable to each other. Even if the public and private intersect in society, there remains an impasse of knowability that parallels Michael Warner's question of the reader: "Would it ever be possible to know anything about the public to which, I hope, you still belong?"[5] Warner, following Benedict Anderson, reminds us that the imaginary construes the public's and the private's conceptions of each other. Radio exists within these colliding realms of imagined public and private audiences, particularly in the case of a national broadcaster such as the CBC.

Radio travels down airwaves to the real or imagined listener. Ideally, this listener is paying attention. As Roland Barthes has articulated in his writing on listening (notably, he distinguishes between listening and hearing: "*Hearing* is a physiological phenomenon; *listening* is a psychological act." Listening to human speech, then, involves attention to and recognition of an body outside of oneself who is speaking: "Corporeality of speech, the voice is located at the articulation of body and discourse, and it is in this interspace that listening's back-and-forth movement might be made."[6] In the case of radio, this "interspace" occupies the airwaves, creating a "back-and-forth movement" for speakers and listeners, or what we might call a dialogue. Listening practice inevitably differs from listener to listener, but there is a general practice of radio listening that has provided a basis for the past century of radio studies. Given that listening is an embodied practice in this way, I want to push the concept of embodiment further to suggest that the radio archive itself constitutes a *body*.

Rather than following Marinetti's concept of radio as "wireless imagination," Ellen Waterman suggests that we might consider "the performative force of radio bodies."[7] Although Waterman uses this term more in the context of experimental radio, I apply her phrase *radio bodies* to radio archives because the body *of* radio is a performative site of acoustic production and consumption. The question of where the body ends and the archive begins has been contested by theorists such as Diana Taylor, who, instead of seeing the body and archive in opposition, suggests that the body plays a central role in remembering, performing, and recording cultural knowledge. For Taylor, the archive and the repertoire are neither sequential nor a binary: "This means that the repertoire, like the archive, is mediated."[8] In Taylor's exploration of the limits of embodied knowledge, the body poses a challenge for the archive, asking us to consider how to record the body's presence. This challenge applies directly to the radio archive because it records the body's presence through sound. I would further suggest that we reorient the terms of *body* and *archive* so that the body *in* the archive then becomes the body *of* the archive. In other words, the archive becomes a body. The archive as body then allows us to engage with what Taylor characterizes as an archival crisis: "Now on the brink of a digital revolution that both utilizes and threatens to displace writing, the body again seems poised to disappear in a virtual space that eludes embodiment."[9] Indeed, radio is an early precursor to that "virtual space that eludes embodiment," yet, fundamentally, radio is an embodied medium. Thus, in this digital age, radio provides a much needed model through which to conceptualize the digital not as "ephemeral" but rather as rooted in the physicality of the body. I make this case for radio because it reminds us that, in a digital world in which we are constantly rethinking our engagement with recorded archives of poetry readings, there is an important precedent in radio. But to complicate matters further, what radio brings to this digital debate is a medium that is rooted in the sound of the body. It is this physicality that, I would argue, links radio to poetry—and, as unpacked in the second section of this essay, it is this physicality that comes to the forefront of the 1968 episode of *Anthology* and its discussion of the state of poetry and poetry publications. Recalling Taylor's concern that "the body again seems poised to disappear in a virtual space that eludes embodiment," I am suggesting that the physicality linking radio and poetry opens up a pathway through this digital terrain and that this very same idea informs the statements on the future of poetics as articulated in 1968.

Returning briefly to the archive as body, this concept holds particular relevance for the institutional body of the CBC and its archival holdings as a public broadcaster. Keeping in mind the origins of the word archive as *arkheion* (as home or dwelling of a public figure, *archon*), the CBC's archival holdings in its main building in Toronto constitute a national home of public broadcasting—to quote a recent motto of the CBC, "Canada lives here." Importantly, in this motto, it is not in one place that the nation lives; rather, it lives *here*. In this way, the motto, when spoken on the radio, results in the *here* (and *hear*) of radio expanding, dispersing, and spilling across the reaches of its transmission signals. "Canada lives here" brings to the forefront the body of the CBC itself in the making of culture as well as the broadcasting of it. In the case of *Anthology*, the fact that it included many writers who went on to become canonical further increases its value as an archive of literary production in Canada. It is an archive that documents the very act of anthologizing on air—that is, again, if we are to listen. In the case of *Anthology, who* is listening?

Radio enacts one of the key features in Warner's definition of a public: it is "a relation among strangers."[10] Warner translates this audience of the self and the stranger into relations that compose a national public. As he contends, "a nation or public or market in which everyone could be known personally would be no nation or public or market at all. This constitutive and normative environment of strangerhood is more, too, than an objectively describable *gesellfschaft;* it requires our constant imagining."[11] Even when concrete figures do exist on the listening audiences of radio, for speakers on the program and for listeners to it, the public itself still "requires our constant imagining." For instance, Mark Abley's article on Weaver in *Books in Canada* estimates the number of people who listened to *Anthology:* "The audience for *Anthology* is not only loyal, it is also surprisingly large. Weaver could be contented if 30,000 listened regularly; the best estimate is about 45,000, and one rating recently suggested that 75,000 people tuned in. Whatever the exact figure, more Canadians listen to *Anthology* than buy all the little magazines put together."[12] While Abley's observation already links readers and listeners, it is worth noting that in the 1968 episode of *Anthology* focusing on small presses, the listening public is not only imagined but also aligned with an *imagined* reading public. The marketplace for the distribution of literature then becomes part of that imagining—an imagining of potential readers vis-à-vis airwaves. Situating the distribution of poetry and the audience for poetry in Canada in terms of airwaves brings even more complexity to the imagined audience, specifically to the extent that the distribution of literature to a reading public is invested in the very same act that radio performs best: transmission.

As Debra Rae Cohen points out, radio performs via transmission rather than reproduction.[13] Thus, transmission is not only the mode of representation in radio but also a process that underscores the objective of *Anthology*, which is to disseminate new works of literature to a listening audience—an objective that speaks to the decision to broadcast Toppings's documentary as part of the episode on 21 December 1968. It is in terms of this metaphoric paralleling of transmission and dissemination vis-à-vis publishing that I turn to this episode and its discussion of the state of poetry publication in Canada. How did the medium of radio shape this discussion, and how did it enact the kind of immediate connection between poetry and public that small press publishers in Canada were attempting through their publications? But before turning to this seminal episode of 1968 to answer these questions, I want to situate the episode in the context of *Anthology* as a literary program.

"Literary Magazine of the Air"
Robert Weaver was hired by CBC Radio in 1948 to manage the short story program *Canadian Short Stories*. He explains how his work evolved on CBC radio's literary programs:

> [Canadian Short Stories] was a weekly 15-minute program, which meant that the stories we broadcast all had to be about 2,000 words long, and the writers were paid $35 for their work...In a year or so we managed to increase the fee for short stories to $50. Writers always need money and we, alas, had little enough to offer them. But writers also need to be published, to be read in the magazines, to have their voices heard. We sent begging letters across the country, not only to writers but also to other editors and to book publishers, saying that there was a market at the CBC, and manuscripts began to find their way to us.[14]

Weaver's dedication to finding new voices led to the emergence of *Anthology* in 1954, a program that often slipped between the terminology of anthology and magazine. In the CBC Radio Archives database, a search to find what was broadcast on each episode reveals that both terms appear in program descriptions:

> ANTHOLOGY
> Network: Trans-Can
> Literary magazine of the air. First program of the season and the beginning of the 4th year on the air.

While its title proclaimed the program as an anthology, Weaver fondly claimed that *Anthology* became "by far the largest of Canadian 'little magazines.'"[15] The audio archives of *Anthology*, however, call for a different *reading* than a printed text of a magazine or anthology. Audio records of *Anthology* have been documented on DAT tapes and CDs. These are the instruments through which we access the audio archive. The tapes themselves are the durable yet fragile objects that contain these recordings of a national literature in the making. These archives record events that many of us were not present to listen to—we turn to these tapes to be *present*. We play them and, as listeners, we feel as if we are almost present at, for instance, a reading of poetry by Lenard Cohen during an episode of *Anthology* in 1958, one of the few audio clips of *Anthology* easily accessible on the CBC Digital Archives.

While we await full episodes of *Anthology* to be made available online for the public, we can consider what archival limitations are imposed by having to visit the CBC building itself in order to listen and what this tells us about the body of the archive. Archival theorist Brien Brothman has noted that archivists are constantly faced with the question of what is to be saved. He has suggested that this question needs to be deconstructed—or rather, as he puts it, "What are the limits of the concept of archiving?"[16] In the case of *Anthology*, I would suggest that the limits of the concept are inseparable from the limits of our listenings. What is at stake in these limits is articulated in the series of questions that Brothman so poignantly asks:

> What are the limits of the concept of archiving? Is to archive to give future generations our transmittal slips? Is to archive inevitably to give future (and past) generations—or perhaps even ourselves—the archival slip? How in our practice and in our writing are the limits of archives constituted? To what extent is it possible for one generation to give another its words, its terms?"[17]

In the case of audio archives for a program such as *Anthology*, Brothman's problematizing of the transference of an archive from one temporality into another is central to the challenge of listening, again, to *Anthology*. Words are heard by different publics than would have listened at the time of its broadcast—and even at the time of its broadcast, listening publics were disparate. Thus, as a literary *event*, a broadcast of *Anthology* exceeded the concept of an event as happening in one place. The literary event took place *at once*—and as a shared experience—but this was an at-once-ness that relied on airwaves to create the experience of listening together. In this regard, Weaver was adamant that *Anthology* be broadcast on the Trans-Canada AM frequency, the principle network of CBC Radio, the one that reached the most Canadians, rather than on the FM Stereo network, which was tested in the 1960s before being established 1975. Thus, as producer, Weaver influenced not only the structure of the program but also its transmission. On the twenty-fifth anniversary of the program, he reflected: "It's pretty well unique...and the CBC deserves some respect for that. There have been no moves, not even covert, to get it onto FM. I've always wanted *Anthology* to stay on the AM network: the writing community in Canada is small-town as well as big-city."[18] Heard through these words, *Anthology* itself performs its own version of imagining a public listening. Moreover, although we cannot know all of the publics who listened, we *can* know that it was a program designed to reach audiences across the nation. Hearing it as *transmission*, intriguingly enough, allows us to understand it as a literary publication performing by travelling across, inhabiting the *trans* of transmission and, indeed, the *trans* of the Trans-Canada Network.

Public Poetics on Air

Opening the 21 December 1968 episode of *Anthology* is a reading aloud of two short stories by Morley Callaghan, a detail that gives a sense of the larger soundscape in which listeners hear Toppings's documentary.[19] After these stories, Toppings's documentary begins with a reference to the recent boom in small press publications in Canada. He then turns to British Columbia, and we hear Patrick Lane and Seymour Mayne of Very Stone House Press (Vancouver) explaining that their press is responding to a "lack of interest in young writers" (transcribed) by larger publishing houses. Rather than letting the larger presses determine what made it into print, Lane and Mayne asked themselves, "Why don't we publish it ourselves[?]" They then explain that bill bissett got involved, as did Jim Brown, and "we started publishing our own books" (transcribed). As Lane and Mayne narrate:

Small press can do things that a large press can't. In a way that usually a large press has a built-in set of ideas that are usually pretty conservative. Some of the small presses have been bringing out, for example, records. One of the things that people involved with poetry today know this is that some of the best poetry being done today is being done on records. One way to reach people is to give them records. Everybody has a phonograph. Poets realize that poetry is not just a matter of a simple written art. It's a public art—it's an oral art. (transcribed)

Significantly, the words "one way to reach people is to give them records" are spoken on air—on radio, one of the other ways "to reach the people." They say of poetry, "it's a public art," thus foregrounding the public-ness of poetry itself. The last few words—"it's an oral art"—are interjected, and without knowing Mayne's voice as opposed to Lane's, one cannot know who is uttering those words. It is fitting that we are reminded of radio's orality at the precise moment that the words spoken foreground the oral medium. It is at this same moment that radio takes on an added dimension of anonymity—"a relation among strangers"—even though the voices themselves signify the presence of individuals.

Despite our ability as critics to listen to this moment as a moment of self-reflexivity upon the medium of radio, neither the interviewer nor the interviewees draw attention to radio as being part of this dissemination of an oral art. However, I would argue that we can still hear the parallel between what is being said and the medium through which it is being conveyed. It is the task of the listener to hear this parallel, an enactment of what I call radio poetics—radio poetics in the sense that the broadcast is simultaneously about the making public of poetry vis-à-vis small presses *and* about the making public of poetry itself. A public-making rooted in the transmission of words to a listening audience.

Attention to the reading and listening publics continues in Toppings's next interview, this one with Dennis Lee of Anansi. In observing that Anansi can "get a book out quickly" (transcribed), Lee characterizes the connection between the writer and his/her reading audience as one of necessary immediacy. As Lee explains of publishing houses that take longer to publish: "In terms of establishing any kind of galvanizing connection between the writer and the people who are reading him this is completely lamentable ('cause he's someplace different when the thing appears)" (transcribed). In the interview, Toppings asks Lee what informs his choice to publish certain texts:

Toppings: I'm interested in how the so-called little presses reach an audience [...] How do you go about sensing what kind of need there is for the books you're doing?

Lee: What our nerve ends tell us. So far, in public affairs, among the two books we've done so far, one—*The University Game* [1968]—[we were] told it might be possible to publish it within a year's time and a thousand copies if done in paperback. And we did it ourselves... And the first edition of 2,500 copies sold out in eight weeks... The subject of university discontent is pretty much to the fore. (transcribed)

In the same way that Layne and Mayne speak of reaching a reading audience, Toppings frames his question in terms of *reaching* a literary audience vis-à-vis print (a question that equally applies to radio). This act of reaching returns to the body by reminding us that, in reaching an audience, the airwaves literally *touch* a listener as sound enters her ears. Reaching the listening public is just as difficult as reaching the reading public, but the terms in which the conversation between Toppings and Lee unfolds reiterate the physicality of the public bodies reached by texts, whether in print or on the airwaves.

This is similar to the impasse of knowability that underscores Warner's question about the reader: "Would it ever be possible to know anything about the public to which, I hope, you still belong?"[20] What can we know of listening publics *or* reading publics? The publishing industry measures book sales to determine whether the reading public has been reached; but this measurement is more unreadable than ever before in the digital world of downloadable texts—not unlike the challenge faced by the world of sound to know who is listening. Nevertheless, even though Lee refers to a tangible knowing of Anansi's public with sales figures (proving that "the subject of university discontent is pretty much to the fore"), his initial answer to the question of knowing the audience responds with the same affective language that Toppings uses to ask it. Publishing "what our nerve ends tell us" suggests an intimate knowledge of the reading public; publishers, like radio producers, must undertake an intuitive yet distanced imagining of their public. Furthermore, when Toppings asks, "How do you go about sensing what kind of need there is for the books you're doing?," he phrases the knowing of one's audience in terms of affect. And, in many ways, this "sensing" constitutes an affective reading of the public and its needs—a reading that requires both a tuning-in-of and a being-in-tune-with the reading public. In the case of *The University Game*, this reading public extended beyond imagined readers for a specific text or genre and became a public engaged with and invested in higher education. A public that extended and spilled across distances and disciplinary boundaries, not unlike radio's public.

At the same time, when listening to Toppings's interview with Lee, one might ask: Is not the public always at the forefront of any publisher's mind? What makes this interview different in terms of imagining a reading public? Here, I would argue that it is important to compare this interview with other forums for public critical discussions about poetry and its publication by small presses. In 1967, *Canadian Literature* ran an assessment of publishing in Canada that gave little attention to what would later be called the "new wave in publishing." It was not until the 1973 issue on publishing that this journal reflected the "new wave" of the 1960s and George Woodcock's questionnaire included representatives from small presses such as Anansi, Coach House, Talonbooks, and Oberon.[21] As Woodcock himself noted in "Publishing Present" (1973), the 1967 issue had anticipated the boom in small presses and had acknowledged the need for further discussion of them (with the nod to small press publication of magazines in the article by Wynne Francis in the 1967 issue); however, the changes on the publishing scene—changes that Woodcock himself noted were "radical"—were acutely felt and conveyed to a listening public in Toppings's radio documentary on publishing that *Anthology* broadcast in 1968. One could argue that radio was more *in touch* than print with literary publics in Canada.

In Toppings's interviews, listeners hear of palpable changes in the Canadian literary landscape—for example, in Al Purdy's comments on the imminent folding of Contact Press at the time of the interview. Purdy mentions this contextual detail towards the end of the documentary, when Toppings asks him about his publishing history, which he then narrates through the stages of self-publishing, Ryerson Press, and a chapbook, followed by Contact Press, which he notes was working almost in a vacuum at the time: "no one else was doing this" (transcribed). Whether it is Purdy's oral history or Dennis Lee's vocalized anticipation of Anansi's publication of *Technology and Empire* by George Grant that transports us to a specific moment—*in medias res*—in Canadian publishing, this, I would argue, is what allows the radio program to speak a different version of public poetics. The oral history embedded in the radio program functions as what Charles Bernstein calls "a public tuning"—and in this case, it is a public tuning not through a poetry reading but rather through a discussion of poetry publications.

Future Transmissions

In the introduction to the *Studies in Canadian Literature* special issue on poetics and public culture in Canada, Diana Brydon, Manina Jones, Jessica Schagerl, and Kristen Warder turn to Bernstein's notion of the poetry reading as a generative space in order to point to new challenges in conceptualizing poetry communities through new media (2007). As they suggest, "the face-to-face community renewed through the public reading remains an important site for performing poetry's social function, yet increasingly that public tuning takes place as well on internet sites devoted to sharing those moments with a wider audience, which no longer needs the immediacy of the initial moment to feel connected to an extended poetics community."[22] Here they speak of Internet sites, but we could easily replace this term with radio, a medium that is complex both as a forum for poetry's social function *and* as sound to be listened to as paradoxically disembodied embodiment.

When Bernstein argues that readings "rival publishing as the most significant method of distribution for poetic works," he situates this argument within a call to examine the ways in which the reading-as-event is documented, or, rather, not documented. For Bernstein, "this absence of documentation together with the tendency among critics and scholars to value the written over the performed text, has resulted in a remarkable lack of attention given to the poetry reading as a medium in its own right, a medium that has had a profound impact on twentieth-century poetry, and in particular the poetry of the second half of the century."[23] Radio recordings are not the only way of approaching this lack of documentation; they do, though, offer a compelling point of entry through which we can access the reading-as-event, even if only as an audible trace of the event. The present essay has not discussed poetry readings in their most recognizable form; rather, it has focused on a rare self-reflexive moment in which we hear publishers discussing the distribution of poetry through a medium that itself is a distributor of poetry. In short, the radio distributes poetry by transmitting sound waves. Thus, in Toppings's documentary we can access a discursive forum that foregrounds that very same social activity of poetry and how this action, as conceptualized by each speaker, connects poetry to its publics. However, just as in the social events that Bernstein has in mind when he posits readings as "the central social activity of poetry,"[24] the question remains as to what happens to these signals once they are disseminated across the airwaves of the nation. To access the CBC Radio Archives, one must visit them in person, and this presents an obstacle to hearing this trace—although in the near future this reality may change. Here, we might imagine what could be possible if the public were given full online access to the archival descriptions and recordings of *Anthology*—an act of making public that recalls the statement by Lane and Mayne regarding phonographs, although this statement could easily be heard as referring to records from the public body of an audio archive: "one of the ways to reach the people is to give them records."

In a 2008 issue of *Open Letter*, Ashok Mathur and Smaro Kamboureli revisit this notion of "a public tuning" in order to ask how "public pedagogy" takes place within and through poetry readings. Bringing the term public pedagogy into dialogue with a radio broadcast that strives to attune us to a moment in Canadian publishing, I ask: What does radio teach us? To answer this through the acoustic lens of a "a public tuning," I turn to Purdy's concluding words in Toppings's documentary, where he comments on the future of poetry and publishing: "At the present moment poetry seems to be the most thriving of all the arts but also the most doomed" (transcribed). He then mentions the possibility of writers moving into prose or "going into singing, records, music," pointing to Leonard Cohen as an example of this new direction. He then makes this qualifying statement: "But he's come to the understanding that basically the written poetry in small publications is a doomed thing" (transcribed). (It is worth noting that here, announcer Harry Manis leaps in with hurried closing words reminding the audience that they have been listening to "a documentary about the small presses prepared by Earle Toppings [and] edited by Robert Weaver" [transcribed].) Listening beyond Purdy's rather gloomy forecast of poetry's future, we hear in his words a turn to sound—audio records as a new direction in poetry. In asking ourselves why he turns to sound at this moment, we may recall the moment in the Very Stone House Press interview with Lane and Mayne when they too turn to sound, reminding us that poetry is "a public art...an oral art," and we remember that we are listening. This is radio. A public art. An oral art.

The CBC has been recognized for its contribution to Canadian literature through the commissioning and broadcasting of plays, poetry, and fiction in support of national culture. What is often not recognized is the much more self-reflexive role the CBC has played through programs like *Anthology*, in which literary distribution itself is the primary topic of conversation. What I would suggest is most important about this attention to distribution is the heed it pays to new and emerging writers; this sets *Anthology* apart from recent literary program such as *Canada Reads* (a program that does contribute to literary distribution but often promotes authors already known to the listening public). As Danielle Fuller and DeNel Rehberg Sedo argue in their assessment of *Canada Reads*, the program functions as both "a mass reading event and a media spectacle."[25] Even though the program succeeds in making new readers of Canadian literature, Fuller and Sedo suggest that "CBC's cultural nationalist project imbricates *Canada Reads* within twenty-first-century globalized publishing structures that favour a handful of highly commodified texts and writers."[26] In contrast, the broadcasts of *Anthology* that discuss the emergence of small presses can be heard as markedly different radio interventions in the making public of Canada's literature.

Yet within this act of making public, there are multiple publics to be imagined. The CBC as a public broadcaster performs with the expectation that its programming speaks to an imagined community of "the nation" and that, therefore, the programming should reflect that nation—a nation that, hopefully, is listening. However, this nation is composed of heterogeneous publics, or, rather, "prismatic publics," as in the title of Kate Eichhorn and Heather Milne's collection, *Prismatic Publics: Innovative Canadian Women's Poetry and Poetics*. In that collection, poetry speaks from and to fragmented publics, reminding us that the homogeneous *public* is always heterogeneous *publics*. So for radio to be in tune with its publics, the question must not be who is listening but rather who are the publics to which and from which it speaks—in other words, who are the bodies tuning in to embodied sounds on air? Although not as attuned to the politics of these prismatic listening bodies, Weaver was aware that *Anthology* was a literary program that spoke to "smaller, specialized publics" that differed from the homogeneous "public" of mass media.[27] During his talk on broadcasting at the Canadian Writers' Conference in 1955, Weaver proposed that any consideration of "the public" and "the writer" vis-à-vis broadcasting needed to take into account the challenge of smaller publics: "At least part of that challenge comes from the fact that, far from having a single mass public on one side and on the other a devoted and clearly defined minority public, we have in our time a thoroughgoing fragmentation of the public."[28] This fragmentation has only become more pronounced in the digital age, which raises the pressing question that Fuller and Sedo ask while looking ahead to the future of literary radio programming: "the CBC helped to create a nationwide audience for Canadian writing during a crucial period of its development; but how might we characterize the broadcaster's relationship to CanLit in the digital era?"[29] This question, along with the public broadcaster's need to continue reaching its publics, calls for an urgent reimagining of CBC radio as a public forum and, moreover, for us to critically re-listen to it as an archive of public listening.

Notes

The majority of this essay was written while its author was supported by a SSHRC Postdoctoral Fellowship held at TransCanada Institute, University of Guelph. Thank you to Smaro Kamboureli for reading early versions of this research, to Keith Hart at CBC Radio Archives, and to Laura Moss for generously directing me to Robert Weaver's report on broadcasting at the Canadian Writers' Conference.

1. Bernstein, "Introduction," 22.
2. Loviglio, *Radio's Intimate Public*, xvi–xvii.
3. Warner, "Publics and Counterpublics," 417.
4. Loviglio, *Radio's Intimate Public*, xvi–xvii.
5. Warner, "Publics and Counterpublics," 417.
6. Barthes, *The Responsibility of Forms*, 245, 246.
7. Waterman, "Radio Bodies," 119.
8. Taylor, *The Archive and the Repertoire*, 21.
9. Taylor, *The Archive and the Repertoire*, 16.
10. Warner, "Publics and Counterpublics," 417.
11. Warner, "Publics and Counterpublics," 417.
12. Abley, "Bob's Our Uncle," 7.
13. Cohen, Coyle, and Lewty, eds., *Broadcasting Modernism*.
14. Weaver, "Introduction," xvii.
15. Weaver, ed., *The Anthology Anthology*, iv.
16. Brothman, "The Limits of Limits," 206.
17. Brothman, "The Limits of Limits," 206.
18. Abley, "Bob's Our Uncle," 5.
19. It is important to situate this program within previous discussion of small press publications. On 29 April 1959, Paul Wright produced and hosted an episode of "Anthology" that included the following:

    1. Patrick Anderson, poet and novelist, talks to Ronal Hambleton, broadcaster, about *Preview*, a literary journal Anderson was very active with in the 1940s in Canada. He also talks about his recent writing, including *Snake Wine*, an autobiographical work. (32:00) (17:00)
    2. Earle Birney, poet, looks at three "little" literary periodicals and discusses their strengths and shortcomings. The periodicals are *Yes*, *Delta* and *Fiddlehead*. (50:00) (10:00)

20. Warner, "Publics and Counterpublics," 413.
21. In the 1967 issue of *Canadian Literature*, the following people were asked questions about Canadian publishing: Earle Birney, Kildare Dobbs, Arnold Edinborough, Robert Fulford, Roderick Haig-Brown, Carl F. Klinck, Hugh MacLennan, and Robert Weaver ("Canadian Publishing: Answers to a Questionnaire," 1967). Six years later, *Canadian Literature* posed similar

questions to a different set of respondents, reflecting the shift towards small publishing houses: Shirley Jackson, Michael Macklem, Dennis Lee, David Robinson, James Lorimer, Victor Coleman, and Mel Hurting ("New Wave in Publishing," 1973).
22   Brydon et al., "Introduction," 7.
23   Bernstein, *Close Listening*, 22.
24   Bernstein, *Close Listening*, 22.
25   Fuller and Sedo, "A Reading Spectacle for the Nation," 6.
26   Fuller and Sedo, "A Reading Spectacle for the Nation," 7.
27   Weaver, "Broadcasting," 108.
28   Weaver, "Broadcasting," 108.
29   Fuller and Sedo, "A Reading Spectacle for the Nation," 18.

Bibliography

Abley, Mark. "Bob's Our Uncle: The CanLit Community Owes a Huge Debt of Gratitude to Robert Weaver." *Books in Canada* 3, no. 5 (May 1979): 4–9.

Anthology. CBC Radio Archives (CBC, Toronto). 22 April 1959.

———. CBC Radio Archives (CBC, Toronto). 29 April 1959

———. CBC Radio Archives (CBC, Toronto). 8 December 1961.

———. CBC Radio Archives (CBC, Toronto). 21 December 1968.

Barthes, Roland. *The Responsibility of Forms*. 245–56. Berkeley: University of California Press, 1985.

Bernstein, Charles. "Introduction." *Close Listening: Poetry and the Performed Word*. Edited by Charles Bernstein. New York: Oxford University Press, 1998.

Berrigan, Sean. *Anthology: Catalogue and Index 1954–1974*. M.A. thesis, Carleton University, 1980.

Brothman, Brien. "The Limits of Limits: Derridean Deconstruction and the Archival Institution." *Archivaria* 36 (Autumn 1993): 205–20.

Brydon, Diana, Manina Jones, Jessica Schagerl, and Kristen Warder. "Introduction: Surviving the Paraphrase: Poetics and Public Culture in Canada." *Studies in Canadian Literature* 32, no. 2 (2007): 7–27.

"Canadian Publishing: Answers to a Questionnaire." *Canadian Literature* 33 (Summer 1967): 6–15.

Cohen, Debra Rae, Michael Coyle, and Jane Lewty, eds. *Broadcasting Modernism*. Gainesville: University Press of Florida, 2009.

Eichhorn, Kate, and Heather Milne, eds. *Prismatic Publics: Innovative Canadian Women's Poetry and Poetics*. Toronto: Coach House Books, 2009.

Fuller, Danielle, and DeNel Rehberg Sedo. "A Reading Spectacle for the Nation: The CBC and 'Canada Reads.'" *Journal of Canadian Studies* 40, no. 1 (Winter 2006): 5–36.

Kamboureli, Smaro, and Ashok Mathur. "On Public Readings and Pedagogy." *Open Letter: Dialogues on Poetics and Public Culture* 13, no. 7 (Fall 2008): 125-39.

Loviglio, Jason. *Radio's Intimate Public: Network Broadcasting and Mass-Mediated Democracy.* Minneapolis: University of Minnesota Press, 2005.

"New Wave in Publishing." *Canadian Literature* 57 (1973): 50-64.

Taylor, Diana. *The Archive and the Repertoire: Performing Cultural Memory in the Americas.* Durham: Duke University Press, 2003.

Warner, Michael. "Publics and Counterpublics." *Quarterly Journal of Speech* 88, no. 4 (November 2002): 413-25.

Waterman, Ellen. "Radio Bodies: Discourse, Performance, Resonance." *Radio Territories.* Edited by Brandon LaBelle and Erik Granly Jensen. 118-53. Copenhagen and Los Angeles: Errant Bodies Press, 2007.

Weaver, Robert. "Introduction." *The Oxford Book of Canadian Short Stories in English: Selected by Margaret Atwood and Robert Weaver.* Oxford: Oxford University Press, 1988.

———. "Broadcasting." *Writing in Canada: Proceedings from the Canadian Writers' Conference, Queen's University, 28-31 July 1955.* Ed. George Whalley. Toronto: Macmillan Company of Canada, 1956. 103-14.

Woodcock, George. "Publishing Present." *Canadian Literature* 57 (Summer 1973): 3-5.

13

The Public Reading: Call for a New Paradigm

Erín Moure and Karis Shearer

The public poetry reading as an "intentional" site—as a site that is more than reiteration of an authoritative, printed text—has been relatively undertheorized in Canada until very recently. In practice, meanwhile, the public reading has long been a variable space and has encompassed a wide range of visual and aural techniques, some shared with theatre, sound art, dance, the "happening" of the 1960s and 1970s, and so on. Concomitant with the lack of attention to the reading as intentional site, there has been only sporadic scholarly attention to poetry readings as documents—sound files, videos—and to what these documents might reveal of creative—and critical—practice. One important exception has been the special issue of *Open Letter* on "Poetics and Public Culture," guest-edited in 2008 by Lily Cho and Melina Baum Singer, which asked contributors to produce conversations on the subject of the public poetry reading; another is *Listening Up, Writing Down, Looking Beyond: Interfaces of the Oral, Written, and Visual*, edited by Susan Gingell and Wendy Roy (2012). Building on this work in the paragraphs that follow, we examine, and call for a renewal of, the Canadian paradigm of the public reading as set out by the Canada Council, and welcome the current intensification of scholarly work on its particularities, especially insofar as they exist at the crossroads of creative/critical practice. Their study stands to enhance our understanding of textual pleasure and of the creative gesture.

The Current Canadian Model

As Robert Lecker observed in his 1999 article "The Canada Council's Block Grant Program and the Construction of Canadian Literature": "Since its founding in 1957, the activities of the Canada Council have had a profound impact on the definition and articulation of Canadian culture, especially in the field of literature" and, indeed, to its credit, "no other agency has done more to foster the growth of a national literature and to assist in the business of cultural production."[1] However, he goes on to argue, "no form of arts patronage...is ever value free," and his own research does much to expose what he terms its "federal and culturally elitist ideology."[2] Although Lecker's study focuses specifically on the Canada Council's Block Grant Program and the publishing industry, many of his key points have the potential to apply equally to the less frequently discussed Literary Readings Program. In what follows we have taken the liberty of substituting "organizer" for Lecker's "publisher," "writer" for "book," and "invite" for "publish" or "produce" to consider what this application might look like:

> The introduction and evolution of the Council's eligibility criteria, and the very idea of eligibility itself, altered the ways in which Canadian *organizers* decided what *authors* to *invite* and their conception of particular types of *reading series* that it would be valuable to produce.

> To obtain funding, *organizers* had to adapt their programs to the Council's criteria or risk losing their place within the *Literary Readings Program*.[3]

> ...the Council encourages *organizers* to become interpreters... [and] it also encourages the *organizers* to replicate the ideology so central to the Council's own conception of eligibility and status as factors that are interpretively produced. This process of replication carries within it a profound recognition of the Council's authority, simply because it places *organizers* in the position of collectively mimicking the hermeneutic activities of a central interpretive body. Such a process is perfectly in keeping with the way in which institutions usually work: they preserve themselves by encouraging the replication of their self-defining values.[4]

If, as American critic Christopher Beach suggested in 1999, "the poetry reading—as the most public site of poetry and the site of the oral performance rather than its written reception—is a crucial index of the way poetry is defined within a given culture at a given moment," then a sustained and detailed historical study of public readings is required—one that would address which poets have been funded to read, where, how frequently, and in what contexts—in order to carry out a more profound analysis of the poetry reading in Canada.[5] We recognize from the outset, then, that further analysis of the history of Canada Council funding of public poetry readings, from 1959 to present, is surely necessary to fully conceptualize the development of the poetry reading in Canada. Lacking such a study, we restrict our own analysis to the literary reading as it is currently constructed by the discourse on the Canada Council's website, aware that the argument we elaborate has other aspects that need to be teased into the light.

The current public readings paradigm in this country might be called a flat model, largely driven by the administrative goals of the public readings program of the Canada Council for the Arts, which are two:

- to PROMOTE the work of writers (thus there is an emphasis on tours, sales of newly published books)
- to provide writers ACCESS to a live public audience (through reading the published work, but not through discussion or conversation settings that depart from the reading model)

The Literary Readings component provides financial assistance to Canadian organizations that wish to invite writers to give public readings. The purpose is to promote published books of writers and to give audiences across Canada greater access to writers and Canadian literature.[6] The public reading is thus defined as a commercial and access opportunity—as a marketing gesture to promote the "real" literary work of book publication—rather than as a work of art worthy of support and study for what it contributes to creative practice. This jibes with the influential categorizations elaborated by French scholar Gérard Genette in the late 1990s, in which the public reading and its apparatuses (series, recordings, invitations, group formations, along with the reading event itself) are *paratextual*, and the reading itself is a "public epitext," an "interpretation," rather than an act that is creative in its very nature.[7]

Moreover, in the Council's current configuration of the reading, the "authentication of the book" remains primary: it is the authors who "read from their works," thereby "contribut[ing] to the quality of life of a community by their presence." Ironically, this affirmation of authorial presence is precisely what many contemporary writers work against in their writing and performance, their inscriptions and voicings. In a conversation called "'The Public Reading Is a Matter of the Public Reading': the

85 Project," Robert Majzels tells Lianne Moyes that he has "always had an aversion to readings, to the way they reinforce the idea of the author as the source of meaning, to the logocentric illusion of presence."[8] The *85 Project* as a text challenges readers to read against Western conventions of left to right; as a performance, it consists of pre-recorded videos of members of a public, in their role as audience, attempting to read aloud from the text rather than listening to the author do it. As Majzels explains, "the act of reading by an audience rather than by the translator/author also works against that relationship of author, authority, presence, the aural experience that seems to be such an integral part of the tradition of the 'literary' in Canadian letters, which I abhor."[9]

Majzels's work, like many actual public readings, involves acts of performance that can and do often push at the Council's definitional limits, and there is a strong history of this in Canada that has, to some extent, been studied or at least archived.[10] A look at the history, for example, of institutions such as The Music Gallery in Toronto (1976 to present),[11] the Intermedia collective (1965–72)[12] and Western Front (1973–present)[13] in Vancouver, or Vehicule Art Inc. (1972–83), or at the development of spoken word[14] in Montreal,[15] shows a Canada Council–supported (and, later, Heritage Canada–supported, especially for archiving support) multidisciplinary practice of creation and documentation that, although rooted in music/sound or in visual arts, also gave strong support to experiments and events in the reading and recording of poetry readings. Events and gatherings such as Women and Words in 1983 in Vancouver also provided an impetus for groups in different cities to create ongoing events with poets, using Canada Council funding, that were not necessarily conventional poetry readings.

This history of performance, and the recording of performance, extends to the present. Collectives in many Canadian centres create space and provide support for expanding notions of writing practice through live reading practice; examples include Word Iz Bond in Halifax, and Kalmunity Vibe Collective and Les Filles électriques in Montreal. Recordings of some of this work have been archived as performance. Even so, scholarly research into the poetry reading is still in its infancy. The poetry reading remains undertheorized as a creative and compositional act on its own, and literary performance, for its part, is often viewed as occupying a different historical and documentary space, separate from the poetry reading. As well, although the practices of performance and reading do continue to overlap and inform each other, the documentary results of both practices have been, as yet, little studied by critics and students as compositional, creative forms, as creative practice, or in fact, as any sort of practice at all.

Even when its artifacts (recordings, recording devices, devices for extracting information from recordings) do begin to be valorized as objects of study, they are often seen as apparatuses rich with *critical* value, and in this way the performative and embodied event that is the reading is tilted in favour of a science of the apparatus. The actual public reading seems still to be seen as a way of expanding the public for poetry, as merely a means of diffusion: Ashok Mathur has referred to the documentation of readings and the resulting potential for dissemination as the means by which the public poetry reading can "[refuse] the normative delimits of time and space" and reach a significantly broader public.[16]

Yet, authorial resistance, in oral language (as seen with Robert Majzels), in embodiment and voice, and in relation to a poet's own and to other texts, is creative: the reading is an act of literary creation, not just replication of a text whose authentication remains central.

The Canada Council Response to Change

Even the Canada Council acknowledges that different performance manoeuvres jostle the public readings paradigm as they have laid it out. Yet their acknowledgement to date has consisted not of altering the entire paradigm (which would help explode fixed notions of the poetry reading everywhere) but of creating new spaces for support, *outside* the regular public readings program. The current program (2015)—the Spoken Word, Storytelling, and Literary Performance program—includes creation grants as well as grants for series of literary performance events.[17] Requirements for organizing events in the performance program, however, are more onerous than in the regular readings program: at least six events must be organized within a twelve-month period, whereas the regular program requires the organization of four. Canada Council acknowledgement, then, can also be read as *resistance* to a change or new theorization, or as harbouring that resistance:

> Literary performance projects involve media and/or creative collaborations with other disciplines as long as the literary aspect is central. These projects may include film and video performances, digital creation, installation and other creative literary performances that present literature in innovative ways.[18]

For Performance Series Host Organizations

Organizations and collectives that present a minimum of 6 professional, paid spoken word artists, storytellers, and literary performers in performance over a 12-month period may apply to the Performance Series category for support."[19]

While it does provide more open access to funds directed at what it deems to be literary performance, the Canada Council literary performance program continues to maintain its separation from the existing public readings paradigm.

In referring in the guidelines for Literary Performance to "performances that present literature in innovative ways," the Canada Council program guide still promulgates and supports a curiously limiting view: that "literature" exists only prior to performance and is *not* this performance. Under this seemingly new regime or scenario, performances of written text are *not* compositional. They are not works of art in and of themselves—they are not "creations." And because such definitions have consequences, they imply that readings are also not worthy of detailed, consistent study. It seems that literature is only published printed text, as if print gives the work a certain stable quality, an immunity from interference or change, that makes it literature. In it, the creative process is over.

For the Canada Council, the paradigm for including literary performance in the former Spoken Word and Storytelling category resembles the paradigm of the public reading: its role is still one of "presenting" published text, of presenting the book as authoritative and the author as verifier or guarantor of the text and of its stability, and of presenting the author's bodily presence as the source of the text and guarantor of the text's original intentions—assumptions that literary study and textual practice have been calling into question on many fronts, at least since Roland Barthes published "The Death of the Author" more than forty years ago (1968).

As Smaro Kamboureli has noted, "we may call such readings public, but they are really part of a promotion package, and the whole promotion/distribution machinery. In this sense, consumption and commodification are a large part of public readings."[20] Indeed, readings are intended to provide opportunities to sell the text.[21] Because readings have a material impact in the form of book sales, there is pressure on writers to read primarily from books that are also available for sale, rather than other material. This implicitly limits performance possibilities as well as possibilities for recombinatory effects that in performance, might "efface" the presence of this "latest book for sale."

A look at poetry book sales in Canada (and elsewhere) in recent decades shows they have generally been falling.[22] It is increasingly difficult to find a bricks-and-mortar bookstore in a Canadian centre, let alone enter one and find a wide selection of poetry books. Moreover, in our recessionary era, and with the increased costs of education, fewer students—a key audience for poetry—can afford books. And overall, younger people live in smaller apartments with less room for books.[23] Still, public readings thrive in various forms, and people come to them, and get their poetry fix there, and engage in conversations with poets and others. Readings offer opportunities for poets to interact with audiences, to tailor their work to audiences, to elicit responses and conversations that can be creatively fruitful even if—and, even more so, even when—these stray from the reiteration of the "latest book." They offer poets opportunities to co-create, to create live versions of work in an order different from what is in the book; they provide attempts for misreadings, altered readings, responsive readings, collaborative readings. All of these readings have the potential to be recorded, with and without the audience reaction, resulting in a new work of art, a new instance of artistic and writing practice. Poetry is a conversation, and embodied performances by poets of their own work before a live audience are in some way essential to poetry's continuity as an art, and affect its range of possibilities.

Actions and interactions that are part of the contemporary excitement of the public reading (if not its paradigm) actually extend beyond the reading "event." With the ready availability, to authors and audiences equally, of contemporary technology—webcast, podcast, tweetchat, digital video, interactive programs like MUPS at PennSound[24] that allow creation of mash-up readings of other peoples' work—it is possible not just for poets but for poetry audiences to remix poetry, create their own readings, record at readings, relisten to readings, post snippets of readings to YouTube and social media, and post photos to Twitter of the poet with her mouth open. There is also the expanding creation of literary works for the Web that involve visuals, text in movement, text in collision, voice. Live performances of *these* works are *also* literary works, created from what is available on the Web, and different from it. Sometimes the audience itself is orchestrated in the creation of the author's work, as in Robert Majzels's *85 Project* already discussed. Another example is Angela Rawlings's (a.k.a. a.rawlings) collaborative and infinitely generative piece *Gibber,* performed at the 2012 Queensland Poetry Festival in Australia, which involved poetic exchange fields from several continents, and which was even picked up and retweeted by tweetbots;[25] yet another is her "#bpNichol Twitter performance" from 6 June 2013. As more writers see each other's work on the Internet, and travel and perform outside Canada, they return with new views of performance and the written page, of interlingual transfer and contamination, that further disturb the standard readings paradigm and its notion of authorial presence as guarantor for a prior written text.

It is safe to say that the border between the Canada Council–defined literary reading and the Canada Council–defined literary performance has been blurred for some time, or that on the ground, the border never has existed. Some of the most active contemporary Canadian poets work at the point where such a border might blur—a.rawlings, Oana Avasilichioaei, Gary Barwin, derek beaulieu, Gregory Betts, Christian Bök, M. NourbeSe Philip, Jordan Abel, and Rita Wong are examples—and their readings are generative and productive. In particular cases, such as Philip's performances of *Zong!*, the difficulty of the written text itself and its challenges to the printed page necessitate the kind of live reading that is self-consciously performative. In the work of all these poets and more, it is clear that the public reading of poetry by the poet is not just a guarantor of a written text but *is* literature in the making.

The public readings paradigm in Canada, however, both inside and outside the Canada Council, does not yet incorporate these developments; it is still stuck in the twentieth century. Much theorization of the reading in Canada, in its effort to open literary soundworks to deeper study and criticism, has thus had to battle aspects of the paradigm. In his 1998 essay "Sound Reading," Peter Quartermain, a renowned scholar of disjunctive and performative poetics, protests the tendency in the late twentieth century to record poetry readings as if the author's voice would "provide an authoritative and authentic register of the poem's sound," "establishing an orthodoxy" for the poem and for understanding the poem.[26] This tendency, he argues, shuts down both what a poem does and what a voicing can do in terms of production of a work of art. The polyvocality and undecidability in the line,between lines, in the poem, are however, as Quartermain notes, shut down by the "authentic" idea of a reading. A new idea is needed.

Views from Elsewhere
American work on the public reading has moved further than Canadian work (and curiously, Canadian scholars such as Quartermain have found publication more often in the United States and the United Kingdom). Charles Bernstein suggests that "the poetry reading is a public tuning" of the poem; referring to the readings of Creeley, Olson, Ginsberg, and Kerouac in the 1950s, he maintains that "public readings established not only the sound of their work but the possibilities for related work."[27] To establish possibilities for work *is* to work, so why not view the reading itself as a production, as literary, as a creation? Creation is that which establishes possibilities, a ground of possibilities. Texts in performance are torqued, bent, agitated in a physical space with the public before them; the writer is present doing the vocalization or manipulation of vocal information, and is creating the work. What must follow, then, is that the poem, to quote Bernstein again, is "not identical to any one graphical or performative realization of it, nor can it

be equated with a totalized unity of these versions or the manifestations. The poem viewed in terms of its multiple performances...has a fundamentally plural existence. This is most dramatically enunciated when instances of the work are contradictory or incommensurable, but it is also the case when versions are commensurate."[28] The sounding of poetry, the choice of poems, the choice to elide lines or place poems beside each other that are not beside each other in the book, is a creative act, one that re-enacts and repurposes the book. Poetry readings by the best readers enact the poem with the audience; their performance is a further element in the composition, is compositional. Recording (and the ability to re-record and remix) allows study of the reading next to study of the written work (if one exists), so as to examine their co-extensiveness and compositional thrust, not just to study the voice as authoritative reproduction of a prior text.

Bernstein's reconceptualization of the poetry reading as creative production can be supplemented with a critique of the reading made by Hank Lazer in a 1996 essay in *Opposing Poetries*, in which he argued that "readings can and should be part of a broader act of poetic exploration and inquiry. But today that opportunity is being forfeited. So long as poetry readings remain a habitualized form of entertainment, the site of institutionally narrow acts of representation, and the ritualization of brief personalized expression, the poetry reading is condemned to a non-self-reflective act of formal repetition."[29] Feminist critic and poet Rachel Blau DuPlessis, similarly, has pointed out very cogently what is at stake in the reading of poetry and thus in its stagings, and her words point to what begs to be examined and studied in the public reading as creative act:

> "Expressive" (heart to heart) readings of poetry in general and lyric in particular are incredibly naïve about poetry. They overlook any use (i.e. motivated manipulation) of the medium, any particular or selective stagings of subjectivity and its interior clashes, the performances of authenticity, folksiness, seriousness, realness by the writer as the "announced"; they overlook the potential splits among enunciation (textual practices, via the imagined "speaker" of the poem), enounced (semantic, content-laden statement, made by the characters, if any, inside the poem), and the "announced" or the subjective and social agency of the writer as existing person.[30]

The public reading has also been intensively theorized outside the United States. In the United Kingdom, we find, alongside Quartermain, the work of cris cheek on the performances of Bob Cobbing, Bob Cobbing's own work (which began in the 1950s), and the continuing events and acts of the Writers Forum. In cheek's words regarding Cobbing, "No other poet in England in the second half of the twentieth century so persistently and so variously raised issues of *performance* in respect of poetry. Nor did his conception of performance at all rest with the *live* event, as in Phelan's notion of performance only spending and never saving, but with composition and publication." Cobbing held workshops at which, to quote cheek:

> Writing was frequently read by more than voice, two or three voices (or more), reading in close interaction, with syncopation, with overlapping stresses, with partial erasure, foreground and background scripting, staccato narrative assemblages and dialogistic interjection. Texts were sometimes arranged across the floor or cascading from the ceiling or fluttering loose in the hand. Listening with attentive vision was at a premium. Spatial placement of sound became an area of investigation and spatiality of paginated notations, both placement of pages in the room and specialization of writings on the page, were consequent.[31]

That performance of poetry has been strongly considered as creative practice in the United Kingdom is also evidenced by the prestigious and longrunning Performance Writing graduate program at Dartington School of Arts, now based at Falmouth University, which has welcomed practitioners such as the Norwegian-French, but long UK-domiciled, writer Caroline Bergvall[32] and the Canadian writer J.R. Carpenter as theorists and teachers. Bergvall's practice is an excellent example of the ways that, within the program and as a result of the interaction between teaching and practice, theory of performance and text and their interactions has been developed. Also, British journals such as *Performance Research*[33] have provided venues for curation and critical writing by poets working with performative practice. While the conventional poetry reading (unselfconscious and promotional) still dominates in the United Kingdom, as it does in Canada, the level of creative performance and thinking on performance there has been astounding. Because it is rarely if ever cited in Canada (compared to work based in the United States, for example, which is often cited as if we too were Americans), it appears to be insufficiently read by Canadian writers and critics looking outside our borders for examples of theorization of public reading practice.

In South America and Europe, works that theorize public reading and performance space have provoked the thinking of those writers who share their languages in Canada, although the original works are rarely engaged directly by English-speaking scholars of poetry practice. As one example, the Argentinian Adrián Cangi in the Chilean journal *Nomadías* links the oft-cited "whatever singularity" of Italian philosopher Giorgio Agamben to the work on performativity and gender of American philosopher Judith Butler: "Poema y *performance* configuran 'seres de sensación' con reglas expresivas propias, que producen pasajes secretos entre el cuerpo de la escritura y el de la presentación escénica, entre la intimidad del poema y la pública 'histéresis' performática... Todo conduce a la vibración del entrelugar, dominio del 'cuerpo vibrátil' o 'ser de sensación,' donde se amplían los dones poéticos e escénicos a expensas de cualquier pretendida unidad."[34]

Given the seminal and influential late-twentieth-century work of Judith Butler on the repetitivity and inscription of performative regimes, and of Donna Haraway on prosthetic bodies, there is a yet further opportunity insufficiently explored: to productively look at current developments in brain science and in sensory behaviour for data that can be applied critically and creatively to the practice of the poetry reading and to poetic performance. The possibilities of "new sensory modalities"[35] that result from new knowledge of the brain's plasticity provide conjunctions and could have interesting consequences for reading practice and its study, from both the creative and the critical viewpoint. Suffice to say there is much ground that could be covered in the future, and covered jointly with critics and poets, in developing a new paradigm for the poetry reading and its study in Canada and across borders.

Toward Altering the Canadian Paradigm
Our critique of the reliance on an idea or ideal of authorial intention is not new. A similar critique was made in 2008 by Smaro Kamboureli in the special issue of *Open Letter* on the public reading, in which she lamented what she called "*This-is-where-it-came-from readings*, i.e. when a poet spends ten minutes explaining a poem that takes less than a minute to read. Thank you, dear poet, but no. I don't want you reducing your poem to a little tale of origins."[36] But if our argument has its seed in Kamboureli, *she* is preceded by others, including Denise Levertov, who demanded the same change from poets over forty years ago (1965, in fact: a long time to be making the same demands): "Unconfident of the poem as an existence, created and having its own life and power, they talk about it beforehand as if to conjure it into being. They tell you what it is about, out of what circumstances it arose, what it 'tries to say'. By the time the poor poem itself gets read, it seems merely a metrical paraphrase of anecdotes already related."[37] Frank Davey would probably wonder if the poem has managed to "Surviv[e] the Paraphrase" of the poetry reading. Yes, it has, and poets too will survive these demands.

The Poet's View, Performed by Erín and Spoken by Karis

To a poet, a performance of poetry *is* a literary text that takes place off the page. Each time I perform, I find a track through a book or combination of texts, and I extract and reconnect elements of the writing into a new writing and then present it with and through my body, my voice's instrument. My performance of the book each time is singular, just as a performance of a musical composition is singular. Singular and intentional. The passage of the text through my body and the audience response to it then go on to affect my subsequent composition of future readings from the work, and of future works for the page. If we believe Jacques Derrida when he says that "Form belongs to the content of the work," and that writing "creates meaning by enregistering it, by entrusting it to an engraving, a groove, a relief, to a surface whose essential characteristic is to be infinitely transmissible," then the poetry reading, with its possibility of recording, remixing, recontextualization, study, regrooving, also creates meaning.[38] It is not reiteration but is compositional, a response to exigencies of writing practice that arise at the moment when a live audience accompanies the process. It is, thus, a literary act.

It necessarily involves the body. Following developments in feminist and performance critical theory since the 1980s, we now recognize more freely the polyvalent nature of bodies and social demarcations of gendering, the existence of cultural markings on "the body," and the impossibility of saying "the body" without immediately problematizing the term. The "infinitely transmissible" of Derrida demands this polyvalent body, demands compositional loops that enter the transmission process differentially, transversally.

Even in the long moment of initial composition, when the writer is not thinking at all of the human audience (the public may be ideas, trees, dead people, a glint of light), past performances of previous works enter them and affect the composition process. The effect of the public is still present.

The Critic's View, Performed by Karis and Spoken by Erín

We are calling for change not only on the part of poets but perhaps even more so from critics. For a critic, the best poetry readings to see and hear are self-reflexive performances that deliberately disrupt the notion of the author as definitive interpreter of their own work. They may do this by collaborating (the Four Horsemen, Nicole Brossard), by playing with pseudonyms and heteronyms (Moure), by performing cover poems, by having others read poems in their place (Majzels), and the like. But until critics and professors of poetry approach readings as creative productions worthy of critical response in the form of scholarship, discussion, and review rather than as interesting supplements to poetry collections, we are complicit in perpetuating the same old paradigm. As professors of poetry, we need to teach poetry on the page and off the page, to borrow a title from Marjorie Perloff. We need to treat the *reading* as a text worth studying either by bringing students to a live performance or by having them listen to recorded audiotexts or videotexts from archives such as PennSound or SpokenWeb 2.0, and by helping our students develop a theoretical vocabulary to talk about the performances they're witnessing—about the space, the bodies, the audience, the technology. We need to think critically through the role of the poetry reading's public: What would it mean to bring performance theorist Jill Dolan's notion of the feminist spectator to the space of a poetry reading? What would it mean to consistently think about notions of embodiment in the context of a poetry reading? We need a critical space to think these ideas through collaboratively, as poets and critics together, and we need to move beyond the paradigm that centralizes value only in the printed page or book, whether by the Canada Council rules, in university courses, or in criticism.

Chorus to Stand as a Conclusion

Finally, as poet and critic, we share the conviction that a new paradigm for the public reading as performative and creative will help spur the evolution of collaborative critical and creative poetic space, and will also spur the evolution and application of new pedagogies for teaching literature to and among critics and poets, not separately but together, with both positions seen as rife with creative and literary possibilities. These evolving pedagogies can engage poetry on the printed page, the poetry reading and its material documents, and philology and the lived bodies of students, as well as philosophies regarding positionality and incorporation, all to better draw out the potentials, stakes, and new possibilities, and, in understanding, to alter literary roles and free creative possibilities for poets, editors, teachers, and critics. Poetry and its publics will both emerge richer.

Notes

1. Lecker, "The Canada Council's," 439, 446.
2. Lecker, "The Canada Council's," 446.
3. Lecker, "The Canada Council's," 443.
4. Lecker, "The Canada Council's," 446.
5. Beach, *Poetic Culture*, 123.
6. Canada Council for the Arts, "Program Description," n.pag.
7. Genette, *Paratexts*, 370.
8. Majzels, Huot, and Moyes, "'The Public Reading," 15.

9 Majzels, Huot, and Moyes, "'The Public Reading," 15.
10 See, for example, Pauline Butling and Susan Rudy's study *Writing in Our Time: Canada's Radical Poetries in English 1957–2003* (2005).
11 http://www.thecanadianencyclopedia.com/articles/emc/music-gallery.
12 See Glenn Lewis, "Intermedia History," Accessed 12 September 2014 at http://www.videoout.ca/catalog/intermedia-history; "Ruins in Process: Vancouver Art in the Sixties," accessed 12 September 2014 at http://vancouverartinthesixties.com; Michael Lithgow, "Decadent Resistance," accessed 12 September 2014 at http://www.academia.edu/200251/Decadent_Resistance_The_Aesthetics_of_Politics_and_Politics_of_Aesthetics_in_Vancouver_Video_Practice_1967-2006.
13 "The Origins of the Western Front," accessed 12 September 2014 at http://arcpost.ca/articles/arclines-western-front.
14 Stanton and Tinguely, *Impure*.
15 http://archives.concordia.ca/P027.
16 Mathur and Kamboureli, "On Public Readings and Pedagogy," 126.
17 It used to be called the Spoken Word and Storytelling Program. In 2010–11, it was renamed the Literary Performance and Spoken Word Program; in late 2012 it was renamed again the Spoken Word, Storytelling, and Literary Performance Program. The very instability of the nomenclature demonstrates the impossibility of maintaining the existing paradigms for long.
18 http://www.canadacouncil.ca/writing-and-publishing/find-a-grant/grants/spoken-word-storytelling-and-literaryperformance.
19 http://www.canadacouncil.ca/writing-and-publishing/find-a-grant/grants/spoken-word-storytelling-and-literaryperformance.
20 Mathur and Kamboureli, "On Public Readings," 128.
21 We could analyze as well where the poetry text is sold: publicly funded readings are held in public spaces such as bookstores and libraries but also in universities, and many of the bookstore, library, and gallery readings are sponsored by universities. The book or work is often "sold" for academic recognition. The paradigm of the public reading, as it exists, occludes notions of the commerce of canonicity, which merit exploration but are beyond the scope of this presentation.
22 See Gold, *Publishing Lives*, 443; Daniel Zomparelli, "Poetry Is Dead: What the Hell Happened?," accessed 27 May 2013 at http://poetryisdead.ca/content/poetry-dead-what-hell-happened.html; Erín Moure's experience with Anansi as described in the 2010 interview *"Crossing Borders with Our Work*: Interview with Erín Moure," in Dobson and Kamboureli, *Producing Canadian Literature*.
23 Michael Babad, "Why Canadian Houses, Condos, Are Getting Smaller," *Globe and Mail*, 19 September 2012, accessed 11 September 2014 at http://www.theglobeandmail.com/report-on-business/top-business-stories/why-canadian

-houses-condos-are-getting-smaller/article4553323; Jim Adai, "Canada's condos are getting smaller," *RealtyTimes.com*, 19 November 2012, accessed 11 September 2014 at http://realtytimes.com/rtpages/20121120_canadacondos.htm.
24 Visit http://glia.ca/2012/mups/pennsound.
25 Visit "Queensland Poetry Festival," accessed 11 September 2014 at http://www.queenslandpoetryfestival.com; and http://qldpir.tumblr.com, accessed 18 September 2012: "Exciting update on the *Gibber* performance debut this Saturday @ the Queensland Poetry Festival: I'll be joined onstage by fellow sibyl Maja Jantar (via Skype from Belgium), *Gibberbird* response poet Nicholas Powell (read the poem here!), and local writers Chloë Callistemon and Tamara Lazaroff. And, as mentioned in the previous post, we'll have just over 20 fantastic writers from around the world tweeting through video projection."
26 Quartermaine, "Sound Reading," 223.
27 Bernstein, *Close Listening*, 6.
28 Bernstein, *Close Listening*, 7.
29 Lazar, *Opposing Poetries*, 54.
30 DuPlessis, "Lyric and Experimental Long Poems," 28.
31 cheek, "Bob Cobbing."
32 On Bergvall, see cheek at "Reading and Writing: The Sites of Performance," accessed 12 September 2012 at http://www.asu.edu/pipercwcenter/how2journal/vol_3_no_3/bergvall/cheek-reading-writing.html.
33 http://www.thecpr.org.uk/shop/journal.php.
34 "Poem and performance configure 'sensorial beings' that have their own expressive rules, which produce secret passages between the body of writing and its stage presentation, between the intimacy of the poem and its public performative "hysteresis"... Everything leads to the vibration of a 'between-space," where the 'resonant body' or 'sensorial being' reigns, and where poetic and scenic givens amplify at the expense of any supposed unity."
35 Pais-Vieira et al., "Simultaneous Top-down Modulation."
36 Mathur and Kamboureli, "On Public Readings," 128.
37 Levertov, "Some Notes on Organic Form," 447.
38 Derrida, "Force and Signification," 7.

Bibliography

Beach, Christopher. *Poetic Culture: Contemporary American Poetry Between Community and Institution*. Evanston: Northwestern University Press, 1999.

Bernstein, Charles. "Introduction," in *Close Listening: Poetry and the Performed Word*. Edited by Charles Bernstein. 3–26. New York: Oxford University Press, 1998.

Butler, Judith. *Gender Trouble*. London: Routledge, 1990.

Butling, Pauline, and Susan Rudy. *Writing in Our Time: Canada's Radical Poetries in English (1957–2003)*. Waterloo: Wilfrid Laurier University Press, 2005.

Cangi, Adrián. "Impromptu: Aproximaciones a la performance poética." *Revista Nomadías* 16 (November 2012): 177–85.

cheek, cris. "Bob Cobbing." Accessed 1 June 2013 http://www.southampton.ac.uk/~bepc/forum/cheek_cobbing.htm.

Cho, Lily, and Melina Baum Singer, eds. "Dialogues on Poetics and Public Culture." *Open Letter*, Special Issue, 13, no. 7 (2008): i–xvii.

de Lauretis, Teresa. "Eccentric Subjects: Feminist Theory and Historical Consciousness." *Feminist Studies* 16, no. 1 (1990): 115–50.

Derrida, Jacques. "Force and Signification." In *Writing and Difference*. Translated by Alan Bass. 3–30. Chicago: University of Chicago Press, 1978.

Dobson, Kit, and Smaro Kamboureli. *Producing Canadian Literature: Authors Speak on the Literary Marketplace*. Wilfrid Laurier University Press, 2013.

Dolan, Jill. "Materialist Feminism: Apparatus-Based Theory and Practice." In *The Feminist Spectator as Critic*. 1988. Reprint. 99–117. Ann Arbor: University of Michigan Press, 1991.

Drucker, Johanna. "Visual Performance of the Poetic Text." In Bernstein. 131–61.

DuPlessis, Rachel Blau. "Lyric and Experimental Long Poems: Intersections." In *Time in Time: Short Poems, Long Poems, and the Rhetoric of North American Avant-Gardism, 1963–2008*. 22–50. Montreal and Kingston: McGill-Queen's University Press, 2013.

Fanselow, Erika E., and Miguel A.L. Nicolelis. "Behavioral Modulation of Tactile Responses in the Rat Somatosensory System." *Journal of Neuroscience* 19, no. 17 (1999): 7603–16.

Genette, Gerard. *Paratexts: Thresholds of Interpretation*. Translated by Jane E. Lewin. London: Cambridge University Press, 1997.

Gingell, Susan and Wendy Roy, eds. *Listening Up, Writing Down, Looking Beyond: Interfaces of the Oral, Written, and Visual*. Waterloo: Wilfrid Laurier University Press, 2012.

Gold, Jerome. *Publishing Lives: Interviews with Independent Book Publishers in the Pacific Northwest and British Columbia*. Mill Creek: Black Heron, 2010.

Haraway, Donna. "A Cyborg Manifesto: Science, Technology, and Socialist Feminism in the Late Twentieth Century." In *Simians, Cyborgs and Women: The Reinvention of Nature*. 149–81. New York: Routledge, 1991.

Lazar, Hank. *Opposing Poetries: Readings*. Evanston: Northwestern University Press, 1996.

Lecker, Robert. "The Canada Council's Block Grant Program and the Construction of Canadian Literature." *English Studies in Canada* 25, nos. 3–4 (1999): 439–69.

Levertov, Denise. "Some Notes on Organic Form," *Poetry Foundation* 106, no. 6 (1965): 440–55.

Majzels, Robert, with Claire Huot and Lianne Moyes. "'The Public Reading Is a Matter of the Public Reading': the 85 Project." In Cho and Singer. 14–39.

Mathur, Ashok, and Smaro Kamboureli. "On Public Readings and Pedagogy." In Cho and Singer. 125–39.

Rawlings, Angela, et al. *Gibber.* Queensland Poetry Residency and Festival, Queensland Australia, 2012. http://arawlings.is/gibber.

Pais-Vieira, Miguel, et al. "A Brain-to-Brain Interface for Real-Time Sharing of Sensorimotor Information." *Scientific Reports.* http://www.nature.com/srep/2013/130228/srep01319/full/srep01319.html.

Pais-Vieira, Miguel, Mikhail A. Lebedev, Michael C. Wiest, and Miguel A.L. Nicolelis. "Simultaneous Top-down Modulation of the Primary Somatosensory Cortex and Thalamic Nuclei during Active Tactile Discrimination." *Journal of Neuroscience* 33, no. 9 (2013): 4076–93. http://www.jneurosci.org/content/33/9/4076.abstract.

Quartermain, Peter. "Sound Reading." In Bernstein. 217–30.

Stanton, Victoria, and Vincent Tinguely. *Impure, Reinventing the Word: The Theory, Practice, and Oral History of Spoken Word in Montreal.* Denver: Conundrum Press, 2001.

14

We Are the Amp: A Poetics of the Human Microphone

Michael Nardone

Poetic forms emerge out of public contexts of language, as response, as confrontation. The emergent contexts of forms more traditionally situated within poetic practice have been explored and described widely—for example, the metrical devices of Ancient Greek verse as mnemonic aids for the oral circulation of information across space, and the sestina's repetitive structure that allowed one to showcase both craft and improvisation during feasts or gatherings. Yet the fetishization of these forms—their replication as static modes emptied of histories—is all too often executed to produce works that fit safely within an untroubled concept of a genre called "poetry." It is in this context, Charles Bernstein argues, that poetry, a poetics, is absent. "*Poetry is aversion to conformity* in the pursuit of new forms, or can be," he writes at the beginning of *A Poetics*. He continues: "When poetry averts conformity it enters into the contemporary: speaking to the pressures and conflicts of the moment with the means just then at hand."[1] Formal innovation and deviation can energize and innervate language—creating new possibilities for content, alternative circulations—and thus act as a transfigurative and transfigurating element of public life.

This chapter focuses on a poetics of the human microphone, the method of sound amplification and multivocalic mode of collective composition, communication, and intervention utilized at Occupy protests. As described by Richard Kim, the basic method of the human microphone is simple:

"Mic check?" someone implores.
"MIC CHECK!" the crowd shouts back, more or less in unison. [...]
After the mic check, the meeting proceeds:
>   with every few words/
>   WITH EVERY FEW WORDS!
>   repeated and amplified out loud/
>   REPEATED AND AMPLIFIED OUT LOUD!
>   by what has been dubbed/
>   BY WHAT HAS BEEN DUBBED!
>   the human microphone/
>   THE HUMAN MICROPHONE![2]

From texts, videos, and images compiled from social media sites, digital repositories, and other online sources, I contextualize the emergence of the human microphone at Occupy protests, locating specific moments of formal variation in its practice during the period 17 September to 19 November 2011, from the start of the protests at Zuccotti Park to the days immediately following the park's forced closure. In this historical sketch, I focus on five distinct modes: (1) the specific context in which the human microphone as a form and method emerged; (2) the human microphone's various tunings as a technique to relay communications; (3) its application as an interventionist form that draws attention to and disrupts specific transmissions; (4) the human microphone as a form in which collective bodies can speak to and against brutalities carried out by state-sponsored forces; and, finally, (5) the human microphone as a device to frame silence with new semantic affect. Finally, I begin to outline a concept of sonic disobedience, a mode of phonemic composition that interrupts particular transmissions while at the same time encoding alternative transmissions in a mesh of noise.

To situate this essay for a book concerned with literary practices and publics, I want to offer a theoretical framework by which I approach a poetics of the human microphone. As opposed to the public event of the poetry reading—one, say, in which a text written by an individual in a private writing space serves as a score for a public performance—I concern myself with the language event: the temporal site(s) of vocalic space and transitive language. Here, I look to the work of Steven Connor, who develops a concept of *vocalic space*:

> I mean to signal with this term the ways in which differing conceptions of the body's form, measure, and susceptibility, along with its articulations with its physical and social environments. In the idea of vocalic space, the voice may be grasped as the mediation between

the phenomenological body and its social and cultural contexts. Vocalic space signifies the ways in which the voice is held both to operate in, and itself to articulate, different conceptions of space, as well as to enact the different relations between the body, community, time, and divinity. What space means, in short, is very largely a function of the perceived powers of the body to occupy and extend itself through its environment.[3]

Then, to consider elements of verbal composition within this vocalic space, I look to the writings of Lyn Hejinian, who develops an idea of transitive language. Following from, and/or counter to, Charles Olson's projectivist poetics, where the poet attempts to transfer the energy of breath, language, and pace of a privately scripted poem to a public audience or readership,[4] a transitive poetics privileges a live public moment of multivocalic composition, the phonemic moment for which any graphemic poem emergent from that moment might function as a documentative or archival text. Through the experiment of the multivocalic production of a language event and that event's (possible) poem-text(s), the poem functions not as "an isolated autonomous rarefied aesthetic object"; instead, as Hejinian writes, it moves towards a production in which "aesthetic discovery is congruent with social discovery" and "new ways of thinking (new relationships among the components of thought) make new ways of being possible."[5] I connect these compositional elements to two concerns I read as being central to performance writing. As Caroline Bergvall asks: "What is the process of live performance in its relation to writing. Is it writing's role, in that context, to function as a guiding background, as the blueprint of a live piece?"[6] More recently, David Buuck has asked: "How might the performance writing form of 'action' expand beyond the recognizable activist performance model (scripts for street theater, etc.) and/or the much more militant and confrontational modes of direct action which are generally discussed in terms of efficacy (symbolic &/or material) rather than 'as performance' (as if the latter threatens to turn the political into the "merely" aesthetic)?"[7]

Within this poetical framework, a space is opened up to address the formal qualities of the human microphone and its components: the speaker and speakers, their utterances, the locality of their utterances, what and how they convey, the embodied distribution, of voiced language across space, the media and platforms that make this language mobile, the repetition and difference of the language in its movement across networks of communications, and, finally, what sounded language becomes audible and what remains mute. Through an "intertwining of the semantic and the pragmatic"—"what we say and what we accomplish in that saying"[8]—the human microphone exemplifies Bernstein's concept of "poetry as dissent, including formal dissent; poetry that makes sounds possible to be heard that are not otherwise articulated."[9]

Of Amplitude

20 September 2011. Occupy Wall Street, day 4: On the Broadway side of Zuccotti Park—then three days away from being renamed Liberty Plaza—an individual addressed a few dozen demonstrators with regard to the pending execution of Troy Davis in Georgia. "Sisters and brothers, it is ridiculous that I cannot address you with a sound system. I just want you to think about it, how petty and stupid and insulting it is that on such a serious occasion, trying to stop a racist murder—" ... then the sound of his words faded out.

The man continued to speak and gesture with his hands opened up before him, but the sound of city traffic and murmur of talk filled the public space, drowning out his words. Only occasional bursts of accented speech became audible. After several seconds, these words could be be heard: "Thank you very much for nothing." He uttered this sentence at a sustained volume above his previous words. Then, again, his voice faded out. Various phrases continued to rise above the ambient din: "who spent half of his life in prison" ... "is going to be murdered" ... "racist murder" ... "that we're talking about here at Wall Street" ... "where you've been camping" ... "three nights." Over the next minute and a half, again, occasional phrases could be heard: "Wall Street responsible" ... "profits instead of needs" ... "motives behind wars" ... "death penalty" ... "very powerful thing" ... "very necessary thing" ... "occupying Wall Street" ... "stop the execution of this innocent man" ... "march united."[10]

Earlier that morning, members of the New York Police Department had informed the occupiers of Zuccotti Park that if they wanted to use amplified sound in a public space, they would need a permit from the NYPD. This meant that microphones and loudspeakers—used throughout the previous three days' events and demonstrations—would from that point on be banned at Zuccotti. And as Kim reported a few days later on *The Nation*'s blog, "the NYPD has also been interpreting the law to include battery-powered bullhorns. Violators can be sentenced for up to thirty days in prison."[11] Thus, on the evening of 20 September, the only spoken words to reach an amplitude loud enough to cross the space of Zuccotti Park were ones spoken in a call-and-answer unison. Two voices shouted: "They say death row!" A crowd voice responded: "We say hell no!" Two voices: "Death Row!" Crowd voice: "Hell No." Following this repetition, an individual voice called out: "We Are," and a crowd voice replied: "Troy Davis." In this collective articulation of a single voice—in the figurative embodiment of a We in the individual Troy Davis, and the literal embodiment of individuated, multivocal speech voiced in collective unison—we have one of the first annunciations of a vocalic body in the Occupy movement.

On 21 September, the general assembly at Zuccotti convened at one o'clock in the afternoon. There were several items on the agenda: the still-pending execution of Troy Davis, assembly procedures, arrest procedures, and methods for sharing documentary footage, specifically, footage capturing the previous day's arrests. This was followed by reports from the various subgroups forming peripherally to the general assembly. The two facilitators, "Katchup" and "Emery," announced to all assembled that "it's going to be hard to hear people with different ability to vocalize what they're saying" and that people "need to be patient with the process and each other."[12] Twice, they called for everyone involved to move closer together. Before continuing to the first items, the facilitators asked for two people to step forward "to act as human mics," one on each end of the assembly. As the agenda moved on to announcements, the initial two human mics grew to several dozen people repeating each speaker's phrases, whose voices carried across the assembly space information regarding child care, news of occupations planned in other American cities and abroad, a proposal to found a Zuccotti Park cleanup crew, and a message from Noam Chomksy in solidarity with the movement's cause. Then a man who called himself Radio Raheem, self-described as "one of the pioneers of the conscious hip-hop movement," stood before the assembly and, with the most enthusiastic support yet from the human microphone, declared:

We don't need
an amplifier.
We are
the amp![13]

(For excerpts transcribed from documented uses of the human microphone, I have enjambed the lines at the moment in which the primary speaker's words are repeated by those involved in the human microphone.) From this moment forward, those gathered at Zuccotti Park began to utilize this new form of communicative exchange.

At this point, it is useful to recall the nearly complete mainstream media blackout on the subject of Occupy Wall Street in its first days. "After five straight days of sit-ins, marches and shouting and some arrests, actual

Figure 1 *The apologetic tweet from @YahooCare after Yahoo blocked occupywallst.org*

North American coverage of [Occupy Wall Street]—even by those who have thought it farce or failure—has been limited to one blurb in a free newspaper in Manhattan and a column in the *Toronto Star*," Keith Olbermann broadcast on his 21 September show. Olbermann then makes note of one media venue that acknowledged the uprising: Yahoo, "which blocked any email containing the group's website with the message, 'Suspicious activity has been detected on your account.'"[14] To situate the first utilizations of the human microphone within a more broadly defined network context, mainstream media were refusing to acknowledge the Occupy Wall Street demonstrations as an event—indeed, various regulators of user-driven social media sites were blocking users from disseminating information about the event. It is also worth noting that over this specific span of time—from the afternoon of 20 September to the evening of 21 September—in the hours of heightening media attention and speculation concerning whether Troy Davis would receive a last-minute stay of execution, a controversy with regard to Twitter allegedly blocking "#TroyDavis" from trending was rising across social media and blogs, and would continue to do so until after Davis's execution at 11:08 (EST), when, in minutes, "#RIPTroyDavis" went to the top of worldwide trending topics.[15] So, it was within this extended blackout moment when—

September 22, 2011 | Technology

Did Twitter Block the #TroyDavis and #TooMuchDoubt Hashtags?

With Troy Davis' life hanging in the balance Wednesday night, people around the world took to social media, and Facebook and Twitter timelines were flooded with pleas to judges and prosecutors to spare his life.

In the days leading up to the execution, Twitter's "trending topics," a daily list of the most talked about items, noticeably were missing Troy Davis' name. The hashtag, #toomuchdoubt, used to describe the prosecution's case, was also absent from the list.

As of this morning, a story that had attracted worldwide media attention couldn't even crack the list of trending topics in Atlanta. Instead, #youknowyoughetto was trending #1 worldwide for the better part of the day.

Did Twitter block Troy Davis and #toomuchdoubt from trending?

Figure 2 *Screen capture from politics365.com*

(1) police banned Occupy Wall Street demonstrators from using electric sound systems;

(2) North American major news media services, applying news censorship comparable to media suppression at the start of the Tunisian and Egyptian revolutions, for five days refused to acknowledge the thousands of organized protesters demonstrating amidst the central hub of global capital in Lower Manhattan;

(3) social media networks such as Yahoo and Twitter, major venues of information exchange for revolutionary undertakings during the Arab Spring, intentionally blacked out various politically volatile subjects from being relayed and thus from building some kind of public consensus, otherwise known as "digital repression;" and, finally,

(4) an African American man charged with killing a police officer in Georgia, after nearly two decades of appeals and petitions and three stays of execution, despite testaments of racial prejudice and questions about the validity of evidence in the trial, and despite

the accused's ongoing protestations of innocence and nearly a million people voicing their objections in petition and in protest to his capital punishment, was executed—

that the occupiers of Zuccotti Park had to seek out some new mode of communication, a new amplitude.

Mic Check
During the first days of the human microphone at Occupy Wall Street, many of those who participated in it did so with audible frustration and impatience. Breaking up the uttered language into phrasable units that carried from one to three times in repetition throughout a collective body made for a slow process. If a speaker included too long a phrase or fell out of rhythm with the phrasal repetitions, the human microphone was prone to being jammed, requiring the speaker to begin all over again.

One can hear moments of both hesitation and satisfaction in a video documenting the General Assembly on 25 September. The assembly went in and out of using the human microphone. In some moments, speakers became impatient to communicate their message and abandoned it, raising their voices to shout their words to the assembly. Then one member of a subgroup finished her report with the statement, "We still call for questions and concerns." This is a simple sentence divided into two phrasal units, the first involving sentence subject and preposition, the second the two mutual objects of the preposition. The statement was tuned to the microphone in that it was carried across in full register. Then the facilitator asked: "How do you feel about that?" He called for a vote from all of those in attendance, yet oddly, the call was not carried across the human microphone. After the vote, a member made a suggestion on the point of concern. None of her words, as she spoke them, got carried across the human microphone. Members of the assembly, even those near her, began to shout: "We can't hear!" So the facilitator spoke:

> What she said
> was that
> the proposal
> be written in paper
> so we can see it
> when we discuss
> whether or not
> to approve it.[16]

This delivery was tuned to the human microphone, and the speaker's emphasized pauses after the only a few syllables per each uttered unit allowed the words to move across it with ease.

The facilitator then introduced an additional speaker in regard to the point under discussion. This new speaker began: "Hello, I am very glad to see you all. Here are many good people gathered together."[17] In the second of these two eleven-syllable phrasal units, the speaker lost half the human microphone. People began to relay "Here are many good people" as the primary speaker continued to speak "gathered here together." One portion of the human microphone finished on the word "people" as the other portion of the human microphone began "Here's many good people gathered here together." The speaker continued: "We need more people." As the human microphone began to relay, the primary speaker attempted to continue his sentence. The process then collapsed into disassembled noise. Someone interrupted the primary speaker by shouting "Mic check." This reorganized the vocalic body, and the crowd voice responded: "Mic check!" The primary speaker then attempted to begin again, and to reground his own speaking, he called again: "Mic check," which, too, the human microphone repeated. The primary speaker then began to organize his utterances into four or five syllables each, but a change of a different order took place. Much of the vocalic body of the human microphone seemed to have lost patience with this speaker, and with each utterance, the volume of those responding decreased until only a few voices echoed his words.[18] This exemplifies well Kim Wanenchack's point that the human microphone "cannot be co-opted by one person with one specific interest, because the components of the microphone must consent to their own participation. In that sense it helps to build and maintain a feeling of consensus in an environment that many have framed as ideologically fractured and unclear."[19] The human microphone may create some kind of cohesion at the level of language among those participating, yet one aspect of this technique is that those participating can intentionally alter the volume, making it higher in some kind of concordance or lower in some form of disagreement.

Over the following days, protesters at Zuccotti Park tested and developed the human microphone during general assemblies and with the growing number of visitors who came each day to address the occupiers, from Judith Butler to Joseph Stiglitz to Slavoj Žižek. The human microphone resounded for the first time across mainstream media after Michael Moore's visit to the encampment on the night of 26 September.[20] Moore was uncertain at first about what he might be getting himself into, pausing for a several moments after saying "Mic check" as though he were a new user of a personal recording machine, rewinding and playing back his first recorded utterances. "Does this thing work?" he seemed to be pondering. "Can you hear me now?" His impromptu speech, delivered through the human microphone to an audience of several hundred in the plaza, tuned in with the human microphone even as he uttered phrasal units of ten to fifteen syllables per unit. Although occasionally clunky, and often textured with subclausal phrases within a single phrasal unit, his off-the-cuff directness translated surprisingly well through the crowd voice.

Cornel West, professor and civil rights activist, began his words to the General Assembly on 27 September in a language mixture at once homily, jazz, and rhetoric, a style harking back to an earlier period of American civic declamation.[21] As the primary speaker in the human microphone, West's phrasal units followed an iambic pattern with variations into spondees, dactyls, and anapests. More often than not these rhythmic variations were the final syllables of each phrasal unit and functioned as kind of sending off of the phrase, an envois. West's language moved from a kind of civil rights affirmation of community and good feeling—

There is a sweet spirit in this place.

—to a jargonized political activism—

We oppose
the greed of Wall Street oligarchs
and corporate plutocrats
who squeeze the democratic juices.

—to humble playfulness—

I am so blessed to be here.
You got me spiritually break dancing all the way here.

—and ended in the longest phrasal unit of his speech, a Baptist-styled benediction—

This is the general assembly consecrated from your witness
 and your body and your mind.

West's rhythmic language and fluctuation of tones harnessed the energy of the human microphone to an exceptional degree. In doing so, it seemed more than fitting that at the end of the human microphone's sixth day at

Occupy Wall Street, the first phrases spoken by the vocalic body after West's speech were:

> We the people
> have found our voice.[22]

Interventionist Form
Within two weeks the Occupy movement had expanded from Zuccotti Park to a number of other North American cities. There were encampments and rallies in cities from Edmonton to Boston, Vancouver to Tallahassee, Los Angeles to Halifax. Within a month, Occupy-related protests had spread to 951 cities in 82 countries. In many of these manifestations, these events and encampments adopted various practices from the camp at Zuccotti Park, while also developing practices specific to the site and its particular concerns. In many locations where there was no ban on electric amplifiers, demonstrators took up the human microphone as though it were the *de facto* rhetorical mode for how collective communications ought to be carried out. I have no interest in discussing those sites that simply repeated the form of the human microphone so as to experience or express some form of solidarity with those at Zuccotti Park. Instead, I focus on those moments where the use of the human microphone, to echo Bernstein again, averted conformity and entered into the contemporary, "speaking to the pressures and conflicts of the moment with the means just then at hand."

One such instance took place on 3 November, when protesters utilized the human microphone's ability to relay communications as a means to *interrupt* transmissions, as a direct protest. When Wisconsin governor Scott Walker, proponent of the union-breaking Budget Repair Bill, came to speak at a breakfast at Chicago's Union League Club, he was welcomed with a "mic check!"[23] Here is a transcription of that event, with some notation. After the "mic check" on Governor Walker, the primary speaker shouted across the room:

> It's an outrage and a shame
> that we sit here at this fancy breakfast
> to listen to someone

The human microphone delivered these phrases with precision and great amplitude. Walker, attempting to interrupt and speak over the human microphone, could be heard commenting: "Their voices are a little bit different than others out there."

who has wreaked havoc

Then, as the primary speaker in the human microphone gets confronted by several people, possibly security, the role of primary speak shifted to another person:

> on the lives of working families.
> Governor Walker has vilified unions
> and insulted the 99%,

Then, again, the primary speaker in the human microphone shifted:

> who depend on living wages
> and adequate benefits to support their families,

At this point, a speaker from the ULCC, who was quite upset, took the microphone from Walker and attempted to drown out the human microphone with his electrically amplified voice or perhaps to lure it into quietude with the utterances: "Hey hey hey hey hey woh woh woh woh woh woh woh." Yet the human microphone continued:

> while on the payroll
> of the right-wing billionaire Koch brothers.
> It is not so different from our state

A man from a nearby table, possibly a security guard, then came over to where the video was being made and asked, "How's it going, guys?" He was attempting to get the camera to stop recording. When this failed to work, he tried to pull the camera out of the cameraman's hands, saying "Put the camera down." This did not work, and the filming continued:

> where corporations and bought-off politicians
> clamor to find ways to grant
> a $100 million tax break

The speaker from the ULCC then said, "Can we have a round of applause here?" This was another attempt to drown out the human microphone:

> to the Mercantile Exchange,

The applause worked much better than the prior attempts to hush out the human microphone. In response, the primary speaker in the human microphone shifted again, this time to a speaker with a more resonant voice:

> one of the most profitable companies in the state,
> while social services are being slashed,
> while workers' pensions are being threatened

When clapping failed to drown out the words of the human microphone, the crowd began to boo loudly while continuing to applaud:

> and homelessness, poverty, and joblessness
> continue to rise.[24]

As the applause and boos faded, the primary speaker's voice rose to its greatest amplitude.

> The CME has already taken
> $15 million in our TIF dollars.[25]
> That's our tax money that would have gone
> to help the students in the Chicago Public Schools.

So far, every attempt to counter the human microphone had failed. The human microphone had full control of the sonic space:

> It is ironic that we give Governor Walker
> free rein to say what he wants
> while the Mayor has ordered the arrest
> of over 300 people in Occupy Chicago
> who have simply tried to express
> their rights to freedom of assembly.

The ULCC speaker, over the electrically amplified microphone, tried one more time to interrupt, shouting, "Ladies and Gentlemen, hey hey hey hey." It had little effect:

> and working people will not honour
> anyone seeking to undermine our lives
> for the benefit of the 1%.

The protesters had used the human microphone to deliver their entire message. As a conclusion, in unison, they shouted in repetition: "Union busting is disgusting!" Throughout the event, Walker had stood at the podium with his arms behind his back. The ULCC spokesman stood beside him, speaking, gesturing with his hands, as if he were trying to convey to Walker an important fact.[26]

This first instance of the human microphone used as an interventionist form clearly caught every person in the banquet hall off guard. The people in attendance—the ones there to actually hear Walker—had no idea how to respond to such a seizure of vocalic space. Walker's initial attempt to undercut the intrusion—"Their voices are a little bit different than others out there"—did nothing to invoke his possible support, nor did it do anything to quell the human microphone. Attempts to physically preside over the primary speaker, to intimidate, silence, or disrupt that first speaker, were easily overcome by a nomadic shifting of the role of primary speaker. This occurred twice in the first seconds of the intervention. When a security guard confronted the primary speaker or a person from the audience tried to intervene, the role of primary speaker was simply taken up by a different body, another voice. This rhizomatic shifting of the primary speaker's role meant that the one central to the many could be any and all ones within the many.

The use of applause by those attempting to drown out the human microphone was quite efficient within the space of the banquet hall. Other countervocalic bodies would resort to this technique against future utilizations of the human microphone as an interventionist form—for example, with Senator Ron Paul,[27] Karl Rove (who responded to the human microphone disruption by stating that "if you believe in free speech then you demonstrate it by shutting up and waiting until the Q&A."),[28] and President Obama.[29] Again, however, in the Chicago manifestation, the strength of the counterapplause did not have the organizational force behind it that the human microphone had. So, in seconds, it dissolved.

In this event, the human microphone occupied a space of officially recognized power by means of its organized vocal amplitude. This established a technique that would continue to disrupt spaces of power during political campaigns (for example, the mic check on GOP presidential candidate Michelle Bachmann).[30] Student groups would utilize it to disrupt campus recruitment drives by banks (Princeton University students disrupted a J.P. Morgan Treasury Services info session)[31] and energy companies (Ohio State University students disrupted a gas industry panel intending to promote hydro-fracking practices).[32] The technique would also be used by protesters to disrupt the COP17 climate talks in Durban on behalf of nations and peoples who lacked representation at the conference.[33] Yet, if the human microphone used as an organized interventionist technique were to continue to be a stratagem of impact, it would—like the rhizomatic primary speaker in a public intervention full of contingencies and impromptu adaptations—have to shift in form and practice depending on the specific contexts in which it was utilized.

"You Use Weapons. We Use Our Voice."
On 18 November, at the University of California, Davis, in the moments leading up to and immediately after Lieutenant John Pike pepper-sprayed students protesting tuition increases in solidarity with the Occupy movement, the initial chaos of verbal reactions did little to halt the ongoing police brutality.[34] In the lead-up to the spraying, bodies were scattered across the quad and demonstrators' voices could be heard from all directions. At times, vocalic bodies formed momentarily, one group repeating several times: "Don't shoot students!" Various individuals shouted to their friends or fellow protesters or at the police: "Keep your eyes closed!" "Protect yourselves!" "They're going to come through." "Don't do this." "Move!" "Stand your ground!" "The whole world is watching." The protesters and onlookers on the quad all spoke to similar concerns: for their friends to protest and for the police not to brutalize their friends. In these tense moments, the crowd failed achieve any kind of response in language, one that might have collectively engaged the police to deter their mobilization.

In the wake of the pepper spraying, the situation changed. After Pike's eighteen-second spraying, it took about fifteen seconds for a chorus of those not sprayed to begin shouting "Shame on you!" This phrasal unit lasted another fifteen seconds, until it dispersed into individual utterances, one of the loudest being a person shouting out the name of the pepper-spraying cop: "I want his name! What's his name? Pike! Pike! J. Pike!" At the moment he was identified, Pike had been kneeling on the back of a young man—whose face was covered in pepper spray—as if he were attempting an arrest. When, from the periphery, a speaker began to shout Pike's name, Pike stood up and disappeared into a group of police clad in riot gear. As the police began to forcefully arrest the seated individuals who had just been pepper-sprayed, calls and shouts continued among those present: "Why?" in repetition, "He's not resisting!" "Why are you doing this?" "These are children!" "This is America!" "This will be seen around the world!" One person began to yell out a list of media—"YouTube! Ugo! Facebook! Twitter! ABC! CNN!"—as if simply shouting these names might make the violent scene appear on those sites. The cacophony of individuated utterings from the crowd continued for more than two minutes. Then the "Shame on you" repetition began again, gathering amplitude. As this phrasal unit escalated in volume, the police, at Pike's direction, began to back out. The crowd then amassed in a discharge both physical and verbal that overwhelmed the police, who, although well armed with batons, shields, pepper spray, and rubber bullets, began to retreat. As the police backpedalled en masse, the crowd's voice shifted to a call-and-response: "Who's university?" "Our university!" This continued for another minute. Then, with the police at one edge of the quad, a voice yelled out "mic check!" three times to summon the human microphone. Once it had assembled, he was able to deliver a message:

> We are willing
> to give you a brief moment
> of peace
> so that you can take your weapons
> and our friends
> and go.
> Please do not return.
> We are giving you a moment of peace.
> You can go.
> We will not follow you.

The crowd voice again returned, in full amplitude: "You can go!" They repeated it, again and again—"You can go! You can go!"—with force. The police dispersed.

It is in contrast to this instance of a vocalic body that I want to position a second example of a vocalic body at UC Davis, but one of an entirely different amplitude. The day after the campus police used force to halt the demonstrations, UC Davis chancellor Linda Katehi faced criticism from both the university and the public. Videos of the previous day's protest and the police response had gone viral. The UC Davis Faculty Association, the Department of English, and a majority in the Department of Physics held her responsible for the excessive force that had been be used against a peaceful assembly of university students. All called for her immediate resignation. Katehi's delay in offering any reply or disciplinary action further angered the university community. In the late afternoon, she held a press conference in a campus building in which she did not respond to the calls for her resignation and stated that she would be dealing with the situation by creating a task force to investigate the previous day's events. Afterwards, upon leaving the building, she was greeted by several hundred protesters lining the paths leading from the building to her car and to the street. They sat in absolute silence.³⁵ The video of Katehi's confrontation with the crowd is wonderfully eerie. The only audible sounds are the thick clunk of her heels on the cement sidewalk as she moves amid the bodies that crowd around her exit path. After the previous day's attempts to use state-sponsored police forces to silence a public, to evict a vocalic body, the protesters' assembled silence came across louder than ever.

On Sonic Disobedience

In *On the Outskirts of Form: Practicing Cultural Poetics*, Michael Davidson asks what poetics might look like "when it is based not around individual [literary] movements, manifestos and school, but around geopolitical policies that impact not only the production of culture but the definition of what it means to be cosmopolitan, a 'citizen of the world.'"³⁶ In this pursuit, Davidson revises his earlier explorations of poetics and community—ones he had situated in aesthetic tendencies rooted in a specific locale and framed within the construct of the nation-state in the Cold War era—to speak to an age of multinational corporations, labor outsourcing, and free trade agreements.³⁷ He argues for a poetics that factors in subjective positions and relations shaped by neoliberal trade policies, transnational capital flows, and the spread of digital information. Alliances exist, certainly, at the level of the nation-state, yet they assemble outside this imaginary, across numerous locales, languages, and cultural perspectives at any site where individuals and collectives confront global capital.

It's with Davidson's provocation in mind that I offer the present research for a collection of writings that frame poetics and conceptions of publics within a construct of the nation-state of Canada. I do so not simply because the human microphone was a technique utilized at Occupy encampments throughout Canada. (There were, of course, many compositional tactics utilized at Occupy-related sites in Canada on which I could have focused this research. One example could have been the bilinguality of the human microphone at Occupons Montréal. Also of interest was how, through the human microphone, certain locations were able to articulate the interrelation of Occupy-related protests with coexisting struggles—for example, anti–Tar Sands organization at Occupy Edmonton, and the mobilizations against the excessive urban development or "condofication" of First Nations lands at Occupy Vancouver.) The intervention, however slight, that I want to assert here is that these compositional modes, these attempts to confront and disrupt, are all vital for individuals and collectives everywhere, not just in Canada. The same can be said of the capacity to establish ad hoc vocalic bodies. As the current governing regime in Canada systematically privatizes the country's nationalized entities—

from natural resources to media, from health care to heritage—while at the same time offering strong political support and financial incentives to the large-scale environmental and social violences that multinational corporations are executing within and outside the country's borders, the frame for which Davidson argues seems especially apt.

In the immediate space of primary speaker and directly addressed audience acting extemporaneously in tandem; in the formation of new and urgent assemblies, however temporary, through a process of active listening and the embodied revocalization of another person's language; in the rhizomatic shifting and tuning of voices; in effectively disseminating communications while asserting a collective agency in vocalic space, the human microphone is an important mode of composition for this moment. As poetic, the human microphone realizes a number of tactics theorized and partly advanced in practice in the latter half of the twentieth and early twenty-first centuries, ones aimed at countering the poetics of an individual's privately scripted and privately consumed text: the improvisation and direct address of a David Antin talk poem; the attention to the phonemic that one might expect in a performance by N.H. Pritchard, The Four Horsemen, Maggie O'Sullivan, Bob Cobbing, or Fred Moten; the momentary sonic dissonance of a Jackson Mac Low performance; the polemics of an Amiri Baraka reading; an emphasis on discourse in one of Bob Perelman's poet talks; and, finally, the collective and collaborative compositional practices developed in a number of Language writings such as *Leningrad* and *The Grand Piano*. As politic, the human microphone provides a powerful example of a way to form and address and form vocalic bodies in particular spaces, as well as a means to collectively articulate dissent either in address or in the interruption of transmissions.

To this extent there is a formal affinity between the human microphone and the casserole marches that began at the height of the 2012 Quebec student uprising. Echoing the *cacerolazo*—used in Chile in 1971 during Salvador Allende's rule in Chile, and then against Pinochet little more than a decade later—thousands of people armed with pots and pans would emerge from their homes each evening to bang and clang and make as much noise as possible. This racket was a signal for people to come out on the streets and make audible their support for the student movement. It also provided an opportunity for those unable physically to join those gathered on the streets to instead show their support from their window or balcony. In Quebec these gatherings were declared illegal under Law 78, the provincial government's emergency measure to quell the student uprising by limiting the protesters' right to assemble. But they would often morph into hours-long demonstrations and ad hoc neighbourhood assemblies where citizens voiced their concerns and listened in return. Throughout the student strike, an ongoing battle for control over sonic space persisted. Because the provincial government refused to listen to what the student leaders had to say about the tuition hikes, those same leaders called on students to make themselves heard on the streets. Once the amplitude of the protests reached a decibel level deemed dangerous by the government, legions of riot cops would be sent in to force those assembled to be silent. The frequent police brutality and the provincial politicians' continued disregard for it only inspired greater numbers to gather in defiance. Thwarted by the escalating demonstrations, the Quebec legislature adopted Law 78, the anti-democratic law that repressed the freedom of assembly, the freedom of expression, and the right to protest. During the nightly student marches, riot cops would beat their shields with their batons, in unison, before violently charging the assembled protesters. The police used this well-known intimidation tactic to magnify their presence. Montreal's casserole protests were effective because they were able to seize that aural space from the police. The state-sponsored weaponry of baton and shield was defused by otherwise innocuous domestic cookware.

These tactics of communication and intervention are of increasing importance in a moment defined by austerity measures, rampant privatizations of previously socialized initiatives, and the wholesaling of non-renewable resources. From the Idle No More round dance protests to the general strikes and street battles in Greece, from the anti-development demonstrations surrounding Gezi Park in Istanbul to the many fronts organizing against the Enbridge Northern Gateway pipeline in British Columbia, an array of public poetics and practices will need to be developed so as to form momentary vocalic bodies, for communication and confrontation. The human microphone opens up a space to consider collective modes of composition—using the voice, sounding objects, the body, printed materials, architectural spaces—to imagine and to experiment with what might be achieved at other sites, in other struggles. Various constraints particular to other sites and other struggles will, of course, play a determining role in each situation, as was the case with the human microphone and the deamplification of Zuccotti Park. So, too, will the specific sets of protest tactics previously utilized by those engaged in the particular site—from songs and chants to banner drops, black bloc to occupations. Sonic composition in these spaces will be a crucial tactic for these emergent publics to form, to accumulate amplitude, and to make their demands resound.

Notes

1. Bernstein, *A Poetics*, 1–2.
2. Kim, "We Are All the Human Microphone Now."
3. Connor, *Dumbstruck*, 12.
4. Olson, *Collected Prose*, 240.
5. Hejinian, *Language of Inquiry*, 323.
6. Bergvall, "What Do We Mean by Performance Writing."
7. Buuck, "Unsettling Scores."
8. Protevi, "Semantic, Pragmatic, and Affective."
9. Bernstein, *A Poetics*, 2.
10. "Occupy Wall Street, Justice for Troy Davis," YouTube.
11. Kim, "We Are All."
12. NYC General Assembly Minutes.
13. "Radio Raheem," YouTube.
14. Since Current TV terminated its relationship with Olbermann in March 2012, the broadcast from this show is no longer available on the Internet.
15. There are numerous reports documenting the "#TroyDavis" blackout. For examples, see these articles: "Did Twitter stop #troydavis from trending," *Clutch Magazine*; "Did @Twitter Kill #TroyDavis," *Flaimahmy*, "Troy Davis Tweets Spark Trending Topic Controversy," *BET*; "Troy Davis and the Twitter Black Out Conspiracy," *Single Black Male*; "Did Twitter Block the #TroyDavis and #TooMuchDoubt Hashtags?" *Politic 365*.
16. "How it works at Occupy Wall Street 9/25/11," YouTube.
17. Kim, "We Are All."
18. Kim, "We Are All."
19. Wanenchak, "Mic check!"
20. "Michael Moore @ Occupy Wall Street," YouTube.
21. "Dr. Cornell West," YouTube.
22. "Dr. Cornell West," YouTube.
23. "Gov. Scott Walker get checked," YouTube.
24. "Gov. Scott Walker get checked," YouTube.
25. Tax Increment Financing (TIF) is "a special funding tool used by the City of Chicago to promote public and private investment across the city. Funds are used to build and repair roads and infrastructure, clean polluted land and put vacant properties back to productive use, usually in conjunction with private development projects." See the City of Chicago's official site on the tax increment financing program: http://www.cityofchicago.org/city/en/depts/dcd/supp_info/tax_increment_financingprogram.html.
26. "Gov. Scott Walker get checked," YouTube.
27. "Ron Paul Town Hall Gets Occupied," YouTube.
28. "Karl Rove #MIC #CHECK in Baltimore," YouTube.
29. "Video: OWS protesters," YouTube.

30 "Michele Bachmann Gets Mic Checked," and "Back Angle of Michele Bachmann getting Mic-Checked by Occupy Charleston," YouTube.
31 "Mic Check! Ohio Students," YouTube.
32 "JP Morgan-Chase Mic-Checked," YouTube.
33 "Flashmob Protest on last day of COP17," YouTube.
34 For better coverage prior to the pepper-spraying, see "Police PEPPER SPRAY," YouTube. For better coverage after the spraying, see "Police pepper spraying," YouTube.
35 "UC Davis Chancellor Katehi," YouTube.
36 Davidson, *On the Outskirts of Form*, 15.
37 For Michael Davidson's chartings of community poetics during the Cold War, see his *The San Francisco Renaissance*; and *Guys Like Us*.

Bibliography

"Back Angle of Michele Bachmann Getting Mic-Checked by Occupy Charleston." YouTube. Accessed 10 April 2013 at http://www.youtube.com/watch?v=Q9e34kHANHs.

Bergvall, Caroline. "What Do We Mean by Performance Writing." Personal website. Accessed 10 April 2013 at http://www.carolinebergvall.com/content/text/BERGVALL-KEYNOTE.pdf.

Bernstein, Charles. *A Poetics*. Cambridge, MA: Harvard University Press, 1992.

Buuck, David. "Un/Settling Scores: Actions for Torture Justice." *Jacket2*. Accessed 10 April 2013 at https://jacket2.org/commentary/unsettling-scores-actions-torture-justice.

Connor, Steven. *Dumbstruck: A Cultural History of Ventriloquism*. New York: Oxford University Press, 2000.

Davidson, Michael. *On the Outskirts of Form: Practicing Cultural Poetics*. Middletown: Wesleyan University Press, 2011.

———. *The San Francisco Renaissance: Poetics and Community at Mid-Century*. Cambridge: Cambridge University Press, 2011.

———. *Guys Like Us: Citing Masculinity in Cold War Poetics*. Chicago: Chicago University Press, 2004.

"Did Twitter Block the #TroyDavis and #TooMuchDoubt Hashtags?" *Politic 365*. Accessed 10 April 2013 at http://politic365.com/2011/09/22/did-twitter-block-the-troydavis-and-toomuchdoubt-hashtags.

"Did Twitter stop #troydavis from trending," *Clutch Magazine*, Accessed 10 April 2013 at http://www.clutchmagonline.com/2011/09/did-twitter-stop-troydavis-from-trending.

"Did @Twitter Kill #TroyDavis." *Flaimahmy*. Accessed 10 April 2013 at http://www.flaimahmy.com/2011/09/22/did-twitter-kill-troydavis.

"Dr. Cornell West—We the People Have Found Our Voice." YouTube. Accessed 10 April 2013 at http://www.youtube.com/watch?feature&v=H31XN8zgXlI.

"Flashmob Protest on last day of COP17—Durban South Africa." YouTube. Accessed 10 April 2103 at http://www.youtube.com/watch?v=XHHAM-fMKHU.

"Gov. Scott Walker get checked, Mic Checked!" YouTube. Accessed 10 April 2013 at http://www.youtube.com/watch?feature&v=1oHRdiklTlU.

Hejinian, Lyn. *Language of Inquiry*. Berkeley: University of California Press, 2000.

"How it works at Occupy Wall Street 9/25/11." YouTube. Accessed 10 April 2013 at http://www.youtube.com/watch?v=xIK7uxBSAS0&list=UUxsec0r8nYS3xKSG7AUYcgA&index=38.

"JP Morgan-Chase Mic-Checked at Princeton University." YouTube. Accessed 10 April 2013 at http://www.youtube.com/watch?v=NJ0J_HusRaI.

"Karl Rove #MIC #CHECK in Baltimore." YouTube. Accessed 10 April 2103 at http://www.youtube.com/watch?v=6cJCqw8XVw0.

Kim, Richard. "We Are All the Human Microphone Now." *The Nation*. Accessed 10 April 2013 at http://www.thenation.com/blog/163767/we-are-all-human-microphones-now.

"Mic Check! Ohio Students Interrupt Gas Industry." YouTube. Accessed 10 April 2103 at http://www.youtube.com/watch?v=9jQXop_6RiU&feature=share.

"Michael Moore @ Occupy Wall Street." YouTube. Accessed 10 April 2013 at http://www.youtube.com/watch?&v=XCZLhEOJ8XA.

"Michele Backhmann Gets Mic Checked by Occupy Charleston, South Carolina." YouTube. Accessed 12 September 2014 at http://www.youtube.com/watch?v=Q9e34kHANHs.

New York City General Assembly Minutes. 9/21/2011. Accessed 10 April 2013 at http://www.nycga.net/2011/09/nycga-minutes-9212011.

"Occupy Wall Street—Justice for Troy Davis." YouTube. Accessed 10 April 2013 at http://www.youtube.com/watch?v=fsUJJ04tuqk.

Olson, Charles. *Collected Prose*. Edited by Donald Allen and Benjamin Friedlander. Berkeley: University of California Press, 1997.

"Police PEPPER SPRAY UC Davis STUDENT PROTESTORS!" YouTube. Accessed 10 April 10 2013 ar http://www.youtube.com/watch?feature&v=wuWEx6Cfn-I.

"Police pepper spraying and arresting students at UC Davis." YouTube. Accessed 10 April 2013 at http://www.youtube.com/watch?feature&v=WmJmmnMkuEM.

Protevi, John. "Semantic, Pragmatic, and Affective Enactment at OWS." *Theory & Event* 14, no. 4 (2011). Accessed 10 April 2013 at http://muse.jhu.edu/journals/theory_and_event/v014/14.4S.protevi.html.

"Radio Raheem—September 21st General Assembly—Day 5." YouTube. Accessed 10 April at http://www.youtube.com/watch?v=ISZm_o2567Y&list=UUmgdwP45wF5XfNOG2XQHigA&index=11.

"Ron Paul Town Hall Gets Occupied." YouTube. Accessed 10 April 2013 at http://www.youtube.com/watch?v=6cJCqw8XVw0.

"Troy Davis Tweets Spark Trending Topic Controversy." *BET.* Accessed 10 April 2013 at http://www.bet.com/news/national/2011/09/21/troy-davis-tweets-spark-trending-topic-controversy.html.

"Troy Davis and the Twitter Black Out Conspiracy." *Single Black Male.* Accessed 10 April 2013 at http://www.singleblackmale.org/2011/09/20/troy-davis-and-the-twitter-black-out-conspiracy.

"UC Davis Chancellor Katehi walks to her car (higher quality)." YouTube. Accessed 10 April 2013 at http://www.youtube.com/watch?feature&v=8775ZmNGFY8.

"Video: OWS protesters interrupt Obama's speech," YouTube. Accessed 10 April 2013 at http://www.youtube.com/watch?v=p7kS3Ic4-lE.

Wanenchak, Kim. "'Mic check!': #occupy, technology & the amplified voice." *Cyborgology.* Accessed 10 April 2013 at http://thesocietypages.org/cyborgology/2011/10/06/mic-check-occupy-technology-the-amplified-voice.

15

Canadian Public Poetics: Negotiating Belonging in a Globalizing World

Diana Brydon

In 2007, proceeding from the Poetics and Public Culture conference at the University of Western Ontario,[1] Manina Jones, Jessica Schagerl, Kristin Warder, and I published a co-edited special issue of *Studies in Canadian Literature/Études en littérature Canadienne* on the topic. Since that time, concerns about globalization and culture have intensified, but there may also be a growing clarity about what is at stake in negotiating the changing dynamics of public and private in the twenty-first century. Poetry is undergoing a revival. Calls for new modes of worldly inscription to engage with twenty-first-century technologies and imaginaries associated with neoliberalism, alter-globalization, and decolonial social movements are leading poet-critics such as Roy Miki to describe our times as "in flux"[2] and writers such as Kate Eichhorn and Heather Milne to describe the audiences for poetry as "prismatic publics"[3]—that is, as multifaceted, partial, and overlapping publics rather than a singular, monocultural public sphere, as is still idealized in many political desires for a homogeneous nation.

"Prismatic publics" may include "counterpublics," as theorized by Michael Warner for addressing "subordinate status"[4] in situations of unequal power, but do not privilege that relation. The suggestive metaphor of prismatic publics may better accommodate the diversity and dynamism of these relations without necessarily abandoning their contestatory power, but it also raises a concern that resistance may become diluted when its multiple entanglements are recognized. With the rise of Internet-enabled and social media, the borders separating public and private are becoming more fluid, adding to the prismatic character of how these spheres interact and co-construct one another. Literary and cultural critics are struggling with the challenge of understanding poetic experimentation with modes of address appropriate to the compressed time–space relations of transnationalism and the associated fluidity, frictions, and commodifications of global engagements, in print and Internet-based formats. Postcolonial and decolonial critics who wish to emphasize the unequal power relations that still shape these publics also seek a new vocabulary that can do justice to the positive power of alternative imaginings without downplaying the oppressions that continue and change their shape with the changing shape of global market, social, and state relations.

In this context of ongoing "semiotic struggle" to control how reality is defined,[5] poets have an important role to play. To think about the relations between neoliberalism and applied linguistics as the authors just cited do, is to further blur some of the distinctions conventionally drawn between poetics as the art of representation, imitation, and invention, and rhetoric as the art of persuasion. This is the territory claimed by postcolonial studies. As David Slater notes, postcolonial studies works at "the intersection between intervention"—the terrain of rhetoric—"and representation"—the terrain of poetics.[6] To develop transnational literacies, which is the focus of my current SSHRC partnership development grant, "Brazil/Canada Knowledge Exchange," is to seek ways of thinking about poetics, rhetoric, and the literacies to which they give rise together in the transnational contexts that characterize many people's lives today. Literacy, at its highest level, refers to skill in meaning-negotiation. When negotiating across languages, cultures, and their various value systems, literacy becomes both more complex and more necessary.[7]

Poetry, with its heightened attention to the suggestive slipperiness of language, may help readers, listeners, and learners develop modes of understanding open to facilitating cooperation without having to deny the value of difference. My collaborative, transnational research team experiences have convinced me that Stefan Collini is incorrect to insist that work in the humanities is ill suited to team-based, transdisciplinary research because it must begin with being able "to assume an extended shared world." For him, that founding assumption necessitates bracketing off multicultural and postcolonial critique, as well as refusing cross-disciplinary dialogue that could put different epistemic communities into relations of friction or even collision. His polemic, *What Are Universities For?*, is unapologetic about its contemporary situatedness within debates that are rocking the

United Kingdom, while paying almost no attention to the challenges posed by internationalization and the emerging global higher education regime. While I agree that rhetoric may need to assume a shared audience or, at least through its skilled employment, call one into being, the strength of poetics is its ability to challenge assumptions about what is given.

To achieve transnational forms of literacy in educational systems, the borders between literary critics and specialists in composition, rhetoric, and literacy studies need to be crossed more often.[8] Within literary studies, the US-based poet-critic Charles Bernstein suggests that "in some ways, literary theory, in its many forms, has displaced poetics as a model for scholarship."[9] He distinguishes between the two as follows: "Theory suggests a predilection for consistency and explanation and, like philosophy, may take the form of stand-alone arguments. Poetics, in contrast, is provisional, context-dependent, and often contentious."[10] However we might wish to blur these distinctions, I suggest that the way he poses them here not only makes a rhetorical argument for the value of poetics to literary study but also reflects some of the shifts now taking place in our post-theory times. Theory is not being abandoned, but it is being placed in closer dialogue with questions of context-specific analysis of all kinds. That requires developing more complex sensitivities to how to function in a world of flux, where words mean multivalently, conjuring multiple associations that each demand attention and where it is not possible to begin with the assumption of a shared starting point for the collaborative work of making meaning, through writing or reading a poem, either within a single language such as English, or in translation.

In response to globalizing processes, Bernstein advises poets to "read globally, write locally."[11] Good advice, but what does that mean in practice? The guest editors of the special 2011 issue of the journal *Canadian Literature* ask how contemporary avant-garde poets in Canada might read hegemonic theorists such as Slavoj Žižek and Alain Badiou in relation to contemporary Indigenous theorists John Borrows and Dale Turner.[12] In my work, I am exploring the various postcolonial frames articulated as "globalectics,"[13] "tidalectics,"[14] "decoloniality,"[15] "ecology of knowledges,"[16] "Asia as method,"[17] and "planetarity."[18] Each of these coinages seeks to capture the spatial and temporal stretching, back-and-forth movement, and interconnectedness that characterize worldly engagements today, from specifically local situations, and they express an increasing impatience with older formulas for describing human worldly engagements, such as Descartes's "I think, therefore I am" and Hegelian dialectics. Each stresses the importance of finding alternative starting points for understanding what Homi Bhabha describes as "the force of writing, its metaphoricity and its rhetorical discourse, as a productive matrix which defines the 'social' and makes it available as an objective of and for action."[19]

Language gives writing its force, yet many studies of globalization tend to shortchange language. In "Comparative Literature and the Global Languagescape," Mary Louise Pratt asks:

> What are the linguistic dimensions of this set of planetary realignments people call globalization?...Astonishing as it may seem, language has not even been a category of analysis in the now vast academic literature on globalization. Though some of the people who think about language think about globalization, almost none of the people who think about globalization think about language. Yet globalization has changed the linguistic landscape of the world, and global processes are directed and shaped by language at every turn.[20]

Indeed, much of the popular and social science writing on globalization, including discussions of cosmopolitanism, has silently assumed global English as the default norm. Those of us teaching and studying English need to pay more attention to this situation, and poetics can help us with this task.

Many studies of globalization and literature also tend to shortchange or ignore poetry. Jahan Ramazani in *A Transnational Poetics* (2009) considers poetry but limits his transnational attention to work in English only. Ramazani argues that "the elasticity of poetry—its figural and allusive traversals of space, its rhythmic and sonic coordinations of distances, its associative suspension of rational boundaries—is well suited to evoking global modernity's interlinking of widely separated sites."[21] His defence of poetry resonates in my mind with Bernstein's endorsement of poetics "as the foundation for a realm of values that is neither scientific nor moralistic."[22] Bernstein makes an important distinction here between the scientistic and the scientific, the formulaic and the exploratory, linking this distinction to the one he draws between the moralistic and the ethical. For Bernstein, poetics is "the ethical engagement with the shifting conditions of everyday life."[23] As Jacob Edmond notes in *A Common Strangeness: Contemporary Poetry, Cross-Cultural Encounter, Comparative Literature*, Bernstein repeatedly insists "on the importance of the mode of communication—or poetics—to the message conveyed. Bernstein's writing emphasizes the place of rhetoric in thinking comparatively and cross-culturally and in addressing the relation of literature and culture to globalization."[24] He also attends to the key issue of language. Bernstein's online Penn sound archive is an important resource for anyone interested in contemporary poetry. This archive and Bernstein's poetics play an important cross-border role for Canadian thinking.

Canadian poetry has never confined its imagination within the borders of the Canadian state. However, the shifting conditions of scholarly fashion mean that transnationalism currently seems more relevant than ever to the theorizing of a public poetics. Ramazani discusses many of the elements of modern life that thwart "mononational narratives,"[25] and he deplores the resilience of national categories for labelling writers and their work. Seeing transnationalism as the norm for writing in the modern period, he asks: "What is the cultural politics of [the] nationalization of transnational writing?"[26] It is a valid question, but it is equally important to ask the opposite: What is the cultural politics of the transnationalization of national writing? And how closely are these politics linked to economics?[27] These are questions about how literature gets institutionalized and used to reinforce specific agendas. They are questions asked by Smaro Kamboureli's TransCanada project, which has led to a number of conferences and publications addressed to the changing contexts for understanding Canadian literature in the contemporary period.[28] Ramazani expresses the hope that "as identitarian ways of structuring knowledge come under increasing scrutiny, as postcolonial and global studies make deeper inroads, English studies and other humanistic disciplines will be better able to project and delineate models of cross-national imaginative citizenship that are mobile, ambivalent, and multifaceted."[29] This challenge of articulating how the national and transnational work together to create new modes of understanding and new ways of imagining belonging seems at odds with the earlier priorities of Canadian literary studies to articulate a national sense of belonging associated with a multicultural identity or a postcolonial critique. To focus on Canadian engagements with these questions today is less to seek a national identity than it is to recognize the multifaceted nature of situatedness in contemporary contexts. The national remains an important frame, or "cultural grammar"[30] for articulating a public poetics, but singular notions of national identity are yielding to more complex formations of diasporic, racialized, and classed relations to belonging.[31]

The title of Gerald L. Brun's book, *What Are Poets For?: An Anthropology of Contemporary Poetry and Poetics*, reflects the contemporary obsession with the use-value of everything, even as it also raises more substantive questions about alternative poetic values.[32] If Brun answers this question at all, he does so implicitly, through describing what several poets do with language. The Canadian poets he discusses, such as Christian Bök, Steve McCaffery, and Karen MacCormack, experiment with the materiality of language and form, resisting calls for an immediately accessible public poetry, such as that promoted on the Canadian Athletes Now website, where Priscilla Uppal as 2012 Poet in Residence wrote daily in response to the 2012 London Olympics and Paralympic Games. Here I do not endorse one mode and disparage the other; rather, I point to the broad continuum of address that characterizes poetry's "prismatic publics," in which various modes of address may call into being different but also potentially overlapping communities.

Here is a poem by Uppal, called "Patience," posted on the Web on 28 July 2012. The poet is in line to buy tickets to Olympic events, reporting on conversations overheard, before intervening. She writes:

> And I capture my captive audience,
> offering up a sonnet and haiku to chase
> boredom away, 'POET' emblazoned
> On my shoulders—a nation of its own,
> With lots of citizens but few fans.[33]

In fact, from the picture on the site, she wears the word POET emblazoned on the back of her jacket. The fear that poetry has been reduced from Shelley's imagined legislative role or Bernstein's ethical engagement to become merely another device for chasing boredom away, and the self-deprecating acknowledgement that poetry, in contrast to elite athletics, attracts "few fans," may at first seem to reinforce a common lament that many wish to be poets but few actually read poetry anymore. However, if one believes that it is better to be a citizen than a fan, then poetry appears to be more publicly meaningful than athletics, for all its hype. The idea that all aspiring poets may constitute a nation assigns a publicly recognizable value to their community. Here, Uppal expands on Margaret Laurence's invocation of writers as a "tribe" to imagine a poetic nation.[34] The terminology suggests that the reach of poetry is broader than might be assumed, that writing poetry speaks to a human need as strong as the one for citizenship, creating sociality as much as meeting any private need, and thereby serving a function greater than that of mere distraction in an empty moment. "Patience," Uppal suggests, may be what poetry requires and what it can teach—a slowing down of pace that enables a shift in perspective. The wordplay around capturing a "captive audience" is simple but it effects this transition, which in turn leads to contemplation of how an audience may be converted into a nation of citizens, and what such citizenship of affinity and aspiration might imply about shared public identities and responsibilities.

The poet-in-residence role in various city, state, and university positions provides some financial support for the poet, a public profile for poetry, and endorses an occasional poetry that can engage with the daily public life of the nation. Poetry awards such as the Griffin Prizes and the more recent

Walrus competition, supported by the Hal Jackman Foundation, also seek to give poetry a wider public profile and poets some financial compensation for their work. Most of the scholarly attention devoted to the politics of literary prizes addresses fiction, even when prizes are awarded to both genres by the same body, such as with the Governor General's Awards. Nonetheless, observations such as those made by Gillian Roberts, that prizes dependent on citizenship qualifications, especially if offered by the nation-state, may be tied in complex ways to national projects, are worth considering. Roberts suggests that in a liberal democratic nation, "prize-winning writers may both contest the nation-state and be celebrated for doing so."[35]

The Occupy movement has prompted renewed attention to the complications of such roles, leading to questions such as Maria Damon's: "How can the poetic as a shared project illuminate our public and civic relations?[36] At issue here is the implied further question: Who constitutes this collective named as "we"? How does poetry call an audience into being? And what is the relation between an audience and a public? To what extent can poetry mirror experience and to what extent can it create it? Is there a space outside market forces? If so, can poetry help readers and listeners experience it? A conference in May 2012 on "Poetry and Revolution" at Birkbeck and a special issue of *Marxism Today* (24.3 [2012]) show the renewed interest in these questions that the Occupy protests are helping to highlight. Many of the Birkbeck papers are freely available online, further expanding the audience for thinking about these issues.

Becky Cremin, in a paper called "to initiate a poetics of occupation: Occupy as poetics, poetics as occupy," plays with the multiple meanings of this word and claims: "I wish to consider how occupation can take place in and around language. To rethink how we can occupy space, textually, poetically and bodily. To explore the possibility of a bodily occupation creating a textual occupation."[37] Susan Bernofsky performs similar serious play with her poem "To Occupy: An Evolution." Her poem has two epigraphs: "I was born to occupy love, not hatred," from Anne Carson's translation of *Antigone,* and "A riot is the language of the unheard," from Dr. Martin Luther King, Jr. For Bernofsky, "it all began as an exercise in listening. We came to occupy words. Then it was a revolution."[38] Her poem imagines how this peaceful revolution might lead towards humanity's evolution into less exclusory forms of community.

Such a conclusion, ostensibly celebratory in its immediate context of the Occupy Wall Street movement (alternatively named in global contexts "Occupy World Street"),[39] cannot help but also problematically recall the politically fraught significance of the word "occupy" in invader-settler contexts, a significance not lost on Indigenous poets and activists. As Adam J.

Barker argues in his article "Already Occupied: Indigenous Peoples, Settler Colonialism and the Occupy Movements in North America," "the concerns of indigenous communities are not necessarily those of the 99% and 'occupation' as a term needs to be fundamentally reconsidered."[40] As Dionne Brand reminds her readers, "no language is neutral."

Damon suggests that "to listen to someone who's really listening—to *hear* people listening—initiates collaborative communities."[41] She implies that the poet's role is at least as much that of a listener as an articulator or creator—that is, someone whose interaction with community is central. She finds promise in dimensions of poetry not usually associated with public engagement, arguing that "because of poetry's *permission* for subjectivity or hermeticism, poetry becomes a completely appropriate venue for clarifying identities, evolving and devolving, that contributes to a rich, ahierarchic heterogeneity composing a thus far hypothetical democracy."[42] Her challenge to a common sense that would require poets to write transparent, publicly accessible poetry if their work is to connect with people's lives opens alternative ways of thinking about connections both democratic and poetic. Public discourse need not be transparent to be effective. Sometimes apparent transparency disguises more fundamental discrepancies between the ways words are used in different contexts. Poetry can highlight the opacity and multiform meanings at the heart of even simple words, alerting readers and listeners to disagreements they need to explore.

For the past ten years, I have often felt that my work with the international teams investigating "Globalization and Autonomy" and "Building Global Democracy" was difficult to reconcile with my work as a literary scholar; although I have also believed that both were essential to the decolonizing agenda of my chosen field of postcolonial literary and cultural studies. Bridging the disciplinary gaps between social science and humanities perspectives remains a challenging task, but there are signs of a new openness on both sides of this divide. At a workshop on Priorities in Global Governance held at the University of Warwick in July 2012, there was a recognition that performance studies, ethnography, and applied linguistics were bringing valuable perspectives to concepts originally developed within economics, law, and politics, changing the lens through which contemporary issues were being viewed and drawing increased attention to the slipperiness of words themselves, their materiality as not just a medium of exchange but also as a mediating technology that is far from transparent. As Homi Bhabha insists, writing is "not a medium; it's a mediation." Writing should not be "relegated to a transparency, as if it is following on from positions, objects, subjects already constituted."[43] Here postcolonial theory meets L=A=N=G=U=A=G=E poetics.

Bernstein's prescription for poetic innovation is equally true for other disciplines. He writes: "We have to constantly reinvent our forms and vocabularies so that we don't lose touch with ourselves and the world we live in."[44] But he also cautions: "What's needed is a transvaluation of the concept of innovation, so that we can think of innovation in a modest and local way, as responses to historical and contemporary particulars—as situational, not universal."[45] And he warns: "Poetic innovations are often noisy, messy, disruptive, disorienting... This may be because they are not only reconceiving the nature of the poem but reconstituting the audience for the poem, reevaluating the contexts that give the poem not only its meaning but its social force."[46] This process is what many have been discovering through events as diverse as the poetry of the Occupy movement, contemporary Indigenous reclamations of the local and transnational in dialogue, and the 2012 Pussy Riot trial in Russia, each of which bridges conventional notions of high and low to fuse new perspectives on injustice.

In one less obviously political example of reciprocal listening and writing across borders of time, language, and space, James Thomas Stevens, a Mohawk poet, and Caroline Sinavaiana, a Samoan poet, have created the volume *Mohawk/Samoa Transmigrations*. The poems in the first half of the book start with the Mohawk and the second half with the Samoan. Each section begins with a traditional poem in its original language, followed by a literal translation into English, then by a pen-and-ink drawing of the relevant cultural item by Stevens, a personal poem by the first poet, another image by Stevens, and a response poem by the other poet. The multimodality of the translation process highlights not just the communication of meaning but also the gaps that accompany any translation. As Sinavaiana writes: "After exchanging our initial poetic 'translations,' I began to see dialogue flowing across layers of time and space: the Americas, Ocean, antiquity, and the present. Vivid experience of a teaching from another Native American colleague: that when we meet each other, our ancestors are meeting each other as well."[47] Furthermore, she finds in her own poems "a third subterranean stream of meaning" derived from her immersion in Tibetan (Vajrayana) Buddhism, another "cultural/spiritual framework" she finds to be "profoundly congruent with that of traditional Samoan world view."[48] Even apparently simple poems can resonate beyond their immediate, apparently transparent representational dimensions. The movement of "Okariahta:ne Kare'ma/Mosquito Song" runs from the Mohawk into the English transcription: "The mosquito is bringing a message. / He comes to tell us how poor he is. / In truth, he is repetitive / and brings the same old message."[49] After a free meditation, the second, Samoan voice responds to contradict that apparent truism:

that sting again,
Wings and tail
a moment's blur...
It's both the same
as before & not.
Lapse & awaken
wander & return. [...]
into arms of
echo and refrain.⁵⁰

This call and response of community formation that crosses oceans and cultures moves to a tidalectic rhythm that seems well suited to our times, with its reconstitution of temporal as well as spatial distances and intimacies. These poets write for a community that includes their ancestors along with their readers in the current moment, and the future generations. These poems are joyful conversations that perform the delight of discovered affinities and differences; they are not overtly resistance writing, nor are they especially innovative in style. Yet in their alternative namings and invocations of their "prismatic publics," they challenge what Jacques Derrida called a "violence of the letter."⁵¹ David Spurr describes this violence as "the rhetoric of empire," which arises from the colonial and capitalist "act of naming and leaving unnamed, of marking...lines of division and uniformity, of boundary and continuity."⁵²

Spurr's book was published in 1993, yet the rhetorical strategies he identifies continue to operate, in reconfigured formations, in mainstream media depictions of non-Western cultures today. It's not enough to identify and deconstruct these images. They also need to be interrupted in ways that enable seeing them afresh, giving the reader pause, and space for contemplating alternatives. Two contemporary Canadian long poems perform these interruptions as acts of aesthetic and political resistance that operate "primarily through wordplay."⁵³

Marvin Francis's *city treaty: a long poem*, works through the interactions and dialogue between two characters: Joe TB, the "treaty buster" and "bush poet," and a mysterious character named "the clown." They move in and out of a playfully bewildering flurry of words that expose the deceptiveness of the treaties signed between the Crown and various First Nations, the ongoing links of treaty trickery with the everyday discourses of global capitalism, and the literatures of English empire and Indigenous resistance in the Americas. The poem asks: "how about a / mcTreaty™ / would you like some lies with that?," where ™ has been footnoted earlier as "treaty manuscript" rather than its more usual signifying function as trade mark.⁵⁴ No wonder a passage a few pages later claims, in bold type: "the translator holds his head and cries / nobody believes me."⁵⁵ The play with trademark, which commodifies the treaty manuscript and signals its role within a capitalist system of commodity exchange, indicates the alternative cultural understandings of the original treaties, a point made forcefully by legal scholar Aimeé Craft in her book *Breathing Life into the Stone Fort Treaties: An Anishinabe Understanding of Treaty One*.⁵⁶ Francis's *city treaty* may be read as the poetic equivalent of this act of historical reinterpretation, which insists that treaties must be seen as living documents rather than as frozen in time.⁵⁷ The poem enacts the contrast between the "word cannibals" who "stole my words"⁵⁸ and the "word drummers" who reclaim and renew them.⁵⁹ The poem can "follow the word drummers to the city treaty,"⁶⁰ to redefine what a treaty means and how it can make its meanings: "no more drunk words / you cannot lie in a treaty / many languages, customs, environments, have to be included / everyone has some voice."⁶¹ This is a renewed vision of what negotiation can mean, when the participants recognize that we are all "edgewalkers": "we all walk edges uncertain / on border slippery / between…"⁶² The poem substitutes "the risky birth of muskeg metaphor"⁶³ for the old treaty language, with its "easy translate / you will lose / 'you taught me language I know how to curse.'"⁶⁴ Addressing the challenge of "*how to write a / treaty who cares*" by recalling both "*the names / of your ancestors*" and "*the / names that you / got called*"⁶⁵ and responding to the call of the word drummers, *city treaty* engages in some word cannibalizing of its own—"peter rabbit for lunch"⁶⁶—before the narrator claims: "we sit / me and this clown / and now have / just recently begun / to right / the city treaty."⁶⁷ The belief that writing can right wrongs and open more inclusive and complex understandings expresses one dimension of the ways in which "global cognitive justice" might lead the way towards "global social justice,"⁶⁸ a belief that animates much of the counterglobalization and decolonial analysis of the twenty-first century.

Just as *city treaty* expands and explodes the given meanings of its two key words, so Jeff Derksen's poems in *Dwell* exploit the different dimensions of his title metaphor (and its Heideggerean associations) to explore the implications of inhabiting contemporary capitalist relations within the reconfigured global system named by Hardt and Negri as a new form of Empire. In this apparently borderless world, Derksen notes sardonically: "The fish instinctively know where the international / boundaries are."⁶⁹ Later in the same poem, "Interface," he places a found fragment: "'We can see a day when borders will mean nothing / more than knowing where to cut your lawn.'"⁷⁰ Here Derksen re-creates what it feels like to "dwell upon" the contradictions of "dwelling in," as seen from a location within

British Columbia's resource-based economy and Vancouver's overheated residential markets, surveying southwards towards the world of American politics and eastward towards tourist travels through Egypt and Europe. At a time when commodification threatens to become the dominant mode of relation, Derksen's poetry explores the deep complicities that shape such a dilemma, prompting tougher interrogation of these questions.

Derksen's destabilizing poetics may be read, in Roy Miki's terms, as a "poetics of the apprehensive." Accepting that "globalization involves a struggle over knowledge of global affairs,"[71] in which marketplace logics play a dominant role, Derksen writes, in this long opening poem, "Interface": "the structure I hate also hates me, but it makes me, / and that's where the problem starts."[72] He notes: "Interface of self and place passes me through a / translation machine. / But when my left eye is jumping, I don't know where / I'm at."[73] He questions the capacities of either brand Canada or brand postcolonial to provide routes through the commodifying logics of the current system, noting that

> Something like postcolonial packaging taken
> Personally in a resource-based economy; I look out my
> Window and see history *versus* I look out my window
> And see a window.
> Visually complicated, overlapping and lapsing.[74]

Here earlier theorizations of poetics as mirror or lamp[75] are replaced by a renewal of the simple metaphor of the window. No longer a clear medium providing ready visual access to the world, Derksen's poetic window is complicated and unstable, clouded by contestations of past, present, and future. The poet, partially blinded by what he terms "Bright and long-lasting negative effects of Cartesian / perspectivalism"[76] moves outward, from his own location, into the kind of alternative thinking described by Mignolo as "I am where I think." The poems in Derksen's *Dwell* provide multiple takes on what such a revised formula for thinking/being might mean. These include the comical/cynical—"If I am alienated from the production of me, then I am / in a commodity relation with myself, hence big / bargains";[77] and the more hopeful/celebratory—"There are so many ones I want to be—beyond the / cardboard maquette stage, more at the prototype level, / the 'working model' example. / A subject-in-process with a horn section."[78]

The co-authored Introduction to our "Poetics and Public Culture in Canada" special issue concluded with a section called "Contested Poetics." My transnational partnership work of the last ten years[79] has deepened my sensitivity to the contested nature of knowledge production, its disputed vocabularies, and learning cultures today, and also to the necessity of engaging these debates with an openness to change. If mobile imaginaries provide the dominant view of how people understand themselves today, then perhaps Lionel Kearns's stance of "just standing here / being a Canadian," which we cited in our "Introduction,"[80] now takes more imagination than ever, but it may also no longer prove a viable option. Derksen's *Dwell* addresses a later time in which Canadian diffidence takes a different form. One of the many voices in "Interface" says: "I wanted to argue but was locked into my role of / simply trying to be nice, or to conciliate an agreement / so I just tapped on the glass and walked away."[81] The cumulative logic of *Dwell* refuses to just stand there and refuses to walk away. In this essay, I have offered a personal engagement with the changing scene of poetics and public culture in Canada and suggested that the poetics of "occupy," "transmigration," "treaty," and "dwell" carry complicated histories that readers cannot ignore as we seek more equitable ways of living together in the world we call home.

Notes

1. I am grateful to the organizers of the Public Poetics conference, Bart Vautour, Travis Mason, Christl Verduyn, and Erin Wunker, for the opportunity to share my thoughts at the conference held at Mount Allison University in Sackville, New Brunswick, September 2012; and to the audience, including the other speakers, for their penetrating questions and discussion. The research for this paper was conducted, in part, with support from the Canada Research Chairs program, and the paper was revised while I was in residence at Linnaeus University, Växjö, Sweden, at the Concurrences Institute for Colonial and Postcolonial Studies. Sections of the revised paper draw on my opening plenary addresses, "Global Rhetoric and the Practice of Transnational Literacies," delivered to the Western States Rhetoric and Literacy conference at the University of Winnipeg, and "Reclaiming the Global Sphere" at "'Narratives of Difference' in the Global Marketplace," University of Northampton, both in October 2012, where once again I benefited from informed and lively audience engagement. I am also grateful to my two terrific research assistants, Riley McGuire and Katie Thorsteinson, for their help with the research for this paper.
2. Miki, *In Flux*.
3. Eichhorn and Milne, eds., *Prismatic Publics*.
4. Eichhorn and Milne, eds., *Prismatic Publics*, 56.
5. Hasan, quoted in Block, Gray, and Holborow, *Neoliberalism and Applied Linguistics*, 38.
6. Slater, *Geopolitics and the Post-Colonial*, 224.

7 Negotiation emerged for me as the central concept for thinking about community autonomy under conditions of globalization when I worked with our research team on putting together the book *Renegotiating Community: Interdisciplinary Perspectives, Global Contexts*. We insisted on using renegotiating because we wished to stress that negotiation is necessarily an ongoing process that is continually tested and revised in practice. Since then, Terence C. Halliday's and Bruce G. Carruthers's book, *Bankrupt*, has elaborated how negotiation works within global policy-making in even more detail. They write: "The term *negotiation* has several meanings relevant to the global/local encounter. Negotiation between the global and local manifests itself cognitively as 'translation' (Merry 2005). Negotiation between national lawmakers and domestic players unfolds as 'bricolage' (Campbell 2004). Negotiation among international and domestic interest groups produces 'recursivity' since a stable political settlement emerges through cycles of enactment and implementation. Moreover, negotiation requires that the so-called weak are treated by global actors with the respect that their local power demands. Local knowledge and power mean that nation-states can (implicitly) veto global actions, so global actors can truly 'globalize' only on terms approved by their local counterparts" (422).
8 See Hesford for an eloquent argument to this effect.
9 Bernstein, "The Practice of Poetics," 76.
10 Bernstein, "The Practice of Poetics," 75.
11 Bernstein, "The Practice of Poetics," 77.
12 Burnham and Stewart, "Afterword."
13 Ngũgĩ wa, *Globalectics*.
14 Brathwaite, "Caribbean Culture."
15 Mignolo, "I Am Where I Think."
16 See Santos, Nunes, and Meneses. "Introduction," ix–xvix.
17 Chen, *Asia as Method*.
18 Spivak, *Death of a Discipline*.
19 Homi Bhabha, quoted in Olson and Worsham, "Staging the Politics of Difference," 8.
20 Pratt, "Comparative Literature," 274.
21 Ramazani, *A Transnational Poetics*, 14.
22 Bernstein, "The Practice of Poetics," 78.
23 Bernstein, "The Practice of Poetics."
24 Edmond, *Common Strangeness*, 165.
25 Ramazani, *A Transnational Poetics*, 25.
26 Ramazani, *A Transnational Poetics*, 37.
27 Justin Read expresses his concern about this potential relation and its effects in *Modern Poetics and Hemispheric American Cultural Studies:* "This is perhaps the primary question posed by this book: In raising culture as integrally related, and perhaps forcefully resistant, to the integrated Free Trade

Agreement of the Americas, how do we avoid creating a homogenized Free Trade Agreement of Hemispheric American Cultural Studies?" (xvi–xvii). Ann Marie Fallon is more optimistic. She writes: "I argue that transnational literary aesthetics furthers our ability to imagine and inhabit cultural differences and interactions beyond the acquisition of knowledge about such difference and interaction" (3). And Françoise Lionnet and Shu-Mei Shih argue that "globalization increasingly favors lateral and non-hierarchical network structures, or what Gilles Deleuze and Félix Guattari call a rhizome" (2). This debate has not been resolved.

28 See Kamboureli and Miki and Coleman and Kamboureli.
29 Ramazani, *A Transnational Poetics*, 48.
30 See Kim, McCall, and Singer, eds., *Cultural Grammars,* for an elaboration of the metaphor of cultural grammar in relation, including "grammars of exchange" (Martin-Lucas) in relation to national belonging and citizenship.
31 For a thoughtful engagement with the ways in which the national frame still matters, see Stam and Shohat, *Race in Translation*.
32 See Stefan Collini's *What Are Universities For?* for a work that seeks an expanded definition of use-value in a related sphere.
33 Uppal, "Patience."
34 See The Writers Union of Canada webpage: "'Writers are a tribe,' said Margaret Laurence...," Accessed on 3 May 2013 at http://www.writersunion.ca/content/history.
35 Roberts, *Prizing Literature*, 6.
36 Damon, *Postliterary America*, 125.
37 Cremin, "To Initiate a Poetics," 1.
38 Susan Bernofsky, "To Occupy," 420.
39 See Jackson.
40 Barker, "Already Occupied," 3.
41 Damon, *Postliterary America*, 124. Emphasis in original.
42 Damon, *Postliterary America*, 124. 125. Emphasis in original.
43 Bhabha, quoted in Olson and Worsham, "Staging the Politics," 10.
44 Bernstein, "Invention Follies," 34.
45 Bernstein, "Invention Follies," 36.
46 Bernstein, "Invention Follies," 37.
47 Stevens and Sinavaiana, *Mohawk/Samoa Transmigrations*, 12.
48 Stevens and Sinavaiana, *Mohawk/Samoa Transmigrations*, 12.
49 Stevens and Sinavaiana, *Mohawk/Samoa Transmigrations*, 25.
50 Stevens and Sinavaiana, *Mohawk/Samoa Transmigrations*, 29.
51 Derrida, quoted in Spurr, *The Rhetoric of Empire*.
52 Spurr, *The Rhetoric of Empire*, 4.
53 Cariou, "'How Come These Guns Are So Tall,'" 151. Cariou describes *city treaty* "as a streetwise anti-globalization manifesto for the indigenous world" (140).

54 Francis, *city treaty*, 6.
55 Francis, *city treaty*, 12.
56 Winnipeg: University of Manitoba Press, 2013.
57 Francis explains in his proposal description for the creative master's thesis that became *city Treaty:* "The main thrust of *city treaty* is that treaties are living documents that evolve along with society. Since an increasing percentage of Native people are urban, their perceptions differ from those who signed the original treaties" (1). See Francis, "Description of Proposal."
58 Francis, *city treaty*, 60.
59 Francis, *city treaty*, 68.
60 Francis, *city treaty*, 69.
61 Francis, *city treaty*, 64.
62 Francis, *city treaty*, 28.
63 Francis, *city treaty*, 58.
64 Francis, *city treaty*, 49.
65 Francis, *city treaty*, 65.
66 Francis, *city treaty*, 59.
67 Francis, *city treaty*, 67.
68 Santos, Nunes, and Meneses, "Opening Up," ix.
69 Derksen, *Dwell*, 1.
70 Derksen, *Dwell*, 2.
71 Cox and Shechter (2002), quoted in Santos, Nunes, and Meneses, "Opening Up," xxxviii. Italics in original.
72 Derksen, *Dwell*, 2.
73 Derksen, *Dwell*, 3.
74 Derksen, *Dwell*, 5.
75 Abrams, *The Mirror and the Lamp*.
76 Derksen, *Dwell*, 8.
77 Derksen, *Dwell*, 72. From "If History."
78 Derksen, *Dwell*, 9. From "Interface."
79 Conducted through "Globalization and Autonomy," "Building Global Democracy," the "Brazil/Canada Knowledge Exchange," and the co-production, with Marta Dvořák, of *Crosstalk: Canadian and Global Imaginaries in Dialogue*.
80 Brydon, Jones, Schagerl, and Warder, "Introduction," 7.
81 Derksen, *Dwell*, 6.

Bibliography

Abrams, Meyer. *The Mirror and the Lamp: Romantic Theory and the Critical Tradition*. Oxford: Oxford University Press, 1971.

Barker, Adam J. "Already Occupied: Indigenous Peoples, Settler Colonialism, and the Occupy Movements in North America." *Social Movement Studies:*

Journal of Social, Cultural, and Political Protest 11, nos. 3–4 (2012): 327–34.
Bernofsky, Susan. "To Occupy: An Evolution." *Rethinking Marxism: A Journal of Economics, Culture, and Society* 24, no. 3 (2012): 420.
Bernstein, Charles. "Invention Follies." In *Attack of the Difficult Poems: Essays and Inventions*. 33–41. Chicago: University of Chicago Press, 2011.
———. "The Practice of Poetics." In *Attack of the Difficult Poems: Essays and Inventions*. 73–80. Chicago: University of Chicago Press, 2011.
Brun, Gerald L. *What Are Poets For?: An Anthropology of Contemporary Poetry and Poetics*. Springfield: U of Illinois Press, 2012.
Block, David, John Gray, and Marnie Holborow. *Neoliberalism and Applied Linguistics*. London: Routledge, 2012.
Brathwaite, Kamau. "Caribbean Culture: Two Paradigms." In *Missile and Capsule*. Edited by Jurgen Martini. 9–54. Bremen: University of Bremen, 1983.
Brydon, Diana, and Marta Dvořák, eds. *Crosstalk: Canadian and Global Imaginaries in Dialogue*. Waterloo: Wilfrid Laurier University Press, 2012.
Brydon, Diana, Manina Jones, Jessica Schagerl, and Kristin Warder. "Introduction." In Brydon et al., eds., "Poetics and Public Culture in Canada." *Studies in Canadian Literature / Études en Littérature Canadienne* 32, no. 2 (2007): 7–27.
Burnham, Clint, and Christine Stewart. "Afterword: 21st-Century Poetics." *Canadian Literature* 210–11 (Autumn 2011): 263–68.
Cariou, Warren. "'How Come These Guns Are So Tall': Anti-Corporate Resistance in Marvin Francis's *city treaty*." *Studies in Canadian Literature / Études en littérature canadienne* 31, no. 1 (2006). Web. 20 November 2014.
Chen, Kuan-Hsing. *Asia as Method: Towards Deimperialization*. Durham: Duke University Press, 2010.
Coleman, Daniel, and Smaro Kamboureli, eds. *Retooling the Humanities: The Culture of Research in Canadian Universities*. Edmonton: University of Alberta Press, 2011.
Collini, Stefan. *What Are Universities For?* Harmondsworth, UK: Penguin, 2012.
Craft, Aimeé. *Breathing Life into the Stone Fort Treaties: An Anishinabe Understanding of Treaty One*. Winnipeg: University of Manitoba Press, 2013.
Cremin, Becky. "To Initiate a Poetics of Occupation: Occupy as Poetics: Poetics as Occupy." In *Poetry and Revolution Conference*. London, UK: Birkbeck, University of London, 2012.
Damon, Maria. *Postliterary America: From Bagel Shop Jazz to Micropoetries*. Contemporary North American Poetry Series. Iowa City: University of Iowa Press, 2011.
Derksen, Jeff. *Dwell*. Vancouver: Talonbooks, 1993.
Edmond, Jacob. *Common Strangeness: Contemporary Poetry, Cross-Cultural Encounter, Comparative Literature*. New York: Fordham University Press, 2012.
Eichhorn, Kate, and Heather Milne, eds. *Prismatic Publics: Innovative Canadian Women's Poetry and Poetics*. Toronto: Coach House, 2009.
Fallon, Ann Marie. *Global Crusoe: Comparative Literature, Postcolonial Theory*

and Transnational Aesthetics. Farnham: Ashgate, 2011.

Francis, Marvin. *city treaty: a long poem.* Winnipeg: Turnstone Press, 2002.

———. "Description of Proposal." Marvin Francis Fonds. University of Manitoba.

Halliday, Terence C., and Bruce G. Carruthers. *Bankrupt: Global Lawmaking and Systemic Financial Crisis.* Stanford: Stanford University Press, 2009.

Hesford, Wendy S. "Global Turns and Cautions in Rhetoric and Composition Studies." *PMLA* 121.3 (May 2006): 787–801.

Jackson, Ross. *Occupy World Street: A Global Roadmap for Radical Economic and Politics Reform.* White River Junction, VT: Chelsea Green, 2012.

Kamboureli, Smaro, and Roy Miki, eds. *Trans.Can.Lit: Resituating the Study of Canadian Literature.* Waterloo: Wilfrid Laurier University Press, 2007.

Kim, Christine, Sophie McCall, and Melina Baum Singer, eds. *Cultural Grammars of Nation, Diaspora, and Indigeneity in Canada.* Waterloo: Wilfrid Laurier University Press, 2012.

Lionnet, Françoise, and Shu-mei Shih, eds. *Minor Transnationalism.* Durham: Duke University Press, 2005.

Martin-Lucas, Belén. "'Grammars of Exchange': The 'Oriental Woman' in the Global Market." In Kim, McCall, and Singer, eds., *Cultural Grammars*.

Mignolo, Walter. "I Am Where I Think: Remapping the Order of Knowing." In *The Creolization of Theory.* Edited by Françoise and Shu-mei Shih Lionnet. Durham: Duke University Press, 2011.

Miki, Roy. *In Flux: Transnational Shifts in Asian Canadian Writing.* Edmonton: NeWest Press, 2011.

Ngũgĩ wa, Thiong'o. *Globalectics: Theory and the Politics of Knowing.* Wellek Library Lectures in Critical Theory. New York: Columbia University Press, 2012.

Olson, Gary A., and Lynn Worsham. "Staging the Politics of Difference: Homi Bhabha's Critical Literacy." In *Race, Rhetoric, and the Postcolonial.* 3–42. Albany: SUNY Press, 1999.

Pratt, Mary Louise. "Comparative Literature and the Global Languagescape." In *A Companion to Comparative Literature.* Edited by Ali and Dominic Thomas Behdad, 273–95. Malden: Wiley-Blackwell, 2011.

Ramazani, Jahan. *A Transnational Poetics.* Chicago: University of Chicago Press, 2009.

Reed, Justin. *Modern Poetics and Hemispheric American Cultural Studies.* London: Palgrave Macmillan, 2009.

Roberts, Gillian. *Prizing Literature: The Celebration and Circulation of National Culture.* Toronto: University of Toronto Press, 2011.

Santos, Boaventura de Sousa, J.A. Nunes, and M.P. Meneses. "Opening Up the Canon of Knowledge and Recognition of Difference." In *Another Knowledge Is Possible: Beyond Northern Epistemologies.* Edited by Boaventura de Sousa

Santos. lx–lxii. London: Verso, 2007.

Slater, David. *Geopolitics and the Post-Colonial: Rethinking North–South Relations.* Oxford: Blackwell, 2004.

Spivak, Gayatri Chakravorty. *Death of a Discipline.* New York: Columbia University Press, 2003.

Spurr, David. *The Rhetoric of Empire: Colonial Discourse in Journalism, Travel Writing, and Imperial Administration.* Durham: Duke University Press, 1993.

Stam, Robert, and Ella Shohat. *Race in Translation: Culture Wars Around the Postcolonial Atlantic.* New York: NYU Press, 2012.

Stevens, James Thomas, and Caroline Sinavaiana. *Mohawk/Samoa Transmigrations.* Oakland: Subpress, 2005.

Uppal, Priscilla. "Patience." *Literary Review of Canada.* Accessed 12 September 2014 at http://games.reviewcanada.ca.

Nota bene; or, notes toward a poetics of work...

Bart Vautour and Christl Verduyn

> In divers tones I sing,
>   And pray you, Friend, give ear!
> My medley of song I bring
>   You, who can rightly hear.
>
> Themes gathered far and near,
>   Thoughts from my heart that spring,
>   In divers tones I sing,
> And pray you, Friend, give ear!
>
> Here's many a serious thing—
>   You'll know if it's sincere.
> Where the light laughters ring
>   You may detect a tear.
> In divers tones I sing,
>   And pray you, Friend, give ear!
>   —Charles G.D. Roberts

This collection makes clear that its contributors and editors consider "public poetics" in divers tones. Indeed, the preceding essays and poems comprise a chorus closer to a contemporary mash-up than an orthodox oratorio. This configuration is purposeful and has been curated to represent a current conjuncture of Canadian work on poetics. In our brief concluding contribution, we wish to add our voices to the chorus by casting a wide net and thinking out loud about the work of poetics and the conditions under which poetics are produced and reproduced in an English Canadian context.

In the first instance, poetics *qua* poetics demand and exemplify a language economy different from prose and the prosaic, which is the dominant mode of communicating—of being public—within a liberal order framework. By recognizing that poetics operate as a language economy, we acknowledge its reliance on more than poems: poetics becomes both the "stuff" of poetry as well as the action that poetry demands. Poetics, in this rendering, stands for the circulation of ideas by other means—other, in this case, because poetics is always up against its prose sibling. As we know, prose-dominated life was born out of Western Enlightenment and raised alongside the novel, bourgeois culture, and imperial imposition, among other things. While it is difficult to make an epistemological claim for either poetic or prosaic modes, it is easier to claim narrative prose as an ontologically dominant mode of social and political organization in contemporary Canada. Prose has something to do with power. With subjugation. With emancipation. With dominantly structuring the enabling and disabling conditions of everyday lives. Poetics, we think, has some of the same characteristics, but also some different things to offer.

We would like to suggest that poetics is prose's sibling demanding attention. Poetics, as a representational system, has the capacity to collapse and refill the rut of conventional thinking and to make less opaque those habits of inattention that are otherwise obscured. Of course the prosaic mode has the facility to enable these things as well, but when it does, it does so from a position of ascendency. Again, poetics is the circulation of ideas by other means. Poetics is a sibling demanding attention *and* refusing to accept the hand-me-downs of prosaic thinking. As Andrea Hasenbank suggests in her contribution to this collection, "refusal becomes powerful in the speaking: a new movement crawls up out of the breach in the formation of a new language that makes it intelligible."[1] Like other alternative economies, poetics operates within an (language) economy that requires us to understand shifting modes of valuation in order for intelligibility to materialize. We don't always understand the shifts. We don't always transvaluate. Given the increasing sovereignty of a prose-based capitalist economy that hides its abstractions in plain sight, poetics in particular requires us to understand its work as always already radical.[2] With clarity and generosity, Tanis MacDonald, in her essay in this collection, suggests that it is usual in Canadian criticism to speak of antipathy between avant-garde and lyric poetics, or to distinguish between radical and more conventional poetic practices, but in the addressable, flawed, contextual, and shifting publics of Canadian poetry, beleaguered as we are by desultory pain, the more we position these ways of proceeding as competing or oppositional, the more we lose. Every time I write poetry, every time I teach it, every time I begin a conversation in any kind of public forum, be it academic, literary, or among people who do not read poetry, I feel radical, no matter what poetry I am talking about and no matter what my method.[3]

If we agree with Tanis, how then do we purposefully shift our understanding of knowledge production through a non-dominant language economy? Moreover, how can we talk of different generations or formal practices within Canadian poetics without projecting them through a lens of competition or hostility? Take for example, the banter that continues to circulate around F.R. Scott's "The Canadian Authors Meet":[4] it has been variously underwritten and overdetermined by dissimilar critical practices and narratives. On the one hand, some of these critical narratives have emerged, taken office for brief or not-so-brief critical moments, and left only residual traces in contemporary assessments. On the other hand, some critical accounts of the poem have found a healthy persistence well into the contemporary moment. We do not want to rehearse the debates here...or at least not in full.[5] We return to this poem because we see the potential for "The Canadian Authors Meet" and the example of the critical debate surrounding the poem to (re)model a general and expansive conversation about poetic work (the work of poetics) and a poetics of work (a different way of working).

Rather than highlight "The Canadian Authors Meet" as a "brilliant *tour-de-force* in the Modernist battles against Canadian Victorian poetry of the 1920s"[6] or as "a masculinist self-birthing...through the rejection of maternity and women's collegial presence and influence,"[7] we instead ask what the poem says about poetic work.[8] What Scott's poem points to (and what more recent poetic attacks on poets do not) is a clear critique of a "poetry scene" in which poetic possibilities do not headline the show. In other words, Scott's satire takes aim at poetic inaction just as much as at actual individuals (Lampman, Roberts, Carman, Campbell, Scott) and stock characters (Miss Crotchet). Scott's portrayal is of a group who care less about the strength of a Canadian poetics than about extra-literary social interrelation. He questions the point and direction of the meeting: "Shall we go round the mulberry bush, or shall / We gather at the river, or shall we / Appoint a poet laureate this Fall, / Or shall we have another cup of tea" (17–20). Scott's blatant echoing of Eliot here suggests more than derivativeness; it suggests that he is using the cultural authority of transnational literary production to energize a Canadian contingent of poetics. Included among the list of unliterary acts is an extremely public literary act of appointing a poet laureate, but when couched within a framework of nursery rhymes and tea, the possible appointment and institutional post of the poet laureate is stripped of urgency, seriousness, and potential cultural and political influence. More than just calling on the cultural authority of Eliot, though, Scott's critique of a "tea party" atmosphere has an actual historical referent, as Watson Kirkconnell suggests:

> The 1926 [annual CAA] convention was held in Vancouver, with a leisurely social epilogue in Victoria. As a matter of fact, the social side of the convention had tended, even in Vancouver, to crowd out the more legitimate activities of the gathering. Thus an afternoon session devoted to the basic business of authorship was simply scrapped in order to give the delegates more leisure to prepare for a tea-party at the new chalet on Grouse Mountain.[9]

Scott was able to mobilize transnational poetic production alongside a critique of the functioning of the Canadian Authors Association on an institutional level that would have been recognizable to the audience of his occasional poem. His satire was aimed at inaction and the devaluation of the labour involved in sustaining a viable Canadian poetics.

In many ways, this collection of essays and poems (and the conference that preceded it) hopes to reverse the rhetorical situation of Scott's poem and the critical debates that followed its publication: to take seriously the ways in which poetics can invigorate a public through attentive work rather than allow poetics to be dulled by uncritical, isolating, or vitriolic discourse. In this, we have hoped not to make the same mistake as Scott in dismissing the breath of Canadian poetics across temporal or formal contingencies. Instead, we hope to have widened and welcomed broader, keener understandings and practices of poetics that attend to the labour inherent in poetics and to the generative approaches such substantial labour might initiate. The contributions to this collection compel us to consider how poetics can and does attend to the political, social, legal, economic, and ecological—as well as the literary and artistic—realms and realities of human life. Mapping a historicity of public poetics in Canada, exploring current manifestations of public poetics, and pointing to future possibilities, the essays in this collection demonstrate that poetics can and does address the "ugly times" of cuts to social programming (Miller), engage issues of urban alienation and unaffordable housing (Ballantyne), confront racial prejudice (Jones), expose gender inequality (Queyras), and express class and political protest—past or present (Hasenbank and Nardone). The essayists locate poetics beyond print on the page, pushing past boundaries of genre to places and parts played by the political pamphlet (Hasenbank), the human microphone (Nardone), the radio broadcast (McLeod), the body in pain (MacDonald), the role of poet laureate re-examined and reconceptualized (Smith and Miller), and the poetry reading itself (Moure and Shearer). These explorations alert us to how poetics works, how poetics provides a different model for human organization and community, a different understanding of power, and ultimately new and different knowledge. In its attention to detail, to listening and awareness, to being alert to the world through words that express it, poetics works to reach past abstraction, beyond pettiness, self-centredness, lack of generosity, and even hostility of the kind evidenced by F.R. Scott's "The Canadian Authors Meet." Poetics perceived and understood for its public work and call to action greets the world beyond national and literary borders (Brydon) and across lines drawn around literary movements, critical discourses (Milne, Stout, McNeilly), or the private (Jernigan). As presented and discussed in the essays of this collection, poetics bridges the word and the world.

It is in this context that we make a final turn to a poetic manifesto written by derek beaulieu, whose work graces the cover of this book. In "Please, No More Poetry" (considered in this collection by John Stout), beaulieu takes F.R. Scott's rhetorical stance further, pushing beyond a satiric critique of poets whose "muse" has "failed to function" to critique poets and poetry of his contemporary moment more generally.[10] "Poetry is the last refuge of the unimaginative," beaulieu tells us.[11] Further, in what we read as mock lament, he notes that "Poetry, sadly, knows / it's poetry, while writing doesn't always know it's writing."[12] In two lines beaulieu both highlights poetry's condition as exception and the potential privilege of prose as simply writing that is subject to its own inattention. Importantly, as the manifesto continues beaulieu maintains a critique of poets and poems, not poetics: his manifesto suggests to us that a poem or a poet in isolation does not do a good job of connecting the dots—that poetry *by itself* will make nothing happen (à la Auden). "Art," he writes, "is a conversation, not a patent office."[13] We take beaulieu seriously here: poetry will only make something happen in the context of a larger, well-informed, and generous conversation that is poetics—object and action. Just as poets must see their work as part of a broad conversation, critical practices must attend to the varied shape of Canadian poetics with more generosity. We must continue to do the work of building a public poetics in Canada, but we must do it within a broad framework that looks to make connections across artistic practices. So, in closing we humbly ask: Please, no more poetry without poetics…

Notes

1 Hassenbank, page 231 in this volume.
2 For studies that explore this collusion between prose and capitalist economy, see Dobson and Kamboureli, *Producing Canadian Literature,* as well as Godard, "Notes from the Cultural Field."
3 MacDonald, page 61 in this volume.
4 The poem was first published the *McGill Fortnightly Review* (27 April 1927) and subsequently published without the original final stanza in *Canadian Forum* (1935) and then again in *New Provinces: Poems by Several Authors* (1936).
5 While we are well aware of the import and weight of these debates, especially about the poem's apparent misogyny, we refrain (slightly), in this *nota bene,* from fully attending to that discussion. For a detailed critical discussion of critical accounts of the poem see: Gerson, "The Canon Between the Wars," 54; Bentley, *The Gay Grey Moose,* 259–61; and, Irvine, "Introduction," 1–4.
6 Trehearne, *Aestheticism and the Canadian Modernists,* 170.
7 Brandt, "A New Genealogy," 3.
8 We don't speak of Scott to rehearse masculinist genealogies, though we do think the poem is useful for highlighting generational and formal shifts. While we wish the poem's misogynist resounding of Eliot through the figure of "Miss Crotchet" were something of the past, we have seen the Canadian "poem about other poets" take on even more acute (read violent and sexualized) forms in recent years. For a critique of this historic trend in contemporary poetics, see Fiorentino, "Sexism and Silence in the Literary Community."
9 Kirkconnell, "The Embattled Authors," 293. Many thanks go to Christopher Doody for bringing this to our attention. His work-in-progress on the CAA will, no doubt, prove important for Canadian literary history.
10 beaulieu, "Please, No More Poetry," 1.
11 beaulieu, "Please, No More Poetry."
12 beaulieu, "Please, No More Poetry."
13 beaulieu, "Please, No More Poetry."

Bibliography

beaulieu, derek. *Please, No More Poetry: The Poetry of derek beaulieu*. Edited by Kit Dobson. Waterloo: Wilfrid Laurier University Press, 2013.

Bentley, D.M.R. *The Gay Grey Moose: Essays on the Ecologies & Mythologies of Canadian Poetry, 1690–1990*. Ottawa: University of Ottawa Press, 1992.

Brandt, Di. "A New Genealogy of Canadian Literary Modernism." *Wider Boundaries of Daring: The Modernist Impulse in Canadian Women's Poetry*. Edited by Di Brandt and Barbara Godard. 1–25. Waterloo: Wilfrid Laurier University Press, 2009.

Dobson, Kit, and Smaro Kamboureli, eds. *Producing Canadian Literature: Authors Speak on the Literary Marketplace*. Waterloo: Wilfrid Laurier University Press, 2013.

Fiorentino, Jon Paul. "Sexism and Silence in the Literary Community." *Huffington Post*. Accessed 12 September 2014 at http://www.huffingtonpost.ca/jon-paul-fiorentino/sexism-literary-community_b_3188385.html.

Gerson, Carole. "The Canon Between the Wars: Field-notes of a Feminist Literary Archaeologist." *Canadian Canons: Essays in Literary Value*. Edited by Robert Lecker. 46–56. Toronto: University of Toronto Press, 1991.

Godard, Barbara. "Notes from the Cultural Field: Canadian Literature from Identity to Hybridity." *Essays on Canadian Writing* 72 (2000): 209–58.

Irvine, Dean. "Introduction." *The Canadian Modernists Meet*. Edited by Dean Irvine. 1–13. Ottawa: University of Ottawa Press, 2005.

Kirkconnell, Watson. "The Embattled Authors." *A Slice of Canada: Memoirs*. 290–303. Toronto: University of Toronto Press, 1967.

Scott, F.R. "The Canadian Authors Meet." *McGill Fortnightly Review* 2, nos. 9–10 (27 April 1927): 73; rpt. in *Canadian Forum*, December 1935, 388; rpt. in *New Provinces: Poems by Several Authors*. Toronto: Macmillan, 1936.

Trehearne, Brian. *Aestheticism and the Canadian Modernists: Aspects of a Poetic Influence*. Montreal and Kingston: McGill–Queen's University Press, 1989.

Contributors

Emily Ballantyne is a doctoral candidate in English at Dalhousie University, where she is a Killam Fellow and a SSHRC Canada Graduate Scholarship recipient. Her dissertation places modernism in the context of transnational travel writing. She recently co-edited (with Michèle Rackham Hall and Emily Essert) a special issue on the oeuvre of P.K. Page for *Canadian Poetry* (Spring 2015), and is at work on a collection of Page's non-fiction prose for the *Collected Works of P.K. Page*.

derek beaulieu is the author or editor of sixteen books, the most recent of which are *Please, No More Poetry: The Poetry of derek beaulieu* (Wilfrid Laurier University Press, 2013) and *kern* (Les Figues press, 2014). He is the publisher of the acclaimed no press and is the visual poetry editor at *UBUWeb*. beaulieu has exhibited his work across Canada, the United States, and Europe and is an award-winning instructor at the Alberta College of Art + Design. He holds a Ph.D. from the University of Roehampton (London) and is the 2014–2016 Poet Laureate of Calgary.

Diana Brydon, Ph.D., FRSC, is Canada Research Chair in Globalization and Cultural Studies and Director of the Research Centre for Globalization and Cultural Studies at the University of Manitoba. A specialist in Canadian and postcolonial literary and cultural studies, she edited *Renegotiating Community: Interdisciplinary Perspectives, Global Contexts* (2008) with W.D. Coleman; and with Marta Dvořák, *Crosstalk: Canadian and Global Imaginaries in Dialogue* (2012). She co-edited (with Manina Jones, Jessica Schagerl and Kristin Warder) *Poetics and Public Culture in Canada* (*SCL/ÉLC*, 2007). She is currently investigating transnational literacies and literary theories of globalization.

Brad Cran is a writer, accountant, and social entrepreneur. Cran served as Poet Laureate for the City of Vancouver from April 2009 until October of 2011. He published his first book, *The Good Life*, in 2001. In 2008 *Hope in Shadows: Stories and Photographs of Vancouver's Downtown Eastside* (with Gillian Jerome) won the City of Vancouver Book Award, was shortlisted for the Roderick Haig-Brown Regional Prize, was long-listed for the George Ryga Award for Social Awareness in Literature, and has raised over $50,000 for marginalized people in Vancouver's Downtown Eastside. Cran's essay "Notes on a World Class City" defended Vancouver's progressive history and went viral in the lead-up to the 2010 Winter Olympic games. His second book of poetry, *Ink on Paper*, was published in 2013.

Andrea Hasenbank is a Ph.D. candidate at the University of Alberta, where she is a Killam Memorial Scholar and a past Doctoral Fellow of both the Social Sciences and Humanities Research Council of Canada and the Editing Modernism in Canada (EMiC) project. Her research focuses on the common material and linguistic tactics shared at the intersection between literary modernism and the leftist pamphleteering culture of 1930s Canada. As part of EMiC, she is currently the editor of *Between Poetics and Polemics: Canadian Manifestos, 1910–1960*.

Amanda Jernigan is the author of two books of poetry, *Groundwork* (Biblioasis, 2011) and *All the Daylight Hours* (Cormorant, 2013), and of the prose monograph *Living in the Orchard: The Poetry of Peter Sanger* (Frog Hollow, 2014). She has worked as a freelance editor for Anchorage Press, Gaspereau Press, and Porcupine's Quill (the proprietors of which are the dedicatees of the poem "Routine," included here). Jernigan edited *The Essential Richard Outram* (2011) for Porcupine's Quill, and is currently at work on a critical edition of Outram's poems. She lives in Hamilton, Ontario, with her family.

El Jones is a spoken word activist and teacher. She is dedicated to using spoken word to tell the histories and stories of her community and to encourage those voices most silenced to speak. She is active in prison outreach and youth work. She is the fifth Poet Laureate of Halifax and teaches in the Creative Writing Program at Dalhousie University.

Vanessa Lent is a writer and teacher in Halifax, Nova Scotia. Her Ph.D. dissertation examined the works of Elizabeth Smart, John Glassco, Sheila Watson, and Malcolm Lowry within the context of late-modernist counter-narratives to nationalism in Canada. She currently teaches and develops curriculum at Immigrant Services Association of Nova Scotia (ISANS). In particular, her work focuses on ways of teaching storytelling and life writing to adult refugees with little or no formal education.

Tanis MacDonald is Associate Professor of English and Film Studies at Wilfrid Laurier University in Waterloo, Ontario. She is the author of *The Daughter's Way: Canadian Women's Paternal Elegies* (WLUP, 2012), and three books of poetry, including *Rue The Day* (Turnstone, 2008).

Shannon Maguire is a doctoral candidate in the Department of English and Film Studies at Wilfrid Laurier University. Her dissertation project is entitled "On Noise: Queer and Métis Unsettlements in Canadian Poetry." Her first collection of poetry, *fur(l) parachute* (BookThug, 2013), was the finalist for several awards, including the Robert Kroetsch Award for Innovative Poetry. She was also a finalist for the bpNichol Chapbook Award for *Fruit Machine* (Ferno House, 2012). Her second full-length collection, *Myrmurs*, is forthcoming from BookThug in fall 2015. Shannon holds an MFA in Creative Writing from the University of Guelph and an M.A. in English from Brock University.

Travis V. Mason has taught ecocriticism, poetry and poetics, and Canadian and postcolonial literatures on the west and east coast. The recipient of both a Mellon and a Killam Postdoctoral Fellowship, he has published several articles and reviews in Canadian and international journals and books. *Ornithologies of Desire: Ecocritical Essays, Avian Poetics, and Don McKay* (2013) is available as part of Wilfrid Laurier University Press's Environmental Humanities series.

Kathleen McConnell, as Kathy Mac, published *The Hundefräulein Papers* (Roseway, 2009) and *Nail Builders Plan for Strength and Growth* (Roseway, 2002). In 2012, Wolsak & Wynn published her book of lyric scholarship *Porn, Pain and Complicity*. She teaches creative writing and Atlantic Canadian poetry at St. Thomas University, Fredericton.

Katherine McLeod is a Postdoctoral Fellow with SpokenWe/Department of English, Concordia University, where she is researching audio archives of poetry readings in Canada. Her SSHRC-funded postdoctoral research (TransCanada Institute / U of Guelph, 2010–12) focused on the early years of CBC Radio's literary programming and her doctoral dissertation (U of Toronto, 2010) examined performances of poetry by The Four Horsemen, Michael Ondaatje, George Elliott Clarke, and Robert Bringhurst. Along with reviews in *Canadian Literature* and *Canadian Theatre Review*, she published an article on Clarke in *Mosaic* that has been republished in *Africadian Atlantic: Essays on George Elliott Clarke* and her chapter in *Theatre and AutoBiography: Writing and Performing Lives in Theory and Practice* has been republished in *Critical Perspectives on Canadian Theatre in English: Solo Performance*.

Kevin McNeilly is an Associate Professor in the English Department at the University of British Columbia, where he teaches cultural studies and contemporary literatures. He's a member of the "Improvisation, Community and Social Practice" research initiative. His book of poems is *Embouchure* (Nightwood Editions). See kevinmcneilly.ca for more.

Geordie Miller is a Ph.D. candidate in the English department at Dalhousie University. His research assesses the political value of American literature within neoliberalism, a project for which he was awarded a Killam Scholarship and a SSHRC Fellowship. He has published articles on the work of Anne Carson, Stephen Collis, and Adeena Karasick, as well as a collection of poetry entitled *Re:union* (Invisible Publishing).

Heather Milne is an Associate Professor in the Department of English at the University of Winnipeg. She is currently writing a book that examines recent American and Canadian feminist poetry and poetics. She is the co-editor of *Prismatic Publics: Innovative Canadian Women's Poetry and Poetics*.

Erín Moure writes in English and Galician and translates poetry from French, Galician, Spanish and Portuguese into English by, among others, Nicole Brossard, Chus Pato, and Fernando Pessoa. Her work has also appeared in short films, theatre, and musical compositions. In 2014, her *Insecession*, a translational echo to Chus Pato's biopoetics, was published alongside her translation of Pato's *Secession* (BookThug, 2014). In 2015, she was writer in residence at Green College, UBC, and launched *Kapusta* (Anansi)—a book-length poem-play-cabaret and outcry against genocide.

Michael Nardone is a Ph.D. candidate at Concordia University's Centre for Interdisciplinary Studies in Society and Culture. He writes on poetics, media, and sound. He is managing editor of *Amodern* and assistant editor of *Jacket2*. Nardone's research has been awarded a Social Science and Humanities Research Council CGS Doctoral Award, a J.W. McConnell Fellowship, a Concordia University Doctoral Award of Excellence, and an Editing Modernism in Canada Doctoral Stipend. He is the author of *Transaction Record* (Gauss PDF) and, with artist Jude Griebel, *O. Cyrus & the Bardo* (JackPine).

Sina Queyras is a writer, teacher, and cultural critic. She has published six books of poetry: *Someone from the Hollow* (1995), *Slip* (2001), *Teethmarks* (2004), *Lemon Hound* (2006), *Expressway* (2009), and *M x T* (2014). She received the Pat Lowther Award and a Lambada Literary Award for *Lemon Hound* and the A.M. Kline Award for *M x T*. She has also published a novel, *Autobiography of Childhood* (2011) and a collection of criticism (*Unleashed*, 2009), and has edited an anthology of Canadian poetry (*Open Field: 30 Contemporary Canadian Poets*, 2005). Between 2005 and 2007 she co-curated the path-breaking feminist belladonna* reading series in New York and has been instrumental in bringing Canadian poets into conversation with American poets. Queyras is the founder and editor of the digital cultural hub *Lemon Hound* (www.lemonhound.com). She teaches at Concordia University.

Karis Shearer is an Assistant Professor in the Faculty of Creative and Critical Studies at UBC (Okanagan) and held the 2010 Canada–US Fulbright Visiting Research Chair at Vanderbilt University. She is the editor of *All These Roads: The Poetry of Louis Dudek* (2008), has published critical work on George Bowering, Tomson Highway, Jane Urquhart, and has published a co-authored chapter on Sina Queyras's work.

Will Smith is an Associate Lecturer and Knowledge Exchange Fellow (2014–15) at Lancaster University in the Department of English and Creative Writing. His doctoral thesis, *Torontos: Representations of Toronto in Contemporary Canadian Literature*, was conducted at the University of Nottingham. He has reviewed for *Matrix Magazine*, *The Bull Calf*, and *The Malahat Review*. He is currently researching the history and legacy of Toronto literature, with an article forthcoming on Peter Donovan and Hopkins Moorhouse in the *British Journal of Canadian Studies*.

John Stout teaches literature at McMaster University. He is currently beginning work on a project exploring innovative poetries of France, the United States, and Canada from recent decades. In 2010 he published the book *L'Énigme-poésie: Entretiens avec 21 poètes françaises*.

Bart Vautour is Assistant Professor at Dalhousie University in the Department of English. His research interests involve Canadian cultural production, social justice and political movements in Canada, literary history, textual studies, and transnational articulations of modernism. He is editor of Ted Allan's Spanish Civil War novel, *This Time a Better Earth* (1939), and co-editor, with Emily Robins Sharpe, of Charles Yale Harrison's *Meet*

Me on the Barricades (1938), both with University of Ottawa Press. He is co-director, with Emily Robins Sharpe, of Canada and the Spanish Civil War (spanishcivilwar.ca).

Christl Verduyn is cross-appointed to the Department of English and the Canadian Studies Program at Mount Allison University, where she is the Davidson Chair in Canadian Studies and Director of the Centre for Canadian Studies. Her research interests include Canadian and Québécois literatures, women's writing and criticism, multiculturalism and minority writing, life writing and archival approaches to literature, and the interdisciplinary field of Canadian studies.

Rob Winger is an Assistant Professor at Trent University, and author of three books of poetry, including *Muybridge's Horse* (2007) and *Old Hat* (2014). His second book, *The Chimney Stone* (2010), complements his critical study of the *ghazal*'s appearance Canadian poetry, *Between the Sky and the Stove*.

Erin Wunker is Chair of the Board of Canadian Women in the Literary Arts (CWILA). She has taught at the University of Calgary, Mount Royal University, Dalhousie University, and Mount Allison University. Her research is in the field of Canadian literature, namely poetry and poetics, cultural production, and critical and cultural theory. She is at work on a manuscript project that addresses the poetics of collapse. She is co-founder, weekly contributor, and co-editor of the feminist academic blog *Hook & Eye: Fast Feminism, Slow Academe*.

Index

Abatos (Sanger), 122–25, 126, 129, 130, 131
Abel, Jordan, 278
Abley, Mark, 257
Acconci, Vito, 39
Acorn, Milton, 10–11
activism. *See forage* (Wong); human microphone; *Human Resources* (Zolf); *Ossuaries* (Brand); pamphlets; poetic activism; political activism; Project Rebuild (Murakami); *Rebuild* (Murakami)
"Address at Simon Fraser" (Page), 212
Adorno, Theodor: on mimesis, 53, 54; "On Lyric Poetry and Society," 200–201
"After Monteverdi" (Sanger), 133
Against Expression (Goldsmith and Dworkin), 88
Agamben, Giorgio, 281
agitprop, 235, 240–41, 242, 245–46, 248n21, 249n39
Aiken Drum (Sanger), 123, 128, 129, 130, 131. *See also Abatos* (Sanger)
Ai Weiwei, 32
Akmakjian, Hiag, 89
Alexander, M. Jacqui, 173n57

Ali, Kazim, 39
"Already Occupied" (Barker), 319–20
Altieri, Charles, 3
Alyokhina, Maria Vladimirovna, 34. *See also* Pussy Riot
"Ambling in the Streets of Affect" (Blair), 194n17
Anatomy of Criticism (Frye), 70, 126–27
Angus, Ian, 244
Annihilated Time (Derkson), 181–82
Anthology (CBC program): 1959 episode, 267n19; 1968 episode, 253–54, 258, 260–63, 265; approach to, 16–17, 253; as archive of literary production, 257; archives of, 254, 259, 264–65; audience of, 257–58, 266; focus of on literary distribution, 265; introduction to, 254; as literary event, 260; objective of, 258; and poetry readings, 253; as public tuning, 263; transmission of, 260; Weaver on, 259. *See also* radio broadcast
Antin, David, 306
"Apiary of Underclothes" (Jerome), 208–9

Apostrophe (Wershler and Kennedy), 88
a.rawlings (Angela Rawlings), 277, 278, 285n25
Arborealis (Sanger), 129
"Archaic Torso of Apollo" (Rilke), 212
archives, 13, 256–57, 259–60
Aristotle, 243
arrière-garde, 61
art, 39, 212, 337
artifacts, 51, 55, 57, 275
"At the Mermaid Inn" (*Globe* column): announcement in *Globe* about, 6; approach to, 5; contents of, 7–8, 8–9; critical consideration of, 6–7; end of, 6; Hogg on, 7; importance of, 7; purpose of, 5–6; transnational reach of, 5
"At the Mermaid Inn" (MacLennan's column), 5, 8, 9, 10–11
Auden, W.H.: "In Memory of W.B. Yeats," 1; on poetry, 2, 18; "The Watchers," 128
audience, 3, 31, 199, 202, 313–14, 319. *See also* performance; poetry readings; public speech
Austin, J.L., 122
Autobiography of Childhood (Queyras), 37
avant-garde, 61. *See also* experimental poetry
Avant-Garde Canadian Literature (Betts), 52, 60
Avasilichioaei, Oana, 278
"Avian Flu, The" (Cran), 225–28
awards, literary, 170n12, 318–19

Babstock, Ken, 202
baby boomers, 195n33
Bankrupt (Halliday and Carruthers), 326n7
Baraka, Amiri, 169, 306
Barker, Adam J.: "Already Occupied," 319–20

Barrett, Paul, 171n26
Barthes, Roland, 61, 170n12, 255–56, 276
Barwin, Gary: *frogments from the frag pool*, 90, 92–95; poetry readings of, 278; "Words Cannot Express," 90–91, 92
Bashō, 92. *See also frogments from the frag pool* (Barwin and beaulieu)
Basho Variations, The (McCaffery), 94
Bates, Walter. *See Abatos* (Sanger)
Bateson, Gregory, 130
Beach, Christopher, 272–73
beaulieu, derek: "26 Statements on Poetry," 90, 92; *frogments from the frag pool*, 90, 92–95; and Moure at Public Poetics conference, 17; "Please, No More Poetry," 337; poetry readings of, 278; "Prose of the TransCanada," 17; on sharing and existence, 40
Bentley, D.M.R., 8
Berger, Ben, 142–43
Bergvall, Caroline, 84n59, 280, 291
Bernofsky, Susan: "To Occupy: An Evolution," 319
Bernstein, Charles: *Close Listening*, 254; and globalization, 315; on innovation in poetry, 289, 299, 321; on literary theory, 315; and PennSound, 316; on poetics, 315, 316; *A Poetics*, 289; on poetry as dissent, 292; on poetry readings, 254, 264, 278–79
Bernstein, Eduard, 171n46
Bervin, Jen: *Nets*, 99–100, 101
Betts, Gregory: *Avant-Garde Canadian Literature*, 52, 60; *The Others Raisd in Me*, 98–99, 100–101; plunderverse projects of, 97–98; "Postmodern Decadence in Canadian Sound and Visual Poetry," 88; public readings of, 278

INDEX 349

Bhabha, Homi, 166, 315–16, 320
Biopiracy (Shiva), 71
Birkbeck, University of London: Poetry and Revolution conference, 319
Birney, Earle, 20n28
Birth of the Modern Mind, The (Oppenheimer), 97
bissett, bill, 87, 260
Black-based art forms. *See* slam poetry
blackness, 166
Blades, John, 101
Blair, Jennifer: "Ambling in the Streets of Affect," 194n17
Blamley, Nicholas B.: *Unsettling the City*, 177
Blasing, Mutlu, 200
Blasted Pine, The (Scott and Smith), 51, 54
blogs, 13, 33–34, 38, 248n5. *See also* digital technology; *Lemon Hound* (website)
Bobker, Danielle, 39
body: and archives, 256–57; and consent, 56; as context, 60; and feminist poetics, 82; in *Human Resources* (Zolf), 74–75; in *Lemon Hound* (Queyras poetry book), 77–78, 81; in poetry readings, 282; and radio, 256–57; and structures of belief, 56. *See also* pain
Body in Pain, The (Scarry), 51, 55, 56, 57, 59
body literary, 161–62
body politic, 78, 82, 161–62
Bök, Christian: *Eunoia*, 88; poetics of, 317; poetry readings of, 278
Book of Canadian Poetry, The (Smith), 12
Boone, Laura, 6
Borduas, Paul-Émile, 29–30
Bowering, George, 10, 148
"#bpNichol Twitter performance" (a.rawlings), 277

"Brahms Clarinet Quintet in B Minor, Op. 115" (Zwicky), 213
Braidotti, Rosi, 66
Brand, Dionne: and Cedarbrae library installation, 150, 168; on city council, 160; *Fierce Departures*, 170n11; on Harper's "reckless coalition" statement, 161; *Inventory*, 166–67, 171n23, 171n26, 172n54; on language, 320; poetic and civic projects of, 160, 170n11; as poet laureate of Toronto, 149, 150, 155n35, 168; and Poetry City Challenge, 159–60, 169; Soupcoff on, 168. *See also Ossuaries* (Brand)
Brandt, Di: *Wider Boundaries of Daring*, 52, 60
Breathing Fire 2 (Crozier and Lane), 206–7
Breathing Life into the Stone Fort Treaties (Craft), 323
Brief Immortals (Outram), 136n60
Bringhurst, Robert, 202
Brock Broido, Lucy, 32
Brossard, Nicole: as feminist poet, 65; "Poetic Politics," 87; poetry readings of, 282
Brothman, Brien, 259–60
Brown, Jim, 260
Brown, Wendy, 78
Bruns, Gerald: *What Are Poets For?*, 204, 317
Brydon, Diana: on globalization and identity, 39; on *Inventory* (Brand), 172n54; *Renegotiating Community*, 326n7; *Studies in Canadian Literature* special issue, 264, 313, 324–25; work of, 320, 324–25
Buck, Tim: "An Indictment of Capitalism," 234, 238, 242, 246
Buck-Morss, Susan: "The Second Time as Farce," 160, 169
Buffalo Electronic Poetry Centre, 13

Buffam, Suzanne, 202, 210
Buller, Annie, 237, 245
Burger, Mary, 39
Butler, Judith, 281
Butling, Pauline: *Writing in Our Time*, 11, 88
Buuck, David, 291

caesura, 166
Cain, Stephen, 144, 145, 148
Campbell, William Wilfred, 6, 7, 8–9
Canada Council of the Arts, 272–73, 275–76, 278, 284n17. *See also* poetry readings
Canada Reads (CBC program), 265–66
Canadian Athletes Now website, 317–18
Canadian Authors Association, 336
"Canadian Authors Meet, The" (Scott), 335–36, 338n4, 338n8
Canadian criticism. *See* criticism
Canadian cultural production: and "At the Mermaid Inn," 5, 7–8; and Canada Council, 272; during Confederation period, 8; Glassco and Acorn exchange, 10–11; history of, 4–5, 9–11, 12; and *Lemon Hound* (website), 12, 13; and *Massey-Levesque Report*, 9, 12; surveying, 21n51; on West Coast, 10. *See also* cultural production
Canadian Labor Defense League (CLDL), 234, 235–36, 244, 248n9. *See also* pamphlets; CLDL
Canadian literary history, 4–5, 9–11, 12, 52
Canadian literary studies, 317
Canadian literature. *See* Canadian cultural production
Canadian Literature (journal), 10, 263, 267n21, 315
Canadian modernism, 52
Canadian poetry: counter/public of, 60–61; and criticism, 337–38; desultory pain of, 57, 58, 61–62; and pain, 54, 57; as publics and counterpublics, 52, 53; rewriting in, 88, 104; scholarship on, 11; and "The Canadian Authors Meet" (Scott), 335–36; and transnationalism, 317; unmaking gestures in, 55–56. *See also specific types of poetry*
Canadian Poetry (journal), 12
Canadian radicalism, 231
Canadian review culture, 20n16, 27, 54. *See also* criticism
Canadian Short Stories (CBC program), 258–59
Canadian Women in Literary Arts (CWILA), 27, 54, 214
Cangi, Adrián, 281
Capilano Review, 90
Cariou, Warren, 327n53
Carpenter, J.R., 280
Carruthers, Bruce G.: *Bankrupt*, 326n7
Carson, Anne, 319
casserole marches, 306–7
Caws, Mary Ann, 91–92
CBC (Canadian Broadcasting Corp.): archives of, 257, 264; *Canada Reads*, 265–66; *Canadian Short Stories*, 258–59; contributions to Canadian literature, 265, 266; perceived audience of, 266. *See also Anthology* (CBC program); radio broadcast
Cecil-Smith, Ed, 245
Cedarbrae Public Library, 150, 168
change, 31, 36, 38
"Chaos feary" (Wong), 71
cheek, cris, 279–80
children's literature, 102, 103–4
Chile, 306
Cho, Lily, 166, 271
Christakos, Margaret: *Excessive Love Prostheses*, 102–4; Influency Salon, 101–2

city treaty (Francis), 322–23, 327n53, 328n57
civic, 142–44
civic lyric, 204
civic poetics, 15, 200
civic public, 140, 142, 144, 148, 152, 153
Civil Elegies (Lee), 139, 150–53, 154n14
Clarke, George Elliott: *Odysseys Home*, 52, 60; as poet laureate of Toronto, 155n35
class protest. *See* human microphone; pamphlets
CLDL. *See* Canadian Labor Defense League
Close Listening (Bernstein), 254
Cobbing, Bob, 279–80, 306
Cohen, Debra Rae, 258
Cohen, Matt, 155n36
Coleman, Daniel: *White Civility*, 143–44, 154n14
Collini, Stefan: *What Are Universities For?*, 314–15
Collis, Stephen, 4–5, 31, 40n6
colonialism, 70–71
commodification: and *Canada Reads* (CBC program), 266; of empowerment, 78; and feminist poetics, 76; of home, 178, 179, 185, 187, 188, 190; of identification, 195n33; of language, 72; of poetry, 178, 188; of public readings, 276
Common Strangeness, A (Edmond), 316
Communist Party of Canada (CPC), 234, 244–45
community, 61
"Comparative Literature and the Global Languagescape" (Pratt), 316
Compton, Anne, 11
conceptual writing, 33, 76, 82, 88–89
concrete poetry, 94

Confederation poets, 12
Connor, Steven, 290–91
consent, 56, 59
Contact Press, 155n24, 263
Contemporary Verse, 12
copyright, 255
counterpublics (counter/publics), 59, 60–61, 189–90, 313
Coupland, Douglas, 36
CPC (Communist Party of Canada), 234, 244–45
Craft, Aimée: *Breathing Life into the Stone Fort Treaties*, 323
Cran, Brad: aim of, 205, 211–12; approach to, 16; cultural politics of, 213–14; "Fun-Loving Nickelback Policy Machine (with Kittens)," 210; *The Good Life*, 206, 208; *Hope in Shadows*, 205–6; *Ink on Paper*, 210; as poet laureate of Vancouver, 210, 213–14; public engagement of, 205; self-understanding of own poetry, 199; "The Avian Flu," 225–28; "Thirteen Ways of Looking at a Gray Whale," 210–12; "Today After Rain," 205, 207–8; writing practice of, 204
Crawley, Alan and Jean, 12
Cremin, Becky: "to initiate a poetics of occupation," 319
Criminal Code of Canada, Section 98, 232, 233, 234, 236, 242, 244
criticism: and Canadian poetry, 337–38; Canadian review culture, 20n16, 27, 54; oppositional nature of, 61, 335; responsive and responsible, 204; Starnino on, 131–32; women in, 27–28, 38, 40
critics: approach to, 14–15
Crozier, Lorna: *Breathing Fire 2*, 206–7
cultural grammar, 317
cultural nationalism, 4, 9

cultural production: in hyperlinked world, 13; poetry as, 188. *See also* Canadian cultural production
cultural quotation, 194n17
Custance, Florence, 245
CWILA (Canadian Women in Literary Arts), 27, 54, 214
"Cyborg Manifesto, A" (Haraway), 77, 81

Damon, Maria, 319, 320
"Dark Light" (Wat), 159, 168
Dartington School of Arts: Performance Writing program, 280
Davey, Frank, 10, 281
Davidson, Michael: *On the Outskirts of Form*, 305
Davies, Barrie, 5–6, 7
Davis, Angela, 34
Davis, Tanya, 18
Davis, Troy, 292–93, 294–95, 295–96
Deleuze, Gilles, 327n27
Denning, Michael, 238
Derkson, Jeff: *Annihilated Time*, 181–82; *Dwell*, 323–24, 325; "Interface," 323–24, 325; on rearticulation, 181–82
Derrida, Jacques, 13, 282, 322
desultory pain, 57–58, 59–60, 61–62
deterritorialization, 180, 193n7
Dialogue conference, 66, 82n3
digital: and body, 256–57
digital discourse, 11, 13
digital technology, 4, 38–39, 277, 314. *See also* blogs; Facebook; Internet; social media; Twitter
Dobson, Kit, 151
domestication, 32
Dudek, Louis: *The Making of Modern Poetry in Canada*, 55, 56, 57
DuPlessis, Rachel Blau, 279
Durand, Marcella, 69
Dwell (Derkson), 323–24, 325
Dworkin, Craig: *Against Expression*, 88

Early, Len, 87
"Earrings, The" (Sanger), 127–28
ecopoetics, 69–70
Edmond, Jacob: *A Common Strangeness*, 316
Eichhorn, Kate: in *Open Letter*, 65; *Prismatic Publics*, 11, 60, 102, 140, 266, 313–14
Eighteenth Brumaire (Marx), 166
Eight Men Speak (play), 242, 245
85 Project (Majzels), 274, 277, 282
elegy, 54
Elrick, Laura, 72, 84n59, 84n60
Empire, 180, 323
Engels, Friedrich: *The Origin of the Family, Private Property, and the State*, 165
English, James, 170n12
English Canadian Poetics, An (Hogg), 7, 11
Enpipe Line poetry project, 5, 31
"Enterprise" (Rensch), 17–18
Eunoia (Bök), 88
Excessive Love Prostheses (Christakos), 102–4
"Exile" (Sullivan), 150, 168
experimental poetry, 15, 76, 78, 87–88, 101, 104. *See also* haiku; lullaby; sonnet

Facebook, 32–33
"Fact of Blackness, The" (Fanon), 166
Fallon, Ann Marie, 327n27
Falmouth University: Performance Writing program, 280
Fanon, Frantz: "The Fact of Blackness," 166
female subjectivity, 66, 77–81, 82
feminism, 173n57, 245
feminist literary criticism, 65
feminist poetics, 15, 65–68, 75–76, 82, 82n5. *See also* post-feminism
Ferron, Marcelle, 34

fiction theory, 65–66
Fierce Departures (Brand), 170n11
Filling Station, 90–91
Fiorito, Joe, 144, 145
Fireship (Sanger), 129, 132, 133
Firestone, Shulamith, 54
First Statement, 12
Fitterman, Robert, 76
flâneur, 77
Flowers of Delight (Vries), 103
forage (Wong): approach of, 67–68, 81–82; ecopoetics of, 69–70, 71; and genetic modification, 70–71; handwritten texts in, 83n23; and humanist subject, 69, 70; place in, 69; political concerns of, 68
Ford, Rob, 173n74
"Form of a City, The"/"The Form of a" (Murakami), 183–85
Four Horsemen, 103, 282, 306
Francis, Marvin: *city treaty*, 322–23, 327n53, 328n57
Fraser, Nancy, 195n38
frogments from the frag pool (Barwin and beaulieu), 90, 92–95
Frye, Northrop: *Anatomy of Criticism*, 70, 126–27; on audience and poetry, 3, 19n9, 31; on independent forms, 126–27; on narrative in poetic conversations, 11, 16; on poetry as outside of time, 19n9; on Souster, 145
Fuller, Danielle, 265–66
"Fun-Loving Nickelback Policy Machine (with Kittens)" (Cran), 210

Gardiner, Elee Kraljii: *V6A*, 205
Garner, Dwight, 33
Garrison, Lorianne, 95
Gematria of Nothing, 73
gender, 66. *See also* feminist poetics
gender inequality. *See* women
Generation Y, 195n33

genetic modification, 70–71
Genette, Gérard, 273
gestures, 53, 55, 56. *See also* counterpublics; desultory pain; pain; predicating criticism
Gibber (a.rawlings), 277, 285n25
Gibson, William, 32
Gingell, Susan: *Listening Up, Writing Down, Looking Beyond*, 271
Glassco, John, 10–11
globalization, 68, 69–70, 180
globalization, and Canadian cultural production: approach to, 17, 313, 325; and interdisciplinary approaches, 320–21; interruptions as aesthetic and political resistance, 322; and language, 316; *Mohawk/Samoa Transmigrations* (Stevens and Sinavaiana), 321–22; and negotiation, 326n7; and Occupy movement, 319–20; and poetry, 316–17, 320; and poetry prizes, 319; and prismatic publics, 313–14; and transnational literacies, 314–16; value of poets in, 317–18
Globe, 6, 7. *See also* "At the Mermaid Inn" (*Globe* column)
Gnarowski, Michael: *The Making of Modern Poetry in Canada*, 55–56, 57
Godard, Barbara: and Dialogue conference, 66; on fiction theory, 65–66; in *Open Letter*, 65; on surveying Canadian literature, 21n51; *Wider Boundaries of Daring*, 52, 60
Gold, Michael: "Strike! A Mass Recitation," 240
Goldsmith, Kenneth: *Against Expression*, 88; *Uncreative Writing*, 39, 72
Good Life, The (Cran), 206, 208
Gramsci, Antonio, 172n54
Grewal, Inderpal, 79
Griffin Prizes, 180, 318–19
Guattari, Félix, 327n27

Habermas, Jürgen, 195n38
haiku: in Canadian postmodern poetry, 89–90; *frogments from the frag pool* (Barwin and beaulieu), 92–95; introduction to, 89; *The World Is a Heartbreaker* (Tjia), 95–96; and Zen Buddhism, 94
Halifax, 43, 45
Halliday, Terence C.: *Bankrupt*, 326n7
Halstead, Joe, 150
Haraway, Donna, 77, 81, 281
Hardt, Michael, 180, 193n7, 195n38, 323
Harvey, David, 193n4
Hegel, Georg, 163, 171n27
Heidegger, Martin, 204
Hejinian, Lyn, 291
Henderson, Brian, 94
Heti, Sheila, 28
Higgins, Keith: vancouverspecial.com, 194n22
Hill, Colin, 9–10
Hill, Geoffrey: *The Lords of Limit*, 125, 128; "Our Word Is Our Bond," 122, 125
Hill, Lawrence, 44
Hogg, Robert, 7, 11; *An English Canadian Poetics*, 7, 11
Hölderlin, Freidrich, 204
Hope in Shadows (Cran and Jerome), 205–6
Hopkins, Gerard Manley, 58
House of Anansi Press, 261–62
"House Which Is Not Extension but *Dispositio* Itself, The" (Moure), 223–24
housing. *See* Project Rebuild (Murakami); *Rebuild* (Murakami)
Hsu, Ray, 191
humanist subject, 69, 70, 71–72, 77
humanities, 9, 314–15
human microphone: approach to, 14, 17, 290; basic method of, 289–90; development of at Occupy Wall Street, 292–93, 294, 296–99; framework for, 290–92; importance of, 306, 307; interventionist form of, 302–3; for protest of Scott Walker, 299–302; and silence as protest, 305; at UC Davis pepper spray incident, 303–4; use of in Canadian Occupy protests, 305
Human Resources (Zolf): approach of, 67–68, 81–82; and commodification, 76; composition of, 72–73; as feminist and queer text, 74–75; and feminist poetics, 75–76; and humanist subject, 71–72; influences in, 83n28; language in, 72, 73–74; meaning in, 73
"Hungry" (McNeilly), 219
Hutton, Thomas, 177

Idle No More movement, 4, 5
"In a Station of the Metro" (Pound), 89
Independent Media Center (Indymedia), 13
"Indictment of Capitalism, An" (Buck), 234, 238, 242, 246
Indymedia (Independent Media Center), 13
"inevitability of gravity on glass, The" (Lent), 117–18
Influency Salon, 101–2
Ink on Paper (Cran), 210
"In Memory of W.B. Yeats" (Auden), 1
interdisciplinary approaches, 320
"Interface" (Derkson), 323–24, 325
Intermedia collective, 274
Internet, 11, 16, 40, 248n5. *See also* blogs; digital technology; social media
intimate public, 255
Inventory (Brand), 166–67, 171n23, 171n26, 172n54

Invisibility Project, The (Murakami), 193n8
Ironworks (Sanger), 121
"Ivan and the Chestnut Horse," 127

Jacket 2, 13
Jailbreaks: 99 Canadian Sonnets (Wells), 97
Jameson, Fredric, 170n19
Jernigan, Amanda: and *Aiken Drum* (Sanger), 129–30; "Routine," 112–13
Jerome, Gillian: aim of, 205; "Apiary of Underclothes," 208–9; approach to, 16; Buffam on, 210; on critical work and artistic practice, 214; cultural politics of, 213, 214; *Hope in Shadows*, 205–6; "Midsummer," 202–3; public engagement of, 205; *Red Nest*, 208; self-understanding of own poetry, 199; "Tenement Song," 212–13; writing practice of, 204
John Stoke's Horse (Sanger), 125–26, 127, 128–29, 130–31, 133
Jones, El, 18, 43–49
Jones, Manina, 264, 313
journals, 10

Kalmunity Vibe Collective, 274
Kamboureli, Smaro: on body literary and body politic, 161; on poetry readings, 265, 276, 281; TransCanada project, 317; *Trans.Can.Lit*, 161
Katehi, Linda, 304
Kearns, Lionel, 10, 325
Keats, John: "Lines on the Mermaid Tavern," 5
Keenan, Edward, 146
Keller, Lynn, 32
Kennedy, Bill: *Apostrophe*, 88
Kim, Christine, 68
Kim, Richard, 289–90, 292

King, Martin Luther, Jr., 319
Kingwell, Mark, 144, 152
Kirkconnell, Watson, 336
knowledge production, 324–25, 335
Kootenay School of Writing (KSW), 180–81, 202

Lampman, Archibald, 5–6, 7, 8, 20n26
Lane, Patrick: *Anthology* episode (CBC program), 260–61, 265; *Breathing Fire 2*, 206–7
language: bissett's use of, 87; Brand on, 320; Brossard on, 87; and Canadian radicalism, 231; as commodity, 72; and ecology, 69–70; and experimental poetry, 104; and globalization, 316; in *Human Resources* (Zolf), 73–74; and love, 122, 131; and poetic forms, 289; as prisonhouse, 170n19; and reality, 130, 167
L=A=N=G=U=A=G=E poetry, 201, 306
Lasn, Kalle, 31
Lau, Evelyn, 210
Laurence, Margaret, 318
Lazer, Hank, 279
Lazy Bastardism (Starnino), 131–32
"Leaping Time" (Sanger), 127, 129
Lecker, Robert, 272
Leclerc, Christine, 31
Lee, Dennis: *Anthology* episode (CBC program), 261–62; approach to, 15–16; civic public poetics of, 153; *Civil Elegies*, 139, 150–53, 154n14; critical opinions on, 139, 150; introduction to, 139; as poet laureate of Toronto, 148–49, 150, 155n35
Lefebvre, Henri, 141, 142, 154n7, 182
Lemon Hound (Queyras poetry book), 37; approach of, 67–68, 76, 81–82; empowerment and displacement in, 78; female subjectivity in, 77–78,

81; figure of Lemon Hound in, 77, 84n53; and humanist subject, 77; irony in, 81; motherhood in, 78–80; politics of, 81; and post-feminism, 80–81; repetition and variation in, 78–79; and Woolf and Stein, 76–77; Zelazo on, 84n53
Lemon Hound (website): introduction to, 11; new version of, 39; post on about reviews, 27; and public poetics, 13–14; start of, 12, 33
Lenin, Vladimir, 240, 248n21
Lent, Vanessa: "The inevitability of gravity on glass," 117–18
Lesbian Body, The (Wittig), 74
Les Filles éléctriques, 274
Less Than Nothing (Žižek), 171n27
"Let the Home" (Murakami), 186
Levertov, Denise, 281
Lewis, Desiree, 13
Lewitt, Sol, 39
Lilburn, Tim, 202
"Lines on the Mermaid Tavern" (Keats), 5
Lionnet, Françoise, 327n27
Lippard, Lucy, 39
Lista, Michael, 27, 28
listening, 205, 255–56, 320
Listening Up, Writing Down, Looking Beyond (Gingell and Roy), 271
literacy, 314–15
literary awards, 170n12, 318–19
literary geography, 141–42, 154n4
literary performance, 274, 275–76, 277–78
literary readings. *See* poetry readings
literary studies, 315
literary theory, 315
Livesay, Dorothy, 4
lords of limit, 128, 136n44
Lords of Limit, The (Hill), 125, 128
love, 122, 131
Loviglio, Jason, 255

lullaby, 103–4
Luxemburg, Rosa, 171n46
lyric mode. *See* poetry
lyric philosophy, 202
lyric poetry: Adorno on, 200–201; and audience, 199–200; in contemporary Canadian poetry, 202; critiques of, 90–91; and language, 200, 201; as promise of and refrain from knowledge, 209–10, 212. *See also* poetry

Mac, Kathy: "Potter's Hearing Is Not Khadr's Ruling," 220–22
MacCormack, Karen, 317
MacDonald, Tanis: at Public Poetics conference, 53; "The Sexual Politics of Bluestockings," 111
Mackenzie, William Lyon, 146
MacLennan, Hugh, 5
maclennan, rob, 13
Mac Low, Jackson, 306
Maguire, Shannon: "Volume," 114–15
Majzels, Robert: *85 Project,* 274, 277, 282
Making of Modern Poetry in Canada, The (Dudek and Gnarowski), 55, 56, 57
Manifesto (Caws), 91–92
manifestos, 91–92
Marinetti, F.T., 91, 256
Marlatt, Daphne, 10, 65
Marshall, Tom, 144–45
Martynov, Aleksandr, 248n21
Marx, Karl: *Eighteenth Brumaire,* 166
Marxism Today, 319
Masses, 9–10, 12
Massey-Levesque Report, 9, 12, 52
mass recitation, 240–41, 242
Mathur, Ashok, 265, 275
Mayne, Seymour, 260–61, 265
Mayor's Poetry City Challenge, 159–60, 169

McCaffery, Steve: *The Basho Variations*, 94; poetics of, 317
McGill group, 12
McKay, Don, 202
McKay, Ian, 231, 244
McKinnie, Michael, 143
McKittrick, Katherine: "Plantation Futures," 172n54
McLuhan, Marshall, 38
McNeilly, Kevin: "Hungry," 219
McWhirter, George, 210
media studies, 248n5
Me Generation, 195n33
Mermaid Tavern, 5
"Midsummer" (Jerome), 202–3
Mignolo, Walter, 324
Miki, Roy, 313, 324
Milne, Heather: *Prismatic Publics*, 11, 60, 102, 140, 266, 313–14
mimesis, 53
Minkus, Kim, 214
modernism, Canadian, 52
Modern Poetics and Hemispheric American Cultural Studies (Read), 326n27
Mohawk/Samoa Transmigrations (Stevens and Sinavaiana), 321–22
Moon, Henry. *See Abatos* (Sanger)
Moore, Michael, 297–98
Moretti, Franco, 145
Moten, Fred, 306
motherhood, 78–80
Moure, Erín: and beaulieu at Public Poetics conference, 17; Queyras on readings by, 30; "The House Which Is Not Extension but *Dispositio* Itself," 223–24
Mudwoman (Oates), 54
multitude model, 195n38
Murakami, Sachiko: *The Invisibility Project*, 193n8; poetic roots of, 180. *See also* Project Rebuild; *Rebuild*
Music Gallery, 274

Nathan Phillips Square, 152
nature poetry, 208, 209, 210–11
"Necklace" (Sanger), 129, 130, 134
negotiation, 323, 326n7
Negri, Antonio, 180, 193n7, 195n38, 323
neoliberalism, 76, 82, 181–82, 193n4. *See also Rebuild* (Murakami)
Nets (Bervin), 99–100, 101
New Frontier, 9–10, 12
Ngai, Sianne, 54, 57–58
Nichol, bp: and *fragments from the frag pool* (Barwin and beaulieu), 94; *Translating Translating Apollinaire*, 93
Nietzsche, Friedrich: *The Will to Power*, 170n19
"Not Guilty!" (pamphlet), 234, 241–42, 246

Oates, Joyce Carol: *Mudwoman*, 54
Occupy movement: ban of electronic sound systems at, 292, 295; in Canada, 305; and Canadian cultural production, 5; and human microphone, 292–93, 294, 296–99; Indigenous concerns with, 319–20; media blackout of, 293–94, 295; poets involved in, 31; questions raised by, 319; and Troy Davis, 292–93
"Ocean Views" (Murakami), 179–80
Odysseys Home (Clarke), 52, 60
Olbermann, Keith, 294, 308n14
Old Man Luedecke, 18–19
Olson, Charles, 291
Olympics, Winter (2010), 213–14
One Hundred Frogs (Sato), 92
"On Lyric Poetry and Society" (Adorno), 200–201
Ono, Yoko, 39
On the Outskirts of Form (Davidson), 305
Open Field (Queyras), 12–13

Open Letter, 65, 265, 271, 281
Oppenheimer, Paul: *The Birth of the Modern Mind*, 97
opposition, 181
Origin of the Family, Private Property, and the State, The (Engels), 165
Orion and Other Poems (Roberts), 8
Orwell, George, 232–33, 239, 244, 246–47, 247n4
Ossuaries (Brand): "Acknowledgment" section, 165; approach to, 15–16; effect of, 169; enjambment in, 163, 164; features of, 161; Griffin Prize won by, 160, 170n12; organization of, 162; and politics, 160, 161; protagonist in, 160–61, 162–64, 165–67, 171n46; punctuation in, 165–67; repetition in, 167; tercet stanza structure of, 162–63
O'Sullivan, Maggie, 306
Others Raisd in Me, The (Betts), 98–99, 100–101
Oulip law, 194n26
"Our Word Is Our Bond" (Hill), 122, 125
Outram, Richard: *Brief Immortals*, 136n60; on marriage ceremony, 122; and Sanger, 129

Page, P.K.: "Address at Simon Fraser," 212
pain: approach to, 15; and Canadian poetry, 54, 57; as clarifying process, 58; desultory, 57–58, 59–60, 61–62; and reality, 55; and structures of belief, 55, 59; as ugly feelings, 54, 57
pamphlets: in 1930s Canada, 232, 239; approach to, 16; early, 240; Orwell on, 232–33, 239, 244, 246–47, 247n4; potential and power of, 247
pamphlets, Canadian Labor Defense League: agitprop in, 235, 240–41, 242, 245–46; "An Indictment of Capitalism" (Buck), 234, 238, 242, 246; audience of, 238; authorship and assembly of, 246; class narrative in, 245; dating, 235; forensic approach of, 239–40; importance of trial of the Eight in, 244–45; lack of feminist critique in, 245; and mass recitation, 241, 242; "Not Guilty!," 234, 241–42, 246; and pamphlet form, 243; poetic legacy of, 243–44; political value of, 244; publication and distribution of, 234; purpose of, 233, 235–36; strategy of, 236–38; "The 'Sedition' of A.E. Smith" (Ryan), 234, 236–37, 242; "Workers' Self-Defense in the Courts," 234, 235, 237–38, 245
"Patience" (Uppal), 318
PennSound, 277, 316
Perelman, Bob, 306
performance, 11, 152, 291. *See also* literary performance; poetry readings
Performance Research, 280
Performance Writing program, 280
performative utterance, 122
Perloff, Marjorie: on arrière-garde, 61; on procedural poems, 194n26; *Unoriginal Genius*, 61, 72
Petryshyn, Jaroslav, 234, 237, 245
Philip, M. NourbeSe: *Zong!*, 278
Pike, John, 303–4
place, 66, 68, 81–82
Place, Vanessa, 76
plagiarism, intentional, 124
"Plantation Futures" (McKittrick), 172n54
"Please, No More Poetry" (beaulieu), 337
poet, 29, 39, 72, 318, 320
poetic activism, 4–5
poetic forms, 289
"Poetic Politics" (Brossard), 87

poetics: Bernstein on, 315, 316; Elricks on, 72; function of, 337; as language economy, 334; *vs.* prose, 334; *vs.* rhetoric, 314–15. *See also* poetry; public poetics
Poetics, A (Bernstein), 289
poetic values, 317
poet-in-residence, 318
poet laureate, 139–40, 149, 168. *See also* Brand, Dionne; Clarke, George Elliott; Cran, Brad; Lee, Dennis; Souster, Raymond
poetry: Altieri on, 3; Auden on, 1–2; Bruns on, 204; context needed for, 30, 37; function of, 320; making of, 51–52; as public and oral art, 261, 265; Purdy on, 265; revival of, 313, 314; Warner on, 3, 14. *See also* Canadian poetry; poetics; public poetics; *specific types of poetry*
Poetry and Revolution conference, 319
poetry awards, 170n12, 318–19
poetry book sales, 276, 284n21
Poetry Canada Review, 28–29
Poetry City Challenge, 159–60, 169
Poetry Is Public Is Poetry (installation), 150, 168
poetry readings: American criticism on, 278–79; approach to, 17; Bernstein on, 254, 264, 278–79; blurring of distinction between reading and performance, 277–78; and body, 282; and brain science and sensory behaviour, 281; British criticism on, 279–80; and Canada Council, 272–73, 275–76, 278; critic's view of, 282–83; as events, 253; Genette on, 273; Glassco on, 10–11; Kamboureli on, 265, 276, 281; as literary creation, 275, 277, 278, 282; new paradigm for, 281, 283; poet's view of, 282; and public pedagogy, 265; pushing of boundaries, 274;

Quartermain on, 278; scholarship on, 271, 274–75; for selling poetry, 273, 276, 284n21; South American and European criticism on, 280–81, 285n34; teaching, 283; and technology, 277. *See also Anthology* (CBC program)
political activism, 76, 160. *See also* human microphone; *Ossuaries* (Brand); pamphlets
Pollock, Griselda, 77
postcolonial studies, 314, 315
post-feminism, 80–81. *See also* feminist poetics
"Postmodern Decadence in Canadian Sound and Visual Poetry" (Betts), 88
postmodernism, 15, 61, 88. *See also* experimental poetry
"Potter's Hearing Is Not Khadr's Ruling" (Mac), 220–22
Pound, Ezra: "In a Station of the Metro," 89
power, 51
Pratt, E.J., 12, 55
Pratt, Mary Louise: "Comparative Literature and the Global Languagescape," 316
predicated visibility, 61
predicating criticism, 56–57
presses, university, 10
Prevallet, Kristin, 84n60
Preview, 12
Printemps d'erable student protests, 4, 306–7
Priorities in Global Governance workshop, 320
Prismatic Publics (Eichhorn and Milne), 11, 60, 102, 140, 266, 313–14
Pritchard, N.H., 306
private poetics, 7
prizes, literary, 170n12, 318–19

procedural poems, 82, 194n26. *See also* conceptual writing
projectivist poetics, 291
Project Rebuild (Murakami): approach to, 16; collaborative nature of, 189, 192–93, 195n40; as counterpublic, 189–90, 193; decentralization of power in, 190–91; and dissent, 191; evolution of poetry on, 192; extending limits of poetry, 191–92; introduction to, 178; and poetry ownership, 188–89. See also *Rebuild* (Murakami)
Prolet-Bühne, 240, 249n39
prose, 334, 337
"Prose of the TransCanada" (beaulieu), 17
protests, 306–7. *See also* Enpipe Line poetry project; human microphone; Idle No More movement; Occupy movement; Quebec student protests
public discourse, 320
public participation. *See* public speech
public pedagogy, 265
public poetics: in action, 18–19; Altieri on, 3; approach to, 2, 4, 18, 336–37; Campbell on, 8–9; in Canada, 4; contemporary field of, 14–15; embedded field of, 15–16; expanding field of, 16–17; history of in Canada, 4–5, 9–11, 12, 14; and *Lemon Hound* (website), 13–14; not participating in, 40; and private poetics, 7. *See also* poetics; poetry
Public Poetics conference, 3, 17–19, 53
"Public Reading Is a Matter of the Public Reading" (Majzels), 274
public readings. *See* poetry readings
publics: as autotelic, 59, 202; Canadian poetry as, 52; as dominant discourses, 2; existence of, 14, 202; functioning of, 141; as heterogeneous, 266, 313–14; individuation of, 195n38; on Internet, 13; and literary texts, 140–41, 142; need for to be self-organized, 59; and reciprocity, 62; reflexivity of, 3, 202; as relation among strangers, 3, 31, 60, 257; as works in progress, 60. *See also* counterpublics; Warner, Michael
Publics and Counterpublics (Warner), 2. *See also* Warner, Michael
public speech: and CLDL pamphlets, 233, 238, 240; and pamphlets, 239; and space and audience, 31; Warner on, 247, 255; and women, 27–28, 38, 40
public tuning, 263, 264, 265
publishers, 262–63
Purdy, Al, 263, 265
Pussy Riot, 30, 34

Quartermain, Peter: "Sound Reading," 278
Quebec student protests, 4, 306–7
QueryCount, 72–73
Queyras, Sina: anxiety of, 34–35; Atwood paper by, 28–29; *Autobiography of Childhood*, 37; and Bobker, 39; and difficult poetry, 30; on domestication, 32; early career of, 34–35; introduction to, 12–13; master's thesis, 34, 35–36; in Montreal, 35; oath to place, 30; *Open Field*, 12–13; poetry of, 30–31, 32; and public speaking, 28–29, 35–36, 40n5; review of *The Weather* (Robertson), 201; and technology for writing, 38–39; "The Sturdiness," 109–10; *Unleashed*, 13, 34; at Vermont retreat, 36–37. See also *Lemon Hound* (poetry book); *Lemon Hound* (website)
Quiet Revolution, 29–30

racism: in slam poetry community, 15, 43–49
radicalism, Canadian, 231
radio broadcast: audience of, 255, 262; as body, 256–57; and digital archives of poetry, 254; and listening, 256; and literary publics, 263; and poetry readings, 253, 264; as public, 255, 257; transmission of, 258. *See also* Anthology (CBC program); CBC
radio poetics, 17, 261. *See also* Anthology (CBC program); radio broadcast
Ramazani, Jahan: *A Transnational Poetics*, 316–17
Rankine, Claudia, 201
Rashley, R.E., 12
Rawlings, Angela (a.rawlings), 277, 278, 285n25
"Ray Hsu *vs.* Sachiko Murakami: Vancouver Specials," 191
Read, Justin: *Modern Poetics and Hemispheric American Cultural Studies*, 326n27
readings. *See* poetry readings
reality, 55, 167, 314
rearticulation, 181–82
Rebellions of 1837, 146, 152
Rebuild (Murakami): approach to, 16; as architectural poetics of community, 178, 192; central dilemma of, 179–80; and globalization, 180; home in, 185–86, 188; on home ownership, 190; introduction to, 177–78; "Let the Home," 186; and neoliberalism, 178, 183, 188, 193; "Ocean Views," 179–80; and rearticulation, 181; revision as renovation in, 182–83; "The Form of a City"/"The Form of a," 183–85; urban in, 180; use of Google's translation software, 186, 194n26;

"Vancouver Special" poems, 186–88. *See also* Project Rebuild (Murakami)
Red Nest (Jerome), 208
refusal, 231–32, 334
Refus global manifesto, 29–30, 34
Reid, Jamie, 10
"Rejected Preface, A" (Smith), 55–56
Renegotiating Community (Brydon and Coleman), 326n7
Rensch, Evan: "Enterprise," 17–18
re poetics, 88
representational space, 141–42
resistance, 181
review culture, Canadian, 20n16, 27, 54. *See also* criticism
revision, 182–83
rewriting, 87–88
rhetoric, 314–15
Rhetoric of Empire, The (Spurr), 322
Rich, Adrienne, 182
Rifkind, Candida, 9, 242, 243
Rilke, Rainer Maria: "Archaic Torso of Apollo," 212
Roberts, Charles G.D., 8, 333
Roberts, Gillian, 319
Robertson, Lisa: *The Weather*, 201
Rock, Chris, 43
"Routine" (Jernigan), 112–13
Rove, Karl, 302
Roy, Wendy: *Listening Up, Writing Down, Looking Beyond*, 271
Rudy, Susan: *Writing in Our Time*, 11, 88
Ryan, Oscar: and feminine contributions, 245; "The 'Sedition' of A.E. Smith," 234, 236–37, 242
Ryan, Toby Gordon, 240, 245, 249n39

Said, Edward, 172n54
Sanders, Leslie C.: *Fierce Departures*, 170n11
Sanger, Peter: *Abatos*, 122–25, 126, 129, 130, 131; "After Monteverdi,"

133; *Aiken Drum*, 123, 128, 129, 130, 131; approach to, 15; binocular view of, 134; childhood of, 133–34; children in poetry of, 126–27; and cock-horse nursery rhyme, 126; dance in work of, 131; *Fireship*, 129, 132, 133; focus of on gaps, 122, 125, 136n44; on intentional plagiarism, 124; and interpenetration of critical and poetic modes, 130, 132, 133; *Ironworks*, 121; and "Ivan and the Chestnut Horse," 127; *John Stoke's Horse*, 125–26, 127, 128–29, 130–31, 133; "Leaping Time," 127, 129; and lords of limit, 128, 136n44; on moon, 128; "Necklace," 129, 130, 134; and Outram, 129, 136n60; as private poet, 121–22; prose and poetry in work of, 129; public ethics of, 122, 132; review of *The Lords of Limit* (Hill), 125, 128; on signs, 133; "The Earrings," 127–28; *Through Darkling Air*, 133–34; trickster/poet in work of, 128–29; Wells on, 121–22, 123, 130, 132–33; and Wolverine figure, 131, 136n45
-scape, 206
Scapperttone, Jennifer, 84n59
Scarry, Elaine: *The Body in Pain*, 51, 55, 56, 57, 59
Schagerl, Jessica, 264, 313
Scott, Duncan Campbell, 6, 7
Scott, F.R.: *The Blasted Pine*, 51–52, 54; and "Not Guilty!" pamphlet, 242; "The Canadian Authors Meet," 335–36, 338n4, 338n8
Scott, Gail, 65
"Second Time as Farce, The" (Buck-Morss), 160, 169
Section 98, Criminal Code of Canada, 232, 233, 234, 236, 242, 244

"'Sedition' of A.E. Smith, The" (Ryan), 234, 236–37, 242
Sedo, DeNel Rehberg, 265–66
Selected Poems (Glassco), 11
self-conscious poetics, 232
selfhood, 77–78
"September Still" (Winger), 116
sexism: in slam poetry community, 46–49
"Sexual Politics of Bluestockings, The" (MacDonald), 111
Shakespeare, William, 97, 99, 101
Shih, Shu-Mei, 327n27
Shiva, Vandana: *Biopiracy*, 71; and transgenic modification, 70
silence, as protest, 305
Sinavaiana, Caroline: *Mohawk/Samoa Transmigrations*, 321–22
Singer, Melina Baum, 271
Skelton, Robin, 31
sKincerity (Elrick), 84n60
slam poetry: Black artists in, 43–46; Black female artists in, 46–49; and poetry readings, 274
Slater, David, 314
Smith, A.E, 245. *See also* "'Sedition' of A.E. Smith, The" (Ryan)
Smith, A.J.M: "A Rejected Preface," 55–56; *The Blasted Pine*, 51–52, 54; *The Book of Canadian Poetry*, 12
Smith, Russell, 154n24, 208
social media, 32–33, 56, 57, 60, 295, 314. *See also* blogs; digital technology; Facebook; Twitter
social space, 142
Solie, Karen, 202
"Somebody Blew Up America" (Baraka), 169
Song Fishermen's Song Sheets, 12
sonnet: introduction to, 97; *The Others Raisd in Me* (Betts), 98–99, 100–101; Shakespeare's, 101; Sonnet 150 (Shakespeare), 99, 100

Sonnet 150 (Shakespeare), 99, 100
sound poetry, 94, 103
"Sound Reading" (Quartermain), 278
Soupcoff, Marni, 149, 168, 169
Souster, Raymond: approach to, 15–16; civic public poetics of, 153; critical opinions on, 139, 144–45, 154n24; introduction to, 139; literary output of, 145; obituaries of, 154n24; public role of, 148; *Ten Elephants on Yonge Street*, 145; "Ten Elephants on Yonge Street," 145–48, 153; and Toronto, 144
space, 181–82
Spahr, Juliana, 201
Spar: Words in Place (Sanger), 129
spatial metaphor, 141
SPEAK! slam series, 45
spirituality, 173n57
spoken word. *See* slam poetry
Spurr, David: *The Rhetoric of Empire*, 322
Starnino, Carmine: *Lazy Bastardism*, 131–32
Stevens, James Thomas: *Mohawk/Samoa Transmigrations*, 321–22
Stevens, Wallace: "Thirteen Ways of Looking at a Blackbird," 210
"Strike! A Mass Recitation" (Gold), 240
structures of belief, 55, 56
Studies in Canadian Literature, 264, 313, 324–25
stuplimity, 57–58
"Sturdiness, The" (Queyras), 109–10
Sublime Object of Ideology, The (Žižek), 171n46
Sullivan, Rosemary: "Exile," 150, 168
Surette, Leon, 142
Sutherland, John, 57, 145
Suzuki, Daisetz T., 89

Tax Increment Financing (TIF), 308n25

Taylor, Diana, 256, 257
teachers, 36
technology. *See* digital technology
Ten Elephants on Yonge Street (Souster), 145
"Ten Elephants on Yonge Street" (Souster), 145–48, 153
"Tenement Song" (Jerome), 212–13
Tessera, 66
textual space, 142
Thacker, Andrew, 141–42
"Thirteen Ways of Looking at a Blackbird" (Stevens), 210
"Thirteen Ways of Looking at a Gray Whale" (Cran), 210–12
Through Darkling Air (Sanger), 133–34
TIF (Tax Increment Financing), 308n25
TISH, 10, 12
Tjia, Sherwin. *See World Is a Heartbreaker, The* (Tjia)
"Today After Rain" (Cran), 205, 207–8
"to initiate a poetics of occupation" (Cremin), 319
Tolokonnikova, Nadezhda Andreyevna, 34. *See also* Pussy Riot
"To Occupy: An Evolution" (Bernofsky), 319
Toronto, 142, 149–50, 151, 159–60
Tostevin, Lola Lemire, 65
TransCanada project, 317
Trans.Can.Lit (Kamboureli), 161
transgenic modification, 70–71
transitive language, 291
Translating Translating Apollinaire (Nichol), 93
transnationalism, 317
transnational literacies, 314, 315, 327n27
Transnational Poetics, A (Ramazani), 316–17
transparency, 320
transtranslation, 92–93
treaties, First Nations, 322–23, 328n57

"26 Statements on Poetry" (beaulieu), 90, 92
Twitter, 32–33, 38–39, 294

UC Davis, 303–5
uncreative writing, 88
Uncreative Writing (Goldsmith), 39, 72
universities, 20n28
University of California, Davis, 303–5
university presses, 10
Unleashed (Queyras), 13, 34
Unoriginal Genius (Perloff), 61, 72
Unsettling the City (Blamley), 177
Uppal, Priscilla: and Canadian Athletes Now website, 317–18; on Dennis Lee, 151; "Patience," 318
Upper Canada Rebellion, 146, 152
urban alienation. *See* Project Rebuild (Murakami); *Rebuild* (Murakami)

V6A (Gardiner), 205
Valentine, Jean, 39
Valverde, Mariana, 152
Vancouver, 177, 193n2, 210, 213–14. *See also* Project Rebuild (Murakami); *Rebuild* (Murakami)
Vancouver 125 Poetry Conference, 214
Vancouver Special, 185–86, 194n22
vancouverspecial.com (Higgins), 194n22
"Vancouver Special" poems (Murakami), 186–88
Vautour, Bart, 232, 242
Vehicule Art Inc., 274
Vermeersch, Paul, 29
Very Stone House Press, 260–61
vocalic space, 290–91
"Volume" (Maguire), 114–15
von Hallberg, Robert, 200
Vries, Leonard de: *Flowers of Delight*, 103

Wah, Fred, 10, 30, 88
Walker, Scott, 299–302
Wallace, David Foster, 54
Wanenchack, Kim, 297
Warder, Kristen, 264, 313
Warner, Michael: on actions of publics, 14; on counterpublics, 189, 313; and Frye, 19n9; individuation of publics, 195n38; on poetry, 3, 14; public and private conceptions of each other, 255; public as autotelic, 59, 202; public as created by discourse, 3, 60, 141; public as dominant discourses, 2–3; public as relation among strangers, 3, 31, 60, 257; public beyond the public sphere, 233; *Publics and Counterpublics*, 2; on public speech, 247, 255; on readers, 262; on reflexivity of publics, 202; on self-organized publics, 58; on technology and public discourse, 4; on university presses and journals, 10
Warner, Patrick, 131–32
Wat, Aleksander: "Dark Light," 159, 168
"Watchers, The" (Auden), 128
Waterman, Ellen, 256
Watts, Jim, 245
Wayman, Tom, 202
Weather, The (Robertson), 201
Weaver, Robert, 258–59, 260, 266
Weinrich, Peter, 234, 248n9
Wells, Zachariah: *Jailbreaks: 99 Canadian Sonnets*, 97; on Sanger, 121–22, 123, 130, 132–33
Wershler, Darren: *Apostrophe*, 88; and Project Rebuild, 191
West, Cornel, 298
Western Front, 274
What Are Poets For? (Bruns), 204, 317
What Are Universities For? (Collini), 314–15
White Civility (Coleman), 143–44, 154n14

White Salt Mountain (Sanger), 129
Whynacht, Ardath, 18
Wider Boundaries of Daring (Brandt and Godard), 52, 60
Willkie, Wendell, 146–47
Will to Power, The (Nietzsche), 170n19
Winger, Rob: "September Still," 116
Wittig, Monique: *The Lesbian Body*, 74
women: approach to as poet, 14–15; Black women in slam poetry, 46–49; and CLDL pamphlets, 245; consequences for radical protests, 34; and *flâneur*, 77; and public participation, 27–28, 38, 40; Queyras on, 78–80. *See also* Canadian Women in Literary Arts; female subjectivity; feminist poetics; *Human Resources* (Zolf)
Women and Words conference, 4, 19n11, 66, 274
Wong, Rita, 278. *See also forage* (Wong)
Woodcock, George, 10, 263
WordCount, 72, 73
Word Iz Bond, 274
"Words Cannot Express" (Barwin), 90–91, 92
"Workers' Self-Defense in the Courts" (pamphlet), 234, 235, 237–38, 245
World Is a Heartbreaker, The (Tjia), 90, 95–96
writing, 315–16, 320, 323
Writing in Our Time (Butling and Rudy), 11, 88
Writing Thru Race conference, 4, 19n11

Yeats, William Butler, 204
Yonge Street (Toronto), 145–46, 147

Zelazo, Suzanne, 80, 84n53
Žižek, Slavoj: *Less Than Nothing*, 171n27; *The Sublime Object of Ideology*, 171n46
Zolf, Rachel. See *Human Resources* (Zolf)
Zong! (Philip), 278
Zwicky, Jan: "Brahms Clarinet Quintet in B Minor, Op. 115," 213; and Lista, 27, 28; lyric philosophy of, 202; on lyric thought, 199

Books in the TransCanada Series
Published by Wilfrid Laurier University Press

Smaro Kamboureli and Roy Miki, editors
Trans.Can.Lit: Resituating the Study of Canadian Literature / 2007 /
ISBN 978-0-88920-513-0

Smaro Kamboureli
Scandalous Bodies: Diasporic Literature in English Canada / 2009 /
ISBN 978-1-55458-064-4

Kit Dobson
Transnational Canadas: Anglo-Canadian Literature and Globalization /
2009 / ISBN 978-1-55458-063-7

Christine Kim, Sophie McCall, and Melina Baum Singer, editors
Cultural Grammars of Nation, Diaspora, and Indigeneity in Canada / 2012 /
ISBN 978-1-55458-336-2

Smaro Kamboureli and Robert Zacharias, editors
Shifting the Ground of Canadian Literary Studies / 2012 / ISBN 978-1-55458-365-2

Kit Dobson and Smaro Kamboureli
Producing Canadian Literature: Authors Speak on the Literary Marketplace /
2013 / ISBN 978-1-55458-355-3

Eva C. Karpinski, Jennifer Henderson, Ian Sowton, and Ray Ellenwood,
editors
Trans/acting Culture, Writing, and Memory / 2013 / ISBN 978-1-55458-839-8

Smaro Kamboureli and Christl Verduyn, editors
*Critical Collaborations: Indigenity, Diaspora, and Ecology in Canadian
Literary Studies* / 2014 / ISBN 978-1-55458-911-1

Larissa Lai
*Slanting I, Imagining We: Asian Canadian Literary Production in the 1980s
and 1990s* / 2014 / ISBN 978-1-77112-041-8

Bart Vautour, Erin Wunker, Travis V. Mason, and Christl Verduyn,
editors
Public Poetics: Critical Issues in Canadian Poetry and Poetics / 2015 /
ISBN 978-1-77112-047-0

www.ingramcontent.com/pod-product-compliance
Lightning Source LLC
Chambersburg PA
CBHW072142100526
44589CB00015B/2050